Militarization and the
American Century

New Approaches to International History

Series Editor:
Thomas Zeiler, Professor of American Diplomatic History, University of Colorado Boulder, USA

Series Editorial Board
Anthony Adamthwaite, University of California at Berkeley (USA)
Kathleen Burk, University College London (UK)
Louis Clerc, University of Turku (Finland)
Petra Goedde, Temple University (USA)
Francine McKenzie, University of Western Ontario (Canada)
Lien-Hang Nguyen, Columbia University (USA)
Jason Parker, Texas A&M University (USA)
Glenda Sluga, University of Sydney (Australia)

New Approaches to International History covers international history during the modern period and across the globe. The series incorporates new developments in the field, such as the cultural turn and transnationalism, as well as the classical high politics of state-centric policymaking and diplomatic relations. Written with upper level undergraduate and postgraduate students in mind, texts in the series provide an accessible overview of international diplomatic and transnational issues, events and actors.

Published
Decolonization and the Cold War, edited by Leslie James and Elisabeth Leake (2015)
Cold War Summits, Chris Tudda (2015)
The United Nations in International History, Amy Sayward (2017)
Latin American Nationalism, James F. Siekmeier (2017)
The History of United States Cultural Diplomacy, Michael L. Krenn (2017)
International Cooperation in the Early 20th Century, Daniel Gorman (2017)
Women and Gender in International History, Karen Garner (2018)
International Development, Corinna Unger (2018)
The Environment and International History, Scott Kaufman (2018)
Scandinavia and the Great Powers in the First World War, Michael Jonas (2019)

Militarization and the American Century

War, the United States and the World since 1941

David Fitzgerald

BLOOMSBURY ACADEMIC
LONDON • NEW YORK • OXFORD • NEW DELHI • SYDNEY

BLOOMSBURY ACADEMIC
Bloomsbury Publishing Plc
50 Bedford Square, London, WC1B 3DP, UK
1385 Broadway, New York, NY 10018, USA
29 Earlsfort Terrace, Dublin 2, Ireland

BLOOMSBURY, BLOOMSBURY ACADEMIC and the Diana logo are
trademarks of Bloomsbury Publishing Plc

First published in Great Britain 2022

Series design: Catherine Wood

Cover image: Liberation of Paris, August 1944.
Photo © AGIP / Bridgeman Images

A catalogue record for this book is available from the British Library.

Library of Congress Cataloging-in-Publication Data
Names: Fitzgerald, David, 1984– author.
Title: Militarization and the American century : war, the United States and
the world since 1941 / David Fitzgerald.
Other titles: War, the United States and the world since 1941
Description: London ; New York : Bloomsbury Academic, 2022. |
Series: New approaches to international history | Includes bibliographical
references and index.
Identifiers: LCCN 2021033268 (print) | LCCN 2021033269 (ebook) |
ISBN 9781350102224 (hardback) | ISBN 9781350102231 (pdf) | ISBN 9781350102248 (ebook)
Subjects: LCSH: United States–Politics and government–1945–1989. |
United States–Politics and government–1989– | War and society–United
States–History–20th century. | National security–United States–History–20th century. |
Militarization–United States–History–20th century. | Militarization–United
States–History–21st century. | United States–History, Military–20th century. |
United States–Foreign relations–1945– | United States–Military policy–0th century.
Classification: LCC E743 .F89 2022 (print) | LCC E743 (ebook) | DDC 355/.033073–dc23
LC record available at https://lccn.loc.gov/2021033268
LC ebook record available at https://lccn.loc.gov/2021033269

ISBN: HB: 978-1-3501-0222-4
ePDF: 978-1-3501-0223-1
eBook: 978-1-3501-0224-8

Series: New Approaches to International History

Typeset by Newgen KnowledgeWorks Pvt. Ltd., Chennai, India

To find out more about our authors and books visit www.bloomsbury.com
and sign up for our newsletters.

For Sarah and Daniel.

Contents

Figures

Series Editor Preface

New Approaches to International History takes the entire world as its stage for exploring the history of diplomacy, broadly conceived theoretically and thematically, and writ large across the span of the globe, during the modern period. This series goes beyond the single goal of explaining encounters in the world. Our aspiration is that these books provide both an introduction for researchers new to a topic, and supplemental and essential reading in classrooms. Thus, *New Approaches* serves a dual purpose that is unique from other large-scale treatments of international history; it applies to scholarly agendas and pedagogy. In addition, it does so against the backdrop of a century of enormous change, conflict and progress that not only informed global history but also continues to reflect on our own times.

The series offers the old and new diplomatic history to address a range of topics that shaped the twentieth century. Engaging in international history (including but not especially focusing on global or world history), these books will appeal to a range of scholars and teachers situated in the humanities and social sciences, including those in history, international relations, cultural studies, politics and economics. We have in mind scholars, both novice and veteran, who require an entrée into a topic, trend or technique that can benefit their own research or education into a new field of study by crossing boundaries in a variety of ways.

By its broad and inclusive coverage, *New Approaches to International History* is also unique because it makes accessible to students current research, methodology and themes. Incorporating cutting-edge scholarship that reflects trends in international history, as well as addressing the classical high politics of state-centric policymaking and diplomatic relations, these books are designed to bring alive the myriad of approaches for digestion by advanced undergraduates and graduate students. In preparation for the *New Approaches* series, Bloomsbury surveyed courses and faculty around the world to gauge interest and reveal core themes of relevance for their classroom use. The polling yielded a host of topics, from war and peace to the environment; from empire to economic integration; and from migration to nuclear arms. The effort proved that there is a much-needed place for studies that connect scholars and students alike to international history, and books that are especially relevant to the teaching missions of faculty around the world.

We hope readers find this series to be appealing, challenging and thought-provoking. Whether the history is viewed through older or newer lenses, *New Approaches to International History* allows students to peer into the modern period's complex relations among nations, people and events to draw their own conclusions about the tumultuous, interconnected past.

Thomas Zeiler
University of Colorado Boulder, USA

Acknowledgements

The vast bulk of this volume was completed during periods of relative isolation, first during the chaotic but joyful months after the birth of my son, and then during long stretches of pandemic-related lockdowns. This means that writing this book was a somewhat unusual experience: there were few opportunities to chat about it with colleagues over coffee, or to bounce ideas off friends at conference hotel bars, while bouts of writing had to be timed to coincide with toddler naps or for periods when public health restrictions eased enough for life to return to something approaching its normal rhythms. It does not, though, mean that the book was created alone. Working on this book gave me a wonderful opportunity to put myself in conversation with so much excellent scholarship on American war and militarization. Even if I could not engage with colleagues in person, I learned so much from reading their work, and I hope the book does their accumulated insights justice.

This book starts with the words of the late Marilyn Young and that is for good reason. Like so many people, I am enormously in debt to Marilyn for both her kindness and her brilliance. So much of my thinking on war and American culture was shaped by her scholarship, and I often wished I could email her for advice as I worked my way through drafts of this book. I would have loved to have sent her a copy of the finished product.

I am deeply grateful to Tom Zeiler for inviting me to contribute a volume to this series, and to Maddie Holder and Abigail Lane for helping me see it through to completion. I would also like to thank the anonymous readers who reviewed the book proposal and the manuscript and who provided helpful and constructive feedback that helped me to fine-tune the book.

There are two non-anonymous readers that I need to thank. David Ryan and Ruth Lawlor both read draft chapters of the manuscript as they emerged, and provided me with a stream of suggestions, corrections and words of encouragement throughout. I have benefitted from David's wisdom for nearly over fifteen years now, and I remain grateful for his mentorship, his generosity and his friendship. As for Ruth, so many of the ideas contained in this book were hashed out in conversations with her that there are places in it where I struggle to see where her ideas end and mine begin. I can't thank her enough for her support and her friendship.

Finally, there is my wife Sarah and my son Daniel, to whom this book is dedicated. Sarah both read over drafts with a keen editorial eye and kept me on an even keel throughout. Her love, support and kindness have been constant throughout, and I am incredibly lucky that we have embarked on this journey through life together. I am grateful for all the things she did to make sure I could finish the book, from taking on extra childcare shifts to dealing with the piles of dishes that had been languishing on the counter for too long to helping me see the wood for the trees when dealing with tricky parts of the manuscript. I am even grateful for her often-futile efforts to prevent the cats from interrupting my writing. Throughout the entire process, Daniel remained mercifully oblivious to the book and its inevitable frustrations. While I worried about historiography and structure, he was only concerned with trips to the park and access to snacks. His complete lack of interest was invaluable, and I am so glad that he gave me a good incentive to close the laptop and go help him with his Duplo construction projects. For that, and for so much else, I am thankful.

Introduction

The story of the United States in the twentieth century and its place in the world is, in some sense, a story about war. Revolutionary wars, civil wars, world wars, cold wars and wars on terror have all provided milestones in the course of American history. In recent decades, though, historians have worked to show that wars were not just isolated episodes – punctuation marks in an otherwise peaceful narrative – but rather events that were deeply woven into the fabric of American politics, culture and society. War's effects never ceased to reverberate, even if they were not immediately visible to many Americans. The historian Marilyn Young called attention to this tension in her 2011 presidential address to the Society for Historians of American Foreign Relations (SHAFR), when she argued that it must be the 'continuous task' of scholars of American foreign relations 'to make war visible, vivid, an inescapable part of the country's self-consciousness, as inescapable a subject of study as it is a reality'. For Young, a lifetime of thinking and writing about war had convinced her that 'the shadow of war … seems not to be a shadow but entirely substantial: the substance of American history'.[1] Responding to Young and reflecting on his own long career writing about the relationship between the United States and war, the historian Michael Sherry confessed that he had previously underestimated the depth of that relationship. For Sherry, 'War constituted modern American history as much as race, class, gender, religion, capitalism – you name it – just as each threaded through the others', and he complained that 'too few historians fully engage that fact'.[2] While he once regarded the United States as a state that was,

---

[1] Marilyn B. Young, '"I Was Thinking, as I Often Do These Days, of War"': The United States in the Twenty-First Century', *Diplomatic History* 36, no. 1 (1 January 2012): 1–2, https://doi.org/10.1111/j.1467-7709.2011.01004.x.

[2] Michael Sherry, 'War as a Way of Life', *Modern American History* 1, no. 1 (March 2018): 93, https://doi.org/10.1017/mah.2017.12.

at heart, reluctant to engage in conflicts overseas, he admitted that 'now I think of it as a nation deeply wedded to and defined by war, though maddeningly reluctant to admit it.'[3]

This study responds to Young and Sherry by taking up their challenge to consider the centrality of war in American history. It makes use of an outpouring of new scholarship on Americans and war to demonstrate how deeply war has affected diverse facets of American society and culture. Notwithstanding Sherry's complaint that too few historians engage with the topic, there has been a wave of excellent and nuanced scholarly work on different aspects of American militarization in recent years.[4] Not only do we have several studies that look at the broad sweep of war's impact on the United States and offer compelling critiques of militarism, such as Sherry's own authoritative book *In the Shadow of War*, but also numerous books and articles that showcase imaginative and important work on the ways in which strategy, culture and politics collide.[5] Taken together, this flood of publications reveals a deep and abiding interest in the study of war and its effects. Few facets of American history have been left untouched by this work: when we consider topics as diverse as the environment, gender, social welfare policy, citizenship or popular culture, we can quickly see that war has affected them all.

My aim here is to draw together this scholarship in order to tell the story of how the American preparation for – and the conduct of – war has left its mark both on the United States and on the world more broadly. Taking American mobilization for the Second World War as its departure point, this book offers an introduction not just to the ways in which the United States has been 'wedded to and defined by war' since 1941 but also reflects on the extent to which war has shaped American relations with the rest of the world in that same period. By exploring the causes and consequences of militarization since the dawn of the 'American Century', it establishes the centrality of war in American identity, state making and foreign relations. The book highlights connections between

---

[3] Sherry, 'War as a Way of Life', 95.

[4] A related plea has come from Daniel Bessner and Fredrik Logevall, who argue that scholars need to pay more attention to the American state and domestic history in the historiography of foreign relations. Daniel Bessner and Fredrik Logevall, 'Recentering the United States in the Historiography of American Foreign Relations', *Texas National Security Review* 3, no. 2 (2020): 38–55, https://doi.org/10.26153/tsw/8867.

[5] Michael Sherry, *In the Shadow of War: The United States since the 1930s* (New Haven, CT: Yale University Press, 1995). In addition to Sherry's book, the following also provide excellent introductions to militarization in the United States: David Kieran and Edwin A. Martini, eds, *At War: The Military and American Culture in the Twentieth Century and Beyond* (New Brunswick, NJ: Rutgers University Press, 2018); Andrew J. Bacevich, *The New American Militarism: How Americans Are Seduced by War* (New York: Oxford University Press, 2005).

domestic, international and transnational developments and demonstrates that the lines between military history and other fields are often blurred when we put militarization at the centre of our analysis.

What do we mean by militarization? The German historian Michael Geyer describes militarization as 'the contradictory and tense social process in which civil society organizes itself for the production of violence'.[6] Militarization does not require a society to celebrate martial values, and it is about more than the armed forces. It is an ongoing and open-ended process that extends outside the realm of politics, connecting all sorts of social and cultural phenomena. This, in turn, makes it a concept that is particularly useful in the American context, as scholars have pointed out that the society which produced the American national security state was vastly different to the openly militarist societies of nineteenth-century Prussia or 1930s Japan. These societies, which had politicized and powerful armed forces at their core, have often been the template for popular and scholarly understandings of militarism.[7] However, as we will see, for much of their history Americans have defined themselves *against* this form of militarism, a political stance that can sometimes obscure the extent to which the preparation for war has helped to shape the contemporary United States. Certainly, there have been various times where cultures of militarism have taken hold in American society, but it is the ongoing process of militarization that provides a thread which runs much of recent American history. In other words, it is not moments of crisis or the ostentatious celebration of martial culture which pulls back the curtain to reveal the significance of militarization in American society but rather the more anodyne and even mundane: draft exemptions encouraging young men to take up a career in science during the Cold War, or international agreements giving the American military justice system jurisdiction over bar districts in South Korea. What we are talking about, then, is not brief moments of punctuation but an American grammar.

This book has three core objectives. Firstly, it seeks to convey just how deeply militarization has affected the course of American history and to demonstrate that it has been a virtually omnipresent factor in American political culture and broader American society since the 1940s. Much of the recent scholarship on Americans and war has gone beyond histories of high politics and statecraft to

---

[6] Michael Geyer, 'The Militarization of Europe, 1914–1945', in *The Militarization of the Western World*, ed. John R. Gillis (New Brunswick, NJ: Rutgers University Press, 1989), 65–102.

[7] For useful discussions of the differences between American militarism and these earlier forms, see Catherine Lutz, 'Making War at Home in the United States: Militarization and the Current Crisis', *American Anthropologist* 104, no. 3 (2002): 723–35; Michael Mann, 'The Roots and Contradictions of Modern Militarism', *New Left Review* 1, no. 162 (1987): 35–50.

demonstrate not only the ways in which top-down militarization has affected American society and culture but also how this militarized society has in turn influenced the formulation of American diplomacy and strategy. This book draws on that scholarship and focuses not just on generals and statesmen – although it does discuss the ideas and actions of both – but also on the broader impact of wars, both real and imagined, on American society. It examines how militarization affected categories as diverse as the American family, the development of the welfare state, notions of citizenship and the industrial geography of the United States. The potency of invoking 'national security' as a justification for policy meant that issues seemingly unrelated to war, such as the federal regulation of homosexuality or debates over property rights in Western states, were influenced by the politics of militarization.

That said, while it is vital to map out the extent and depth of militarization in the United States, it would be a mistake to think of militarization as an inevitable or unchanging phenomenon. Indeed, the second objective of this book is to demonstrate that its progress has been uneven and contingent. If we return to Geyer's definition of militarization, it is important to note that he describes it as a contentious process, and part of the task of this book is to map out its tensions and contradictions. Some of the early scholarship on militarization has, in its eagerness to demonstrate its centrality in American history, at times given the impression of a monolithically militarized garrison state. Instead, as the historian Gary Gerstle has argued, while 'national security' has been a centrally important concept in American political discourse since the Second World War, it is also one that has at times been used as a cover for other ideas and for the expansion of the central state in ways that are, at their core, not directly related to militarization.[8] For instance, the National Interstate and Defense Highway Act was, to be sure, partly about national defence, but to consider the post-war interstate highway system as *solely* a product of militarization would be an oversimplification.

Moreover, while the trajectory of American history in the twentieth and twenty-first centuries may seem to have been towards ever-greater militarization, there have been moments of rupture and retreat. In the wake of the Second World War, it looked as though the United States might demobilize, as it had done after previous wars. And with defeat in Vietnam, Americans openly questioned the centrality of war in their society and in their culture and ended the draft, thus significantly

---

[8] Gary Gerstle, *Liberty and Coercion: The Paradox of American Government from the Founding to the Present* (Princeton, NJ: Princeton University Press, 2015), 252–3.

reducing the proportion of the population who would be exposed to military service. More recently, there was a brief and limited retreat from militarism in the 1990s, as a defence drawdown and talk of a 'peace dividend' followed the end of the Cold War. To observe this is not to downplay or minimize the significance of militarization as a force in American history but to point out that this centrality was not inevitable and that at various times Americans imagined and campaigned for other possibilities. Studying how these alternative trajectories did not come to pass can help us understand how they might arise again. Indeed, it is entirely possible that the current moment, with its oversaturation of adulation for the military and veterans, and a public that has lost all interest in long wars such as the multi-decade intervention in Afghanistan, may represent such a turning point. Therefore, while the book emphasizes long-term processes, it also seeks to demonstrate how important agency and contingency have been when it comes to the particular form of militarization that grew in the United States.

Finally, the book argues that to fully understand militarization and its impacts, it is necessary to look at it through an international and transnational lens. Focusing solely on developments within the United States can have the effect of obscuring many of the external sources and effects of militarization. In order to more fully account for this broader story, this study seeks to synthesize the global history of US militarization and to offer readers an introduction to a large and growing body of literature that examines connections between and across different countries. In one sense, the international origins of militarization are clear: for example, few would deny that the architects of that great foundational document of Cold War militarization, NSC-68, were unaffected by what they saw as a perilous international situation. But scholars have gone beyond this to show the myriad ways in which American relations with the rest of the world have been deeply affected by war, not just in the obvious geopolitical sense but also via transnational connections and processes. This has meant examining how American statesmen conceptualized their military–industrial complex by contrasting it with the militarisms of other states, but it has also involved uncovering more quotidian links that have been based on the experiences of ordinary people.

Of particular importance here is the study of the global history of the US military. The historian Gretchen Heefner has argued that scholars of foreign relations at times treat the military like a 'black box' that has not warranted the same scrutiny as other organizations.[9] By unpacking the contents of that black box,

---

[9] Gretchen Heefner, '"A Slice of Their Sovereignty": Negotiating the U.S. Empire of Bases, Wheelus Field, Libya, 1950–1954', *Diplomatic History* 41, no. 1 (1 January 2017): 52–3, https://doi.org/10.1093/dh/dhv058.

we can get a much clearer sense of the international and transnational aspects of militarization. For instance, the experiences of armed Americans overseas, both during wartime and via the American 'empire of bases' that emerged during the Second World War, were central to interstate relations and had their own effects both on the host countries and on the United States itself. These encounters, along with the flow of people – from war brides to refugees – moving in the other direction as a result of American wars, have shaped American foreign relations in profound ways. Thus, militarization has been at once a domestic, an international and a transnational process. By highlighting both the global effects of American militarization and the ways in which external factors have shaped its evolution within the United States, the connections between what may seem at times to be disparate social, cultural and political changes, as well as both the depth and pervasiveness of militarization become clearer.

The notion that these connections are important is central to this book. In previous generations, the fields of diplomatic history, military history, social history and cultural history were somewhat walled from each other, but that is certainly no longer the case, and has not been for some time. In many ways, *Militarization and the American Century* is both a celebration of and an introduction to scholarship that breaks down barriers between subfields. Some of the very best work on militarization, and indeed in the fields of diplomatic and military history more broadly, is that which not only borrows concepts and ideas from different subfields but puts those subfields into conversation as well. As the work cited in this book demonstrates, these conversations have been incredibly rich and productive, and point to new avenues for historical research that takes a broad view of militarization and that works to integrate different historiographical traditions.

In order to emphasize the global consequences of American militarization, the book largely focuses on what journalist Henry Luce has called 'the American Century', an epoch first identified when the United States mobilized for the Second World War and whose ending continues to be the subject of debate. Scholars may disagree whether or not it ended with the 2008 financial crash, the Trump presidency, the onset of the Covid-19 pandemic or indeed whether or not it has ended at all, but all agree that the middle of the twentieth century saw the United States achieve almost unparalleled global political and military power. It was in this era that militarization began to take on an inexorable logic and moved to the centre of American political, economic and cultural life. Certainly, scholars of earlier periods have done invaluable work in demonstrating both how earlier crises provided precursors to the national security state and how war shaped the United States in all manner of ways, but if we take the size of the permanent armed forces as a proxy for militarization, then we can see that the 1940s marked a decisive break with past practices. The fact that the vast American armies of the Second World War did not follow the pattern of previous eras and demobilize is a clear indication that something had changed, and the presence of American troops on every continent meant that this change would have global implications. Crucially, it was the Second World War itself, not the Cold War that followed it, that marked the beginnings of both the American Century and the national security state that shaped so much of the course of that century. There may have been an opportunity to dismantle that national security apparatus after the end of the war, but it was the institutions, the bases, the strategic choices and the politics of the Second World War that were at the heart of the process of militarization. Not only that, but the experiences of that war provided the template for both popular and elite thinking about war and the United States' role in the world for decades to come.

In order to more effectively trace the various processes and effects of militarization, the book adopts a thematic approach to the topic. The first chapter examines militarization before the American Century, and then the following five chapters focus on different aspects of militarization to give a clearer sense of how the process played out in various domains. Chapter 1 looks at the long arc of militarization in the United States before 1941. It describes the evolution of the relationship between the US military and broader American society, as well as the experiences of armed Americans both on the frontier and overseas. By tracing debates over war, empire and 'preparedness', it shows how the militarization of American society ebbed and flowed from the Revolution to the 1930s. Anti-militarism was part of the founding myth of the United States, as Jeffersonians condemned standing armies even as they called for continental expansion and the United States became embroiled in several regional wars. While the Civil War saw the mobilization of society for total war and the deployment of vast armies, it did not permanently erode this anti-militarist tendency, as Americans immediately sought to return the military to its pre-war status when the war ended.

This equilibrium began to shift towards the end of the nineteenth century, as a generation of veterans who had initially turned away from the horrors of war began to embrace the notion of military service as the pinnacle of active masculine citizenship as the more traumatic memories of war faded. This change coincided with the overt embrace of empire and overseas intervention at the turn of the century; as war in Europe loomed, Americans first debated how best to be prepared for such a conflict, and then built the apparatus necessary to assert military power overseas and to make the United States a global power on both land and sea. Throughout this period however, there was significant resistance to militarization and militarism was never an unquestioned virtue, nor were the armed forces ever anything like the size of their European counterparts. From the anti-imperialists protesting wars in the Philippines and Cuba, to the pacifists opposing American entry into the First World War and advocating for worldwide disarmament after the war, to the Nye Committee's investigations into the armaments industry in the 1930s, to the America First Committee opposing entry into the Second World War, anti-militarist movements found significant purchase in American political culture in the first part of the twentieth century.

Chapter 2 begins with a moment of rupture and examines how the concept of 'national security' altered both the structures of American government and the ways in which policymakers have understood the world. With the United States' entry into the Second World War, the machinery of state had to adapt itself to manage the vast demands of a global conflict. Not only that, but the coming of the Cold War meant that, unlike previous wars, no significant demobilization would happen after the end of the Second World War. Instead, defence spending stayed well above pre-war levels and the consequences of a nuclear weapons build-up dominated the thoughts of policymakers and strategists. The Cold War and the subsequent conflicts also blurred the lines between war and peace, as the imminence of the nuclear threat along with the indistinct beginning and ending of wars meant that the United States was perpetually between war and peace.[10] New institutions such as the Joint Chiefs of Staff, the National Security Council and the Department of Defense gave the military a much larger role in the formulation of foreign policy. This chapter demonstrates how this move, along with the growing use of 'national security' as a lens through which to view policy problems, has led to a steady militarization of American foreign policy. Not only that, but wartime practices were applied at home, as militarized police forces began to act like occupiers in the communities they served, and surveillance systems designed to apprehend terrorists were turned inwards. From Henry Wallace's dissent from the Cold War consensus to more recent complaints about celebrity generals and the militarization of foreign aid, various Americans, including many within the

---

[10] Mary Dudziak, *War Time: An Idea, Its History, Its Consequences* (New York: Oxford University Press, 2012).

military itself, critiqued and resisted the growing influence of the armed forces on foreign affairs and the drift towards militarization. Despite these reservations, over the course of American century and into the twenty-first century, the military steadily became the primary actor and face of the United States abroad and the state at home became increasingly animated by militarized logics.

Given the pervasiveness of militarization's effects on both foreign and domestic policies, it is no surprise that the physical manifestations of the phenomenon were profound and far-reaching. Chapter 3 investigates the ways in which militarization has shaped landscapes and spaces, in both the United States and overseas. The Cold War deeply affected the industrial geography of the United States, with the creation of a 'gun belt' stretching from high-tech aircraft manufacturing in California to the armament factories of the industrializing South to the research laboratories of New England. Indeed, militarization contributed substantially to the modernization of the South and the emergence of the Sunbelt, a development that in turn affected American electoral politics. Further, the military became more southern as it increasingly consolidated on large bases in the South, a trend that accelerated with the post–Cold War draw down. The politics of military basing were complex: for instance, the placement of intercontinental ballistic missiles (ICBMs) in pastures across the Great Plains both inspired environmental protests and led local politicians to advocate for further integration into the military–industrial complex. Militarization has had physical consequences beyond the United States as well, nowhere more so than in the 'Empire of Bases' that sprang up during the Second World War. The history of these bases and the ways in which their existence shaped American foreign relations has been the subject of an explosion of scholarship in recent years, pointing to how the study of militarization can effectively draw on the scholarship of foreign relations, the military, the environment and social and cultural histories. Similarly, we can see the value of broadening our disciplinary lens when we look at the wide range of scholarship that has examined the heavy and growing militarization of the United States' southern border. This work has highlighted how easily the restrictive practices associated with military spaces and bases overseas can migrate back to the United States.

Chapter 4 follows American service members out in the world as they deployed for the Second World War and subsequent conflicts and examines the various encounters they had with people in other lands. These could be commercial, sexual, political or even violent, but they all in some way involved the remaking of local cultures, while service members were also vehicles for the transmission of foreign ideas back to the United States. Whether as armed tourists, military occupiers or in senior roles such as attaché or advisor, armed Americans overseas were, for many, the embodiment of US foreign policy. Often, Americans came 'armed with abundance' and symbolized the strengths of American consumerism, while on other occasions, their interactions were much less benign and much more violent, particularly and most obviously during combat operations. These encounters also frequently involved sexual violence, a phenomenon that has been the subject of considerable scholarly attention in recent years. The military did not just send soldiers overseas, however; and the families and dependents that travelled with them are also worthy of study, particularly for the ways in which they sought to recreate some version of the United States abroad. Finally, the chapter outlines the flow of people and ideas that went in the other direction – whether it be ideas about civil rights that Black soldiers brought home from Europe, the Second World War era 'war brides' or the large flows of refugees produced by American wars in Southeast Asia, Latin America and the Middle East. By studying these more personal encounters and the movement of people to and from the United States, we can better understand the transnational dimensions of militarization.

While the concept of 'national security' became an organizing principle of American foreign policy, similar notions also influenced domestic policy and shaped the nature of American citizenship. Chapter 5 focuses on the interaction between national security imperatives and debates over the rights and obligations of citizenship, a complex relationship that produced unexpected results at times. Militarization's reach extended into social policy, where the GI Bill shaped federal welfare policies, while debates over Universal Military Training and the implementation of both desegregation and Selective Service meant that the military was both an engine for social change and a marker of full citizenship for men. The relationship between the military and broader American society changed profoundly with the advent of the All-Volunteer Force, as the military found itself competing with other employers in the marketplace and military service became the preserve of fewer and fewer Americans. The All-Volunteer Force necessitated the construction of military welfare state to support it and had the contradictory effects of placing soldiers on pedestals as 'warriors' while at the same time promoting what the sociologist Charles Moskos called 'occupationalism' within the military – the sense that the military was 'just another job.'[11] Even as the

---

[11] Charles C. Moskos, ed., *The Postmodern Military: Armed Forces after the Cold War* (New York: Oxford University Press, 2000).

nature of military service changed, militarization continued to have a profound impact on notions of citizenship as well as the nature of the American state.

The final chapter of the book introduces readers to the ways in which war has figured in American culture since 1940. From the celebratory to the condemnatory, popular culture has always reflected how Americans have thought about war. Culture has also shaped and framed those thoughts, however, as can be seen by the large-scale investment of the Department of Defense in Hollywood productions and the importance attached to cultural resistance to militarization. Cultural depictions of war feed into broader ideas about American identity and the United States' role in the world, but they also have profound effects, ones that are often missed by even those who invest significant time and money in them, such as Pentagon Public Affairs officers. For much as television, film and literary portrayals of war have influenced how the American public thought about war, gender roles and race, they also shape, in subtle ways, the worldviews of strategists and policymakers. Marilyn Young has argued that much as war has been in a constant in American history, it has also been the subject of constant erasure in American culture. That erasure has contributed to the impoverishment of American thinking about war, as the inability of American culture to depict its consequences, particularly its consequences for those outside the United States, has limited the imagination of policymakers as well as citizens.

1

Liberal empire and the paradoxes of war: Militarization before 1941

In the spring of 1898, Americans were gripped by enthusiasm for war. In the wake of the sinking of the USS *Maine* in February, the public clamoured for revenge against Spain, whose agents had purportedly sabotaged the ship as it lay at anchor. As the McKinley administration equivocated over its response, public pressure mounted, and an angry crowd burned President William McKinley's effigy in Colorado.[1] When McKinley finally asked Congress for authorization to send troops to Cuba in early April, Congress swiftly gave its assent and then declared war on Spain. Since the regular Army only had a strength of 28,100, the next order of business was to raise volunteers for the war.[2] McKinley first called for 75,000 volunteers, then 125,000, then 200,000; ultimately, over a million Americans responded.[3] We can get some sense of the depth of the zeal for conflict by looking at the range of people who offered to raise troops for the War Department. Impresario William F. Cody, popularly known as 'Buffalo Bill', published an article in the *New York World* entitled 'How I Could Drive Spaniards from Cuba with Thirty Thousand Indian Braves', while Frank James, brother of the outlaw Jesse James, offered to raise a company of cowboys. Publisher William Randolph Hearst proposed assembling a regiment of professional boxers and baseball players who 'would overawe any Spanish regiment by their mere appearance'.[4]

While none of these more outlandish proposals were accepted, the ranks were swelled by large numbers of volunteers. Most famously, assistant secretary of the

---

[1] Clay Risen, *The Crowded Hour: Theodore Roosevelt, the Rough Riders, and the Dawn of the American Century* (New York: Simon & Schuster, 2020), 53.

[2] 'The U.S. Army in the 1890s', US Army Center of Military History, April 2000, https://history.army.mil/html/forcestruc/usa-1890.html.

[3] Kristin L. Hoganson, *Fighting for American Manhood: How Gender Politics Provoked the Spanish-American and Philippine-American Wars* (New Haven, CT: Yale University Press, 1998), 107.

[4] David F. Trask, *The War with Spain in 1898* (Lincoln: University of Nebraska Press, 1996), 156.

Navy Theodore Roosevelt and Army colonel (and veteran of frontier campaigns) Leonard Wood formed the 1st U.S. Volunteer Cavalry Regiment, which took the nickname of 'Rough Riders' from Cody's travelling Western show, 'Buffalo Bill's Wild West and Congress of Rough Riders of the World'.[5] The make-up of the regiment reflected the breadth of popular enthusiasm for war, as it included veterans, Ivy League athletes, Texas Rangers and Native Americans. As historian David Blight observes, this enthusiasm for war was widespread on both sides of the Mason-Dixon line.[6] The former Confederate General Joseph Wheeler, now a member of the House of Representatives, was granted a commission as a Major General by McKinley and commanded a Division in Cuba, while news of the first war death, a Naval ensign from North Carolina named Worth Bagley, united a north and south still steeped in the bitterness of civil war and Reconstruction. The *New York Tribune* declared that 'the South furnishes the first sacrifice of this war. There is no North and no South after that … we are all Worth Bagley's countrymen'.[7] The mobilization for war, then, marked a moment where reconciliation between North and South was almost complete.

The Spanish-American War also represented an important moment where the United States announced itself as a global military power, defeating a European empire on land and at sea, and operating not only in the Caribbean, where US forces routed the Spanish Army in Cuba and seized Puerto Rico, but also across the Pacific, where a US Navy squadron steamed from Hong Kong, defeated the Spanish fleet in Manilla Bay and then occupied the Philippines (an occupation that would soon descend into a brutal counterinsurgency campaign) and Guam.[8] Given that the US census bureau had declared the frontier on the continental United States closed in 1890, the events of 1898, which also included the annexation of Hawaii, marked a decisive shift towards a formal overseas empire.[9]

Yet at the same time, many of the patterns from previous wars held. Americans were certainly enthusiastic for war, but it was an amateurish enthusiasm.

---

[5] Paul Andrew Hutton, 'Col. Cody, Rough Riders, Spanish American War', *Points West*, Fall 1998, https://centerofthewest.org/2014/08/06/cody-rough-riders-spanish-american-war/.

[6] David W. Blight, *Race and Reunion: The Civil War in American Memory* (Cambridge, MA: Harvard University Press, 2002), 347–54; Richard E. Wood, 'The South and Reunion, 1898', *The Historian* 31, no. 3 (1969): 415–30.

[7] Blight, *Race and Reunion*, 352.

[8] For a useful popular history of US imperial expansion, see Daniel Immerwahr, *How to Hide an Empire: A History of the Greater United States* (New York: Farrar, Straus and Giroux, 2019), 59–107.

[9] Gerald Nash has questioned the significance of 1890 as a marker in the history of western United States, but there is no question that the 1890s marked an important moment of overseas expansion. Gerald D. Nash, 'The Census of 1890 and the Closing of the Frontier', *Pacific Northwest Quarterly* 71, no. 3 (1980): 98–100.

The regular Army remained small and relatively poorly equipped, and while Americans rushed to volunteer for military service, the vast majority of these volunteers never left the United States. Preparations for war were shambolic, as quartermasters struggled to manage railway timetables and to select debarkation ports, and the Army's performance in Cuba was not particularly impressive, with much of the American success due to the aid of Cuban rebels.[10] After the fighting had ended, over three quarters of the force was incapacitated by yellow fever, and they had to be quarantined at Montauk Point, New York, on their return to the United States.[11] While the Navy's strong performance in the war was due to sustained investment in the fleet that began in the 1880s, the Army's struggles were testament to the long-standing American suspicion of standing armies.[12] Both the struggle to transport the Army to Cuba and the offers of privately raised regiments of Indian braves and professional boxers stemmed from a consensus that amateurs could be perfectly capable soldiers and generals and that the vast distances that separated the United States from the European powers provided adequate protection from invasion. This meant that a large and well-equipped force was both a luxury and potential long-term threat to democracy. For the American volunteers of 1898, war was a passing thing, as it had been for previous generations: certainly important, possibly deeply affirming of their manhood, but not something that they need to organize their lives or society around.

The Spanish-American war, then, does not so much represent a sharp break with American tradition, but rather another moment in its transition from a regional to a global actor. As American power grew, the issue of what sort of role military instruments might have in advancing that power remained an open question. This chapter considers the long history of debates over militarization in the United States up to 1941, the moment that this book takes as the truly decisive turning point where both political culture and socio-economic structures changed in a permanent way. It looks at the evolution of the relationship between the US military and broader American society, as well as the experiences of armed Americans both on the frontier and overseas. By tracing debates over war, empire and 'preparedness', it shows how the militarization of American society ebbed and flowed from the American Revolution to the 1930s.

---

[10] J. P. Clark, *Preparing for War: The Emergence of the Modern U.S. Army, 1815–1917* (Cambridge, MA: Harvard University Press, 2017), 169–76.

[11] Graham A. Cosmas, *An Army for Empire: The United States Army in the Spanish-American War* (Columbia: University of Missouri Press, 1971), 245–63.

[12] Fred Anderson and Andrew Cayton, *The Dominion of War: Empire and Liberty in North America, 1500–2000* (New York: Penguin Books, 2005), 323.

In drawing a distinction between militarization prior to and after 1941, the intent here is not to deny the central place of war, expansion and settler colonialism in American history. In *The Dominion of War*, their sweeping history of five centuries of war in North America, Fred Anderson and Andrew Cayton rightly critique the tendency of previous generations of historians to approach 'the imperial dimension of the nation's history obliquely, treating occurrences of jingoism like the war fevers of 1812, 1846 and 1898 as unfortunate exceptions to the anti-militarist rule of republicanism'.[13] What the first century and a half of the nation's history does demonstrate, though, is that American imperial expansion took on a particular cast due to both the ideological visions of the American Revolution and the favourable geography that put vast oceans between Americans and potential threats.[14] This meant that the United States was an expansionist power, but that that expansion largely did not require the nation to orientate itself around the preparation for war. That distinction might have made little difference to those on the receiving end of American violence, but it did matter in that it had an effect on American political culture, the role and status of the military, and the stories that Americans told themselves about war.

The early part of the chapter examines debates about militarism in the early Republic and pre–Civil War era, focusing on how broad scepticism about the value of a standing army and fears of a 'man on horseback' in the form of a military leader who would overthrow democracy contended with the need to raise forces to fight on the frontier and the celebration of military heroes such as George Washington, Andrew Jackson and Zachary Taylor, all former generals who were elected president.[15] Even as war heroes were elected to high office, military officers never cohered as an influential political class. While the Civil War wrought immense social change and effectively brought about a second American Revolution, it did not resolve these contradictions, given that the Union Army rapidly demobilized at the end of the war and white southerners successfully opposed Reconstruction in part by claiming that the deployment of federal troops to enforce the law violated their rights.

After the conflict ended, a generation of veterans initially turned away from the horror of war, before re-embracing the notion of military service as the

---

[13] Anderson and Cayton, *The Dominion of War*, xi.
[14] Richard H. Immerman, *Empire for Liberty: A History of American Imperialism from Benjamin Franklin to Paul Wolfowitz* (Princeton, NJ: Princeton University Press, 2010); Walter Lippmann, *U.S. Foreign Policy: Shield of the Republic* (Boston, MA: Little, Brown, 1943); Anders Stephanson, *Manifest Destiny: American Expansion and the Empire of Right* (New York: Hill and Wang, 1996).
[15] David A. Bell, *Men on Horseback: The Power of Charisma in the Age of Revolution* (New York: Farrar, Straus and Giroux, 2020).

pinnacle of active masculine citizenship as the more traumatic memories of war faded. The Civil War never became a unifying national touchstone the way later wars did, but the celebration of military virtue became a useful reconciliation tactic between North and South. This change coincided with the overt embrace of empire and overseas intervention at the turn of the century; as war in Europe loomed, Americans first debated how best to be prepared for such a conflict, and then built the apparatus necessary to assert military power overseas and to make the United States a significant force on both land and at sea.

This global power was exercised with a decisive intervention in the First World War, breaching George Washington's long-standing admonition not to become embroiled in European conflicts. In order to prosecute that war, the Wilson administration built a proto-national security state, enacting sweeping domestic surveillance and policing powers, criminalizing forms of dissent and instituting a draft to supply manpower for the trenches in France. Even if these structures provided a blueprint for later efforts to build a national security state during the Second World War and the early Cold War, they were still seen as largely temporary impositions, and much of the wartime expansion of state power was rolled back in the conflict's aftermath, as Americans were divided over the role of the United States in maintaining the post-war order. The First World War did not provide the same sort of validation as 1898 had done, and those Americans who had been horrified by the slaughter on the Western Front joined with activists across the Atlantic in imagining how they might end war once and for all.

The twenty-year-long debate over American power that followed the end of the First World War was in keeping with the sort of tendencies that had dominated American politics since the foundation of the Republic. Throughout this period, there was significant resistance to militarization and militarism was never an unquestioned virtue, nor were the armed forces ever anything like the size of their European counterparts. From those who opposed the war with Mexico in 1846 to the anti-imperialists protesting wars in the Philippines and Cuba, to the pacifists opposing American entry into the First World War and advocating for worldwide disarmament after the war, to anti-interventionists of the 1920s and 1930s, anti-militarist movements found significant purchase in American political culture. In reading the long history of militarization in the United States, it is worth bearing these movements and the possibilities they imagined in mind, rather than treating the centuries before the Second World War as mere prelude to what must inevitably follow.

* * *

The United States was created through war. Even as delegates debated what the post-independence political order would look like, the Continental Congress expended much of their energies on organizing and equipping the Army and Navy while military leaders, especially General George Washington, were among the most popular figures in the colonies. From the outset though, the particular character of the American Revolution meant that many of the founders were ill-disposed towards standing armies. Colonists had objected to taxes levied by Parliament to pay for a standing army, while the misconduct of British soldiers and legislation passed by Parliament to ensure that any soldiers arrested for that misconduct would be tried in Britain rather than the colonies was the source of outrage prior to the Revolution.[16] While some of this hostility towards the military abated during the Revolutionary War, as the Continental Army proved to be a much more effective fighting force than the various local militias, questions of civil–military relations were immediately put back on the table when news of the Newburgh conspiracy reached Congress in 1783. While waiting for word of the outcome of the negotiations in Paris that would formally end the war, a group of soldiers agitated to take action against Congress in order to claim unpaid wages and secure the pensions that had been promised to them but never funded. While historians have disagreed over whether or not these soldiers were planning a coup d'état, it is clear that only the intervention of General George Washington, who pled with the Army to remain loyal to Congress, prevented matters from getting out of hand.[17] Very early on then, the spectre of militarism loomed over American politicians.

Washington's own resignation as commander-in-chief of the Continental Army provided a template for civilian supremacy over the military, but questions about the role of the military in American society were still a matter of fierce debate during the early years of the Republic. The Federalists, who were in the political ascendency for the first decade of the United States' existence, argued for the necessity of a strong state and a strong military to go with it.[18] Washington, along with allies such as Treasury Secretary Alexander Hamilton, thought that the young Republic was uniquely vulnerable to the predations of

---

[16] Robert Middlekauff, *The Glorious Cause: The American Revolution, 1763–1789*, rev. edn (Oxford: Oxford University Press, 2007), 152, 179.

[17] Richard H. Kohn, 'The Inside History of the Newburgh Conspiracy: America and the Coup d'Etat', *William and Mary Quarterly* 27, no. 2 (1970): 188–220, https://doi.org/10.2307/1918650; C. Edward Skeen and Richard H. Kohn, 'The Newburgh Conspiracy Reconsidered', *William and Mary Quarterly* 31, no. 2 (1974): 273–98, https://doi.org/10.2307/1920913.

[18] Richard H. Kohn, *Eagle and Sword: The Federalists and the Creation of the Military Establishment in America, 1783–1802*, 1st edn (New York: Free Press, 1975).

European powers and argued for a standing army and a strong navy to defend its independence. Hamilton also believed that the Army would have an important role in crushing internal dissent, and the events of Shays's Rebellion in 1787, where General Benjamin Lincoln had to solicit funds from private merchants in order to put together a force to suppress a rebellion that was attempting to overthrow the government of Massachusetts, further reinforced this belief.[19] Hamilton took advantage of the war crisis of 1798–9, when it seemed like a French invasion of United States was imminent, to argue again for a standing army.[20] He succeeded in having Congress appropriate enough funds for a 12,000-strong force to be put together and persuaded a reluctant Washington to come out of retirement to lead it. Even other Federalists were sceptical of the need for a standing army though, and President John Adams' reluctance to actually appoint officers and make provisions for this new force meant that it had petered out by mid-1800.[21] The Regular Army remained a small force of 5,400 men, primarily concerned with campaigning on the frontier.[22]

Thomas Jefferson's victory in the hotly contested presidential election of 1800 effectively ended Federalist dreams of a standing army. The Jeffersonians had a radically different view of foreign affairs: where Federalists saw a world full of danger that necessitated a strong military, the Jeffersonians believed that the expansion of commerce could bring peace to the world, and strongly associated war with monarchism and dictatorship.[23] Jefferson pointed to Napoleon's coup in France and Oliver Cromwell's track record as a dictator in England as examples of what could happen if a standing army was left in place.[24] Local, democratically controlled militias that could muster at short notice and then disperse when the threat had passed were far more preferable than risking a coup and impinging on liberties by taxing the citizenry to pay for an army. Jefferson cut the Army to a strength of 3,300 and even proposed replacing the Navy's half-dozen frigates with a 'militia' of several hundred small gunboats that would be incapable of waging offensive operations.[25]

---

[19] Leonard L. Richards, *Shays's Rebellion: The American Revolution's Final Battle* (Philadelphia: University of Pennsylvania Press, 2014).

[20] Gordon S. Wood, *Empire of Liberty: A History of the Early Republic, 1789–1815* (Oxford: Oxford University Press, 2011), 263–5.

[21] William J. Murphy, 'John Adams: The Politics of the Additional Army, 1798–1800', *New England Quarterly* 52, no. 2 (1979): 234–49, https://doi.org/10.2307/364841.

[22] Theodore J. Crackel, 'Jefferson, Politics, and the Army: An Examination of the Military Peace Establishment Act of 1802', *Journal of the Early Republic* 2, no. 1 (1982): 23, https://doi.org/10.2307/3122533.

[23] Wood, *Empire of Liberty*, 189.

[24] Wood, *Empire of Liberty*, 292.

[25] Crackel, 'Jefferson, Politics, and the Army', 23; Wood, *Empire of Liberty*, 293.

This proposal never came to pass. Instead, in an effort to root out Federalist political influence in the officer corps, Jefferson founded the Military Academy at West Point. Jefferson hoped to train not only officers who embodied Republican ideals but also the engineers and surveyors who would be needed for westward expansion.[26] The failures of the militia during the war of 1812, when some New England governors even refused to send their militias to war with Britain and where the American invasion of Canada collapsed in defeat due to the poor performance of militia units, further underlined the need to maintain some form of permanent military establishment, even if the size of that force was minimal in comparison to the sort of armies raised by European powers.[27] Not only that but, as historian Daniel Walker Howe observes, the militia system gradually faded away over the course of the early nineteenth century simply because militia duty was seen as onerous and unpopular.[28] The need to protect commerce from privateers and the fact that sailors tended to be less of a threat to liberty than soldiers meant that Jeffersonians were more sympathetic to the Navy, and Jefferson did dispatch a squadron of frigates to the Mediterranean to protect American shipping there.

Even if Americans in the early Republic turned away from formal military power and hoped for a coming world of peaceful democracies, their society was still shaped to some degree by war. Americans were instrumental in providing what historian Brian DeLay has called an 'iron river' of guns that flowed throughout the Americas, as federal armouries at Springfield, Massachusetts, and Harper's Ferry, Virginia, along with private contractors such as Eli Whitney, pioneered the use of interchangeable parts in musket manufacturing and sold arms to all comers.[29] The flow of American armaments had repercussions for revolutionaries in Latin America and Native tribes in the interior of North America, while it also helped spark the American industrial revolution.[30]

Memories of the Revolution and ongoing wars with Native American tribes on the frontier also provided a steady stream of military heroes for Americans, even if they hardly venerated peacetime military service.[31] General Andrew Jackson, who

---

[26] Wood, *Empire of Liberty*, 292.
[27] Clark, *Preparing for War*, 17–22; Wood, *Empire of Liberty*, 693.
[28] Daniel Walker Howe, *What Hath God Wrought: The Transformation of America, 1815–1848* (Oxford: Oxford University Press, 2009), 491.
[29] Brian DeLay, 'How Not to Arm a State: American Guns and the Crisis of Governance in Mexico, Nineteenth and Twenty-First Centuries', *Southern California Quarterly* 95, no. 1 (1 February 2013): 6, https://doi.org/10.1525/scq.2013.95.1.5; Howe, *What Hath God Wrought*, 532.
[30] Lindsay Schakenbach Regele, 'Manufacturing Advantage: War, the State, and the Origins of American Industry, 1790–1840', *Enterprise & Society* 17, no. 4 (2016): 721–33.
[31] James Edward Wright, *Those Who Have Borne the Battle: A History of America's Wars and Those Who Fought Them* (New York: Public Affairs, 2012), 66–70.

launched an unauthorized invasion of Spanish Florida in the first Seminole War of 1818, became a national celebrity and then a candidate for president in 1824. When Jackson won the presidency in 1828, he brought with him an expansionist zeal that accelerated an already-existing policy of aggression towards Native Americans.[32] Jackson's belligerence was representative of the emerging annexationist impulses of 'manifest destiny', the idea that American settlers were destined to colonize the entire continent of North America. Many proponents of manifest destiny, such as the journalist John L. O'Sullivan, believed that expansion could happen without the involvement of the military, as groups of settlers would organically set up democratic governments and then apply for admission to the United States.[33]

These Jeffersonian impulses were not shared by all expansionists, however. Nationalists such as John C. Calhoun continued to argue for the need for a strong army and navy, coastal fortifications and military roads that would allow that army to quickly traverse the country.[34] While Calhoun advocated for an expansible national army that would retain all of its regiments and officers but double the number of its enlisted ranks in time of war, other advocates for greater military spending envisioned a more static but no less expensive arrangement.[35] The Fortifications Board claimed that a building programme of coastal fortifications could, once complete, offer absolute security and that 'war and all of its terrors' would be 'shut from our territories by our fortresses, and transferred by our navy to the bosom of the ocean.'[36]

While many southerners, wary as they were of a strong government, did not share Calhoun's enthusiasm for a standing army, the historian Matthew Karp has demonstrated how 'southerners claimed almost exclusive control over the military politics of the republic' in the 1840s and 1850s and that many of them were willing to acquiesce in building a bigger military in order to achieve their goals of further expansion.[37] For southern expansionists, their institution of slavery would inevitably die out absent the acquisition of more territory in which it could grow, so the risk of a stronger military was one worth taking. Among their number was secretary of the Navy Abel P. Upshur, who unsuccessfully advocated quadrupling the size of the Navy in the 1840s so that it could stand

---

[32] Anderson and Cayton, *The Dominion of War*, 202–46.

[33] Robert J. Scholnick, 'Extermination and Democracy: O'Sullivan, the Democratic Review, and Empire, 1837–1840', *American Periodicals* 15, no. 2 (2005): 123–41.

[34] Clark, *Preparing for War*, 25–7.

[35] Clark, *Preparing for War*, 25–7.

[36] Brian McAllister Linn, *The Echo of Battle: The Army's Way of War* (Cambridge, MA: Harvard University Press, 2007), 17.

[37] Matthew Karp, *This Vast Southern Empire: Slaveholders at the Helm of American Foreign Policy* (Cambridge, MA: Harvard University Press, 2016), 199.

up to any European power, and Secretary of War Jefferson Davis, who increased the size of the Army to its largest ever peacetime level in the 1850s in order to subdue the Indians on the Great Plains.[38]

The culmination of the proslavery vision for expansion was the Mexican American War of 1846–8, when the United States followed its annexation of Texas with an invasion of Mexico intended to force the Mexicans to cede vast swathes of territory in the west. The war was fought by a combination of Regular Army and volunteer units, but the bulk of the responsibility for actual fighting fell on the shoulders of Regular units.[39] Much like the War of 1812, opinion on the war split along partisan lines, with most Whigs deeply critical of the Polk administration's aggressiveness.[40] The Whig-controlled House of Representatives did not vote to cut off support to the armies deployed to Mexico but otherwise denounced the president's war policy. Among them was the freshman Congressman Abraham Lincoln, who declared that Polk had fixed 'the public gaze upon the exceeding brightness of military glory – that attractive rainbow that rises in showers of blood – that serpent's eye, that charms to destroy'.[41] Like many Whigs, Lincoln feared the expansion of the Slave Power, and worried that a despot could take over the United States from within. In an earlier speech, his Lyceum Address of 1838, Lincoln gave perhaps the clearest possible expression of the geostrategic position of the United States in the mid-nineteenth century:

> Shall we expect some transatlantic military giant to step the ocean and crush us at a blow? Never! All the armies of Europe, Asia, and Africa combined, with all the treasure of the earth (our own excepted) in their military chest, with a Bonaparte for a commander, could not by force take a drink from the Ohio or make a track on the Blue Ridge in a trial of a thousand years.[42]

Of course, the point Lincoln was making was that the danger to the Republic was internal in nature. What followed in the years after the Mexican American War was a slide into Civil War that both vindicated these fears and ensured that the United States itself would be remade in the crucible of war.

* * *

---

[38] Karp, *This Vast Southern Empire*, 32–5, 208–16.

[39] Howe, *What Hath God Wrought*, 749.

[40] Amy S. Greenberg, *A Wicked War: Polk, Clay, Lincoln, and the 1846 U.S. Invasion of Mexico* (New York: Vintage, 2013).

[41] Anderson and Cayton, *The Dominion of War*, 284.

[42] Abraham Lincoln, 'The Perpetuation of Our Political Institutions (Address by Abraham Lincoln before the Young Men's Lyceum of Springfield, January 27, 1838)', *Papers of the Abraham Lincoln Association* 6, no. 1 (1984), http://hdl.handle.net/2027/spo.2629860.0006.103.

It is difficult to overstate the impact of the Civil War on the United States. With some justification, many historians refer to the conflict as 'the Second American Revolution', so far-reaching were its consequences for the political order.[43] The war touched every part of the United States and remains by far the bloodiest conflict in the nation's history. In order to raise and sustain the massive armies needed for the war, both the Union and the Confederacy greatly expanded the powers of the state.[44] The war ushered in the first national income tax, passed by Congress in 1861, and both North and South instituted conscription to help fill the ranks of their armies. Both sides allowed draftees to hire a substitute to take their place, while the Confederates carved out a series of exemptions, notably the Twenty Negro Law, which exempted one white man from military service for every slave owned on a plantation.[45] Not surprisingly, conscription proved hugely unpopular, prompting riots and anti-Black violence in New York City, and sparking such resistance in the South that the draft became nearly impossible to enforce in many parts of the Confederacy.[46] Notwithstanding the controversy it caused, the Civil War–era draft only directly touched on the lives of a few. The vast majority of soldiers were volunteers and only about 2 per cent of the US Army was composed of draftees, with another 6 per cent made up of substitutes hired by draftees (Figure 1.1).[47]

In keeping with previous wars, rapid demobilization followed the surrender of Confederate forces at Appomattox. The US Army quickly dropped from a peak strength of 1,000,000 in the spring of 1865 to 54,000 the following year down to 25,000 in 1875.[48] However, similar to those earlier wars, the army's strength was still greater than it had been prior to the war. Many of those who remained in uniform were immediately committed to the task of occupying and reconstructing the defeated South.[49] The commanders of the Army, Generals Grant and Sherman, found themselves at the centre of a power struggle between

[43] James M. McPherson, *Battle Cry of Freedom: The Civil War Era* (Oxford: Oxford University Press, 1988).

[44] Richard Franklin Bensel, *Yankee Leviathan: The Origins of Central State Authority in America, 1859–1877* (Cambridge: Cambridge University Press, 2008).

[45] David Williams, *Bitterly Divided: The South's Inner Civil War* (New York: New Press, 2010), 58.

[46] James Geary, *We Need Men: The Union Draft in the Civil War* (Dekalb: Northern Illinois University Press, 1991); Williams, *Bitterly Divided*.

[47] John Whiteclay Chambers, *The Oxford Companion to American Military History* (New York: Oxford University Press, 2000), 181.

[48] Richard W. Stewart, ed., *American Military History, Volume 1: The United States Army and the Forging of a Nation, 1775–1917* (Washington, DC: US Army Center of Military History, 2005), 304, 323.

[49] Eric Foner, *Reconstruction: America's Unfinished Revolution, 1863–1877* (New York: HarperCollins, 2011); Gregory P. Downs, *After Appomattox: Military Occupation and the Ends of War* (Cambridge, MA: Harvard University Press, 2015).

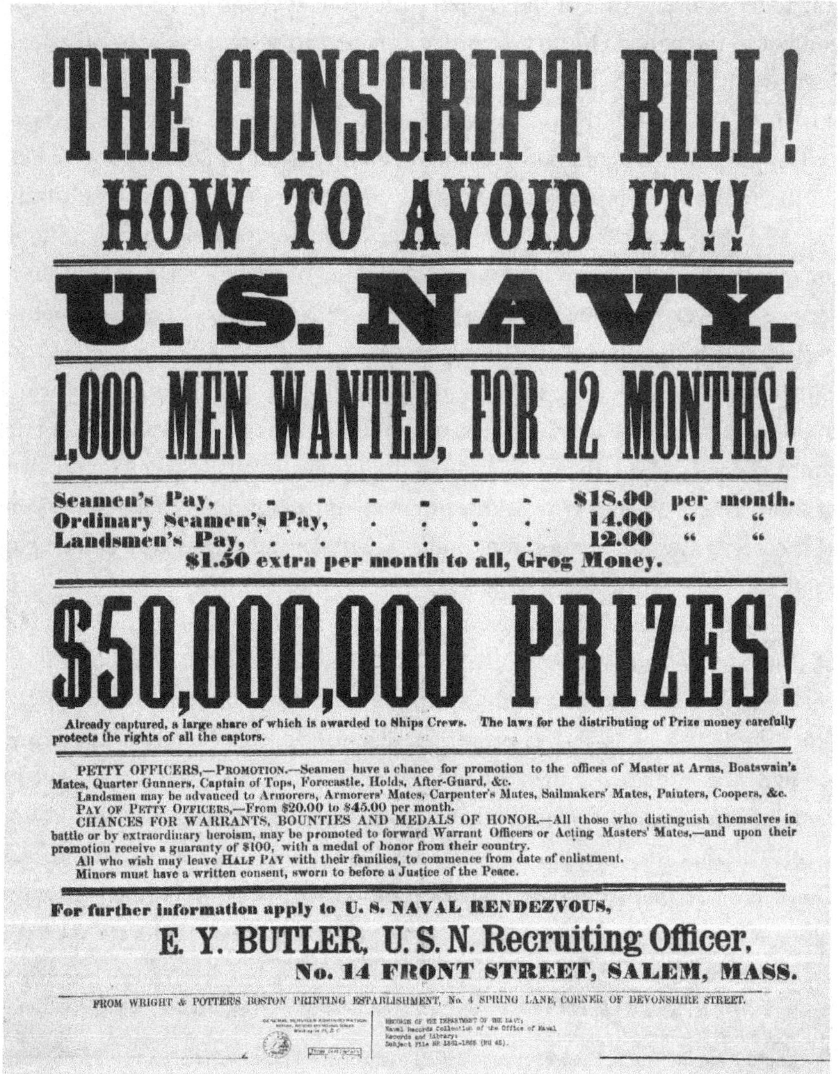

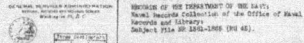

Figure 1.1 US Navy recruiting poster, 1863. Sailors who enlisted under this recruiting drive could avoid being conscripted into the Army. Credit: US National Archives.

President Andrew Johnson and the Radical Republicans in Congress, both of whom sought to impose their own vision of Reconstruction. The crisis came to a head when Johnson defied Congressional authority by removing Secretary of War Edward Stanton and appointing Grant in his stead. Grant ultimately sided with Congress by resigning when the Senate voted to reinstate Stanton, but, as historian J. P. Clark observes, the fact that Johnson's overreach forced Grant and Sherman 'to selectively defy the president [was] one of the lowest points in civilian control of the military in America'.[50]

Under the direction of Congress, the former Confederacy was divided into five military districts and 20,000 troops were sent to enforce the Reconstruction Acts, which enabled Black male suffrage and promoted civil rights. However, enforcing these acts proved to be difficult, and the now-President Grant was forced to re-impose martial law in parts of the South in order to combat a growing white supremacist insurgency.[51] The military's prominent role in governing the former Confederacy was presented as an outrageous infringement on liberty by Southern opponents of Reconstruction. One Southern academic later complained about white men being made 'to be the trembling subject of a major-general clothed with almost despotic power' before proclaiming that 'no people of English blood could be long subjected to military government'.[52]

While such a situation may have seemed anomalous in the old South, it was much more common further west. Indeed, the New Mexico Territory had spent four years under direct military government following its conquest in the Mexican American War, and army-protected trading posts in Indian Country had long been a pivotal part of the American presence in the west of the continent, while roads, river improvement and railroads that facilitated military movements further opened up what had been foreign lands for trade and exploitation.[53] Indeed, after a weary North abandoned Reconstruction in the face of armed white resistance, what was left of the Army was chiefly dedicated to campaigns in the Great Plains against the Ute, the Lakota and the Cheyenne, while the 1870s saw the beginning of the final push to conquer the Trans-Mississippi

---

[50] Clark, *Preparing for War*, 116.
[51] Andrew F. Lang, 'Republicanism, Race, and Reconstruction: The Ethos of Military Occupation in Civil War America', *Journal of the Civil War Era* 4, no. 4 (2014): 559–89; Downs, *After Appomattox*, 137–60.
[52] W. P. Trent, 'A New South View of Reconstruction', *Sewanee Review* 9, no. 1 (1901): 13, 19–20.
[53] Howe, *What Hath God Wrought*, 761; Brooke L. Blower, 'Nation of Outposts: Forts, Factories, Bases, and the Making of American Power', *Diplomatic History* 41, no. 3 (1 June 2017): 439–59, https://doi.org/10.1093/dh/dhx034; Robert Wooster, *The American Military Frontiers: The United States Army in the West, 1783–1900* (Albuquerque: University of New Mexico Press, 2012).

West for the United States.[54] These bloody campaigns, which took place far from the population centres of the East, rarely penetrated public consciousness at the time, apart from rare defeats like the battle of Little Bighorn, where a large detachment of 7th Cavalry Regiment under the command of Lieutenant Colonel George Custer was wiped out in an engagement with a mixed force of Lakota, northern Cheyenne and Arapaho tribes.[55]

News of the defeat of Little Bighorn reached the east just as the nation was preparing to celebrate its centennial on 4 July 1876.[56] While it was met with shock and prompted some calls for increased funding for the army and yet-harsher measures against the tribes of the Great Plains, appeals for a larger army went unheeded as its post-Reconstruction drawdown continued. Americans were more concerned with looking inwards at the still-raw wounds of the war than outwards at the frontier. Aside from the all-consuming question of Reconstruction, the government strove to provide pensions for more than 3 million war veterans, pioneering a large-scale social welfare system.[57] These veterans made up a substantial proportion of the all-male electorate, which helps explain why Grant's two-term presidency was followed by the election of two former brevet-generals, Rutherford B. Hayes and James Garfield. Indeed, every president from Grant's election in 1868 to the end of the nineteenth century could claim veteran status, bar the Democrat Grover Cleveland, who had hired a substitute to take his place in the war.

Elections were largely contests about the meaning of the Civil War – the historian David Blight argues that 'postwar American politics was still war by other means' – and politicians accused each other of 'waving the bloody shirt' of sectional divides in order to mobilize their supporters.[58] The response, as Blight has suggested, was to evacuate the political meaning of Civil War memories and to reduce white soldiers' narratives about the war to reconciliatory accounts emphasizing that all had 'fought heroically and deserved recognition, regardless of which side of a stone wall they had stood upon.'[59] As the decade progressed, and memories of the war's trauma faded, these narratives cohered into a new

[54] Sherry L. Smith, 'Lost Soldiers: Re-Searching the Army in the American West', *Western Historical Quarterly* 29, no. 2 (1 May 1998): 149–63, https://doi.org/10.2307/971327.

[55] Pekka Hämäläinen, *Lakota America: A New History of Indigenous Power* (New Haven, CT: Yale University Press, 2019), 364–72.

[56] Heather Cox Richardson, *West from Appomattox: The Reconstruction of America after the Civil War* (New Haven, CT: Yale University Press, 2007), 174.

[57] Theda Skocpol, *Protecting Soldiers and Mothers: The Political Origins of Social Policy in the United States* (Cambridge, MA: Harvard University Press, 1995).

[58] Blight, *Race and Reunion*, 102–3.

[59] Blight, *Race and Reunion*, 189–90.

nationalism, and by 1895 the jurist and Civil War veteran Oliver Wendell Holmes Jr. was standing before the students of Harvard, bemoaning that 'war is out of fashion, and the man who commands attention of his fellows is the man of wealth'.[60] Critiquing the culture of the gilded age which led to 'rootless self-seeking search for a place where the most enjoyment may be had at the least cost', Holmes argued that the antidote to capitalism could be found in the austere pleasures of war.[61] Holmes argued that 'noble enemies' in Virginia, Georgia and on the Mississippi taught that a soldier's life was an honourable one and that 'War, when you are at it, is horrible and dull. It is only when time has passed that you see that its message was divine.'[62]

* * *

While Holmes complained that 'the aspirations of the world are those of commerce' and denigrated the 'moralists and philosophers' who were declaring 'that war is wicked, foolish and soon to disappear', in truth, it was his world view that was ascendant by the time he spoke.[63] Holmes spoke of being inspired by the 'sword-slashed faces' of the young German fencers he saw at the University of Heidelberg, and he regarded that prospect of a polo player breaking their neck in a fall 'not as a waste, but as a price well paid for the breeding of a race fit for headship and command'.[64] This embrace of war, then, was part of a transatlantic turn towards militarism that was partly inspired by the creed of social Darwinism.[65] Imperialists like Senator Henry Cabot Lodge believed that the United States needed to join the European race for empire and not to shrink from the martial consequences. In a letter to a friend, Lodge echoed Holmes when he complained that 'the moment any question arises in which the honour of the country is involved and patriotism aroused, the opposition seems always to come from bankers and capitalists', and later he wrote that 'war is a bad thing no doubt, but there are worse things for both nations and men'.[66]

The romanticism of Holmes and Lodge was not entirely incompatible with the interests of capitalism, though. Alfred Thayer Mahan, the American naval

---

[60] Oliver Wendell Holmes, 'The Soldier's Faith', in *The Essential Holmes: Selections from the Letters, Speeches, Judicial Opinions, and Other Writings of Oliver Wendell Holmes, Jr*, ed. Richard A. Posner (Chicago: University of Chicago Press, 1992), 87.
[61] Holmes, 'The Soldier's Faith', 88.
[62] Holmes, 'The Soldier's Faith', 92, 91.
[63] Holmes, 'The Soldier's Faith', 87.
[64] Holmes, 'The Soldier's Faith', 92.
[65] H. W. Koch, 'Social Darwinism as a Factor in the "New Imperialism"', in *The Origins of the First World War: Great Power Rivalry and German War Aims*, ed. H. W. Koch (London: Macmillan Education UK, 1984), 319–42, https://doi.org/10.1007/978-1-349-07437-2_9.
[66] Immerman, *Empire for Liberty*, 145.

strategist whose writings were enormously influential on both sides of the Atlantic, held similar views but couched them very much in cold-blooded calculations about trade and commerce. A devoted Anglophile, Mahan believed, in the words of historian David Milne, that 'the British were doing the world a favour in their colonial expansion during the nineteenth century. They were opening backward nations up to trade, cleansing the arteries of global commerce, and thus doing all exporting nations a great service.'[67] As British power inevitably faded, Mahan believed the United States must take its place by building up a powerful Navy and assuming the duties of global hegemon. When Mahan was attempting to put his ideas on paper in the 1880s, it was clear that the United States was in the midst of eclipsing Britain as the world's pre-eminent industrial power, but, as Milne puts it, 'this bulky economic stature cast a faint military shadow'.[68]

Mahan's book, *The Influence of Sea Power upon History, 1660–1783*, did much to change this state of affairs, helping to build elite support for a great expansion of the Navy.[69] Mahan found an important acolyte in Theodore Roosevelt, then assistant secretary of the Navy.[70] Mahan did not embrace war with Spain in 1898 with much enthusiasm, but both Lodge and Roosevelt were among its most influential supporters. As historian Kristin Hoganson argues, gendered and racialized ideas about white martial masculinity were crucial in securing both popular and elite support for the war.[71] More than anyone, Roosevelt promoted (and attempted to live out) the idea that soldiers were model citizens who embodied the best manly qualities. In a speech delivered in 1899 while he was governor of New York, Roosevelt argued that the United States 'must strive in good faith to play a great part in the world'. If it did not, it need only look to the example of China, a country 'content to rot by inches in ignoble ease within [its] borders, taking no interest in what goes on beyond them, sunk in a scrambling commercialism'. China had found that 'in this world the nation that has trained

---

[67]　David Milne, *Worldmaking: The Art and Science of American Diplomacy*, repr. edn (New York: Farrar, Straus and Giroux, 2017), 31.

[68]　Milne, *Worldmaking*, 32.

[69]　Alfred Thayer Mahan, *The Influence of Sea Power upon History 1660–1783* (London: Sampson Low, Marston & Company, 1892), https://books.google.ie/books?id=DWw-AQAAMAAJ&dq=the%20influence%20of%20sea%20power%20upon%20history&pg=PR1#v=onepage&q=the%20influence%20of%20sea%20power%20upon%20history&f=false.

[70]　Peter Karsten, 'The Nature of "Influence": Roosevelt, Mahan and the Concept of Sea Power', *American Quarterly* 23, no. 4 (1971): 585–600, https://doi.org/10.2307/2711707; J. Simon Rofe, '"Under the Influence of Mahan": Theodore and Franklin Roosevelt and Their Understanding of American National Interest', *Diplomacy & Statecraft* 19, no. 4 (16 December 2008): 732–45, https://doi.org/10.1080/09592290802564536.

[71]　Hoganson, *Fighting for American Manhood*.

itself to a career of unwarlike and isolated ease is bound, in the end, to go down before other nations which have not lost the manly and adventurous qualities'.[72]

Indeed, in its participation in the suppression of the Boxer Rebellion in Beijing in 1900, the United States itself played an active role in the humiliation of China. American intervention in China was only one of a spate of military engagements in these years. Apart from the ocean-spanning invasions of 1898, American troops intervened in Nicaragua, Honduras, Dominican Republic, Panama and the Philippines between 1885 and 1915. It was this last conflict that did the most to discredit the imperialist case for war. As Hoganson points out, anti-imperialists attempted to invert imperial notions of manliness to argue that American war against the Filipino independence movement was degrading the honour of the Army by 'making American soldiers even more savage than the people they were sent to redeem'.[73] Old arguments about the anti-democratic nature of military service were aired again, even if concern this time was more about the corrosive effect on soldiers than on those they were oppressing. If the Spanish-American War had been, in the words of Secretary of State John Hay, 'a splendid little war', then the war in the Philippines highlighted an altogether different set of realities for Americans.[74]

Opposition to the Spanish-American War and the occupation of the Philippines helped to bolster the American peace movement. American internationalists, like the industrialist Andrew Carnegie, feared that the war was part of a 'vortex of militarism' threatening international peace, and agitated for the use of non-military means to advance American power.[75] There was a strong legalist streak to this activism, and proponents of peace emphasized the possibilities of using arbitration, a mechanism that the United States had made frequent use of in the nineteenth century, to resolve international tensions without war.[76] Legalists even advanced the idea that permanent international courts could end war between civilized nations, while Americans became prominent in the international peace

---

[72] Theodore Roosevelt, *The Works of Theodore Roosevelt in Fourteen Volumes*, executive edn, vol. 12 (The Strenuous Life) (New York: P. F. Collier & Son, 1899), 8, https://www.gutenberg.org/files/58821/58821-h/58821-h.htm.

[73] Hoganson, *Fighting for American Manhood*, 183.

[74] Brian McAllister Linn, *The Philippine War, 1899–1902* (Lawrence: University Press of Kansas, 2000); Paul Alexander Kramer, *The Blood of Government: Race, Empire, the United States, & the Philippines* (Chapel Hill: University of North Carolina Press, 2006); Christopher Capozzola, *Bound by War: How the United States and the Philippines Built America's First Pacific Century* (New York: Basic Books, 2020), 13–64.

[75] Duncan Bell, *Dreamworlds of Race: Empire and the Utopian Destiny of Anglo-America* (Princeton, NJ: Princeton University Press, 2020), 74.

[76] Benjamin Allen Coates, *Legalist Empire: International Law and American Foreign Relations in the Early Twentieth Century* (Oxford: Oxford University Press, 2016), 30.

movement. Carnegie funded the construction of a 'peace palace' for the new permanent court of arbitration in the Hague, and Americans were the driving force behind the 1907 Hague conference, which attempted to regulate the conduct of war.[77] The push did not come solely from peace activists – after all, it was Roosevelt who had called for the conference, and he had won a Nobel Peace Prize for his mediation of the Russo-Japanese War in 1906 – but their emphasis on the primacy of international law caused serious splits among American elites. Roosevelt's successor as president, William Howard Taft, negotiated arbitration treaties with Britain and France which attempted to ensure that any international disputes with these powers would be handled peacefully. These treaties helped cause a permanent rupture with his former ally Roosevelt, and they faced fierce opposition in the Senate, where opponents successfully argued that these treaties would unreasonably limit American freedom of action.[78]

Indeed, even as Taft advanced the treaties in the Senate, he told an aide that he hoped that they would 'draw the sting of old Carnegie and other peace cranks' and mute their criticism of naval rearmament.[79] While advocates for international peace won some successes, they did so in the shadow of a global arms race in which the United States was an enthusiastic participant.[80] Mahan's advocacy for sea power had had an effect on virtually all great powers, and all engaged in extensive naval shipbuilding programmes.[81] In the twenty-five years prior to the outbreak of the First World War, the aggregate warship tonnage of the six major powers more than quadrupled.[82] With the encouragement of a Naval enthusiast in the White House in the form of Teddy Roosevelt, the United States greatly expanded its fleet. By 1907, the Atlantic fleet was made up of sixteen modern battleships and the US Navy vied with the Imperial German Navy for second place in the naval power rankings.[83]

---

[77] Coates, *Legalist Empire*, 91–5.

[78] John P. Campbell, 'Taft, Roosevelt, and the Arbitration Treaties of 1911', *Journal of American History* 53, no. 2 (1966): 279–98, https://doi.org/10.2307/1894200.

[79] Coates, *Legalist Empire*, 102.

[80] Dirk Bonker, 'Admiration, Enmity, and Cooperation: U.S. Navalism and the British and German Empires before the Great War', *Journal of Colonialism and Colonial History* 2, no. 1 (2001), https://doi.org/10.1353/cch.2001.0002.

[81] Ronald B. St. John, 'European Naval Expansion and Mahan, 1889–1906', *Naval War College Review* 23, no. 7 (1971): 74–83.

[82] Dirk Bönker, *Militarism in a Global Age: Naval Ambitions in Germany and the United States before World War I* (Ithaca, NY: Cornell University Press, 2012), 2.

[83] The historian Katherine Epstein, however, persuasively argues that 'the impressive steel exoskeleton of the U.S. Navy obscured deficiencies in its supply base, logistics, and readiness for combat … The fleet was top-heavy in capital ships, lacking the smaller vessels necessary to perform myriad functions – protection from torpedo craft, refuelling, and so forth – required to make a navy effective.' Katherine C. Epstein, 'The Conundrum of American Power in the Age of World War I', *Modern American History* 2, no. 3 (November 2019): 351, https://doi.org/10.1017/mah.2019.23.

Figure 1.2 The Great White Fleet at Hampton Roads, 1907. Credit: Library of Congress, Prints and Photographs Division, Detroit Publishing Company Collection.

While this shipbuilding programme was a highly technocratic and elite-led endeavour that, in the words of one historian, fused 'the navy, elite rule, the industrial nation, and global power' to create a particular form of militarism, its proponents also worked hard to promote it in the popular imagination.[84] As with Britain and Imperial Germany, naval reviews drew enormous crowds to watch lines of battleships steam by. The largest naval review, in San Francisco Bay in 1908, attracted more than a million spectators.[85] This parade marked the midpoint of the around-the-world voyage of the 'Great White Fleet'. On the order of Roosevelt, the Navy despatched a fleet of sixteen battleships to tour the world and make ceremonial visits to various friendly ports in order to demonstrate growing American military power and blue-water naval capabilities (Figure 1.2).[86]

---

[84] Bönker, *Militarism in a Global Age*, 6.
[85] Bönker, *Militarism in a Global Age*, 216.
[86] James R. Reckner, *Teddy Roosevelt's Great White Fleet*, new edn (Annapolis, MD: Naval Institute Press, 2001); Kenneth Wimmel, *Theodore Roosevelt and the Great White Fleet: American Sea Power Comes of Age* (Washington, DC: Brassey's, 1998); Margaret Werry, ' "The Greatest Show on Earth": Political Spectacle, Spectacular Politics, and the American Pacific', *Theatre Journal* 57, no. 3 (2005): 355–82, https://doi.org/10.1353/tj.2005.0124.

Even if Naval power could have elitist connotations, it was an easier sell to American sensibilities than substantially increasing the strength of the Army. While there was no momentum for a large expansion, concerns over the Army's performance in Cuba combined with the general modernizing impulse of the age led to a series of reforms at the turn of the century. As late as 1895, the annual survey of the world's military forces published by the German General Staff didn't bother to include the United States.[87] The Dodge Commission, established to investigate the War Department's failings in 1898, gave impetus to change this situation. The new Secretary of War, Elihu Root, both advocated for an increase in the size of the regular Army and worked to standardize and nationalize the militia system, creating a trained force that could be called into federal service more efficiently.[88] Root also established a separate Army General Staff, which would be responsible for war planning, as well as overhauling the officer promotion system and establishing an Army War College to provide the General Staff with adequately trained officers. Root's reforms were typical of the Progressive era in that they emphasized the importance of professionalization, standardization and efficient bureaucracy.

At a strength of 88,000, this reorganized Army would still be too small to hold its own in a war with great powers, but it became 'the vessel into which citizen-soldiers were poured in times of crisis'.[89] As he had done with the Navy earlier in the century, Roosevelt advocated heavily for increased spending on the Army, especially as the prospect of a great war loomed. Roosevelt's old 'Rough Rider' comrade (and by now former Army Chief of Staff) Leonard Wood worked with Roosevelt, Root and others to create a 'preparedness movement' after the outbreak of the First World War that argued for a huge expansion of the Army and for an immediate implementation of a Universal Military Training programme that would train over a million conscripts a year.[90] When the Wilson administration refused to fully commit to the sort of expansion that preparedness advocates wanted, Wood and others organized the Plattsburg camps, a series of privately funded military training programmes that trained 40,000 volunteers in the summers of 1915 and 1916.[91]

---

[87] Jörg Muth, *Command Culture: Officer Education in the U.S. Army and the German Armed Forces, 1901–1940, and the Consequences for World War II* (Denton: University of North Texas Press, 2011), 18.

[88] Clark, *Preparing for War*, 183–96.

[89] Clark, *Preparing for War*, 1.

[90] Clark, *Preparing for War*, 249–54.

[91] J. Garry Clifford, *The Citizen Soldiers; the Plattsburg Training Camp Movement, 1913–1920* (Lexington: University Press of Kentucky, 1972), http://archive.org/details/citizensoldiersp0000clif.

The camps largely attracted upper-class recruits, in part because candidates had to pay for both their uniforms and subsistence, but they reflected the Progressive desire to impose middle-class values and discipline on both the decadent top tier of society and the immigrant working classes.[92] Indeed, many of the preparedness advocates expressed contempt for civilian society; Wood complained to a colleague that 'the people are filled with ignorance and a cheap conceit as to their military ability, which has been catered to and built up by fakers'.[93] As historian Brian Linn has noted, the military intellectuals of the Progressive era mourned the passing of the nineteenth-century citizen solider, 'posthumously transformed into a rugged fighter and national marksman, [who] sparkled as a diamond when compared to the human lumps of coal produced by the industrialized metropolis'.[94] For the militarists of the early twentieth century, war was far less of a threat to liberty and democracy than a degenerate citizenry would be.

* * *

This view was never uncontested but it did mean that the American public was primed to see military service as a worthy endeavour by the time the Wilson administration instituted a draft in 1917. Unlike the Civil War, where the draft only provided a small minority of soldiers while states provided large numbers of troops in volunteer units, the First World War saw the United States assemble a truly national army, in which 72 per cent of troops were conscripted.[95] The deployment of this army to Europe came as a surprise even to some who voted for war, as many in Congress thought that they were voting for a limited war in defence of neutrality in which only a token force would be sent to Europe.[96] The manpower needs of the Allies, though, meant that the United States committed an American Expeditionary Force that would eventually number 2 million. By the end of the war, more than 4 million men had served in the Army, with over 700,000 in other military service branches.[97]

[92] Clark, *Preparing for War*, 250; Ross A. Kennedy, 'Preparedness', in *A Companion to Woodrow Wilson* (New York: Wiley-Blackwell, 2013), 270–85, https://doi.org/10.1002/9781118445693.ch14.

[93] Linn, *The Echo of Battle*, 112.

[94] Linn, *The Echo of Battle*, 111.

[95] Jennifer D. Keene, *Doughboys, the Great War, and the Remaking of America* (Baltimore, MD: Johns Hopkins University Press, 2003), 2.

[96] Chris Capozzola et al., 'Interchange: World War I', *Journal of American History* 102, no. 2 (1 September 2015): 474, https://doi.org/10.1093/jahist/jav474.

[97] David A. Blum and Nese F. DeBruyne, 'American War and Military Operations Casualties: Lists and Statistics' (Washington, DC: Congressional Research Service, July 2020), 2, https://crsreports.congress.gov/product/pdf/RL/RL32492.

In order to raise this Army, and to foreclose the possibility of his rival Theodore Roosevelt recruiting an army of volunteers and taking them to Europe, Wilson turned to a draft. Roosevelt had been authorized by Congress in March 1917 to raise four divisions similar to the Rough Riders, but Wilson rejected Roosevelt's offer and instead chose to send an American Expeditionary Force, under the command of General John J. Pershing, to France instead. Congress passed the Selective Service Act of 1917, which required all men between the ages of twenty-one and thirty to register for potential military service.[98] Draft registration was a major national event: there were three registration days throughout the course of the war. On the first one, 5 June 1917, over 24 million men stood in line for hours at a time to register.[99] Even if the policy was set nationally, the administration of the drafts still relied heavily on voluntarism: 4,648 boards made up of local volunteers were responsible for registering men, classifying them, deciding on exemptions and placing draftees on trains to training centres.[100] In keeping with the ideals of the Plattsburg movement, Progressives hoped that wartime military service would help forge a homogenized male citizen that embodied American values, with reformers focusing their efforts on leisure activities in Army training camps, as they attempted to provide organized activities for working-class draftees that would promote physical fitness and moral instruction and would counter the temptations of alcohol and sex.[101] Draft registration formed only part of the national voluntarist effort. More than 500,000 women collected pledges on behalf of the newly established US Food Administration, where they convinced citizens to commit to conserving food in order to help the war effort.[102]

As the Wilson administration sought to manage the Army's manpower needs while still relying on as much voluntarism from private groups as possible, they also attempted to strike a similar balance with the mobilization of the economy for war. Treasury Secretary William McAdoo embarked on a programme of extensive borrowing to help pay for the war, and much of this financing came from the 'liberty loans' scheme, where citizens were encouraged to purchase war

---

[98] Edward M. Coffman, *The War to End All Wars: The American Military Experience in World War I* (Lexington: University Press of Kentucky, 2014), 25–8.

[99] Christopher Capozzola, *Uncle Sam Wants You: World War I and the Making of the Modern American Citizen* (Oxford: Oxford University Press, 2010), 18.

[100] 'World War I Draft Registration Cards', National Archives, 15 August 2016, https://www.archives.gov/research/military/ww1/draft-registration.

[101] Andrew J. Huebner, *Love and Death in the Great War* (Oxford: Oxford University Press, 2018), 84, 99.

[102] Capozzola, *Uncle Sam Wants You*, 19; Julia Irwin, *Making the World Safe: The American Red Cross and a Nation's Humanitarian Awakening* (Oxford: Oxford University Press, 2013).

bonds as part of their patriotic duty.[103] The government's Committee on Public Information dedicated much of its propaganda effort to the liberty loan drive, deploying thousands of 'four-minute men' to make pro-war speeches at cinemas, restaurants and town halls.[104] McAdoo also used the war to implement a much more progressive system of taxation. Prior to the war, 75 per cent of federal revenues came from customs and excise taxes; after the war, that same share was drawn from taxes on income, profits and estates.[105] Wartime social welfare legislation also focused on the needs of wounded soldiers, hoping to rehabilitate as many as possible so that they would not be a burden of the state in the post-war years.

While the reach of the fiscal state expanded, the economy generally boomed. Notional national income almost doubled over the course of the war, as the United States effectively fed and equipped the Allied side.[106] Arms manufacturers made huge profits during the wartime years. The Savage Arms Corporation made a 60 per cent profit in 1917, while the Bethlehem Shipbuilding Company increased its annual average profits from $6 million at the war's outset to $49 million by the war's end. The DuPont Company multiplied its stock dividends by a factor of sixteen over the course of the conflict, and finished the war with its assets having quadrupled and with a surplus of $68 million in the bank.[107] Given this extraordinary growth, the administration struggled with the question of how to manage a hot economy and service the needs of wartime industries while causing minimal disruption to the rest of the economy. Progressives were split on the question of whether strong anti-trust legislation should be used to ensure a thriving system of small producers or whether the efficiencies of large corporations could be a blessing in wartime. The various bodies set up to coordinate the economy, such as the War Industrial Board and the Food Administration, struggled to find the balance between voluntary cooperation and government direction.[108]

As historian Chris Capozzola points out, though, when it came to ordinary citizens, there was a coercive edge to the culture of wartime voluntarism. The three years of fractious debate over whether or not to enter the war had deeply

---

[103] David M. Kennedy, *Over Here: The First World War and American Society* (Oxford: Oxford University Press, 2004), 100–6.
[104] Susan A. Brewer, *Why America Fights: Patriotism and War Propaganda from the Philippines to Iraq* (Oxford: Oxford University Press, 2009), 62–4.
[105] Kennedy, *Over Here*, 112.
[106] Adam Tooze, *The Deluge: The Great War and the Remaking of Global Order 1916–1931* (London: Penguin, 2015), 242.
[107] Kennedy, *Over Here*, 139.
[108] Kennedy, *Over Here*, 113–43.

polarized American society, which meant that the public did not rise up as one mass to support the war effort. The women who worked on pledge drives convinced others to sign up not just through persuasion but by gossip and public shaming too.[109] In a more directly coercive fashion, the draft was policed by a 500,000-strong vigilante organization, the American Protective League (APL), that, with the blessings of the federal government, sought to clamp down on draft evasion. Outright resistance to the draft was rare, but some 337,000 men evaded conscription.[110] The most spectacular form of vigilante coercion was the 'slacker raid': mass dragnet operations carried out by APL members wearing government-issued badges. In the largest such operation, the New York City slacker raids of September 1918, the APL 'scoured the city's streets and public places' in search of men evading the draft and interrogated between 300,000 and 500,000 men over the course of three days. Anyone without a draft card could find himself dragged to the nearest police station.[111]

Beyond policing the draft, vigilantes focused on fears of espionage and dissent. In April 1918, a mob in Illinois lynched a German-American coal miner who they suspected of being a spy, while in June 1917, a local sheriff in Bisbee, Arizona, mobilized some 2,000 volunteers from the Citizen's Protective League to violently break up a coal miner's strike, and 'deported' the striking miners and their families to New Mexico.[112] In a more official capacity, the Bureau of Investigation focused on striking workers, tarring them as either pro-German or (later in the war) pro-Bolshevik, while the government worked to regulate and control the activities of 'enemy aliens'. In a move heavy with symbolism, the immigration inspection station at Ellis Island, New York, became a detention centre for enemy aliens.[113] Several states moved to mandate that schools teach in English only, banning the German language from their classrooms.[114] Meanwhile, while much wartime rhetoric contrasted American press freedom with oppressive German militarism, the Espionage Act allowed the government to regulate speech by granting the Postmaster General the right to withhold from the mails any material that advocated treason, insurrection or sedition.[115]

---

[109] Capozzola, *Uncle Sam Wants You*, 19.
[110] Capozzola, *Uncle Sam Wants You*, 10.
[111] Capozzola, *Uncle Sam Wants You*, 46.
[112] Capozzola, *Uncle Sam Wants You*, 117, 126–7.
[113] Capozzola, *Uncle Sam Wants You*, 173.
[114] Frederick C. Luebke, *Bonds of Loyalty: German-Americans and World War I* (DeKalb: Northern Illinois University Press, 1974).
[115] Gary Gerstle, *Liberty and Coercion: The Paradox of American Government from the Founding to the Present* (Princeton, NJ: Princeton University Press, 2015), 128–30.

Unsurprisingly, this mix of private and state coercion produced resistance.[116] The socialist politician Eugene V. Debs continued to openly oppose the war and, in a speech in Canton, Ohio, in June 1918, urged resistance to the draft. He was arrested shortly thereafter and convicted of ten counts of sedition.[117] Religious pacifist groups such as the Mennonites and Quakers claimed draft exemptions for their congregants. Some groups assented to draft registration on condition that their draftees be assigned to non-combatant duties, while others rejected any semblance of cooperation with Selective Service. Significantly, conscientious objectors who objected to military service did so by emphasizing their own personal religious and moral objections to war.[118] As the proto-National Security State of the First World War era grew, the opposition to that state increasingly took the form of assertions about the rights of individual citizens. While the Supreme Court largely upheld convictions under laws against anti-war speech, the Court's thinking began to drift towards an emphasis on free speech.[119] Civil society groups worked to advocate for these rights, and the most influential of these groups, the American Civil Liberties Union, was founded in 1920 as a consequence of wartime activism on free speech on conscientious objection.[120] There were few organized protests against the war after American entry, but the three-way contest between pro-war vigilantes, anti-war activists and the state worked to produce both new forms of rights and ideas about 'Americanness' that were based more on obedience to the laws of the state than on the dense web of private obligations that had initially been mobilized to coerce support for the war effort.[121]

Negotiating that dense web was no straightforward matter, though. As state institutions sought to mobilize Americans for war, they found themselves negotiating with citizens who thought that their wartime service gave them particular rights. As historian Jennifer Keene argues, the Army initially aimed to promote a doctrine of '100% Americanism' in its training regime, emphasizing the shedding of Old World attributes in favour of a thoroughly American identity.[122] However, army leaders soon realized that they were dealing with

---

[116] Michael Kazin, *War against War: The American Fight for Peace, 1914–1918* (New York: Simon & Schuster, 2017).

[117] Geoffrey R. Stone, *Perilous Times: Free Speech in Wartime: From the Sedition Act of 1798 to the War on Terrorism* (New York: W. W. Norton, 2005), 192–8.

[118] Capozzola, *Uncle Sam Wants You*, 81.

[119] Richard Polenberg, *Fighting Faiths: The Abrams Case, the Supreme Court, and Free Speech* (Ithaca, NY: Cornell University Press, 1999).

[120] Paul L. Murphy, *World War I and the Origin of Civil Liberties in the United States* (New York: W. W. Norton, 1979).

[121] Capozzola, *Uncle Sam Wants You*, 6–8.

[122] Keene, *Doughboys, the Great War, and the Remaking of America*, 21.

a cohort of men who saw their military service obligation as a social contract that they intended to negotiate. This meant that harsh discipline had to be moderated in the face of objections from draftees, and even the push for '100% Americanism' gave way to a more Progressive approach that accepted the dual identity of citizen soldiers.[123] More darkly, the Army had to contend with the views of its own soldiers when it came to matters of race. Any attempt to put Black soldiers in close proximity to white soldiers or even to put Black soldiers in positions of minor authority faced fierce backlash, and Army commanders typically accommodated the demands of white draftees in spite of the negative effect that segregation had on the war effort.[124]

The travails of Black soldiers hinted at the coming disappointment of Black civil rights activists, such as W. E. B. DuBois, who had reluctantly supported the war and African American participation in it in the hope that it might provide leverage for civil rights at home and precipitate the end of colonialism overseas.[125] The Black press had noted with interest the presence of armed coloured colonial troops in the ranks of Allied armies from 1914 onwards and many hoped that Black American manhood might achieve similar recognition if given the opportunity to fight on European battlefields.[126] While 370,000 Black soldiers were drafted, any hope of using them in combat was dashed by white resistance, both from fellow draftees and from the Southern politicians who objected to hosting large numbers of armed Black soldiers in their states.[127] Indeed, this era was marked by increased racial violence rather than any major advances in civil rights.[128]

White women fared better during the war than African Americans had. The passage of the 19th Amendment, which granted suffrage to white women, owed much to wartime mobilization of women. While Alfred Thayer Mahan had claimed that female suffrage would weaken military preparedness because women voting would 'obliterate the constant practice of past ages by which to men are assigned the outdoor rough action of life and women that indoor sphere which we call the family', women used their wartime roles to make the case for their political rights.[129] Through their fulfilment of wartime obligations, such as

---

[123] Keene, *Doughboys, the Great War, and the Remaking of America*, 62.
[124] Keene, *Doughboys, the Great War, and the Remaking of America*, 82–104.
[125] Chad L. Williams, *Torchbearers of Democracy: African American Soldiers in the World War I Era* (Chapel Hill: University of North Carolina Press, 2013); Adriane Lentz-Smith, *Freedom Struggles: African Americans and World War I* (Cambridge, MA: Harvard University Press, 2010).
[126] Capozzola et al., 'Interchange', 467.
[127] Huebner, *Love and Death in the Great War*, 69–70.
[128] Capozzola et al., 'Interchange', 496.
[129] Huebner, *Love and Death in the Great War*, 6.

food pledge drives, publicly shaming 'slackers' and willingly sending their sons and husbands to war, white women demonstrated that they could be entrusted with voting rights.[130]

* * *

The contrasting fortunes of white women and African Americans in their wartime campaigns to secure citizenship give a sense of the social unrest caused by the war. After the guns fell silent, that tumult continued as Americans started to reckon with what the war had meant. We can get a sense of the trajectory of the reckoning by looking at the thinking of the scholar W. E. B. DuBois, who had seen the war as an opportunity to advance civil rights. Writing in 1919, he still held to this belief, proclaiming that 'for a moment – and it was but a moment, it passed, but for a moment the country seemed to rise to its mightiest stature. I saw it and saw it with streaming eyes. ... here I saw all the hurts, the tears, the pain as in one country and that country was mine.'[131] By 1924, this language of unity had disappeared and DuBois was calling the war 'a Scourge, an Evil, a retrogression to Barbarism, a waste, a wholesale murder'. He now saw it instead as a debasing experience, claiming that 'we found ourselves during and after the war descending to the meanest and most sordid of selfish actions, and we find ourselves today nearer moral bankruptcy then we were in 1914'.[132] This shift in thinking was indicative of broader intellectual trends in the aftermath of the war. Historians such as Charles Beard openly doubted Allied assertions of German culpability for the war. Beard, who had once worried about the spectre of 'Prussian militarism', had become disillusioned during the war and now took on the role of strong critic of military intervention and of war more broadly.[133]

In this context, the War Department's request to Congress in late 1918 to authorize a permanent Regular Army establishment of 500,000 and a universal military training system to go with it was bound to fall flat.[134] Instead, the wartime Army demobilized and the Army shrank from 2 million to an authorized strength of 296,000, which later translated into an actual strength of 140,000.[135] Critics of the Wilson administration's intervention in the Great War, such as Senator Charles Borah, called for a 50 per cent reduction in

---

[130] Capozzola, *Uncle Sam Wants You*, 103; Huebner, *Love and Death in the Great War*, 47.

[131] Chad Williams, 'World War I in the Historical Imagination of W. E. B. Du Bois', *Modern American History* 1, no. 1 (March 2018): 15, https://doi.org/10.1017/mah.2017.20.

[132] Williams, 'World War I in the Historical Imagination of W. E. B. Du Bois', 17, 20.

[133] Milne, *Worldmaking*, 123–67.

[134] Richard W. Stewart, ed., *American Military History Volume 2: The United States Army in a Global Era, 1917–2008* (Washington, DC: US Army Center of Military History, 2010), 55.

[135] Wright, *Those Who Have Borne the Battle*, 60.

the strength of the Navy, while the Harding administration organized the Washington Naval Conference of 1921 in order to pursue an international agreement to end arms races and to bring about universal disarmament. Entire classes of battleships were scrapped and, as they had been in the early years of the twentieth century, American diplomats were at the forefront of the effort to regulate war. Speaking of the performance of Secretary of States Charles Evan Hughes at the conference, one journalist declared that 'Hughes sank in thirty-five minutes more ships than all of the admirals of the world have sunk in a cycle of centuries.'[136]

Some wished to go further than this. The historian James Shotwell, an erstwhile colleague of Beard at Columbia who had advised Wilson at the peace conference at Versailles, shared Beard's disgust at the war and its aftermath.[137] Shotwell argued that this experience had demonstrated that war was an illegitimate and counterproductive policy choice, and he worked in parallel with other efforts originating in the international peace movement to construct a legal regime that would go beyond regulating the conduct of war to outlawing it entirely. The various efforts of Shotwell and a host of other actors such as the attorney Salmon Levison, the philosopher John Dewey and the activist Jane Addams, eventually paid off in the form of the Kellogg–Briand Pact of 1928.[138] This treaty, authored by Secretary of State Frank Kellogg and his French counterpart, Minister for Foreign Affairs, Aristide Briand, was officially known as the 'General Treaty for Renunciation of War as an Instrument of National Policy' and consisted of a short declaration from the fifteen nations that signed it that they condemned 'recourse to war for the solution of international controversies and renounce it as an instrument of national policy in their relations with one another', and that they agreed to solve all conflicts between them by pacific means.'[139] The treaty, which was eventually signed by sixty-two states, attracted a flood of positive press coverage in the United States, and was ratified by the Senate in an 85–1 vote.[140]

---

[136] George C. Herring, *From Colony to Superpower: U.S. Foreign Relations since 1776* (New York: Oxford University Press, 2011), 454.

[137] Katharina Rietzler, 'The War as History: Writing the Economic and Social History of the First World War*', *Diplomatic History* 38, no. 4 (1 September 2014): 826–39, https://doi.org/10.1093/dh/dhu028.

[138] Oona A. Hathaway and Scott J. Shapiro, *The Internationalists: How a Radical Plan to Outlaw War Remade the World* (New York: Penguin Books, 2017), 108–28.

[139] 'Treaty between the United States and other Powers providing for the renunciation of war as an instrument of national policy', Text, The Avalon Project: Documents in Law, History and Diplomacy, accessed 22 April 2021, https://avalon.law.yale.edu/20th_century/kbpact.asp.

[140] Hathaway and Shapiro, *The Internationalists*, 128–9.

The optimism of the Kellogg–Briand Pact did not last long. Following the economic crash of 1929, both the United States and the world more broadly entered another period of tension, in which the status of war and its relationship to the state and American society again came under scrutiny. The Army of the First World War era had hoped that the war would produce a large body of obedient citizen-soldiers who, as veterans, would fight after the war for increased military budgets and a more prominent role for the Army in American society.[141] To some extent, this materialized in the form of the American Legion, a veterans' organization founded in 1919 that provided a strongly nationalistic and pro-preparedness voice in debates over military policy, but veterans were generally more interested in asserting their own rights.[142] In the eyes of those who had gone to war, they had missed out on an economic boom that had led to the highest wages in American history. While others did well, draftees had been conscripted without any choice and earned far less while putting up with the hardships of war.[143] This resentment came to a head in 1932, when thousands of veterans assembled in Washington, DC, to demand the early payment of their wartime service benefit to help them to get through the Great Depression. This 'Bonus Army' set up an encampment on the Anacostia Flats near Capitol Hill and the sight of Army Chief of Staff Douglas MacArthur (accompanied by Majors Dwight D. Eisenhower and George Patton) leading troops and tanks in violently clearing out the cantonment gave a sense of just how frayed the connections between the military and broader American society were in that moment.[144] The war veterans who should have provided a platform for higher defence spending were instead demonstrating for an expanded welfare state, which put them strongly at odds with their erstwhile military leaders.

The international situation darkened even as President Franklin Delano Roosevelt's New Deal sought to stabilize liberal capitalist democracy, making this choice between rearmament and domestic welfare even more stark.[145] The Roosevelt administration attempted to make the case that the two were intertwined; over the objections of MacArthur, the administration deployed military officers to help run the Civilian Conservation Corps, a mass public

[141] Keene, *Doughboys, the Great War, and the Remaking of America*, 1.
[142] Keene, *Doughboys, the Great War, and the Remaking of America*, 158.
[143] Keene, *Doughboys, the Great War, and the Remaking of America*, 162.
[144] Roger Daniels, *The Bonus March: An Episode of the Great Depression* (Westport, CT: Praeger, 1971); Stephen R. Ortiz, 'Rethinking the Bonus March: Federal Bonus Policy, the Veterans of Foreign Wars, and the Origins of a Protest Movement', *Journal of Policy History* 18, no. 3 (July 2006): 275–303, https://doi.org/10.1353/jph.2006.0010.
[145] Ira Katznelson, *Fear Itself: The New Deal and the Origins of Our Time* (New York: W. W. Norton, 2013).

work relief programme that employed a total of over 3 million unemployed young men and First World War veterans (including thousands from the Bonus Army) throughout the course of its existence.[146] Many of these men, who lived a regimented and quasi-militarized life while working to fight forest fires, floods and soil erosion, ended up providing the core of the NCO cadre during the Second World War, but the programme was ultimately much more focused on providing economic relief than on assisting with military preparedness.[147]

The combination of economic distress and negative memories of the First World War experience meant that any effort to reorient the country to prepare for war was always going to be a difficult sell. This was exacerbated by the findings of the Nye Committee, the latest and more effective in a series of Congressional committees that were dedicated to investigating the economic mobilization during the First World War and the relationship between the government and key industries.[148] The Committee's hearings, which took place from 1934 to 1936, uncovered connections between profiteering arms manufacturers, financiers and political elites that constituted an association that it termed, in the words of historian Paul Koistinen, an 'unhealthy, elitist alliance, which was abusive of the public interest and treasury, and more important, which could encourage and perpetuate warfare.'[149] The only way to deter the growth of what we now would call a military industrial complex would be to avoid excessive spending on the military during peacetime and, if possible, to avoid participating in war in the first place.

The committee's findings matched the public mood. Economic depression sharpened resentment at those corporations who had profited from the war and pamphlets such as H. C. Engelbrecht and F. C. Hanighen's *Merchants of Death* and retired Marine general Smedley Butler's *War Is a Racket* sold well in the mid-1930s, while the anti-war film, *All Quiet on the Western Front*, won the 'Best Picture' and 'Best Director' awards at the 1930 Academy Awards.[150] College

---

[146] Benjamin F. Alexander, *The New Deal's Forest Army: How the Civilian Conservation Corps Worked* (Baltimore, MD: Johns Hopkins University Press, 2018).

[147] Charles E. Heller, 'The U.S. Army, the Civilian Conservation Corps, and Leadership for World War II, 1933–1942', *Armed Forces & Society* 36, no. 3 (1 April 2010): 439–53, https://doi.org/10.1177/00 95327X09333944.

[148] Special Committee to Investigate the Munitions Industry, 'Munitions Industry. Report of the Special Committee on Investigation of the Munitions Industry, United States Senate, Pursuant to S.Res. 206 (73d Congress), a Resolution to Make Certain Investigations Concerning the Manufacture and Sale of Arms and Other War Munitions.' (Washington, DC: United States Congress, 24 February 1936).

[149] Paul A. C. Koistinen, *Planning War, Pursuing Peace: The Political Economy of American Warfare, 1920–1939* (Lawrence: University Press of Kansas, 1998), 210.

[150] Michael Sherry, *In the Shadow of War: The United States since the 1930s* (New Haven, CT: Yale University Press, 1995), 24; Lewis Milestone, *All Quiet on the Western Front*, Drama, War (Universal Pictures, 1930); Smedley D. Butler, *War Is a Racket: The Antiwar Classic by America's Most Decorated General, Two Other Anti-Interventionist Tracts and Photographs from the Horror of It*

students protested against the draft even though there wasn't one, and the peace movement reached its height in 1935–7, with over 12 million adherents.[151] This widespread disillusionment with war found political expression in a series of Acts passed by Congress over the objections of the Roosevelt administration between 1935 and 1939 that aimed to reinforce American neutrality. In the words of Senator Bennet Champ Clark, they wished to 'make it plain that Uncle Sam does not intend again to play Uncle Santa Claus to the war lords of the world', which meant forbidding Americans to sell munitions to belligerents, to offer loans to them or to sail on their ships.[152] The fraught debates about the Neutrality Acts and their effects on conflicts in Europe and Asia made it clear that the United States wielded immense power by the 1930s but that it did not automatically follow that power would manifest itself in the form of military supremacy.

* * *

As late as September 1939, the US Army ranked as only the seventeenth largest in the world, behind Romania and other minor powers.[153] This situation would have been familiar to American politicians during any preceding era, but it is worth noting the United States of the late 1930s did possess a powerful and sophisticated Navy and, just as importantly, one of the most technologically advanced air forces in the world. The connections between the armed services and private industry that the Nye Committee had decried were still in existence, even if those ties were not yet strengthened by the massive budgets of wartime. Nonetheless, on the eve of the Second World War, the United States was an immensely powerful international actor, but not one that had committed to organizing itself around the preparation for war. To the extent that the military was prepared for war, it was in defence of the western hemisphere.

Throughout the first 150 years of the United States' existence, American military power had steadily grown along with the state itself. Each time the United States entered a war, it rapidly expanded its military and then almost as swiftly demobilized its forces. Each demobilization, though, left the military

---

(Los Angeles, CA: Feral House, 2005); H. C. Engelbrecht and Frank Cleary Hanighen, *Merchants of Death* (Garden City, NY: Garden City, 1937).

[151] Sherry, *In the Shadow of War*, 26; Huebner, *Love and Death in the Great War*, 280; Stephen Wertheim, *Tomorrow, the World: The Birth of U.S. Global Supremacy* (Cambridge, MA: Harvard University Press, 2020), 32.

[152] Brooke L. Blower, 'From Isolationism to Neutrality: A New Framework for Understanding American Political Culture, 1919–1941', *Diplomatic History* 38, no. 2 (1 April 2014): 369, https://doi.org/10.1093/dh/dht091.

[153] Rick Atkinson, *An Army at Dawn: The War in North Africa, 1942–1943* (New York: Henry Holt, 2002), 8.

stronger than it had been when the conflict had started. As the American military grew, the arms industry grew with it. From Eli Whitney's musket manufacturing enterprise to the collaboration between the Navy and industrialists that produced steam-powered warships to the high-tech aircraft manufacturers of the 1930s, American industry benefitted from military spending, even the sums involved fluctuated wildly depending on the international situation. Similarly, the American state's major bursts of expansion can all be tied to the needs of wartime, as systems of taxation, finance, welfare and domestic surveillance all grew as part of wartime mobilizations.

At the same time, Americans defined and negotiated their identities, political and civil rights during wartime as well. Often though, such identities were defined in opposition to militarism and its demands. Even if Americans never failed to mobilize, few of the wars which the country fought, with the exception of the Civil War and the Spanish-American War, were wildly popular affairs and all provided opportunities for Americans to affirm their long-standing opposition to a standing army or even, as with the First World War, to define themselves in opposition to foreign militarism. American expansion had been a bloody and violent affair, but the stories that Americans told themselves about how they came to acquire power instead generally focused on the figure of the individual and the volunteer rather than on professional military forces. This heritage meant that, in spite of bursts of militarism such as the one typified by Theodore Roosevelt at the turn of the twentieth century, there was no political consensus in favour of ongoing militarization. Many Americans approached the Second World War confident that that state of affairs would endure.

2

'National security' and the militarization of statecraft

For a clear illustration of how radically the American consensus on what was needed to keep the United States safe changed in the early 1940s, we need only look to real estate developments on either side of the Potomac River. In the summer of 1939, the War and State Departments were both housed in the Old Executive Office Building, adjacent to the White House. By the late 1940s, the new Department of Defense (DoD) – which incorporated the former War and Navy Departments, as well as the new Department of the Air Force – was housed across the river in the Pentagon, then and now the world's largest office building. In a move symbolic of their diminished importance, the State Department shifted five blocks west to Foggy Bottom, where it took up residence in a new building that was originally intended to house the War Department, but which the latter had outgrown even before it was complete in 1941.[1] The former State-War-Navy building next to the White House became home to various White House offices, including the newly formed National Security Council (NSC). In less than a decade, these departments had spilled out from the cramped corridors of their Gilded-Era vintage former home into large modernist new offices whose stripped classicist architectural style emulated that of other federal buildings from the New Deal era.

This explosion of office building was not the first time in the history of Washington, DC, that federal agencies had moved quickly to expand their footprint. The Old Executive Office Building had itself been one of the largest office buildings in the world when it was finished in 1888, and the Navy Department

---

[1] For an architectural history of the Old Executive Office Building, see Thomas E. Luebke, *Palace of State: The Eisenhower Executive Office Building* (Washington, DC: US Commission of Fine Arts, 2018). No comparable history of the State Department's post-1947 headquarters exists, but the State Department's Office of the Historian has written a brief historical sketch: 'Buildings of the Department of State – Buildings – Department History – Office of the Historian', accessed 24 October 2020, https://history.state.gov/departmenthistory/buildings/section28.

had long since vacated its old headquarters, moving into temporary 'Main Navy' headquarters on the National Mall in 1918, a site selected by then-Assistant Secretary of the Navy Franklin Delano Roosevelt.[2] In August 1939, the Secretary of War moved into the adjoining Munitions Building to escape overcrowding in the Old Executive Office Building, and more 'tempo' buildings sprang up on the Mall so that all of the land to the immediate north and south of the Reflecting Pool between the Lincoln Memorial and the Washington Monument was taken up by office space. The difference, though, was that these First World War–era buildings were designed to be temporary, and the planners responsible for National Parks in Washington, DC, were campaigning to get rid of them from the moment they were erected. Although the final 'tempo' buildings on the Mall were not demolished until 1970, their makeshift nature was very apparent to all occupants, as they were sweltering in the muggy Washington summer and freezing in the winter; they leaked rain, suffered from constant rodent and insect infestations and had a number of structural defects in their rickety upper floors (Figure 2.1).[3]

By contrast, a series of temporary wooden buildings on the National Mall aside, the federal government's Second World War building boom focused on permanent structures. There was still some tension between wartime emergency and visions of the post-war world, as could be seen in wrangling over the construction of the Pentagon.[4] Asked at an August 1941 press conference about the War Department's proposed new building, President Franklin Delano Roosevelt, remembering the controversy over the 'tempo' buildings on the National Mall, expressed some unease about aesthetic effect that the Pentagon would have on Potomac waterfront vistas:

> Under the name of emergency, it is proposed to put up a permanent building, which will deliberately and definitely, for one hundred years to come, spoil the plan of the National Capital. Quite aside from any question of access to it, or where people live, how you get across the bridge, or anything else, I think that I have had a part in spoiling the national parks and the beautiful water front of the District once, and I don't want to do it again.[5]

[2] *Main Navy Building: Its Construction and Original Occupants* (Washington, DC: Naval Historical Foundation, 1970).

[3] Andrew Friedman, *Covert Capital: Landscapes of Denial and the Making of U.S. Empire in the Suburbs of Northern Virginia* (Berkeley: University of California Press, 2013), 30–1.

[4] For histories of the Pentagon, see Alfred Goldberg, *The Pentagon: The First Fifty Years* (Washington, DC: Historical Office, Office of the Secretary of Defense, 1992); James Carroll, *House of War: The Pentagon and the Disastrous Rise of American Power* (Boston, MA: Houghton Mifflin, 2007); Steve Vogel, *The Pentagon: A History* (New York: Random House, 2008).

[5] Franklin Delano Roosevelt, 'Excerpts from the Press Conference (Online by Gerhard Peters and John T. Woolley)', The American Presidency Project, 19 August 1941, https://www.presidency.ucsb.edu/documents/excerpts-from-the-press-conference-49.

Figure 2.1 Navy Department buildings, Washington, DC. Photographed from the top of the Washington Monument, looking west, in 1943–4. After these temporary buildings were demolished, the area was turned into parkland. Credit: US Naval History and Heritage Command.

He also wondered whether all of that floor space would be needed once the emergency ended, arguing that 'when that time comes, the Army of course will cut down tremendously on its employees … Actually on footage – square feet – the thing can be worked out pretty well. This building that is proposed on the other side of the river is much larger actually than we need in Washington.'[6] Despite FDR's doubts and the strong opposition of influential New Dealers such as Harold Ickes, the project, already authorized by Congress by the time FDR aired his grievances at a press conference, went ahead, albeit at a new and less unsightly location chosen by the President, in Arlington, Virginia. In a nod to FDR's hopes for a rapid post-war demobilization, the building's architects designed it to be able to withstand very heavy floor loads, so that it could be used as a records management facility after the war when the War Department

---

[6] Roosevelt, 'Excerpts from the Press Conference (Online by Gerhard Peters and John T. Woolley)'.

would move back across the river to be under closer supervision from the White House.[7]

The Pentagon, though, never did become an archives building. Even as it was constructed at breakneck speed over 16 months, it was redesigned midway through the build to provide 50 per cent more office space to accommodate the ever-growing War Department. The basement, originally intended for storage, was fitted out with light and heat and planners added a fifth floor to the inner rings so late in the construction process that they had to tear down some roofing that had already been laid over the fourth floor.[8] The completed building had a working population of up to 33,000 when it was completed in 1943, not far off Arlington's 1940 census population of 57,000.[9] The building also included the world's largest telephone exchange, with 125 switchboard positions, and six enormous cafeterias that could seat 1,100 people at once. It also had double the normal number of washrooms, as the design team led by Colonel Leslie Groves, who would soon oversee the Manhattan Project, accommodated Virginia's Jim Crow laws and provided for racially segregated toilet facilities.[10] At its post-war low point, the building's working population still approached 23,000, and the Navy were forced to vacate their premises on the National Mall and join their Army colleagues in the Pentagon after the passage of the 1947 National Security Act created the National Military Establishment (NME) and the beginnings of a unified command structure for the military.

The history of the Pentagon and the State Department buildings at Foggy Bottom indicates just how important issues of war and peace became to the federal government from the early 1940s on. The building boom was symbolic of where federal dollars were going: defence-related spending peaked at over 90 per cent of the overall federal budget in 1945 and, after a brief post-war lull, shot back up to 70 per cent in 1953 before slowly drifting down as Cold War tensions gradually eased.[11] To help direct this spending, a series of presidential administrations constructed an entirely new foreign policy decision-making architecture, centred on the new NSC, and created multiple federal agencies – such as the DoD, the Central Intelligence Agency (CIA), the National Security Agency (NSA) and the Atomic Energy Agency – to manage different aspects of American strategy. Scholars have termed this collection of agencies and the

---

[7] Goldberg, *The Pentagon*, 33.
[8] Goldberg, *The Pentagon*, 82.
[9] Goldberg, *The Pentagon*, 22.
[10] Goldberg, *The Pentagon*, 62, 80, 131.
[11] 'Fiscal Year 2017 Historical Tables: Budget of the U.S. Government' (Washington, DC: Office of Management and Budget, 2017), table 3.1.

laws associated with them the 'national security state'.[12] While other chapters in this book examine the effects of militarization and the manner in which this phenomenon shaped spaces, identities, imaginations and encounters with others, this chapter differs in that it focuses largely on the political processes that drove the growth of the national security state and made it so central to federal governance from the 1940s onwards. So much of American politics, economic policy and governance became oriented around the idea of national security that the origins of the concept and the politics surrounding it need to be sketched out. Crucially, as Andrew Preston and other scholars have pointed out, the term, which originated in the late 1930s, has a much broader meaning than mere military strategy.[13] National security was as much about defending values and a way of life as it was about defending territory from attack. Given such an expansive definition, it was inevitable that its reach was extraordinarily broad and deep.

It is worth recalling, though, that FDR's objections to the construction of the Pentagon were about more than aesthetics. Even though American defence spending has been enormous, and the logic of the national security state has informed huge swathes of federal governance, it is not the case that American policymakers saw themselves as embracing a fully militarized state. In keeping with the patterns of previous American wars, FDR assumed that the military would drastically shrink in size after the Second World War and the presidents most responsible for the construction of the national security state, Harry S. Truman and Dwight D. Eisenhower, were both wary of the growth in military spending. Both Democrats and Republicans feared the emergence of what they termed a 'garrison state' and anti-statist impulses informed many of the Congressional debates on military budgets and legislation governing these new agencies and structures.[14] Conversely, as the historian Gary Gerstle has observed, advocates of various causes, including groups as diverse as university administrators, infrastructure planners and climate activists, have invoked

---

[12] The term 'national security' has been in circulation since the 1940s, but Daniel Yergin popularized the term 'national security state' in the 1970s. Daniel Yergin, *Shattered Peace: The Origins of the Cold War and the National Security State* (Boston, MA: Houghton Mifflin, 1978).

[13] Andrew Preston, 'Monsters Everywhere: A Genealogy of National Security', *Diplomatic History* 38, no. 3 (1 June 2014): 477–500, https://doi.org/10.1093/dh/dhu018; Melvyn P. Leffler, 'National Security', *Journal of American History* 77, no. 1 (1990): 143–52, https://doi.org/10.2307/2078646.

[14] Michael J. Hogan, *A Cross of Iron: Harry S. Truman and the Origins of the National Security State, 1945–1954* (Cambridge: Cambridge University Press, 2000); Aaron L. Friedberg, *In the Shadow of the Garrison State: America's Anti-Statism and Its Cold War Grand Strategy* (Princeton, NJ: Princeton University Press, 2000).

'national security' as a way to gain policy traction for their projects, even if these programmes only had a tenuous connection to issues of war and peace.[15]

These conflicting impulses – to resist the growth of the state lest it fundamentally endanger American democracy, and to use concerns about security to address societal deficits – illustrate that the American national security state was a peculiar edifice, both immensely powerful and frequently worried about its own vulnerability. Its existence was far from inevitable, and its mature form was very much contingent on the particular circumstances from which it emerged. The sociologist Charles Tilly's famous aphorism that 'war made the state and the state made war' gives us some sense of why it took the shape that it did.[16] If war makes the state, then the ambiguous character of the Cold War, which blurred the lines between war and peace and raised the stakes of war to existential levels due to the threat of nuclear war, informed the particular path that the national security state took as it matured in the 1940s and 1950s.[17] Equally, Americans who thought that such a state did not fit within the American political tradition had an influence on its trajectory, and the activists who opposed the different ways in which the American state oriented itself towards the preparation for war did not understand this state of affairs to be preordained.

Even if its emergence was not inevitable, though, the national security state had proven to be a durable institution. It has survived several crises and managed to rejuvenate itself even after the Cold War which had sustained it ended with unquestioned American hegemony. The final part of the chapter examines what national security has meant – and continues to mean – for American relations with the rest of the world. The State Department's relegation to the Department of War's now-unwanted Foggy Bottom headquarters gave an early hint as to just how completely the emphasis in foreign policy would shift to military imperatives. Vast defence budgets meant that the armed forces played an increasingly prominent role in diplomatic affairs, even as the architects of the national security state worked hard to ensure that civilian control over the military would ultimately endure. From the militarization of aid via counterinsurgency campaigns to the 'war on drugs' in Latin America to the growing prominence of four-star 'combatant commanders'

---

[15] Gary Gerstle, *Liberty and Coercion: The Paradox of American Government from the Founding to the Present* (Princeton, NJ: Princeton University Press, 2015), 252.

[16] Charles Tilly, 'War Making and State Making as Organized Crime', in *Violence: A Reader*, ed. Catherine Besteman (Basingstoke: Palgrave Macmillan, 2002), 35–60.

[17] Anders Stephanson has offered perhaps the best-known appraisal of the ambiguity of the concept. Anders Stephanson, 'Fourteen Notes on the Very Concept of the Cold War', in *Rethinking Geopolitics*, ed. Simon Dalby and Gearóid Ó Tuathail (London: Routledge, 1998), 62–85.

who flew around the world to meet with heads of state, the military steadily became a primary diplomatic actor and the face of the United States abroad.

This projection of a militarized foreign policy abroad has itself fed back into the operation of the national security state at home. The post-9/11 concept of 'homeland security', with its array of new security agencies and laws infringing on civil liberties, is the most obvious manifestation of militarized techniques from abroad returning to the United States, but in recent years, scholars such as Stuart Schrader have shown that even phenomena such as the deeply controversial militarization of local police forces can be traced to Cold War–era programmes conducted overseas in the name of national security.[18] The irony of these feedback loops where military measures conducted for the sake of national security abroad were mimicked by domestic law enforcement agencies is that they were the very things that many of the original architects of the national security state wanted to avoid. As we shall see, the move towards 'national security' as a concept was as much about protecting a particular way of life and set of values as it was about defending physical territory.

* * *

As several scholars have argued, the current meaning of the term 'national security' is a relatively recent development. Andrew Preston has noted that presidents rarely, if ever, used the term prior to the Great Depression. After 1931, it began to appear in speeches and pamphlets, but only in reference to economic insecurity. The New Deal aimed to protect individual citizens from the wild fluctuations of the economy, and in this sense the search for 'national security' was a policy response to this economic crisis. The Roosevelt administration's thinking on economic security, though, could not be divorced from its views of the threat posed by hostile powers across the oceans. Influenced in part by hawkish intellectuals like Edward Meade Earle, FDR began to use 'national security' to refer to military affairs as well.[19] Preston argues that this new definition of security was a significant departure, because 'until FDR, no American statesman had presented security as having two equal parts – physical and normative, territorial and ideological – forming an integrated, indivisible whole'.[20]

---

[18] Stuart Schrader, *Badges without Borders: How Global Counterinsurgency Transformed American Policing* (Berkeley: University of California Press, 2019).

[19] Dexter Fergie, 'Geopolitics Turned Inwards: The Princeton Military Studies Group and the National Security Imagination', *Diplomatic History* 43, no. 4 (2019): 644–70, accessed 16 July 2019, https://doi.org/10.1093/dh/dhz026.

[20] Preston, 'Monsters Everywhere', 492.

By Preston's count, FDR used the term more times between 1938 and 1941 than all previous presidents had in the history of the United States.[21] This shift was driven by the disappearance of what the historian C. Van Woodward called 'free security': the sense that the United States was physically protected by two oceans and weak neighbours to the north and south.[22] The spectre of a German-dominated Europe and a British Empire shattered by the Axis powers meant that the oceans would no longer afford protection to the United States, either from bomber fleets or from saboteurs who might already be present on American soil. More importantly, the United States would be cut off from world markets and would struggle to maintain economic growth. 'National security', then, became a way of thinking where the boundaries between the foreign and domestic, peace and war blurred. Its primary goal was to protect citizens from insecurity of all kinds, whether it be economic or military, and New Deal policymakers increasingly orientated towards threats from the outside. The historian Melvyn Leffler defines national security as encompassing 'the decisions and actions deemed imperative to protect domestic core values from external threats', and in the late 1930s, events overseas seemed to directly threaten core American values for the first time, rather than just American interests or power.[23] To many Americans, this crisis seemed existential.

To FDR and other internationalists, it was obvious that the United States was newly vulnerable after the fall of France, and in order to defend American values and the American way of life, the United States would need to actively shape the world around it. As historian Stephen Wertheim has documented, foreign policy elites cohered in 1940 and early 1941 around the idea that the United States would need to pursue global military superiority in order to protect its place in the world.[24] The post-war order would have to be underwritten by American military power. Reflecting on this new disposition in his fourth inaugural address in January 1945, at a time when he was preoccupied with thinking about the shape of the post-war world, Roosevelt declared that 'we have learned that we cannot live alone, at peace; that our own well-being is dependent on the well-being of other nations far away'.[25] The historian Elizabeth Borgwardt has termed

---

[21] Preston, 'Monsters Everywhere', 490.

[22] C. Vann Woodward, 'The Age of Reinterpretation', *American Historical Review* 66, no. 1 (1960): 1–19, https://doi.org/10.2307/1845704.

[23] Melvyn P. Leffler, 'National Security', in *Explaining the History of American Foreign Relations*, ed. Frank Costigliola and Michael J. Hogan, 3rd edn (New York: Cambridge University Press, 2016), 25.

[24] Stephen Wertheim, *Tomorrow, the World: The Birth of U.S. Global Supremacy* (Cambridge, MA: Harvard University Press, 2020).

[25] Franklin Delano Roosevelt, 'Inaugural Address', Online by Gerhard Peters and John T. Wooley, The American Presidency Project, 20 January 1945, https://www.presidency.ucsb.edu/documents/inaugural-address-6.

this outlook as a 'New Deal for the world', where New Deal planners hoped to offer large-scale institutional solutions to global problems in order to protect the American way of life and to expand the New Deal's benefits to the whole world.[26]

This view was certainly not a common one in the late 1930s, when Americans looked on with fear at both continuing economic turmoil and the rise of dictatorships around the world who seemed to offer the key to the future that liberal capitalist democracy could not provide.[27] In the shadow of the 1930s, a great debate over whether or not the United States should intervene in the coming war roiled American society. Both sides of the debate actively supported military rearmament by 1940, as even those who opposed the administration's inclination to either directly or indirectly join the war against the Axis thought that the United States would need to be able to defend the continental United States from invasion, but they diverged greatly on whether or not 'national security' required active military intervention overseas. In order to make his case, Roosevelt had to make it clear to Americans just how vulnerable they really were. The historian John A. Thompson has noted that this was hardly the first time that Americans felt a sense of vulnerability, but it was certainly much more acute in this era.[28]

Cartographers and magazine publishers played their role by publishing maps which showed the United States at the centre of the world and besieged on all sides. Publishers showed the growing Axis control over vast swathes of territory and readers could thus draw their own conclusions as to how easily these powers could end up surrounding the United States and cutting it off from the rest of the world.[29] The popularity of globes, such as the huge 750-pound model that Roosevelt kept in his office, allowed advocates for intervention to demonstrate just how quickly enemy bombers could reach American cities, which lay completely unprotected.[30] The lessons of the war were that time and space were collapsing, as the rapid success of the German Blitzkrieg in Poland and France demonstrated. In a May 1941 fireside chat, FDR warned that 'some people seem to think that we are not attacked until bombs actually drop in the streets of New York or San Francisco or New Orleans or Chicago (Figure 2.2).

---

[26] Elizabeth Borgwardt, *A New Deal for the World* (Cambridge, MA: Harvard University Press, 2007).

[27] Ira Katznelson, *Fear Itself: The New Deal and the Origins of Our Time* (New York: W. W. Norton, 2013).

[28] John A. Thompson, 'The Exaggeration of American Vulnerability: The Anatomy of a Tradition', *Diplomatic History* 16, no. 1 (1992): 23–43, https://doi.org/10.1111/j.1467-7709.1992.tb00482.x; John A. Thompson, 'Conceptions of National Security and American Entry into World War II', *Diplomacy & Statecraft* 16, no. 4 (1 December 2005): 671–97, https://doi.org/10.1080/09592290500331006.

[29] Matthew Farish, *The Contours of America's Cold War* (Minneapolis: University of Minnesota Press, 2010), 8–11; Fergie, 'Geopolitics Turned Inwards', 21–3.

[30] Farish, *The Contours of America's Cold War*, 11.

Figure 2.2 President Roosevelt examines a 750-lb globe presented to him by the US Army. 25 December 1942. Credit: Franklin D. Roosevelt Presidential Library and Museum.

But they are simply shutting their eyes to the lesson that we must learn from the fate of every Nation that the Nazis have conquered.'[31]

The irony was that in playing up this sense of insecurity in the name of national security, Roosevelt was leaving the door open to some of the very threats to domestic core values that he sought to ward off. For many internationalists, the strongest argument for taking up arms against the Axis powers was not that Germany or Japan could ever realistically threaten US territory; it was that a world dominated by these powers would necessitate that the United States permanently mobilize for war in order to defend itself, producing a 'garrison state' dominated by military men, thus fatally undermining the American way of life. They argued that it would be far better to defeat these powers in concert with other nations rather than wait to confront them alone in a long and difficult

---

[31] Franklin Delano Roosevelt, 'Radio Address Announcing an Unlimited National Emergency', Online by Gerhard Peters and John T. Wooley, The American Presidency Project, 27 May 1941, https://www.presidency.ucsb.edu/documents/radio-address-announcing-unlimited-national-emergency.

stand-off.[32] The challenge, then, would be to pursue a form of national security policy that could challenge militarism overseas without promoting it at home.

The Japanese surprise attack on Pearl Harbor (and on the Philippines) in December 1941 formally brought the United States into the war and made plain the need to overhaul intelligence structures and to ensure better coordination between the military services and civilian decision-makers. Wartime requirements also made economic coordination vital, and so the Roosevelt administration worked to establish new federal agencies to oversee the war effort and to plan and manage the wartime economy. Agencies such as the War Production Board, the Office of Price Administration, the Office of War Information and the Office of Scientific Research and Development all sought to mobilize and coordinate American society in a manner reminiscent of the economic planning of the early years of the New Deal.[33] While these agencies worked to ensure that the economy was producing enough materiel to supply both the United States and its allies, the military embarked on a massive mobilization, which meant that over 12 million personnel were serving in uniform by 1945, along with 2.6 million civilians working in national defence (out of a total federal civilian workforce of 3.4 million).[34] In spite of the immense scope of their responsibilities, coordination among these wartime agencies was somewhat haphazard and their efficacy very much depended on the personalities of their administrators rather than any deeper institutional competence. Looked upon with suspicion by Republicans and conservative Southern Democrats alike, these wartime agencies were rapidly dismantled following the end of the war.[35] Similarly, the military worked to demobilize quicky as soon as Japan was defeated, although it was clear to even the most optimistic of planners that its strength would remain far above that of the pre-1940 armed forces.

Despite this demobilization, the Second World War differed from previous major wars in that it was closely followed by the Cold War, which meant this bout of wartime state-building took on a permanent character. Just a few years after the United States began its demobilization, lawmakers contemplated new institutions that would preserve and extend American military hegemony

---

[32] Katznelson, *Fear Itself*, 318–20.
[33] Alan S. Milward, *War, Economy and Society, 1939–1945* (Berkeley: University of California Press, 1979); Mark R. Wilson, *Destructive Creation: American Business and the Winning of World War II* (Philadelphia: University of Pennsylvania Press, 2016); Jeffrey Fear, 'War of the Factories', in *Cambridge History of the Second World War, Vol. 3. Total War: Economy, Society and Culture*, ed. Michael Geyer and Adam Tooze, vol. 3 (Cambridge: Cambridge University Press, 2015), 94–121.
[34] United States Bureau of the Census, *Historical Statistics of the United States, Colonial Times to 1970*, vol. 2 (Washington, DC: US Department of Commerce, Bureau of the Census, 1975), 1102, 1141.
[35] Katznelson, *Fear Itself*, 373–81.

in competition with the Soviet Union. If the early New Deal produced an 'alphabet soup' of new agencies to deal with the economic emergency, then the early Cold War resulted in a profusion of 'three-letter' agencies, as the Truman administration established, in quick succession, the Atomic Energy Commission (AEC) in 1946; the NSC, CIA, the Joint Chiefs of Staff (JCS), and NME in 1947; the DoD, which replaced the NME in 1949; and finally the NSA, founded in 1952.[36] This flurry of institution-building constituted a decisive break with the past, as power flowed from the legislative branch towards the executive. Some of this was due to fears that nuclear war would require rapid decision-making, something which was not always one of Congress's strengths. Consequently, Congressional leaders had no seat on the NSC, which was designed to coordinate national security policy across the federal government.[37] Many of these agencies also prioritized secrecy: for instance, the AEC, established to make permanent the Manhattan Project's nuclear weapons research and manufacturing, operated with minimal Congressional oversight and was exempted from the civil service system, even as the huge scale of the agency meant that its facilities occupied more land than the states of Rhode Island and Delaware combined.[38]

The New Deal origins of many of these ideas could be seen in the provisions of the National Security Act of 1947, the founding document of the national security state. Along with the host of agencies mentioned above, it established a number of bodies to provide oversight for economic and industrial mobilization and preparedness: the Munitions Board, the Research and Development Board, and the National Security Resources Board (NSRB), which was intended to function as the economic equivalent of the NSC. These various boards, though, never acquired the prominence of their Second World War–era equivalents and, hamstrung in their design by a Congress suspicious of the notion of a planned economy and regulatory state, had short and unsuccessful histories, with the NSRB folding in 1953 after six years of ineffectiveness.[39]

The fate of the NSRB demonstrates that the National Security Act and its successor laws were not part of a story of the straightforward expansion and centralization of state power. The United States had just fought a totalitarian power in Nazi Germany and its leaders believed it was confronting another one in the Soviet Union, a reality that the creators of these agencies were only too

---

[36] Hogan, *A Cross of Iron*; Douglas T. Stuart, *Creating the National Security State: A History of the Law That Transformed America* (Princeton, NJ: Princeton University Press, 2009).

[37] Katznelson, *Fear Itself*, 441.

[38] Katznelson, *Fear Itself*, 432.

[39] Stuart, *Creating the National Security State*, 144–79.

aware of. Liberal and libertarian thinkers such as Hannah Arendt, Friedrich Hayek, and Harold Lasswell warned against massive concentrations of power in the hands of the state and it was Lasswell's concept of the 'garrison state' that stuck and that informed public and elite debates about the construction of the national security state.[40] President Harry S. Truman proved to be a reluctant architect of this state. On the one hand, his wartime experience on the Senate Armed Services committee gave him a keen understanding of the extent of duplication and waste present in the armed forces and he had an enduring suspicion of military cliques, a feeling made stronger by witnessing the endless and vicious inter-service squabbling between the Army and Navy throughout the war.[41] He believed that the service secretaries were effectively hostages of their respective branches of the military and, along with Secretary of State (and former Army Chief of Staff) George Marshall, pushed for a unified military establishment and a Secretary of Defense who would be directly accountable to the president.[42] On the other hand, as a New Dealer, he was reluctant to permanently divert resources away from social programmes and into the defence budget.

On the other end of the political spectrum, Republicans led by Senator Robert Taft were suspicious of an overly centralized command structure, preferring a liberal-Republican diffusion of power that maintained a strong voice for each of the services. To that end, they were broadly supportive of the ultimately unsuccessful efforts of the Navy to promote a system of looser cooperation and coordination among the services.[43] Taft was much more reluctant to embrace a global role for the United States and opposed Truman on foreign aid, which had ramped up sharply in the aftermath of the announcement of the Truman doctrine in March 1947 and its extensive commitments to alliances and economic and military aid. Taft rejected proposals for a large standing army and thought that the United States could protect itself by massively expanding the new Air Force and equipping it with atomic weapons, preferring to emphasize hemispheric defence over global containment.[44] While Truman wanted to limit the defence budget in order to further expand the New Deal, Taft worried about deficits, proposed to cut social security to provide for any increase in defence spending and preferred to generally shrink the federal budget in order to cut

[40]   Harold D. Lasswell, 'The Garrison State', *American Journal of Sociology* 46, no. 4 (1941): 455–68; Hannah Arendt, *The Origins of Totalitarianism* (New York: Schoken Books, 1951); Friedrich Hayek, *The Road to Serfdom* (London: Routledge, 1944).
[41]   Hogan, *A Cross of Iron*, 38.
[42]   Hogan, *A Cross of Iron*, 31.
[43]   Hogan, *A Cross of Iron*, 31–6.
[44]   Hogan, *A Cross of Iron*, 101.

the state down to size.[45] Neither were wholly in favour of what the historian Michael Hogan has called 'national security ideology' and both felt some unease as the defence budget climbed steadily upwards in spite of bipartisan fears of the garrison state.

Others within the foreign policy establishment thought that the threat from the Soviet Union was serious enough to make any quibbling over budgets or limits to defence spending unnecessary.[46] This group, which included Secretary of State Dean Acheson (who replaced the more cautious George Marshall in January 1949), thought that the Soviet Union's development of nuclear weapons and its military capabilities posed an existential threat. This viewpoint found its purest expression in the policy paper 'United States Objectives and Programs for National Security', commissioned by President Truman in January 1950.[47] The seventy-page report, authored by a hawkish team led by the head of the State Department's Policy Planning Unit, Paul Nitze, was submitted to the NSC and given the identifier NSC-68 in April of that year. The report adopted an apocalyptic tone, claiming that 'the issues that face us are momentous, involving the fulfilment or destruction not only of this Republic but of civilization itself' and arguing that 'budgetary considerations will need to be subordinated to the stark fact that our very independence as a nation may be at stake'.[48] It called for a rapid build-up of military strength, including both nuclear and conventional forces, along with increased military aid to allies overseas and investment in public diplomacy, propaganda and covert operations. To fund this, it proposed increasing taxes and reducing spending on non-defence-related programmes. The authors of NSC-68 believed, though, that such a massive military build-up need not have a negative effect on the standard of living, 'for the economic effects of the program might be to increase the gross national product by more than the amount being absorbed for additional military and foreign assistance'.[49] Deficit-fuelled spending would provide fiscal stimulus for the economy to the

---

[45] Campbell Craig and Fredrik Logevall, *America's Cold War: The Politics of Insecurity* (Cambridge, MA: Harvard University Press, 2008), 113.

[46] John Lewis Gaddis, *Strategies of Containment: A Critical Appraisal of Postwar American National Security* (New York: Oxford University Press, 1982); Melvyn P. Leffler, *A Preponderance of Power: National Security, the Truman Administration, and the Cold War* (Stanford, CA: Stanford University Press, 1993); Nicholas Thompson, *The Hawk and the Dove: Paul Nitze, George Kennan, and the History of the Cold War* (New York: Picador, 2010).

[47] 'National Security Council Report: NSC 68, "United States Objectives and Programs for National Security"' (Washington, DC: National Security Council, 14 April 1950), History and Public Policy Program Digital Archive, The Wilson Center, https://digitalarchive.wilsoncenter.org/document/116191.pdf; Ernest R. May, ed., *American Cold War Strategy: Interpreting NSC 68* (Boston, MA: Palgrave Macmillan, 1993).

[48] 'NSC-68', 4, 56.

[49] 'NSC-68', 58.

point where economic growth might offset the need for new taxes or spending cuts elsewhere.

NSC-68 initially received a frosty reception from President Truman, who had invested in containment in Europe because he believed it was a cost-effective way to prevent the Soviet Union's influence from expanding while avoiding a large military build-up. The surprise news of North Korean forces crossing the 38th parallel and launching an invasion of South Korea in June 1950 completely changed the character of the discussion on the document within the administration.[50] By September 1950, Truman ordered that NSC-68 be understood as a 'statement of policy to be followed over the next four or five years and … that the implementing programs … be put into effect as rapidly as possible'.[51] These instructions fundamentally changed the character of the Cold War, making it an ideologically charged global campaign that became much more militarized. The defence budget increased nearly sixfold between 1948 and 1953, shooting up from $9 billion to $53 billion.[52] An American public that had been watching the government demobilize its large military and unwind its wartime institutions suddenly found that the preparation for war formed a greater part of their daily lives. This was not quite the garrison state that Lasswell and others had feared, but the quest for national security now involved a substantially greater defence budget than had ever before been approved in peacetime, and a federal state that assumed increased responsibilities for large swathes of American life.

* * *

Speaking to an audience of newspaper editors in April 1953, just a few months into his first term in office, President Dwight D. Eisenhower echoed many of the fears of an overly large defence budget that had haunted both Truman and Taft. He described the Cold War as 'a life of perpetual fear and tension; a burden of arms draining the wealth and the labour of all peoples'. He quantified the trade-off between arms manufacturing and economic welfare in explicit terms, noting how much housing the money used to build a single destroyer could have paid for, or how many schools could have been constructed for the price

---

[50] Hogan, *A Cross of Iron*, 302–5.
[51] James S. Lay, 'Note by the Executive Secretary to the National Security Council on United States Objectives and Programs for National Security', Foreign Relation of the United States, 1950, National Security Affairs; Foreign Economic Policy, vol. 1 (Washington, DC: Office of the Historian, United States State Department, 30 September 1950), https://history.state.gov/historicaldocuments/frus1950v01/d129.
[52] 'Fiscal Year 2017 Historical Tables: Budget of the U.S. Government', table 3.1.

of a heavy bomber. Eisenhower argued that 'every gun that is made, every warship launched, every rocket fired signifies, in the final sense, a theft from those who hunger and are not fed, those who are cold and are not clothed' and claimed that 'under the cloud of threatening war ... humanity [is] hanging from a cross of iron'.[53] He repeated these concerns in his farewell address in January 1961. In what is certainly the best-known speech of this genre, he cautioned that the influence of the military establishment and the arms industry 'is felt in every city, every state house, every office of the Federal government' and worried about its 'grave implications' for liberty and democracy. Eisenhower gave the stark warning, 'In the councils of government, we must guard against the acquisition of unwarranted influence, whether sought or unsought, by the military-industrial complex. The potential for the disastrous rise of misplaced power exists and will persist.'[54]

What is striking about these two speeches is how similar they are, even though they were delivered nearly eight years apart. Those eight years constituted the entirety of Eisenhower's presidency and yet he, much like Truman before him, presided over a deepening of Cold War tensions and an expansion of the national security state, even as he openly and publicly expressed his doubts about aspects of this project. Eisenhower's 'New Look' policy attempted to rein in defence spending by relying extensively on nuclear weapons at the expense of conventional forces and the defence budget did drop below its post-NSC-68 peak, but it remained well above the levels seen from 1946 to 1952.[55] So why did Eisenhower, a popular two-term president with more military experience than virtually every other occupant of the Oval Office, fail to arrest the expansion of the national security state and the military–industrial complex? Geopolitics surely played a role, much as it did with the success of NSC-68, but what's notable about Eisenhower's tenure is how the Cold War and its associated militarization took on a domestic political momentum of its own.

Anti-communism was an important factor in shaping electoral politics in such a way that made it difficult for political leaders to back out of military commitments. The looming threat of war in the early 1940s had seen Congress

---

[53] Dwight D. Eisenhower, 'Address "The Chance for Peace" Delivered Before the American Society of Newspaper Editors', Online by Gerhard Peters and John T. Wooley, The American Presidency Project, 16 April 1953, https://www.presidency.ucsb.edu/documents/address-the-chance-for-peace-delivered-before-the-american-society-newspaper-editors.

[54] Dwight D. Eisenhower, 'Farewell Radio and Television Address to the American People', Online by Gerhard Peters and John T. Wooley, The American Presidency Project, 17 January 1961, https://www.presidency.ucsb.edu/documents/farewell-radio-and-television-address-the-american-people.

[55] Robert R. Bowie and Richard H. Immerman, *Waging Peace: How Eisenhower Shaped an Enduring Cold War Strategy* (Oxford: Oxford University Press, 2000).

pass the Smith Act – which criminalized a wide range of activities by declaring them to be subversion, and which was intended to target communists, anarchists and fascists – and Truman further extended the peacetime restrictions on civil liberties by signing Executive Order 9835, known as the 'loyalty order', which allowed the Federal Bureau of Investigation to examine the backgrounds of all 2 million federal employees and investigate any questionable associations or beliefs.[56] The FBI itself increased in size sevenfold between 1939 and 1953.[57] The historian Mary Dudziak argues that 'the domestic politics of repression' were informed but not determined by geopolitical developments, but in either case this extension of wartime-like restrictions on civil liberties into peacetime enabled a crusading anti-communism that was not seen elsewhere in the Western world.[58] Jonathan Bell has claimed that this Cold War atmosphere severely limited American liberals' room for manoeuvre in electoral politics, preventing the sort of 'popular front' alliances that had powered the New Deal and foreclosing the possibility of the pursuit of social democratic policies, such as those that the British Labour Party had implemented after their general election victory of 1945. Anti-communism instead pushing New Dealers to embrace a Cold War consensus that required acquiescence to high defence spending and to expanding the reach of the national security state.[59]

While the left was constrained by anti-communism, Republicans were able to use fears of external subversion to their electoral advantage, taking control of both house of Congress for the first time since 1933 in the mid-term elections of 1946, after a campaign where many of their candidates, including a young Richard Nixon, ran on a red-baiting platform. The Republican Party found itself constrained in a different way, however. The Taft wing of the party was unable to persuade Eisenhower to withdraw from NATO, even though he was sympathetic to their concerns about military spending, and they found that the ground began to shift under their feet as the political effects of defence spending took hold in electoral politics.[60] The political scientist Aaron Friedberg has argued that the national security state was in fact much smaller than it could have been, given external pressure, and that policymakers emphasized private

---

[56] Katznelson, *Fear Itself*, 328–34; Gerstle, *Liberty and Coercion*, 256–8.
[57] Gerstle, *Liberty and Coercion*, 258.
[58] Mary Dudziak, *War Time: An Idea, Its History, Its Consequences* (New York: Oxford University Press, 2012), 81–4; Ellen Schrecker, *Many Are the Crimes: McCarthyism in America* (Princeton, NJ: Princeton University Press, 1999); Stanley I. Kutler, *American Inquisition: Justice and Injustice in the Cold War* (New York: Hill & Wang, 1984).
[59] Jonathan Bell, *The Liberal State on Trial: The Cold War and American Politics in the Truman Years* (New York: Columbia University Press, 2004).
[60] Craig and Logevall, *America's Cold War*, 143.

industry over state-owned arsenals and shipyards – closing many of the military services' research and production facilities in an effort to shrink the size of the federal state – but this investment in private industry created its own series of institutions and political incentives, many of which would have destructive effects later on.[61] In the absence of the sort of broader welfare state, including the jobs guarantee that FDR had called for in his 1944 State of Union address, military spending allowed the national security state to provide well-paying jobs in the defence industry. Midwestern anti-interventionist Republicans soon lost influence within the party as the military Keynesianism prompted by the Korean War took hold to great effect.[62]

In his study of how Cold War defence spending affected American democracy, Michael Brenes has argued that 'military officials, business executives, local politicians, labour leaders, and unemployed factory workers realized the defence economy's resources could serve their respective ends'.[63] The largesse provided by increased defence spending further entrenched anti-communism among liberals, and made labour unions acquiesce to militarization in the name of providing middle-class jobs for workers. On the right, domestic welfare programmes and infrastructure spending that were couched within the language of militarization became acceptable, or even necessary. This could lead to policymakers using national security as a form of surrogacy. The legislation that authorized the Eisenhower administration's ambitious road building programme creating the interstate highway system was known as the National Interstate and Defense Highways Act. The security rationale for the highway system was that it would allow for the rapid movement of military units across the country in the event of an invasion and for the speedy evacuation of cities that were threatened with atomic attack. As Gary Gerstle has observed, the actual effect of the Act went far beyond military preparedness, as federal funding produced over 40,000 miles of road that reorganized the country around grid of north-south and east-west highways, 'arguably the most comprehensive reorganization of American space since the land surveys launched by the Northwest Ordinances of 1785 and 1787'.[64] Similarly, university administrators and scientists used Cold War imperatives to attract funding for research and development via the National Science Foundation, which acted in part to militarize science, and higher

---

[61] Friedberg, *In the Shadow of the Garrison State*.
[62] Michael Brenes, *For Might and Right: Cold War Defense Spending and the Remaking of American Democracy* (Amherst: University of Massachusetts Press, 2020), 64–7.
[63] Brenes, *For Might and Right*, 49.
[64] Gerstle, *Liberty and Coercion*, 265.

education, but in other ways was just a cover for an expansion of the university system that its advocates desired anyway.[65]

This combination of anti-communism and military Keynesianism had a powerful impact on electoral politics. Eisenhower's warning about the power of the military–industrial complex should be seen in the context of the presidential election of 1960, where Senator John F. Kennedy won a narrow victory against Vice-President Richard Nixon by highlighting a supposed missile gap between the United States and the Soviet Union and by advocating for another military build-up. Kennedy campaigned heavily in districts where the defence industry had suffered job losses and he attracted donations from aerospace contractors. He did particularly well in the industrial regions in the northeast and the Pacific coast that relied heavily on military spending.[66] More broadly, Kennedy thought that military spending could revive a flagging American economy and do so in such a way that would attract the approval of voters and donors who had previously supported Eisenhower. Kennedy reversed course after the Cuban Missile Crisis, commissioning his Secretary of Defense Robert McNamara to cut wasteful defence spending, but he immediately found himself constrained by the politics that he had harnessed in his election campaign.[67] Boeing workers in Washington state who were irked at the company's loss of the TFX fighter contract were rumoured by 1963 to be supporting Kennedy's probable opponent in the 1964 election, Senator Barry Goldwater, and newspaper columnists believed that such was labour's discontent at the loss of the contract and the closure of shipyards that the state of Washington would swing to the Republicans in 1964.[68]

The resilience of the military–industrial complex became clear when the Cold War consensus fell apart in the aftermath of the Vietnam War. Anti-communism's electoral importance had already faded, and the spectacle of American bombs being dropped on Vietnamese villages fuelled widespread resistance, not only to the war itself but also to the power of the military and defence corporations to an extent not seen since the 1930s and the Nye Committee.[69] A new generation of anti-war Democrats entered Congress in the aftermath of the Watergate scandal of 1974, and it seemed as though the United

---

[65] Audra J. Wolfe, *Competing with the Soviets: Science, Technology, and the State in Cold War America* (Baltimore, MD: Johns Hopkins University Press, 2013); Audra J. Wolfe, *Freedom's Laboratory: The Cold War Struggle for the Soul of Science* (Baltimore, MD: Johns Hopkins University Press, 2018).
[66] Craig and Logevall, *America's Cold War*, 177, 192.
[67] Brenes, *For Might and Right*, 96–8.
[68] Brenes, *For Might and Right*, 100–2.
[69] Michael Sherry, *In the Shadow of War: The United States since the 1930s* (New Haven, CT: Yale University Press, 1995), 276–83.

States might seriously reconsider the rationale for the national security state, especially as military spending declined from 46 per cent of the federal budget in 1968 to 29.5 per cent in 1974, and Congressional investigations uncovered a series of abuses committed by intelligence agencies in the name of national security.[70] Yet, as Michael Brenes argues, local opposition to defence spending cuts in industrial communities effectively stymied any attempt to seriously rein in military spending. The economic crises of the 1970s, which saw declining wages and higher unemployment, meant that defence hawks could argue that higher defence spending was necessary to provide well-paying jobs to American workers at a time when many of these jobs seemed to be disappearing.[71] The same logic played out again in the 1990s: even when the end of the Cold War and calls for a 'peace dividend' made the case for the eradication of the military–industrial complex seem inevitable, bipartisan Congressional resistance to cuts meant that the defence budget only declined moderately, and many of the military's major weapons programmes escaped cancellation. Even before the 9/11 attacks launched a new iteration of the national security state, the defence budget had already started to rise again.

To fully understand the particular form the American national security state took, we need to explore how this enormous defence expenditure was financed. If the military–industrial complex and the Cold War combined to close off the possibility of forging an American social welfare state to mirror those built in post-war western Europe, they also meant that conservatives were unable to return to a pre-New Deal equilibrium. Wartime spending in the Second World War was partly financed not only by widely held 'liberty bonds' but also by a newly enlarged system of mass taxation. The number of wage earners subject to income tax increased tenfold between 1939 and 1945, and individual income tax receipts increased $892 million to $18.4 billion between 1940 and 1945.[72] While Republicans hoped to enact large-scale tax cuts after taking both houses of Congress in 1946, growing Cold War tensions ultimately meant that their antitax measures fell afoul of increasing defence budget. When Eisenhower took office in 1953, he worked to defend the federal income tax, an unheard-of stance for a Republican to take at that time.[73] Thus, the national security state helped

---

[70] 'Fiscal Year 2017 Historical Tables: Budget of the U.S. Government', table 3.1.

[71] Brenes, *For Might and Right*, 143–4. Jefferson Cowie argues that this electoral coalition was already visible in the 1972 presidential election, when elements of the labour movement supported Richard Nixon's campaign against the anti-war candidate George McGovern. Jefferson Cowie, *Stayin' Alive: The 1970s and the Last Days of the Working Class* (New York: New Press, 2010), 147–8.

[72] Gerstle, *Liberty and Coercion*, 270; 'Fiscal Year 2017 Historical Tables: Budget of the U.S. Government', table 2.1.

[73] Gerstle, *Liberty and Coercion*, 270.

to usher in a modernized and comprehensive system of mass taxation, one that affected all Americans and which proved very difficult even for its greatest critics to undo.

The Republican revolt against taxation in the late 1940s did have a longer-term effect on American finances though, even if Republicans were ultimately unsuccessful in their effort to dismantle the New Deal. In the early phase of the Korean War, President Truman was initially able to raise taxes thanks to a public that had just recently experienced mass taxation and liberty bonds during the Second World War, only to find that lagging public support for the war as it ground on made raising additional war taxes much more difficult.[74] This experience meant that when President Lyndon Johnson looked to finance the American war in Vietnam, he was much more wary of increasing taxes, imposing a war tax just once, in 1968. Instead, much of his military spending was paid for by issuing government debt. The political scientist Sarah Kreps argues that this represents a crucial turning point in the relationship between popular opinion and elite decision-making on war.[75] Characterized by Kreps as a shift from a 'Liberty Bond' model of war financing to a 'Hide and Seek' model, this strategy was pursued by virtually all leaders after the war in Vietnam. Moving the fiscal costs of war into the future meant that the public was no longer burdened by war taxes and thus much less likely to call for an end to war. Changes in global financial markets in the 1970s and the dollar's hegemony meant that debt-financed war was relatively cheap and the United States never had any trouble selling bonds.[76] The post-9/11 wars represent the purest form of this model, as the Bush administration made sure that a large portion of the costs of the war were off-books and paid for by the 'Overseas Contingency Operations' fund, separate from the Pentagon's normal budget and subject to very little Congressional oversight. Even if the costs of these wars seem to be invisible, they remain extraordinarily high. In 2019, Brown University's Costs of War project estimated the total cost of the post-9/11 wars at $6.4 trillion, including $925 billion in interest due on war debt.[77] The financial cost of these wars was scarcely

---

[74] Steven Casey, *Selling the Korean War: Propaganda, Politics, and Public Opinion in the United States, 1950–1953* (Oxford: Oxford University Press, 2010), 178–88.

[75] Sarah Kreps, *Taxing Wars: The American Way of War Finance and the Decline of Democracy* (New York: Oxford University Press, 2018).

[76] Linda J. Bilmes, Rosella Cappella Zielinski, Matthew DiGiuseppe, Paul Poast, A. Trevor Thrall, Sarah E. Kreps and Joshua Rovner, 'Roundtable 10–32 on Taxing Wars: The American Way of War Finance and the Decline of American Democracy', H-Diplo | ISSF, accessed 26 October 2020, https://issforum.org/roundtables/10-32-taxing.

[77] Neta Crawford, 'United States Budgetary Costs and Obligations of Post-9/11 Wars through FY2020: $6.4 Trillion', 20 Years of War: A Costs of War Research Series (Providence, RI: Watson Institute for International and Public Affairs, Brown University, 13 November 2019), https://

visible to voters and the structure of the All-Volunteer Force meant the human costs were unevenly distributed, while the jobs provided by defence spending were all too apparent. The invisibility of the costs of intervention does much to explain how the United States was able to sustain its military intervention in Afghanistan for nearly two decades.

* * *

The longevity of the newest 'forever' wars, though, is also rooted in other changes to the state wrought by militarization. Increasingly, diplomatic relations with the rest of the world were conducted via military channels. While FDR had hoped to move the headquarters of the post-war Army back across the Potomac so that it could be more easily supervised by the White House, the Second World War and the Cold War meant that military leaders gained a level of autonomy and power within the state that they had rarely held before. The surge of military spending that empowered the DoD and the military more broadly also made the military leaders and policymakers nested in the national security bureaucracy into important diplomatic actors at the expense of the State Department and the diplomatic corps. In the immediate aftermath of the Second World War, soldiers played an important political role as military governors of occupied nations. Figures like Douglas MacArthur and Lucius Clay were given wide-ranging powers to implement reforms, build democratic institutions and rebuild economies.[78] MacArthur, in particular, had extraordinary power, as his staff drafted Japan's post-war constitution and he directly governed the country until handing control back to the Japanese government in 1949.[79] The historian Grant Madsen goes so far as to argue that these soldier-governors had a crucial role in reshaping the global economy, as the sort of balanced-budget anti-Keynesian austerity politics that they promoted in Germany and Japan made their way back to the Eisenhower administration and later provided a blueprint for Western economies more broadly.[80]

Even outside of the confines of military occupation, soldiers became increasingly prominent as diplomatic actors in their own right. Many of the details of the Second World War strategy had been worked out in a series of

watson.brown.edu/costsofwar/files/cow/imce/papers/2019/US%20Budgetary%20Costs%20of%20 Wars%20November%202019.pdf.

[78] Susan L. Carruthers, *The Good Occupation: American Soldiers and the Hazards of Peace* (Cambridge, MA: Harvard University Press, 2016).

[79] John W. Dower, *Embracing Defeat: Japan in the Wake of World War II* (New York: W. W. Norton, 2000).

[80] Grant Madsen, *Sovereign Soldiers: How the U.S. Military Transformed the Global Economy After World War II* (Philadelphia: University of Pennsylvania Press, 2018).

wartime conferences, attended not just by heads of state but by military staffs as well. In the West, the foundation of the North Atlantic Treaty Organization (NATO) gave institutional permanence to cooperation between military staffs, and the presence of large numbers of American troops in Europe and East Asia meant that military issues were always a prominent part of the United States' diplomatic relations with a long list of countries. While the State Department grew in absolute terms in the post-war period – with the size of the Foreign Service increasing sixfold from 4,000 in 1940 to 24,000 in 1950 – its relative influence within the US government waned as questions of military strategy predominated throughout the Cold War.[81]

This was not solely a question of military leaders taking on more explicitly diplomatic roles however. The growth of the NSC itself did much to sideline the State Department. The relative prominence and importance of the NSC varied depending on the preference of individual presidents, but its centrality nonetheless grew steadily over the years.[82] While it was originally intended to be a coordinating body, various National Security Advisors, particularly McGeorge Bundy and Henry Kissinger, empowered the NSC so that it became almost like an independent executive branch agency at times.[83] The fact that foreign policy was routed through an institution that directly focused on national security inevitably militarized aspects of American diplomacy. Indeed, at various stages, the NSC attempted to conduct diplomacy in its own right, leaving the State Department and its formal diplomatic channels under-utilized. The most absurd example of this tendency was the Iran–Contra scandal during the Reagan administration, when the administration illegally sold arms to Iran, a country that was the subject of an American arms embargo, and then channelled the proceeds to the Contra anti-communist guerrillas in Nicaragua. All of this was intended to

---

[81] Katznelson, *Fear Itself*, 409.

[82] John Gans, *White House Warriors: How the National Security Council Transformed the American Way of War* (New York: Liveright, 2019); David Rothkopf, *Running the World: The Inside Story of the National Security Council and the Architects of American Power* (New York: Public Affairs, 2006); John P. Burke, *Honest Broker?: The National Security Advisor and Presidential Decision Making* (College Station: Texas A&M University Press, 2009); Ivo H. Daalder and I. M. Destler, *In the Shadow of the Oval Office: Profiles of the National Security Advisers and the Presidents They Served-From JFK to George W. Bush* (New York: Simon & Schuster, 2011); Amy B. Zegart, *Flawed by Design: The Evolution of the CIA, JCS, and NSC* (Stanford, CA: Stanford University Press, 2000); Loch Johnson and Karl F. Inderfurth, eds, *Fateful Decisions: Inside the National Security Council* (New York: Oxford University Press, 2004).

[83] Andrew Preston, *The War Council: McGeorge Bundy, The NSC, and Vietnam* (Cambridge, MA: Harvard University Press, 2006); Gerry Argyris Andrianopoulos, *Kissinger and Brzezinski: The NSC and the Struggle for Control of US National Security Policy* (Basingstoke: Palgrave Macmillan, 2016); Henry Kissinger and United States Congress Senate Committee on Government Operations Subcommittee on National Security and International Operations, *The National Security Council* (US Government Printing Office, 1970).

circumvent the Boland amendment, a Congressional initiative aimed at limiting US government assistance to the Contras. The details of the affair were byzantine in places, but the NSC staffer and Marine Lt. Col. Oliver North was at the heart of it, as he orchestrated a scheme that effectively constituted an independent foreign policy.[84] While the Iran–Contra scandal resulted in criminal indictments for several prominent Reagan administration officials, including the Secretary of Defense, two National Security Advisors, an Assistant Secretary of State and a number of lesser CIA and military officials, it did not lead to a downgrading of the NSC's importance. Indeed, thirty years later, Washington insiders were again complaining that NSC staffers – this time in the Obama administration – were taking direct operational control of issues and cutting the State Department, and even the Pentagon, out of the decision-making process.[85]

The marginalization of the State Department and the rise of the NSC was not simply a story of sharp bureaucratic politics on the part of characters like McGeorge Bundy and Henry Kissinger however. The centralization of foreign policymaking in the White House and its attendant militarization was also due in part to fears of nuclear war and the perceived need for rapid decision-making.[86] The fact that decisions would need to be made in minutes in the event of a nuclear attack meant that the president was vested with extraordinary power to take the country to war immediately and without any reference to constitutional checks and balances. The role of Congress as the sole institution with the constitutional authority to declare war was effectively rendered moot in a world where the president could launch a world-destroying barrage of missiles without the need

---

[84] Lawrence E. Walsh, *Final Report of the Independent Counsel for Iran/Contra Matters* (US Court of Appeals for the District of Columbia Circuit, Division for the Purpose of Appointing Independent Counsel, 1993); Peter Kornbluh and Malcolm Byrne, *The Iran-Contra Scandal: The Declassified History* (New York: New Press, 1993); James F. Siekmeier, 'The Iran–Contra Affair', in *A Companion to Ronald Reagan*, ed. Andrew L. Johns (Chichester: John Wiley, 2015), 321–38, https://doi.org/10.1002/9781118607770.ch18.

[85] Jeffrey Goldberg, 'A Withering Critique of Obama's National Security Council', The Atlantic, 12 November 2014, https://www.theatlantic.com/international/archive/2014/11/a-withering-critique-of-president-obamas-national-security-council/382477/; Derek Chollett, 'What's Wrong with Obama's National Security Council?', Defense One, 26 April 2016, https://www.defenseone.com/ideas/2016/04/whats-wrong-obamas-national-security-council/127802/; Robert M. Gates, *Duty: Memoirs of a Secretary at War* (New York: Vintage, 2015), 586–588.

[86] Gary Wills, *Bomb Power: The Modern Presidency and the National Security State* (New York: Penguin Books, 2011); Robert S. Singh, 'The United States Congress and Nuclear War Powers: Explaining Legislative Nonfeasance', *Journal of Legislative Studies*, 15 September 2018, http://www.tandfonline.com/doi/abs/10.1080/13572334.2018.1516604; Arthur S. Miller and H. Bart Cox, 'Congress, the Constitution, and First Use of Nuclear Weapons', *Review of Politics* 48, no. 3 (1986): 424–55; William C. Banks, 'First Use of Nuclear Weapons: The Constitutional Role of a Congressional Leadership Committee', *Journal of Legislation* 13, no. 1 (1986): 1–21; Mary DeRosa and Ashley Nicolas, 'The President and Nuclear Weapons: Authorities, Limits, and Process', SSRN Scholarly Paper (Rochester, NY: Social Science Research Network, 10 December 2019), https://papers.ssrn.com/abstract=3595440.

to do more than consult the Secretary of Defense. This slippage was apparent in the early hours of the Korean War, when the Truman administration took the United States to war without bothering to seek any Congressional declaration of war.[87] This precedent would be cited repeatedly by White House Office of Legal Counsel officials in numerous administrations, as lawyers sought to argue that military actions such as troop deployments and air strikes could be justified by Truman's actions on Korea.[88] Following Korea, presidents instead preferred to look for Congressional authorizations rather than formal declarations of war. President Lyndon Johnson's Gulf of Tonkin Resolution, which provided blanket authority for the use of military force in Southeast Asia and precipitated massive escalation of American involvement in the war in Vietnam, represents the best-known example of extreme presidential autonomy in the use of military force.[89]

The growing unpopularity of the American War in Vietnam prompted Congressional efforts to seize back war-making powers from the Executive. As early as 1966, Senator Wayne Morse, one of only two Senators to vote against the Tonkin Gulf Resolution, introduced legislation to repeal it, and both Presidents Lyndon B. Johnson and Richard Nixon had to fight off attempts by members of Congress to pass amendments that would restrict presidential freedom of action in Southeast Asia and, later, that would have forced the withdrawal of all US forces from South Vietnam.[90] Nixon had to engage in extensive political action and mobilization to defeat the McGovern–Hatfield amendment, a move by anti-war Senators in 1970 to require the end of US military operations in the region by the end of that year, and only managed to water down rather than defeat outright the Cooper–Church amendment, which called for an end to US operations in Cambodia and Laos.[91] The Bill that contained the final version of

---

[87] Mary L. Dudziak, 'The Toxic Legacy of the Korean War', *Washington Post*, accessed 22 September 2020, https://www.washingtonpost.com/outlook/2019/03/01/toxic-legacy-korean-war/.

[88] Brian Finucane, 'Presidential War Powers, the Take Care Clause, and Article 2(4) of the U.N. Charter', SSRN Scholarly Paper (Rochester, NY: Social Science Research Network, 14 January 2019), https://doi.org/10.2139/ssrn.3315698; Louis Fisher, 'The Korean War: On What Legal Basis Did Truman Act?', *American Journal of International Law* 89, no. 1 (1995): 21–39, https://doi.org/10.2307/2203888; Jane E. Stromseth, 'Rethinking War Powers: Congress, the President, and the United Nations Symposium: International Law for a New World Order', *Georgetown Law Journal* 81, no. 3 (1993): 597–674; Curtis Bradley and Jean Galbraith, 'Presidential War Powers as an Interactive Dynamic: International Law, Domestic Law, and Practice-Based Legal Change', *Faculty Scholarship at Penn Law*, 1 January 2016, https://scholarship.law.upenn.edu/faculty_scholarship/1600.

[89] Edwin E. Moise, *Tonkin Gulf and the Escalation of the Vietnam War* (Chapel Hill: University of North Carolina Press, 1996), http://archive.org/details/isbn_9780807823002.

[90] Alvin Beggs, 'The Vietnam War Dissent of Ernest Gruening and Wayne Morse, 1964–1968', PhD diss., Bowling Green State University, 1 January 2010, https://scholarworks.bgsu.edu/hist_diss/15.

[91] Sarah Thelen, 'Give War a Chance: The Nixon Administration and Domestic Support for the Vietnam War, 1969–1973' (PhD diss., Washington, DC, American University, 2012); Andrew L. Johns, *Vietnam's Second Front: Domestic Politics, the Republican Party, and the War* (Lexington: University Press of Kentucky, 2010).

the Cooper–Church amendment also included a repeal of the Gulf of Tonkin resolution, marking a serious attempt at controlling executive power in foreign policy.

Nixon's secret bombing of Cambodia and Laos, in defiance of Congressional wishes, prompted Congress to go further, and they passed the War Powers Resolution over Nixon's veto in 1973. The Resolution required the president to consult with Congress in advance of introducing US armed forces into hostilities or situations in which hostilities were imminent. It also forbade the military from remaining in such situations for more than sixty days without a Congressional authorization of the use of force and stipulated that Congress could require the president to remove troops that were engaged in combat without the requisite Congressional authorization at the time by passing a Concurrent Resolution.[92] Nixon immediately declared the War Powers Resolution to be unconstitutional, a stance adopted by every president since then, but this Congressional anti-war action did have a material effect on US military operations around the world. The Case–Church amendment of 1973 effectively ended direct US involvement in the Vietnam War and prevented President Ford from re-intervening when the South Vietnamese regime faced collapse in the spring of 1975.[93] The work of Congressional oversight committees, most notably the Church Committee, highlighted intelligence abuses and produced a body of legislation that restricted the CIA from engaging in paramilitary activity and covert actions, preventing the United States from supplying arms to belligerents in the Angolan Civil War.[94] The Boland amendment similarly limited US support and aid to the Contras in Nicaragua, which prompted Reagan's NSC to engage in the series of illegal

---

[92] Richard F. Grimmett, 'War Powers Resolution: Presidential Compliance', CRS Report for Congress (Washington, DC: Congressional Research Service, November 2010); Stephen L. Carter, 'The Constitutionality of the War Powers Resolution', *Virginia Law Review* 70, no. 1 (1984): 101–34, https://doi.org/10.2307/1072825; Cyrus R. Vance, 'Striking the Balance: Congress and the President Under the War Powers Resolution', *University of Pennsylvania Law Review* 133, no. 1 (1984): 79–95; Eugene V. Rostow, 'Once More unto the Breach: The War Powers Resolution Revisited The Edward A. Seegers Lectures: Lecture', *Valparaiso University Law Review* 21, no. 1 (1986): 1–52; Michael Rubner, 'The Reagan Administration, the 1973 War Powers Resolution, and the Invasion of Grenada', *Political Science Quarterly* 100, no. 4 (1985): 627–47, https://doi.org/10.2307/2151544.

[93] Jeffrey H. Michaels, 'Delusions of Survival: US Deliberations on Support for South Vietnam during the 1975 "Final Offensive"', *Small Wars & Insurgencies* 26, no. 6 (2 November 2015): 957–75, https://doi.org/10.1080/09592318.2015.1095838.

[94] Loch K. Johnson, 'Congressional Supervision of America's Secret Agencies: The Experience and Legacy of the Church Committee', *Public Administration Review* 64, no. 1 (2004): 3–14, https://doi.org/10.1111/j.1540-6210.2004.00342.x; Russell A. Miller, *US National Security, Intelligence and Democracy: From the Church Committee to the War on Terror* (London: Routledge, 2008); Steven O'Sullivan, *Kissinger, Angola and US-African Foreign Policy: The Unintentional Realist* (London: Routledge, 2019); Hannah Bentley, 'Keeping Secrets: The Church Committee, Covert Action, and Nicaragua Comment', *Columbia Journal of Transnational Law* 25, no. 3 (1987): 601–46.

attempts to circumvent it – this ultimately was the scandal that became known as Iran–Contra.[95]

This Congressional activism faded along with the rawness of the memories of defeat in Vietnam, however, and presidents since then both explicitly pushed back against the constitutionality of the War Powers Resolution and worked with Congressional allies and lobby groups to repeal laws that restricted the executive branch's freedom of action in military affairs. The most important change to this struggle of attrition between the legislative and executive branches, though, came with the American response to the attacks of 11 September 2001. Congress's hasty passage of the Authorization of the Use of Military Force (AUMF) on 18 September brought back all of the broad sweeping powers contained in the Tonkin Gulf Resolution, but now effectively applied them to the whole world. In a terse statement, Congress authorized the president:

> to use all necessary and appropriate force against those nations, organizations, or persons he determines planned, authorized, committed, or aided the terrorist attacks that occurred on September 11, 2001, or harbored such organizations or persons, in order to prevent any future acts of international terrorism against the United States by such nations, organizations or persons.[96]

This declaration served as the legal justification for the war in Afghanistan and countless air strikes, drone strikes and Special Forces raids in countries all over the world, and the fact that it was temporally and geographically unbounded meant that it was being repurposed over a decade later to authorize the use of force against organizations that had not even existed in September 2001.[97] The Trump administration even used the AUMF as justification for air strikes against the Assad regime in Syria in 2017, despite the fact that Assad styled himself as an opponent of Al-Qaeda, the organization responsible for the 11 September attacks.[98] Despite attempts by Congressional opponents such as Representative Barbara Lee to terminate or replace the AUMF, it remains operational at the time

---

[95] William M. LeoGrande, *Our Own Backyard: The United States in Central America, 1977–1992* (Chapel Hill: University of North Carolina Press, 2000), 299–305.

[96] United States Congress, 'Authorization for Use of Military Force', Pub. L. No. 107–40 (2001), https://www.congress.gov/107/plaws/publ40/PLAW-107publ40.pdf.

[97] Rosa Brooks, *How Everything Became War and the Military Became Everything: Tales from the Pentagon* (New York: Simon & Schuster, 2017); Rosa Brooks, 'The Trickle-Down War', *Yale Law & Policy Review* 32, no. 2 (1 April 2014): 583–602; Shoon Kathleen Murray, 'The Contemporary Presidency: Stretching the 2001 AUMF: A History of Two Presidencies', *Presidential Studies Quarterly* 45, no. 1 (2015): 175–98, https://doi.org/10.1111/psq.12184; 'AUMF Panel Transcript', *Pepperdine Law Review* 42, no. 3 (1 March 2015): 607; Maria Ryan, *Full Spectrum Dominance: Irregular Warfare and the War on Terror* (Stanford, CA: Stanford University Press, 2019).

[98] Sean Illing, 'Was Trump's Syria Bombing Illegal?', Vox, 16 April 2018, https://www.vox.com/2018/4/16/17239732/trump-syria-strike-bombing-illegal-aumf-constitution-congress.

of writing, nearly twenty years after its passage, and it continues to provide the legal premise for the use of force by the US military around the world.[99]

Congressional wariness of military intervention after the end of the American War in Vietnam did not mean that the legislature provided an extensive critique of the militarization of foreign policy. The Goldwater–Nichols Act of 1986 reorganized much of the national security establishment and, crucially, empowered the commanders-in-chief (CINCs) of the unified regional commands that divided up the world into geographical areas of responsibility.[100] These flag officers would now report directly to the Secretary of Defense and were given a great deal of autonomy to manage military affairs in their regions. Supported by large headquarters (which doubled in size after the end of the Cold War) and substantial budgets, these military leaders became important diplomatic actors in their regions in a manner not seen since MacArthur and Clay were responsible for military governments in Japan and Germany. The smallest of these commands, SOUTHCOM, responsible for Latin America, had a staff of 1,100 in 2003. As the journalist Dana Priest points out, this meant that there were more people in SOUTHCOM working on Latin American affairs 'than at the departments of State, Commerce, Treasury, and Agriculture, the Pentagon's Joint Staff and the Office of the Secretary of Defense combined'.[101] Not only that, but regional CINCs were provided with their own personal long-range air transport and a fleet of helicopters for shorter trips.[102] By contrast, the Secretary of State is the only diplomat afforded this privilege. The CINCs also oversee extensive military training and education programmes and manage defence diplomacy, aided by over 2,200 Foreign Area Officers, who serve as military diplomats.[103] As of 2020, there were approximately eight thousand Foreign Service Officers in the State Department.[104]

[99] John Nichols, 'Barbara Lee Wins a House Vote to Stop the Blank Checks for Endless War', 19 June 2019, https://www.thenation.com/article/archive/barbara-lee-endless-war/.

[100] James R. Locher III and Sam Nunn, *Victory on the Potomac: The Goldwater-Nichols Act Unifies the Pentagon*, rev. edn (College Station: Texas A&M University Press, 2004); Gordon Nathaniel Lederman and Sam Nunn, *Reorganizing the Joint Chiefs of Staff: The Goldwater-Nichols Act of 1986* (Westport, CT: Greenwood Press, 1999).

[101] Dana Priest, *The Mission: Waging War and Keeping Peace with America's Military* (New York: W. W. Norton, 2004), 74.

[102] Priest, *The Mission*, 71.

[103] Amy A. Alrich, Joseph Adams and Claudio C. Biltoc, 'The Strategic Value of Foreign Area Officers' (Alexandria, VA: Institute for Defense Analysis, 20 June 2013), https://apps.dtic.mil/sti/citations/ADA589137; Robert D. Kaplan, *Imperial Grunts: On the Ground with the American Military, from Mongolia to the Philippines to Iraq and Beyond* (New York: Vintage Books, 2006).

[104] Christopher W. Smith, 'The Diplomat and the State', *Foreign Service Journal*, May 2020, https://www.afsa.org/diplomat-and-state.

While Congressional reform of the military command structure inadvertently empowered generals as diplomats, the legislature's enthusiasm for arms exports provided a more direct impetus for the militarization of foreign policy. The popularity of foreign military sales – or at least the largesse to local armament plants provided by those sales – underlines just how difficult a task it has been for opponents to attempt to unwind the military–industrial complex. Congress was a co-equal player in the promotion of foreign military sales as a diplomatic tool. Following Nixon and Kissinger's desire to make sure that allied countries would be primarily responsible for their own security, defence sales boomed through the 1970s.[105] The establishment of the Defense Security Assistance Agency in 1971 provided the structure for the administration of arms exports worth tens of billions a year.[106] While these sales occasionally became a political flashpoint due to human rights concerns, they generally proceeded without undue controversy.[107] Even in instances where there was significant Congressional and public opposition, such as the Reagan administration's sale of AWACS aircraft to Saudi Arabia, the sheer price tag of these deals made them hard to resist.[108] Not only that, but policymakers presented them as a vital part of American national security policy and foreign military assistance became a useful way to manage alliances. Indeed, arms sales were at the heart of the Iran–Contra scandal, as the Reagan administration sold Iran hundreds of TOW anti-tank missiles and Hawk anti-aircraft missiles for use in their war against Iraq. The United States also sold helicopters to Iraq during the war, and the CIA worked to channel non-US weaponry and equipment.

Aside from sales, the United States has also provided grant funding for foreign governments to purchase US military equipment. Military aid currently makes up slightly less than one-third of the overall US foreign assistance budget,

---

[105] Leslie H. Gelb, 'Arms Sales', *Foreign Policy*, no. 25 (1976): 3–23, https://doi.org/10.2307/1148021; Michael T. Klare, *American Arms Supermarket* (Austin: University of Texas Press, 1984); Geoffrey Kemp, 'The Continuing Debate Over U.S. Arms Sales: Strategic Needs and the Quest for Arms Limitations', *Annals of the American Academy of Political and Social Science* 535, no. 1 (1 September 1994): 146–57, https://doi.org/10.1177/0002716294535001011.

[106] John Tirman, *Spoils of War* (New York: Free Press, 1997), 24–5, http://archive.org/details/spoilsofwarhuman00tirm.

[107] Shannon Lindsey Blanton, 'Foreign Policy in Transition? Human Rights, Democracy, and U.S. Arms Exports', *International Studies Quarterly* 49, no. 4 (1 December 2005): 647–67, https://doi.org/10.1111/j.1468-2478.2005.00382.x.

[108] Nicholas Laham and Patrick Murray, *Selling AWACS to Saudi Arabia: The Reagan Administration and the Balancing of America's Competing Interests in the Middle East* (Westport, CT: Greenwood Press, 2002); Charles Mohr, 'Saudi AWACS Deal Passes $8 Billion', *New York Times*, 22 August 1981, https://www.nytimes.com/1981/08/22/world/saudi-awacs-deal-passes-8-billion.html; Christopher S. Raj, 'Controversial US AWACS Sale to Saudis', *Strategic Analysis* 5, no. 8 (1 November 1981): 392–9, https://doi.org/10.1080/09700168109425826.

while at times during the 1980s it made up over 60 per cent of the total figure.[109] The militarization of US foreign policy, however, also had implications for the rest of the overseas aid budget. Throughout the 1960s, as the United States intervened in a number of conflicts by launching counterinsurgency campaigns, most notably in Vietnam, social scientists were directly enlisted in military-led efforts to win hearts and minds.[110] The United States Agency for International Development (USAID), founded in 1961 in order to assist underdeveloped countries, was by 1967 dedicating over $550 million of its overall $2 billion budget to South Vietnam, a nation of some 17 million people, and in that same year began to work jointly with the military and the CIA in the Civil Operations and Rural Development Program (CORDS), a pacification programme run jointly by the United States in South Vietnam.[111] Much of what Elizabeth Borgwardt characterizes as a New Deal for the world had become explicitly tied to military operations by the 1960s. Similarly, in Iraq and Afghanistan, American development aid was channelled in support of counterinsurgency operations, with USAID personnel embedded in Provincial Reconstruction Teams and huge sums allocated to infrastructure projects.[112] Outside of these two countries, USAID has also worked closely with AFRICOM, the military's newest geographical combatant command, to distribute development aid in sub-Saharan Africa in support of American national security objectives, security force assistance and counter-terrorist operations throughout the continent.[113]

[109] 'How Does the U.S. Spend Its Foreign Aid?', Council on Foreign Relations, accessed 29 October 2020, https://www.cfr.org/backgrounder/how-does-us-spend-its-foreign-aid; Chester J. Pach Jr, _Arming the Free World: The Origins of the United States Military Assistance Program, 1945–1950_ (Chapel Hill: University of North Carolina Press, 1991); William Easterly, 'Foreign Aid Goes Military!', _New York Review of Books_, 4 December 2008, https://www.nybooks.com/articles/2008/12/04/foreign-aid-goes-military/; 'Fiscal Year 2017 Historical Tables: Budget of the U.S. Government', table 3.2.

[110] Joy Rohde, _Armed with Expertise: The Militarization of American Social Research during the Cold War_ (Ithaca, NY: Cornell University Press, 2013), https://www.jstor.org/stable/10.7591/j.ctt32b4z5.

[111] Marc Leepson, 'The Heart and Mind of USAID's Vietnam Mission', _Foreign Service Journal_ 77, no. 4 (April 2000): 21; Nick Cullather, 'Miracles of Modernization: The Green Revolution and the Apotheosis of Technology', _Diplomatic History_ 28, no. 2 (1 April 2004): 227–54, https://doi.org/10.1111/j.1467-7709.2004.00407.x; Michael Latham, _Modernization as Ideology: American Social Science and 'Nation Building' in the Kennedy Era_ (Chapel Hill: University of North Carolina Press, 2000), 151–208; Andrew J. Gawthorpe, _To Build as Well as Destroy: American Nation Building in South Vietnam_ (Ithaca, NY: Cornell University Press, 2018).

[112] Office of the Special Inspector General for Iraq Reconstruction, _Hard Lessons: The Iraq Reconstruction Experience_ (Washington, DC: Government Printing Office, 2009); Rajiv Chandrasekaran, _Little America: The War within the War for Afghanistan_ (New York: Vintage Books, 2012).

[113] James J. F. Forest and Rebecca Crispin, 'AFRICOM: Troubled Infancy, Promising Future', _Contemporary Security Policy_ 30, no. 1 (1 April 2009): 5–27, https://doi.org/10.1080/13523260902759753; Dan Henk, 'AFRICOM's Role in an African Future: Bridge or Dam?', _Contemporary Security Policy_ 30, no. 1 (1 April 2009): 39–44, https://doi.org/10.1080/13523260902759928; Paul Jackson, 'Introduction: Mars, Venus or Mercury? AFRICOM and America's Ambiguous Intentions', _Contemporary Security Policy_ 30, no. 1 (1 April 2009): 1–4, https://doi.org/10.1080/13523260902759738; Ken Menkhaus, 'False Start in AFRICOM', _Contemporary Security Policy_ 30, no. 1 (1 April 2009): 53–7, https://doi.org/10.1080/13523260902767905;

This melding of social science, development programmes and military operations could also be seen in the decades-long 'war on drugs' in Latin America. President Richard Nixon coined the phrase in 1971 as he launched a campaign both within American borders and abroad to reduce the illegal drug trade in the United States, militarizing what had been seen as a public health and law enforcement problem.[114] Working with countries like Mexico and Colombia, US authorities provided military aid, training and even troops to break up narcotics supply chains and eradicate coca crops.[115] As the historian Aileen Teague documents, though, not only did these policies fail to slow the flow of drugs into the United States, but militarized aid was gladly accepted by these governments and put to other uses. For instance, the United States succeeded in militarizing Mexico's police force in the 1970s, but these forces were then largely used for domestic political repression rather than for the elimination of narcotics trafficking.[116] The 'war' metaphor may have been initially effective at mobilizing political and financial support for these initiatives, but as a way of dealing with the problem, it was remarkably ineffective.

* * *

Notwithstanding the fact that the limitations of the 'war on drugs' were apparent to many in Washington by the late 1980s, President Clinton appointed recently retired General Barry McCaffrey, who had led the 24th Mechanized Infantry Division in the Persian Gulf War and commanded SOUTHCOM, as his 'drugs czar', with responsibility for both international and domestic anti-drug efforts. In the immediate aftermath of the Gulf War, Mayor Richard Daley of Chicago had asked President George H. W. Bush to put General Norman Schwarzkopf in charge of a renewed 'war on drugs'.[117] Daley's plea and McCaffrey's elevation were symptomatic of how many Americans look to the military as a source

José de Arimatéia da Cruz and Laura K. Stephens, 'The U.S. Africa Command (AFRICOM): Building Partnership or Neo-Colonialism of U.S.-Africa Relations?', *Journal of Third World Studies; Americus* 27, no. 2 (Fall 2010): 193–213.

[114] Jeremy Kuzmarov, *The Myth of the Addicted Army: Vietnam and the Modern War on Drugs* (Amherst: University Massachusetts Press, 2009), 101–88; Vanda Felbab-Brown, *Shooting Up: Counterinsurgency and the War on Drugs* (Washington, DC: Brookings Institution Press, 2009); Dan Baum, *Smoke and Mirrors: The War on Drugs and the Politics of Failure* (Boston, MA: Back Bay Books, 1997).

[115] Jonathan D. Rosen, *Losing War, The: Plan Colombia and Beyond* (Albany: State University of New York Press, 2015).

[116] Aileen Teague, 'The United States, Mexico, and the Mutual Securitization of Drug Enforcement, 1969–1985', *Diplomatic History* 43, no. 5 (1 November 2019): 785–812, https://doi.org/10.1093/dh/dhz035.

[117] Sherry, *In the Shadow of War*, 473.

of competence after the end of the Cold War. Other federal agencies began to mimic military culture in an effort to burnish their own reputations. This tendency accelerated tremendously after the 11 September 2001 attacks, as new agencies such the Department of Homeland Security and Immigration Control and Enforcement (ICE) pursued a 'war on terror' at home, while intelligence agencies led by the CIA took on increasingly paramilitary roles around the world.[118] The surge of legislation in the early 2000s that created these agencies and allowed for increased surveillance of both US citizens and foreign nationals (most notably in the PATRIOT Act) in some ways paralleled the similar cascade of legislation in the late 1940s, although far fewer politicians seemed to worry about the garrison state this time around.[119]

The effects of this era on the character of domestic policing, though, were perhaps most striking. Agencies like ICE and the Border Patrol were able to make extensive use of their new powers and large budgets to equip themselves like a military force and act accordingly, while the Department of Defense's 1033 programme allowed local police departments to acquire some $7.4 billion worth of excess military equipment, including weapons and even armoured vehicles.[120] Not only that, but police forces recruited large numbers of veterans returning from Iraq and Afghanistan, with one 2017 study estimating that up to 20 per cent of police were former military personnel, who often brought with them an aggressive mindset more suited to infantry patrols than police work.[121] In cities like Ferguson and Minneapolis, police responded to complaints about police violence by taking to the streets with armoured vehicles, while wearing camouflage and body armour. These scenes recalled an earlier wave of police militarization: as the sociologist Stuart Schrader has argued, much as 1960s

---

[118] Ron Suskind, *The One Percent Doctrine: Deep Inside America's Pursuit of Its Enemies since 9/11* (New York: Simon & Schuster, 2007); Mark Mazzetti, *The Way of the Knife: The CIA, a Secret Army, and a War at the Ends of the Earth* (New York: Penguin Press, 2013).

[119] Matthew J. Morgan, 'The Garrison State Revisited: Civil–Military Implications of Terrorism and Security', *Contemporary Politics* 10, no. 1 (1 March 2004): 5–19, https://doi.org/10.1080/135697704 10001701224.

[120] Jared Keller, 'The Pentagon Has Funneled $7.4 Billion in Surplus Military Gear to Police Forces That Don't Want or Need It', Task & Purpose, 9 October 2020, https://taskandpurpose.com/news/military-surplus-equipment-inspector-general-audit.

[121] Jasper Craven, 'The Police's 'Sheepdog' Problem', *New Republic*, 11 June 2020, https://newrepublic.com/article/158136/military-veterans-police-sheepdog-problem; Bryan Schatz, "'Are You Prepared to Kill Somebody?" A Day with One of America's Most Popular Police Trainers', *Mother Jones* (blog), accessed 26 October 2020, https://www.motherjones.com/politics/2017/02/dave-grossman-training-police-militarization/; Ben Taub, 'The Spy Who Came Home: Why an Expert in Counterterrorism Became a Beat Cop', *New Yorker*, 30 April 2018, https://www.newyorker.com/magazine/2018/05/07/the-spy-who-came-home; Radley Balko, *Rise of the Warrior Cop: The Militarization of America's Police Forces* (New York: Public Affairs, 2013); Simone Wiechselbaum and Beth Schwartzapfel, 'When Warriors Put on the Badge', The Marshall Project, 30 March 2017, https://www.themarshallproject.org/2017/03/30/when-warriors-put-on-the-badge.

counterinsurgency campaigns militarized development aid, they also involved militarized policing, as police participated as combatants in war. Unlike economic aid, though, the militarization of policing made its way home to urban police departments, as officers who had been involved in professionalizing policing overseas took military logistics, practices and technologies back to the United States with them.[122]

This long-standing blurring of the lines between counterinsurgency and police work fused together with the more recent wave of 'war on terror'–inspired militarization to produce the spectacle of police, federal immigration agents, National Guard and active duty military gathering together on the streets of Washington, DC, in the summer of 2020 to confront protestors demonstrating against the police murder of George Floyd in Minneapolis and police violence more broadly. Secretary of Defense Mark Esper urged governors to 'dominate the battlespace' in responding to these nationwide protests against racialized policing, while on the same call, President Donald J. Trump incoherently declared General Mark Milley, Chairman of the JCS, to be 'in charge' of the response.[123] Much as the military and conceptions of national security had grown to dominate the conduct of American foreign policy, in this moment, the armed forces briefly seemed like they might play a central role in domestic law enforcement as well.

If the military's presence on the streets in the summer of 2020 marked a low point, then the message put forth by the millions of protestors who took to the streets suggested more hopeful possibilities. Much as the George Floyd protests were about racial injustice, they were also about militarization and its discontents. As early as 2014, Iraq and Afghanistan veterans had been to the fore in critiquing police responses to protest as being overly militarized, and now that critique extended to questioning what security was supposed to mean in the first place, and who was being made secure by the forces of the state.[124] Black Lives Matter protestors pushed to either defund or abolish police departments, arguing that the presence of heavily armed police on the streets did nothing

---

[122] Schrader, *Badges without Borders*.

[123] Meghann Myers, 'Esper Encourages Governors to "Dominate the Battlespace" to Put down Nationwide Protests', *Military Times*, 1 June 2020, https://www.militarytimes.com/news/your-military/2020/06/01/secdef-encourages-governors-to-dominate-the-battlespace-to-put-down-nationwide-protests/.

[124] Phillip Carter, 'Ferguson's Cops Are Armed Like I Was in Iraq', *Daily Beast*, 14 August 2014, https://www.thedailybeast.com/articles/2014/08/14/ferguson-s-cops-are-armed-like-i-was-in-iraq; Thomas Gibbons-Neff, 'Military Veterans See Deeply Flawed Police Response in Ferguson', *Washington Post*, 14 August 2014, https://www.washingtonpost.com/news/checkpoint/wp/2014/08/14/military-veterans-see-deeply-flawed-police-response-in-ferguson/.

to keep communities safe. Although the primary thrust of these demands was domestic in nature, many within the movement saw their activism as transnational and also questioned the military foundations of US power, making connections between their own protests and global struggles for justice. While these activists saw the same interlinking of foreign and domestic concerns as the internationalists of the early 1940s had observed, they were moving to unpick the logic of national security that had been brought into being by that earlier generation.[125] While the structural impediments to this reimagining of security are readily apparent, the very scale of these protests (between 15 and 26 million Americans took part) along with widespread scepticism of the merits of military intervention does at least open up the potential for another great debate over the United States' role in the world and what it means to keep Americans safe.[126]

* * *

In his magisterial book, *In the Shadow of War*, the historian Michael Sherry argues that the militarization of the Second World War and the early Cold War – which involved Americans explicitly rejecting militarism as something that characterized Nazi or Communist societies and only reluctantly acquiescing to the national security state while orienting civilian society around the preparation for war – had, by the end of the Vietnam War, morphed into a more symbolic militarism, where the armed forces and military values were glorified and celebrated for their own sake.[127] The scenes that played out in American cities throughout the summer of 2020 certainly pointed to the degradation of the term 'national security' and to a shift towards open militarism in some quarters. Long understood as a concept that encompassed the defence of values and a way of life as well as physical security, the way in which officials now employed the term related only to the repression of domestic political dissent and the display of raw military power.[128] The ubiquity of heavily armed and camouflage-clad security forces on American streets is surely a symbol of how deeply the militarized logic of security has permeated the state and a representation of the fears of early critics of the national security state come to life.

[125] Arun Kundnani, 'Abolish National Security' (Amsterdam: Transnational Institute, June 2021).
[126] Larry Buchanan, Quoctrung Bui and Jugal K. Patel, 'Black Lives Matter May Be the Largest Movement in U.S. History', *New York Times*, 3 July 2020, https://www.nytimes.com/interactive/2020/07/03/us/george-floyd-protests-crowd-size.html.
[127] Sherry, *In the Shadow of War*, 339–40.
[128] Stephen Wertheim, 'How Trump Brought Home the Endless War', *New Yorker*, 1 October 2020, https://www.newyorker.com/news/our-columnists/how-trump-brought-home-the-endless-war.

The history of how that shift occurred is in many ways a cultural one, a story that we will return to in Chapter 6, but we can also see how the political economy of the Cold War helped to produce this change by establishing a large and geographically dispersed defence industry that was difficult to shut down, no matter how pacific the international situation might be. Even as the proportion of the population with a history of military service declined and the number of Americans directly employed in the defence industry fell, the political power of the defence lobby remained largely unchallenged. Thus, even as protestors questioned the logic of the national security state, they were faced with immense structural obstacles to fundamental change. Over the course of the Second World War, the Cold War, the War on Terror, and the myriad minor crises in between, national security has remained centrally important to both American domestic politics and the United States' relations with the rest of the world.

3

Bases, borders and gun belts: The evolution of militarized spaces in the United States and beyond

On 20 December 1970, a car full of American servicemembers hit an Okinawan man in the island's Koza entertainment district. While the injured man was being bundled into an ambulance, a group of taxi drivers who had witnessed the incident angrily accosted a passing American serviceman and his girlfriend. Even as American Military Police rescued the couple from a growing crowd, another American vehicle caused yet another traffic accident nearby. The crowd, now hundreds-strong, became even more incensed and surrounded this second vehicle, attempting to drag the American driver out of the car. Getting word of the fracas, Okinawans in nearby bars emerged with flaming Molotov cocktails and then began overturning American-owned vehicles (identifiable by their distinctive number plates) and setting them on fire. Eventually, some five thousand Okinawans confronted around seven hundred American Military Police on the streets of Koza. As squads of American Military Police rushed to the scene, the crowd threw bricks at them and, ignoring warning shots and tear gas, broke through the gates of nearby Kadena Air Base and threw Molotov Cocktails at several buildings. After the crowds had finally dispersed in the early hours of 21 December, seven hours after the initial traffic accident, US military authorities counted the cost: over sixty Americans injured, more than eighty cars burned out and several buildings damaged.[1]

The explosion of violence in Koza, variously termed a 'riot' and an 'uprising', was the result of years of pent-up frustration at the behaviour of American servicemembers on the island.[2] From petty crimes such as jumping out of

---

[1] Masamichi Inoue, *Okinawa and the U.S. Military: Identity Making in the Age of Globalization* (New York: Columbia University Press, 2017), 53–5.
[2] Christopher Aldous, '"Mob Rule" or Popular Activism? The Koza Riot of 1970 and the Okinawan Search for Citizenship', in *Japan and Okinawa: Structure and Subjectivity*, ed. Glen D. Hook and Richard Siddle (London: Routledge, 2003), 148–66.

taxis without paying the fare to major felonies such as rape and manslaughter, Americans had acted with impunity for years. Just weeks before the incident in Koza, an American serviceman who had killed an Okinawan woman in a car accident had been found not guilty by an American court martial, despite strong incriminating evidence.[3] This incident, though, was about more than boorish behaviour. At the time of the outbreak of violence, Okinawa was under the administrative control of the United States, not Japan. The Ryukyu Islands had been under military occupation since the United States seized them in the battles of 1945. When Japan and the United States signed the Treaty of San Francisco in 1952 to end the US military occupation of Japan, they agreed that the United States would retain control of the strategically located Ryukyu Islands, including Okinawa.[4] From 1950, Okinawa was governed by the United States Civil Administration of the Ryukyu Islands (USCAR), led by an American governor and then a high commissioner. Despite these civilian-sounding titles, the head of USCAR was always a US Army general, and the island became a heavily militarized zone.

Over 25 per cent of the land in Okinawa was given over to military bases while local police had no power over the behaviour of American servicemembers and relied on American Military Police to enforce the law. Okinawans effectively lived in an armed camp where they had little say over what was done with their land or how the tens of thousands of American military personnel living among them would behave. Despite a 1969 agreement that the Ryukyus would revert to Japan in 1972, it was clear by 1970 that the bases – and the troops – would not be going anywhere. Air bases like Kadena and Marine Combat Air Station Futenma sat in the middle of densely populated Okinawan cities, while the construction of both bases and military training areas led to soil erosion, deforestation, toxic dumping and soil and groundwater contamination.[5] Whenever local politicians protested either the behaviour of American servicemembers or the noise created by military aircraft flying low over their cities, the Americans could invoke the spectre of job losses for the civilian workers employed by these bases or the loss of rents paid to the landowners that the Americans leased their bases from. Thus, when Okinawans took to the streets of Koza in December 1970, they were not only giving voice to frustrations about their powerlessness in the face of

---

[3] Christopher T. Nelson, *Dancing with the Dead: Memory, Performance, and Everyday Life in Postwar Okinawa* (Durham, NC: Duke University Press, 2008), 117.

[4] Arnold G. Fisch, *Military Government in the Ryukyu Islands, 1945-1950* (Washington, DC: Center of Military History, U.S. Army, 1988).

[5] Jonathan Taylor, 'Environment and Security Conflicts: The U.S. Military in Okinawa', *Geographical Bulletin* 48 (2007): 3–13.

military occupation but were also protesting issues that would endure long after the formal occupation of the island ended (Figure 3.1).

The frustrations at the presence of American troops and infrastructure on Okinawa that spilled over in the streets of Koza were not unique to that island. Nor were issues around environmental degradation or the dependence of the local economy on the presence of the American military. Wherever the US military went, similar tensions emerged. Crucially, the military left its mark not only on societies and people but on spaces and places as well. The focus of this chapter is on how the process of militarization has shaped landscapes and spaces, both in and around the overseas 'Empire of Bases' and in the United States itself. As of 2017, the Department of Defense (DoD) recorded that there were over 4,800 'defense sites' worldwide and that the DoD occupies 275,504 buildings, totalling 2.2 billion square feet. These buildings sit on 26.1 million acres of land 'owned, leased or otherwise possessed' by the US military; 11.4 million of those acres are within the United States, with individual land parcels ranging from the miniscule to the 2.3 million acres of the White Sands Missile Range in New Mexico. The 14.7 million acres worth of 'defense sites' overseas is spread across

Figure 3.1 Marine Corps Air Station Futenma, surrounded by the city of Ginowan. Credit: Sonata, CC BY-SA 3.0, https://commons.wikimedia.org/w/index.php?curid=10644828.

46 countries and includes a total of 517 sites, of which 213 are in Germany, 122 in Japan and 81 in South Korea.[6]

In one sense, we can say that these spaces like Okinawa are militarized simply because large chunks of them are owned by the military, but militarized spaces are also those where particular sets of laws and restrictions apply. Okinawa – where the US military-led administration made the laws, appropriated land and restricted the access of Okinawans to their own territory – offers a clear illustration of this, but special laws and rules apply not only in military-owned or administered land. Often, this sort of control is less obvious. Geographer Rachel Woodward argues that military activities and purposes can 'exert control over space in ways and through means which frequently render this control invisible.'[7] We can see this phenomenon in action in places like Washington, DC, and Northern Virginia, where Sensitive Compartmentalized Information Facilities (SCIFs) proliferate. These specialized facilities are required in order to store and discuss classified information, which can range from diplomatic cables to technical specifications for weapons systems. The technical specifications required by SCIFs – no windows, soundproofing, secure access, protection from electronic eavesdropping – mean that architects and engineers have to consider detailed security protocols when designing an office building with one or more SCIFs.[8] Thus, even something as banal as office space can be shaped by security requirements. Crucially, SCIFs are not just the sole preserve of the military or the intelligence community; SCIFs can be found in the buildings of the countless private defence contractors who carry out research and manufacturing on behalf of the military. As the office blocks of the DC metropolitan area demonstrate, we can find the process of militarization at work even in the smallest of spaces.

This chapter offers a survey of how the United States has militarized spaces and places, from the vast expanses of the Great Plains and Pacific Ocean atolls to offices in Virginia and Boston and technology campuses in the Bay Area and North Carolina. It is primarily concerned with the physical manifestations of militarization and how people relate to those militarized landscapes and spaces. To understand how militarization shaped landscapes, it is best to start on the

[6] Department of Defense, 'Base Structure Report – Fiscal Year 2017 Baseline: A Summary of the Real Property Inventory' (Washington, DC: Department of Defense, 2017), https://www.acq.osd.mil/eie/Downloads/BSI/Base%20Structure%20Report%20FY17.pdf.

[7] Rachel Woodward, *Military Geographies* (Malden, MA: Wiley-Blackwell, 2004), 3.

[8] Andrew Friedman provides an excellent account of the centrality of SCIFs to the built environment in Northern Virginia. Andrew Friedman, *Covert Capital: Landscapes of Denial and the Making of U.S. Empire in the Suburbs of Northern Virginia* (Berkeley: University of California Press, 2013), 220–93.

outside and then work in. Perhaps the most-studied militarized spaces have been the 'Empire of Bases' that the United States established during the Second World War and then expanded throughout the Cold War and even afterwards. The history of these bases and the ways in which their existence shaped American foreign relations has been the subject of an explosion of scholarship in recent years, pointing to the ways in which the study of militarization can effectively draw on the scholarship of foreign relations, the military, the environment, and social and cultural histories.

As the Cold War expanded, landscapes within the United States itself also became dominated by military considerations. The Cold War profoundly affected the industrial geography of the United States, with the creation of a 'gun belt' stretching from high-tech aircraft manufacturing in California to the armament factories of the industrializing South to the research laboratories of New England. Indeed, militarization contributed substantially to the modernization of the South and the emergence of the Sunbelt, a development that in turn affected American electoral politics. Further, the military became more southern as it increasingly consolidated on large bases in the South, a trend that accelerated with the post–Cold War draw down. As with bases overseas, the politics of military basing were complex: for instance, the placement of ICBMs in pastures across the Great Plains both inspired environmental protests and led local politicians to advocate for further integration into the military–industrial complex.[9]

Finally, the chapter examines perhaps one of the most important ways in which the idea of militarized space has been imported into the continental United States: the heavy and growing militarization of the Southern border. As the Southwest shifted in the American imagination from an ever-expanding 'frontier' to the zone of a static 'border', efforts to forcefully secure that border multiplied over the years, accelerating drastically in the last decades of the twentieth century.[10] Many of the practices at the border, from surveillance technology and hard, concrete infrastructure to special legislation empowering authorities in the border region, would have been familiar to many of those who lived in the vicinity of US bases overseas. Indeed, the fact that the border fence at San Diego is largely made from corrugated steel that once served as helicopter

[9] Gretchen Heefner, *The Missile Next Door: The Minuteman in the American Heartland*, Sew edn (Cambridge, MA: Harvard University Press, 2012).
[10] Greg Grandin, *The End of the Myth: From the Frontier to the Border Wall in the Mind of America* (New York: Metropolitan Books, 2019).

Figure 3.2 Section of the US–Mexico Border Wall near San Diego, seen from Tijuana, Mexico. Credit: Getty/Guillermo Arias.

landing pads during the Vietnam War is deeply symbolic of the connections between militarized landscapes overseas and at home (Figure 3.2).[11]

* * *

In his first telegram to President Franklin Delano Roosevelt after becoming prime minister in May 1940, Winston Churchill set off a chain of events that symbolized the final transition from British to American hegemony. Writing in the shadow of the ongoing collapse of the Allied position in France, Churchill sought material and symbolic support from the United States. He asked Roosevelt for 'forty or fifty of your older destroyers'.[12] Roosevelt, though, struck a harder bargain than Churchill had imagined he would. Taking executive action and bypassing Congress, Roosevelt agreed to give the British the destroyers they had requested, but only in exchange for ninety-nine-year leasing rights for air and naval bases in Newfoundland and the Caribbean. Writing to Congress to inform them of the agreement, Roosevelt argued that these bases were 'essential

---

[11] John Burnett, 'Southern Border Wall: Campaign Slogan Meets Reality', NPR.org, 23 January 2017, https://www.npr.org/2017/01/23/511165471/southern-border-wall-campaign-slogan-meets-reality.

[12] Martin Gilbert, *Finest Hour: Winston S. Churchill 1939–1941* (London: William Heinemann, 1983), 345–6.

for hemispheric defence' and that the agreement marked 'the most important action in the reinforcement of our national defence that has been taken since the Louisiana Purchase'.[13] This moment was crucial to the rise of American power, as it both demonstrated that the United States was beginning to think of its national security in hemispheric and then global terms, and that it considered the acquisition of basing rights overseas as fundamental to that defence.[14]

Of course, these bases were not the first outposts on foreign territories that the United States had acquired. In its race for territorial empire, the United States had built bases in Guantanamo Bay in Cuba, in the Philippines and Puerto Rico, and its Navy had made use of coaling stations in East Asia. It had also of course built countless outposts in the then-foreign territories of Indian Country in North America, as the new nation expanded its territorial empire westwards.[15] What was different about the destroyer-for-bases deal and the Lend Lease Act that followed it was that they signalled that American responsibilities were now global. As early as 1943, Washington's defence planning assumed that the American hegemony over both the Pacific and Atlantic was necessary. Historian Melvyn Leffler has argued that 'these bases were defined as the nation's strategic frontier. Beyond this frontier the United States would be able to use force to counter any threats or frustrate any overt acts of aggression. Within the strategic frontier, American military predominance had to remain inviolate.'[16] With the onset of the Cold War and atomic warfare, the need for bases for American bombers and for radar installations and missile installations became even more acute. Outside of the logic of the Cold War, the Carter Doctrine, which proclaimed the free flow of oil from the Persian Gulf to be a vital US national security interest, pushed the United States to acquire more basing rights in the Middle East.[17] The end of the Cold War did not mean an end to American conceptions of their security interests as global, and thus only led to a limited reduction in the number of overseas bases. The War

---

[13] Franklin Delano Roosevelt, 'Message to Congress on Exchanging Destroyers for British Naval and Air Bases, Online by Gerhard Peters and John T. Wooley', The American Presidency Project, accessed 9 November 2019, https://www.presidency.ucsb.edu/documents/message-congress-exchanging-destroyers-for-british-naval-and-air-bases.

[14] Melvyn P. Leffler, *A Preponderance of Power: National Security, the Truman Administration, and the Cold War* (Stanford, CA: Stanford University Press, 1993), 55–9; Stephen Wertheim, 'Tomorrow, the World: The Birth of U.S. Global Supremacy in World War II' (Columbia University, 2015), https://doi.org/10.7916/D8DB814F.

[15] Brooke Blower argues that it is important for historians to conceptualize these outposts in Indian Country as having been on foreign territory rather than the territorial United States. Brooke L. Blower, 'Nation of Outposts: Forts, Factories, Bases, and the Making of American Power', *Diplomatic History* 41, no. 3 (1 June 2017): 439–59, https://doi.org/10.1093/dh/dhx034.

[16] Melvyn P. Leffler, 'The American Conception of National Security and the Beginnings of the Cold War, 1945–48', *American Historical Review* 89, no. 2 (April 1984): 349, https://doi.org/10.2307/1862556.

[17] Joe Stork, 'The Carter Doctrine and US Bases in the Middle East', *Merip Reports* 90 (1980): 3–14.

on Terror served to further extend the network of bases, as US Special Forces and intelligence officials chasing Islamist militants constructed outposts in places as diverse as Central Asia, the Sahel and the Philippines.[18]

The consequences of the rapid growth of this network of bases after 1940 has led to a large and growing body of literature dedicated to studying what many term 'the Empire of Bases', and this literature has formed a large part of the broader scholarly exploration of the question of what sort of empire the twentieth and twenty-first century United States has been.[19] Indeed, historian Daniel Immerwahr has claimed that this network of bases represents a fundamental transition in the nature of American power, from a more limited territorial empire to what he calls a 'pointillist empire' of bases and outposts that spans the globe.[20] Similarly, anthropologist David Vine argues that these bases no longer represent a 'strategic frontier' as they did in the 1940s but have rather evolved into a series of 'lily pads' from where US forces could launch operations anywhere in the world virtually instantly.[21]

The language of pointillism and lily pads though, while useful in conveying the ubiquity of US bases around the globe, perhaps inadvertently obscures some of the realities of the network of overseas outposts by deemphasizing their material presence. Generally speaking, the most important US bases have not been isolated airfields with austere facilities but rather large, complex and resource-hungry conglomerations. As Gretchen Heefner argues, 'while it is widely appreciated that the United States emerged from World War II a global hegemon with preponderant economic, political, and military power, less attention is paid to how this power was rationalized and made visible in specific locations.'[22]

[18] Maria Ryan, *Full Spectrum Dominance: Irregular Warfare and the War on Terror* (Stanford, CA: Stanford University Press, 2019).

[19] The literature on the 'Empire of Bases' is vast and growing. For a representative sample, see Mark L. Gillem, *America Town: Building the Outposts of Empire* (Minneapolis: University of Minnesota Press, 2007); S. High, *Base Colonies in the Western Hemisphere, 1940-1967*, Studies of the Americas (Basingstoke: Palgrave Macmillan, 2009), https://doi.org/10.1057/9780230618046; Sasha Davis, *The Empires' Edge: Militarization, Resistance, and Transcending Hegemony in the Pacific* (Athens: University of Georgia Press, 2015); Daniel Immerwahr, 'The Greater United States: Territory and Empire in U.S. History', *Diplomatic History* 40, no. 3 (June 2016): 373–91, https://doi.org/10.1093/dh/dhw009; Catherine Lutz, *The Bases of Empire: The Global Struggle against U.S. Military Posts* (New York: New York University Press, 2009); Jana K. Lipman, *Guantanamo: A Working-Class History between Empire and Revolution* (Berkeley: University of California Press, 2008); David Vine, *Base Nation: How U.S. Military Bases Abroad Harm America and the World*, The American Empire Project (New York: Metropolitan Books, Henry Holt and Company, 2015); David Vine, *Island of Shame: The Secret History of the U.S. Military Base on Diego Garcia* (Princeton, NJ: Princeton University Press, 2011).

[20] Daniel Immerwahr, *How to Hide an Empire: A History of the Greater United States* (New York: Farrar, Straus and Giroux, 2019), 372–90.

[21] Vine, *Base Nation*, 299–319.

[22] Gretchen Heefner, ' "A Fighter Pilot's Heaven": Finding Cold War Utility in the North African Desert', *Environmental History* 22, no. 1 (1 January 2017): 68, https://doi.org/10.1093/envhis/emw066.

By examining the history of US military power in specific locations, historians have demonstrated how transformational that power could be, but also how the exercise of that power was itself shaped and constrained by local landscapes and peoples. Often, the base network required extensive construction and reshaping of environments in order to function.[23] David Vine estimated that in 2015 the cost of maintaining US bases overseas totalled $100–$120 billion per annum, which gives some indication of their material needs.[24] The construction of these bases has involved billions of tonnes of concrete and the cumulative efforts of hundreds of thousands of labourers. Not only that, these large bases form part of a global transportation network. Writing of the Second World War, the era in which the United States built over 2,000 bases, Andrew Friedman describes this network as constituting five global 'highways', running from the United States through Brazil and Africa and on to India and China, from northern Canada and Alaska to Siberia, as well as directly across the South Pacific and North Atlantic. These 'highways' necessitated the constructions of hundreds of airfields, ports and military roads that 'had to be driven through steaming jungles, over ice-capped mountains, and through territory held by the enemy'.[25]

As Heefner points out, the engineers tasked with building such networks were given a complex and difficult task, for 'it was their job to take broad international goals and designs and implement them on the ground in specific places where bases were needed'. This meant that the challenges were not merely technical. Heefner records that US military engineers building Wheelus airfield in Libya 'built roads, paved runways, fixed wells and constructed houses. They also acquired property, relocated people, and navigated competing local ideas and attachments to the land.'[26] Indeed, sometimes, as with the US programme of road-building in Afghanistan, reshaping local ideas was the very point of the exercise. There, American counterinsurgents hoped that building paved roads in a country that had very few of them would not only help project military power but would extend the reach of Afghan governance, would provide employment for men who might otherwise become insurgents and

---

[23] Edwin A. Martini, ed., *Proving Grounds: Militarized Landscapes, Weapons Testing, and the Environmental Impact of U.S. Bases* (Seattle: University of Washington Press, 2017); J. R. McNeill and Corinna R. Unger, eds, *Environmental Histories of the Cold War* (Cambridge: Cambridge University Press, 2010).

[24] Vine, *Base Nation*, 9.

[25] Andrew Friedman, 'US Empire, World War 2 and the Racialising of Labour', *Race & Class*, 4 April 2017, 25, https://doi.org/10.1177/0306396816685024.

[26] Gretchen Heefner, '"A Tract That Is Wholly Sand": Engineering Military Environments in Libya', *Endeavour* 40, no. 1 (1 March 2016): 39, https://doi.org/10.1016/j.endeavour.2015.12.002.

would stimulate economic development.[27] In Afghanistan, as in Libya and Okinawa, military construction projects were deeply tied up in local and international politics.

American military activities – both in peacetime and wartime, but especially during the Cold War – could have immense impact on local environments. At the El Uotia training range in Libya, the US Air Force, attracted by clear skies and sparsely populated desert, dropped some 75,000 bombs and expended 250,000 rounds of ammunition a year between 1956 and 1970, littering the desert with unexploded ordinance.[28] As John McNeill and David Painter point out, the Cold War US military needed immense quantities of oil to fuel its daily operations, as a single wing of medium bombers would consume more fuel in an afternoon than the entire Spanish railroad petroleum tanker fleet could transport in a month.[29] During the Cold War, the US military built over six thousand kilometres of buried oil pipelines and fifty petroleum depots in Europe as part of the Central European Pipeline System, one of the largest pipeline systems in the world. Problems associated with this pipeline system included the contamination of the aquifer supplying water to Frankfurt.[30]

These problems multiplied in poorer countries, where the US military had to worry less about local environmental regulations (although in many cases in Cold War Europe, they were able to ignore both local and American environmental rules because of proclaimed security imperatives). In the Philippines, the huge US facilities at Clark Air Force Base and Subic Bay Naval Base, which covered 77,000 hectares, were the site of extensive environmental damage. Both bases generated immense amounts of hazardous waste, which was dumped into landfill or open drains, while leakage from underground petroleum tanks and petroleum pipelines contaminated the groundwater.[31] Chemical weapons caused particularly difficult problems, as dangerous chemical agents such as the defoliant Agent Orange leaked into the soil at testing grounds in Panama and at air bases in South Vietnam. Indeed, as of 2018, Da Nang International Airport in Vietnam contained 162,500 cubic metres of soil contaminated by the dioxin, while the former US Air Base at Bien Hoa contained 850,000 cubic metres

---

[27] Laleh Khalili, 'The Roads to Power: The Infrastructure of Counterinsurgency', *World Policy Journal* 34, no. 1 (1 April 2017): 93–9.

[28] Heefner, ' "A Tract That Is Wholly Sand" ', 44.

[29] J. R. McNeill and D. S. Painter, 'The Global Environmental Footprint of the U.S. Military, 1789–2003', in *War and the Environment: Military Destruction in the Modern Age*, ed. Charles E. Closmann (College Station: Texas A&M University Press, 2009), 23.

[30] McNeill and Painter, 'The Global Environmental Footprint of the U.S. Military, 1789–2003', 23.

[31] McNeill and Painter, 'The Global Environmental Footprint of the U.S. Military, 1789–2003', 22.

of contaminated soil.[32] At least 2 million Vietnamese were exposed to Agent Orange, many of them via contamination at former US base sites long after the end of the war.[33]

Perhaps the most spectacular example of the environmental damage wrought by the US military overseas is the story of the Pacific Proving Grounds. In area of the Pacific Ocean the size of the continental United States and populated by 100,000 people, the United States conducted 106 nuclear weapons tests between 1946 and 1962.[34] These tests carved out giant craters in Pacific atolls and islands, and the fallout contaminated them with radiation. Most infamously, the Castle Bravo nuclear test of 1954 exploded a fifteen-megaton thermonuclear device, which was both two and a half times the yield that scientists had expected, and the largest nuclear device ever tested by the United States. The fallout from the Castle Bravo test affected nearby inhabited islands of Rongelap and Rongerik, prompting an evacuation of residents, and traces of radiation could be detected as far away as Australia, India, Japan and even part of the United States and Europe.[35]

What was unique about American activities in the Pacific though was not just the scale of the nuclear testing but the legal strategies used in order to enable it. The Pacific Proving Grounds were part of the Trust Territory of the Pacific Islands, established by the United Nations in 1947 and administered by the United States until its formal end in 1994.[36] Unusually, this particular trust territory was designated as a 'strategic area', which meant that its trusteeship status could only be ended by a vote of the Security Council rather than by the General Assembly. Five days after the establishment of the trusteeship, the US Atomic Energy Commission established the Pacific Proving Grounds. The United States had effective sovereign control of over two thousand islands, but US domestic laws did not apply in these spaces.

---

[32] Nyugen Dong, 'Dioxin Contamination in Da Nang More Serious Than Expected: Conference', *Vn Express International*, 7 November 2018, https://e.vnexpress.net/news/news/dioxin-contamination-in-da-nang-more-serious-than-expected-conference-3835609.html.

[33] For a full history of the impact of Agent Orange, see Edwin A. Martini, *Agent Orange: History, Science and the Politics of Uncertainty* (Amherst: University Massachusetts Press, 2012).

[34] Nevada Operations Office U.S. Department of Energy, 'United States Nuclear Tests, July 1945 through September 1992' (Las Vegas, NV: Government Printing Office, 2000), xiii.

[35] April L. Brown, 'No Promised Land: The Shared Legacy of the Castle Bravo Nuclear Test', *Arms Control Today* 44, no. 2 (2014): 40; Gary Lee, 'Postwar Pacific Fallout Wider Than Thought; New Data Show Radiation Spread Beyond Limited Area; House Hearing Set Today', *Washington Post*, 24 February 1994, http://search.proquest.com/docview/307731591/abstract/A92540C4687A4272PQ/1.

[36] Lauren Hirshberg, '"Navigating Sovereignty under a Cold War Military Industrial Colonial Complex: US Military Empire and Marshallese Decolonization"', *History and Technology* 31, no. 3 (3 July 2015): 259–74, https://doi.org/10.1080/07341512.2015.1126408.

The relationship between host nation sovereignty and US military bases has often been a vexed one. The oldest US overseas base, in Guantanamo in Cuba, is, in the words of historian Paul Kramer, 'juridically no-man's land', a status that proved to be of immense value after the Cold War when it came both to housing Haitian refugees without allowing them into the United States and indefinitely detaining and torturing prisoners during the 'war on terror'.[37] Conversely, Gretchen Heefner has demonstrated that US diplomats in Libya argued that the fact that the Libyan government was able to negotiate a basing agreement with the United States in 1950 was evidence of their competence as a sovereign government, thus demonstrating that Libya would not need to enter a UN trusteeship that might prevent the United States from leasing bases there.[38] More commonly, Status of Force Agreements between the United States and host countries that carved out exemptions from local laws for American military personnel have made US bases the site of the sort of protests detailed both in Chapter 4 and the introduction to this chapter. Those who lived near American bases often felt powerless in the face of the environmental, political and social costs imposed by them.[39] The specific nature of this discontent varied, as did the impact of these bases, depending on their size, purpose and who was occupying them. According to Catherine Lutz,

> Marine bases create more criminal behaviour than Air Force bases; Air Force bases produce more toxins per square inch than Army bases; and Navy bases produce more episodic and so visible social impacts, as ships dock and spill what are sometimes thousands of men and women into a community, many looking for sex and alcohol.[40]

What has been common to all of these bases, though, is that they have been important sites where US military power has been made visible and shaped the histories and environments of the places where they were located. The very scale of this network of bases has meant that they have had an outsized impact on landscapes and peoples all over the world, while the laws and security requirements associated with military land holdings have constrained the ability

---

[37] Paul Kramer, 'A Useful Corner of the World: Guantánamo', *New Yorker*, 30 July 2013, https://www.newyorker.com/news/news-desk/a-useful-corner-of-the-world-guantnamo.

[38] Gretchen Heefner, ' "A Slice of Their Sovereignty": Negotiating the U.S. Empire of Bases, Wheelus Field, Libya, 1950–1954', *Diplomatic History* 41, no. 1 (1 January 2017): 50–77, https://doi.org/10.1093/dh/dhv058.

[39] Amy Austin Holmes, *Social Unrest and American Military Bases in Turkey and Germany since 1945* (Cambridge: Cambridge University Press, 2014).

[40] Catherine Lutz, 'Bases, Empire, and Global Response', in *The Bases of Empire: The Global Struggle against US Military Posts*, ed. Catherine Lutz (New York: New York University Press, 2009), 32.

of local actors to have much control over the manner in which their daily lives are affected by the American military and its operations.

* * *

Even if questions of sovereignty and power were less fraught, bases on American soil had equally powerful impacts on their surroundings. These were the places where militarization was at its most intense, where a dense cluster of relationships played out in particular landscapes. A network of military outposts and forts had helped to knit the United States together as a nation, but it was the mobilization of a mass army in the First World War that saw the construction of large, permanent bases to train hundreds of thousands of recruits. In the rush to mobilize, the Army built thirty-two National Army cantonments and National Guard training camps across the United States in the summer of 1917, each expected to host a population of 40,000 recruits, trainers and support staff.[41] Over half of these new bases were located in old Confederacy, as the warm climate of the South and cheap rural land suitable for training proved attractive to planners.[42] Along with already-existing posts, such as Camp Benning in Georgia, and training ranges acquired in 1918, such as Camp Bragg in North Carolina, many of these new cantonments were named after Confederate generals, in an appeal to local white sentiment.[43]

The location of these camps had an effect on the Army's plans to organize the American Expeditionary Force. While the War Department initially wanted to mobilize regionally focused units, the imperative to ensure that there was a white majority in the mobilization camps instead meant that the Army sent Black recruits from Southern states to the North, and white men from the West and the Northeast to training camps in Georgia and Arkansas.[44] Despite these efforts, the camps were sites of racial tension. Black soldiers could serve as camp guards, but could not carry weapons. In Charleston, South Carolina, the arrest and beating of a Black soldier in uniform provoked outrage, while Black stevedores working at the docks in Newport News, Virginia, had to live in tents with no floors in the dead of winter.[45] In Houston, nineteen Black soldiers were

---

[41] Edward M. Coffman, *The War to End All Wars: The American Military Experience in World War I* (Lexington: University Press of Kentucky, 1998), 30.

[42] Eric B. Setzekorn, *Joining the Great War, April 1917-April 1918*, US Army Campaigns of World War I, CMH pub 77–3 (Washington, DC: US Army Center of Military History, 2017), 28–9.

[43] Mark Thompson, 'Ten Army Bases Named for Confederate Officers', *Time*, 23 June 2015, https://time.com/3932914/army-bases-confederate/.

[44] Jennifer D. Keene, *Doughboys, the Great War, and the Remaking of America* (Baltimore, MD: Johns Hopkins University Press, 2003), 85.

[45] Keene, *Doughboys, the Great War, and the Remaking of America*, 92, 101.

executed after a group of armed Black soldiers mutinied and marched on the city.[46] Nor were these problems confined to the South. In Camp Merritt, New Jersey, a Black serviceman was shot dead after a race riot broke out when white soldiers from Mississippi attempted to eject five Black soldiers from a YMCA hut where they had been writing letters home.[47]

Black soldiers faced similar problems on American military bases in the Second World War. Race riots took place at Fort Bragg, North Carolina, and Camp Stewart, Georgia, while in Port Chicago, California, fifty Black stevedores were tried for mutiny after refusing to load munitions under unsafe working conditions shortly after a disastrous explosion there killed 390 sailors, most of whom were Black.[48] However, the Second World War also saw unprecedented numbers of troops flowing back and forth across the Atlantic and Pacific, exposing them to different racial orders. As we will see in Chapter 4, Black soldiers in Europe and Japan discovered different societies, but some of this discovery also took place in the United States itself. Close to a million service members of all races were either stationed in or passed through the American territory of Hawai'i. Here, as historians Beth Bailey and David Farber argue, they were exposed to a much more dynamic, multiethnic society where women and ethnic minorities were attempting to claim a more equal status, a place that offered a vision for what the future of the post-war United States might look like.[49]

Hawai'i was also a highly militarized place, with military personnel outnumbering the islanders and large tracts of land given over to military installations. Not only that, but Military Police played an outsized role in policing places like Honolulu, where the military regulated an effectively legalized prostitution industry on Hotel Street.[50] Wherever off-duty military personnel gathered in large numbers, disciplinary problems meant the construction of legal regimes to regulate their behaviour. As historian Aaron Hiltner observes, port cities were particularly problematic places during the Second World War, as soldiers and sailors sometimes ran amok prior to embarkation. The numbers of troops moving through these cities could be staggering. Hiltner notes that up

---

[46] Robert V. Haynes, 'The Houston Mutiny and Riot of 1917', *Southwestern Historical Quarterly* 76, no. 4 (1973): 418–39.

[47] Keene, *Doughboys, the Great War, and the Remaking of America*, 94.

[48] Robert L. Allen, *The Port Chicago Mutiny: The Story of the Largest Mass Mutiny Trial in U.S. Naval History* (Berkeley, CA: Equal Justice Society, 1989).

[49] Beth L. Bailey and David Farber, *The First Strange Place: Race and Sex in World War II Hawaii* (Baltimore, MD: Johns Hopkins University Press, 1994).

[50] Bailey and Farber, *The First Strange Place*, 95–132.

to 75 per cent of American soldiers were stationed in port cities in the build-up to the D-Day landings, while 3 million moved through New York City alone.[51] The global flow of troops meant that these places, both home and abroad, faced similar issues. While Bamber Bridge in England and Camp Stewart in Georgia saw race riots, both Paris and New York City had to reckon with the problem of sexual violence caused by drunken soldiers. Later, in the Vietnam era, bars in Germany and South Korea were the sites of the same 'dark carnival' that anthropologist Catherine Lutz described as taking place in the bars of Hay Street in Fayetteville, North Carolina, where GIs from nearby Fort Bragg recently returned from Vietnam turned to drinking and violence to deal with the trauma of their experiences there.[52]

The scale of the Second World War left its mark on US basing infrastructure. While the War Department scrambled to build thirty-two training camps in the summer of 1917, Florida alone had sixty-four Army Air Corps bases by 1944, while North Carolina counted twenty-four major military installations.[53] The advent of the Cold War meant that this network was only partly rolled back, while the need for extensive training ranges for military aircraft required huge tracts of land in the American West. Even if not quite as extensive as the 'Empire of Bases' which scholars of US foreign relations talk about, this archipelago of military land was immense in its own way. By 1999, even after a wave of post–Cold War base closures, the US military owned 27 million acres of land in the United States, while 40 per cent of Nevada's airspace was given over to military aviation.[54] This meant that while the military did not quite have the sort of free reign it enjoyed in some overseas locations, it was certainly an important presence in large parts of the country, where its particular requirements and effects were visible.

As Lutz argues, this extensive network of bases and training ranges, while hardly disconnected from the broader economy, produced communities that moved to slightly different economic rhythms. These base communities were somewhat insulated from the dangers of economic turmoil, as the steady flow of cash from military personnel and retirees provided relatively reliable income

[51] Aaron Hiltner, *Taking Leave, Taking Liberties: American Troops on the World War II Home Front* (Chicago: University of Chicago Press, 2020), 3.

[52] Catherine A. Lutz, *Homefront: A Military City and the American Twentieth Century* (Boston, MA: Beacon Press, 2002), 134.

[53] David S. Sorenson, *Shutting Down the Cold War: The Politics of Military Base Closure* (New York: Palgrave Macmillan, 1998), 12; Lutz, *Homefront*, 49.

[54] 'Hill Air Force Base (AFB), Establishment of Gandy Range Extension and Adjacent Restricted Airspace for Supersonic Flight Training: Environmental Impact Statement' (Washington, DC: Department of the Air Force, 1985), D-495, https://apps.dtic.mil/dtic/tr/fulltext/u2/a213098.pdf.

streams.[55] Boosts in defence spending could bring in not only more troops but also more money for local contractors and service providers. Conversely, when units rotated out of the United States for lengthy deployments, the effect on local economies could be brutal. For instance, the mayors of several towns surrounding Fort Campbell, Kentucky, reported near recession-like conditions when the 101st Airborne Division and other Fort Campbell-based units deployed to Kuwait in August 1990.[56] Moreover, the class structures of these towns tended to be much more egalitarian, as the gap in pay between senior military leaders and junior personnel was many multiples lower than that of a typical corporation, producing strong middle-class communities.[57]

The economic effect of these bases was not entirely positive, however. Large military installations took up valuable real estate and, as federal land, were exempt from property tax. Soldiers based there might also pay state taxes elsewhere, as many chose to maintain tax status in lower-tax states. Meanwhile, the abundance of on-base shopping and dining opportunities via the PX and Morale, Welfare and Recreation service meant that a large chunk of soldiers' and military retirees' income never circulated in the local economy.[58] Thus, while municipal budgets failed to capture revenue from these bases, military personnel continued to draw on local services and school districts, creating budgetary imbalances and stretching local resources.

To say that these bases and the communities surrounding them had their own particular economic logic is not to say that they were entirely immune from broader trends in the American economy. The end of the Cold War and establishment of the Base Realignment and Closure (BRAC) process saw over 350 bases close in five rounds between 1988 and 2005.[59] While communities and their Congressional representatives fought to preserve the perceived economic boon of these bases for their regions, the post–Cold War military consolidated around fewer but much larger mega-posts, setting off a building boom in places like Fort Hood, Texas, which effectively became cities in their own right.[60] Even

---

[55] Lutz, *Homefront*, 172.

[56] Bill Sloat, 'Kentucky Base Braces for Desert Deployment', *Plain Dealer; Cleveland, Ohio*, 16 August 1990, http://search.proquest.com/newsstand/docview/287823412/abstract/7322CCC5BA31421 EPQ/84; Bill Nichols, 'Kentucky and Tennessee Area: Communities Will Do Their Share', *USA Today*, 21 August 1990; Sheila M. Poole, 'Hinesville: Early Casualty of Gulf Crisis', *Atlanta Constitution; Atlanta, Ga.*, 23 September 1990, sec. A.

[57] Lutz, *Homefront*, 185.

[58] Lutz, *Homefront*, 185.

[59] Sorenson, *Shutting Down the Cold War*.

[60] Kenneth T. MacLeish, *Making War at Fort Hood: Life and Uncertainty in a Military Community* (Princeton, NJ: Princeton University Press, 2013).

as the military cut its overall numbers, there were severe housing shortages in those areas chosen for consolidation.[61] As historian Jennifer Mittelstadt shows, this building boom was of a different character than that of the Second World War. A downsizing military sought to leverage private capital to help alleviate the housing shortage, and so the Army invited construction firms via the Residential Communities Initiative public–private partnership to invest in military housing in return for profit from the rents they produced. This mechanism meant that an investment of $380 million from the DoD leveraged $7.2 billion in private funding and that private construction firms built tens of thousands of military homes each year while getting free title to public land.[62]

Similarly, the Defense Logistics Agency consolidated its operations in the 1990s and began awarding supply contracts to large vendors rather than local producers. As of late 2019, the vast bulk of military food supply contracts in the Continental United States were awarded to just two firms: US Foods, Inc., and Sysco.[63] Thus, these 'defence sites' had an outsized impact on the places in which they were located, in both social and economic terms, but the economic largesse that they brought with them did not necessarily stay in local areas. Military bases in the United States had similar issues to their overseas counterparts in terms of environmental damage and (to a lesser extent) frictions with local populations, but the economic largesse that they distributed, even if unevenly, made them popular across the political spectrum.

* * *

Even if they add up to billions of dollars, food supply contracts represent only a small fraction of the military budget. Instead, any list of the top ten federal contractors is dominated by defence manufacturing giants such as Boeing, Lockheed Martin, Raytheon, General Dynamics and Northorp Grumman.[64] Indeed, if we want to trace the full economic impact of militarization on towns, cities and regions, we need to move beyond military bases to look at the factories, research laboratories and office blocks where weapons systems are developed and made, and where contracts are negotiated and products sold. Defence industrial policy has had profound consequences for the United States and the

---

[61] Jennifer Mittelstadt, *The Rise of the Military Welfare State* (Cambridge, MA: Harvard University Press, 2015), 204.
[62] Mittelstadt, *The Rise of the Military Welfare State*, 206–10.
[63] 'Food Services', accessed 16 December 2019, https://www.dla.mil/TroopSupport/Subsistence/FoodServices/.
[64] 'Top 100 Contractors Report', Federal Procurement Data System, accessed 11 February 2020, https://www.fpds.gov/fpdsng_cms/index.php/en/reports/62-top-100-contractors-report.

development of regional economies. Military spending helped propel California into the first ranks of manufacturing states and transformed the southern economy after the Second World War.[65] Federal spending during the Second World War dwarfed even New Deal–era programmes; while all regions received some form of economic benefit, the money spent on armaments manufacturing was unevenly distributed. Much of the armaments boom centred on aviation, and Army Air Force planners preferred to outsource not only production but also research and development to private industry, rather than follow the lead of the Army or Navy, who preferred in-house development in federal arsenals or Navy yards.[66] The aviation industry had already begun to move West away from its Midwestern origins prior to the war, as the clear skies and warm weather of southern California offered a better environment for metal airframes. Moreover, many factories in the industrial heartland were geared towards civilian production, which meant that more contracts were awarded to factories in the Northeast and West that could be quickly retooled for wartime production.[67]

The effect of this spending on regional growth can be overstated: southern California was already a major aviation manufacturing centre prior to the Second World War, and wartime defence spending did not permanently industrialize the Southern economy.[68] Nonetheless, hundreds of thousands of defence workers and their families moved to California during the war, transforming the state. Between 1940 and 1945, the Pacific Coast's population increased by 2.7 million, or by more than 25 per cent. Cities like Los Angeles and San Diego boomed, as federal dollars flowed in. Wartime defence contracts and facilities investments were worth $27 billion to Western states, one-eighth of the national total and twice the region's pre-war share.[69] The West and the South were also well-positioned to take advantage of the Cold War's massive and sustained defence spending. Local politicians lobbied to divert federal dollars in their direction, a skill that Southern politicians with their Congressional

[65] Gerald D. Nash, *World War II and the West: Reshaping the Economy* (Lincoln: University of Nebraska Press, 1990).

[66] Ann R. Markusen et al., *The Rise of the Gunbelt: The Military Remapping of Industrial America* (Oxford: Oxford University Press, 1991), 31–2.

[67] Markusen et al., *The Rise of the Gunbelt*, 65–6.

[68] Roger W. Lotchin, 'California Cities and the Hurricane of Change: World War II in the San Francisco, Los Angeles, and San Diego Metropolitan Areas', *Pacific Historical Review* 63, no. 3 (1994): 393–420, https://doi.org/10.2307/3640972; Robert Lewis, 'World War II Manufacturing and the Postwar Southern Economy', *Journal of Southern History* 73, no. 4 (2007): 837–66, https://doi.org/10.2307/27649570; Paul Rhode, 'The Nash Thesis Revisited: An Economic Historian's View', *Pacific Historical Review* 63, no. 3 (1994): 363–92, https://doi.org/10.2307/3640971.

[69] Paul W Rhode, 'After the War Boom: Reconversion on the U.S. Pacific Coast, 1943–49', Working Paper (National Bureau of Economic Research, July 2003), 2–3, https://doi.org/10.3386/w9854.

seniority were particularly adept at.[70] More so than the Second World War, the Cold War was transformational in its impact on American industrial geography. The rise of the Sunbelt and the slow deindustrialization of the Midwest was intimately linked to defence spending, so much so that some scholars have preferred to speak of the rise of a 'gun belt'. Writing in immediate aftermath of the Cold War, Ann Markusen *et al* argued that 'the gunbelt is a major – *the* major – phenomenon in the contemporary economic map of America'. They noted that 'no other Western industrial nation has seen so much of its leading-edge industrial capacity located, in so extraordinarily short a time, so far from the original centres of commerce and production'.[71]

This transformation has had far-reaching demographic and political consequences. In terms of political economy, what was unique about many of these manufacturing centres was their complete reliance on government defence spending that was channelled through private firms that also benefitted from right-to-work laws that stopped this new workforce from unionizing.[72] This meant that Keynesian economic policies could be conducted through military spending rather than through more conventional means, obscuring the role of the federal government in transferring wealth between regions. As Gretchen Heefner noted in a different context, speaking about the construction of Air Force nuclear missile fields in the Plains States, 'western South Dakotans accepted the need for federal assistance in developing their economy, but in channelling it through Pentagon funds they could shun the more redistributive programs of the liberal state'.[73] Similarly, states that acquired a reputation for hard-edged conservative politics in the Sun Belt era, such as Arizona and Texas, benefitted from federal spending on defence while eschewing social spending. Bruce Schulman observes that in the 1950s the South aggressively sought federal investment in the form of military spending and the space programme, while at the same time the South ceased to be the primary beneficiary of federal social programs, as it had been in the New Deal era.[74]

---

[70] For a pre–Cold War example of this ability to attract defence spending, see Robert Caro's compelling account of then-Rep. Lyndon Johnson's campaign for the construction of the Corpus Christi Naval Air Station and the award of the construction contracts to his patrons in Brown and Root, see Robert A. Caro, *The Path to Power* (New York: Vintage, 1990), 581–6.

[71] Markusen et al., *The Rise of the Gunbelt*, 8.

[72] James M. Cypher, 'The Origins and Evolution of Military Keynesianism in the United States', *Journal of Post Keynesian Economics* 38, no. 3 (3 October 2015): 460, 462, https://doi.org/10.1080/01603477 .2015.1076704.

[73] Heefner, *The Missile Next Door*, 109.

[74] Bruce J. Schulman, *From Cotton Belt to Sunbelt: Federal Policy, Economic Development, and the Transformation of the South 1938–1980* (Durham, NC: Duke University Press, 1994), 136.

The Gun Belt was not only about manufacturing though. While the Cold War defence boom created significant manufacturing employment, it also generated large clusters of white collar jobs. If we look again at lists of top federal contractors, scattered among the names of major corporations such as Booze Allen Hamilton or Bechtel, we can see universities such as California Institute of Technology or Massachusetts Institute of Technology, who respectively earned $1.8 billion and $1 billion worth of federal contracts in 2015.[75] These more recent figures, while impressive, pale in comparison to the massive investment in research and development during the Second World War and the Cold War. Funding for scientific research exploded during the Second World War, and the US budget for military research and development increased from $23 million to $1.6 billion between 1938 and 1945.[76] After the Soviet Union provoked American anxieties by launching the Sputnik satellite in 1957, federal support for military R&D reached new heights, accounting for $13.7 billion and 2.6 per cent of GDP by 1960.[77] University administrators proved adept at capturing their share of this funding, even if the $838 million the government spent on university-based R&D in 1960 paled in comparison to the money expended on industry.[78] Institutions such as Stanford, Cal Tech and MIT transformed themselves in order to take advantage of federal and industrial patronage.[79]

As with manufacturing, these investments had regional implications. Areas with clusters of research universities were among the primary beneficiaries of these contracts, which added more white-collar jobs in the Northeast and in California. More broadly, the nature of this R&D followed its own particular logic, with investment tending to cluster in specific areas, such as Boston's Route 128 or the Bay Area's Silicon Valley.[80] In Boston, neither Harvard nor MIT wanted to conduct military research on campus, and so set up separate research

[75] 'Top 100 Contractors Report'.

[76] John L. Rudolph, *How We Teach Science: What's Changed, and Why It Matters* (Cambridge, MA: Harvard University Press, 2019), 124.

[77] Steven W. Usselman, 'Research and Development in the United States since 1900: An Interpretive History', Economic History Workshop Working Paper (New Haven, CT: Yale University, 11 November 2013), 21, https://economics.yale.edu/sites/default/files/usselman_paper.pdf.

[78] Usselman, 'Research and Development in the United States since 1900', 23.

[79] Rebecca Lowen argues that scholars need to pay more attention to the role of University administrators in capturing federal defence funding. She notes that Depression-era funding cuts primed administrators to pursue new sources of funding. Rebecca S. Lowen, *Creating the Cold War University: The Transformation of Stanford* (Berkeley: University of California Press, 1997). For an account that traces student opposition to the relationship between universities and the defence establishment, see Matthew Levin, *Cold War University: Madison and the New Left in the Sixties* (Madison: University of Wisconsin Press, 2013).

[80] Margaret O'Mara, *Cities of Knowledge: Cold War Science and the Search for the Next Silicon Valley* (Princeton, NJ: Princeton University Press, 2015); Margaret O'Mara, *The Code: Silicon Valley and the Remaking of America* (New York: Penguin, 2019).

facilities, such as MIT's Lincoln Laboratory, in off-campus locations.[81] These labs in turn produced spin-off companies that also pursued federal R&D contracts, creating regional business subcultures. The success of these companies, which often developed electronics for the military and then civilian markets, led many politicians to understand that research universities had to be at the heart of any regional economic development plan, even as overall spending on military R&D declined in the 1960s and 1970s. Certainly, the 'Massachusetts miracle' of the 1980s, where the state drastically slashed its unemployment rate, was predicated on the success of tech companies along Route 128, many of whom took advantage in the Reagan-era increases in defence budgets. Thus, these research clusters pointed to a model for post-industrial economic success that many mayors and governors wanted to emulate.[82]

However, this military-fuelled success story had implications for the future of American cities. Many of these 'research parks' were both suburban in nature and directly modelled on the aesthetics of college campuses. As Margaret O'Mara has pointed out, 'American colleges and universities were institutions with a long tradition of physical disengagement from the heterogeneous and disorderly urban landscape beyond their gates.' This meant that the design and architectural choices of these institutions reflected the 'deep-seated cultural presumption that the urban environment was no place for intellectual discovery'.[83] Not only that, but Cold War–era federal contracting guidance encouraged dispersion for both manufacturing and R&D, as the need for adequate distance from the ground zero of potential Soviet nuclear strikes pushed development away from city centres.[84] This combination of a preference for campus-like aesthetics and civil defence considerations pushed the tech and scientific clusters that became the engines for economic growth outside of the cities. The model for growth and progress was thus a suburban 'research park' rather an urban core. While defence industrial policy imperatives were far from the sole driving force behind these major changes in American economic and political geography, they were certainly pushing in the same direction as

---

[81] Susan Rosegrant, *Route 128: Lessons from Boston's High Tech Community* (New York: Basic Books, 1993), 16.

[82] Brent Cebul, 'Supply-Side Liberalism: Fiscal Crisis, Post-Industrial Policy, and the Rise of the New Democrats', *Modern American History* 2, no. 2 (July 2019): 139–64, https://doi.org/10.1017/mah.2019.9.

[83] Margaret Pugh O'Mara, 'Uncovering the City in the Suburb: Cold War Politics, Scientific Elites, and High-Tech Spaces', in *The New Suburban History*, ed. Thomas J. Sugrue and Kevin M. Kruse (Chicago: University of Chicago Press, 2006), 69.

[84] O'Mara, 'Uncovering the City in the Suburb', 63–5. See also Matthew Farish, *The Contours of America's Cold War* (Minneapolis: University of Minnesota Press, 2010), 226–31.

the other factors that were relocating the drivers of economic and population growth to the south, the west and the suburbs.

* * *

Of course, like the rise of the Sun Belt and technology parks, suburbanization was about much more than the Cold War and militarization, but it is striking to read in E. B. White's 1949 ode to New York City, *Here Is New York*, some intimation that the mid-twentieth century city that he was describing would have to change. In a book that is widely regarded as a warm celebration of American urban living, White ends on a dark note, describing the 'cold shadow of the planes'. New York, 'for the first time in its long history', was now destructible. He describes how 'a single flight of planes no bigger than a wedge of geese can quickly end this island fantasy, burn the towers, crumble the bridges, turn the underground passages into lethal chambers, cremate the millions. The intimation of mortality is part of New York now: in the sound of jets overhead, in the black headlines of the latest edition.'[85] White's uncharacteristic foreboding signifies a shift in the way in which the United States understood its own vulnerability. While we discussed the broader policy ramifications of that shift in Chapter 2, it is worth exploring in further detail how American landscapes were shaped by its consequences.

More than any other defence initiative, the US nuclear weapons programme reshaped landscapes and regions. The sheer scale of the programme – which cost \$5.5 trillion over the course of the Cold War and constituted possibly the largest public works project in history – made this inevitable.[86] What distinguished this construction programme from other large-scale projects, even military ones, was its secrecy and its environmental implications. Speaking of the network of laboratories, reactor complexes, manufacturing facilities and test sites that constituted the effort to build the first atomic bomb, Herbert Marks, Atomic Energy Commission attorney, noted,

> The Manhattan District bore no relation to the industrial or social life of our country; it was a separate state, with its own airplanes and its own factories and its thousands of secrets. It had a peculiar sovereignty, one that could bring about the end, peacefully or violently, of all other sovereignties.[87]

---

[85] E. B. White, *Here Is New York* (New York: Curtis, 1949), 50–1, http://archive.org/details/in.ernet. dli.2015.166056.

[86] Tom Vanderbilt, *Survival City: Adventures among the Ruins of Atomic America* (New York: Princeton Architectural Press, 2002), 14, 17.

[87] Cited in Farish, *The Contours of America's Cold War*, 197.

Much of this 'sovereignty' took the form of strict secrecy, as the three 'secret cities' of the Manhattan Project – the Los Alamos laboratory in New Mexico, the uranium engineering works in Oak Ridge, Tennessee, and the Hanford Plutonium Works in Washington – were built in geographically isolated areas and operated with such rigorous security protocols that the work of 125,000 staff that laboured to produce atomic bombs remained essentially invisible to the American public and even most of the workers themselves. This culture of secrecy was further deepened by the Cold War, as huge military command centres such as the Cheyenne Mountain complex in Colorado and 'Site R', the bunker complex in Pennsylvania designed to house the US government in time of war, were buried underground, concealing their scale and presence.[88]

If the scale of the nuclear programme was largely invisible to most Americans, it could not be completely hidden from everyone. In the early 1960s, farmers in the Plains States were informed by the Air Force that nuclear missile silos would be built on their land, with national security prerogatives ensuring that there would be no room to negotiate their location. Thousands of these silos were built throughout the West, as, in Gretchen Heefner's phrasing, the heartland was offered up as a 'giant sacrificial sponge' for Soviet missiles.[89] As Heefner notes, the Cold War was physically present for these Americans in a way that wasn't true for the majority of the population: 'Each day they opened their kitchen windows and saw strange antennas poking up from the ground ... they spent extra time plowing around 2-acre "holes" in the middle of their wheat fields; they drove their children to school past missile silos.'[90] More subtly, in the 1960s, most major American cities hosted batteries of Nike missiles, designed to intercept ballistic missiles, and marking the first attempt to directly defend urban areas in the continental United States from air attack. These missile batteries were common sights in American cities until Soviet missile technology outstripped the ability of anti-ballistic missiles to intercept them, making the batteries obsolete.[91]

While the Nike batteries scattered throughout American cities were subtle reminders of the realities of the nuclear arms race, the Nevada Test Site, where the military conducted above-ground and below-ground nuclear tests, was more crude in how it made these realities – and the potential for Armageddon – visible. At times, the mushroom clouds from the test site were visible from downtown

---

[88] Vanderbilt, *Survival City*, 130–45.
[89] Heefner, *The Missile Next Door*, 5.
[90] Heefner, *The Missile Next Door*, 50.
[91] Vanderbilt, *Survival City*, 175–80.

Las Vegas.[92] Residents living close to the site were rhetorically conscripted into national defence: one pamphlet issued by the military told them that they were 'in a very real sense active participants in the Nation's atomic test program' and thanked them for accepting the 'inconvenience' of the risk from flash, blast or fall-out 'without fuss, without alarm, and without panic'. Residents were assured that the tests had contributed greatly to the security of the United States and to 'maintaining the peace of the world' and that no test would be conducted unless public safety was assured.[93]

Similarly, the city of Richland, Washington, which housed the workers of the Hanford plutonium site, was designed to reassure residents and the broader public, even as the plant itself produced the fissile material for more than 60,000 nuclear weapons. The Hanford plant itself was off-limits, so the city of Richland became a showcase for nuclear production. As Kate Brown notes in *Plutopia*, her comparative history of Richland and the Soviet city of Ozersk, the town provided 'a soothing image. The neat green lawns, gently curving streets, stocked stores, and palatial schools filled with high-performing children instilled confidence and a sense of protection.'[94] Residents welcomed the fact that the town was under constant surveillance by a private security patrol and by health physicists. One resident even declared that 'living in Richland is ideal because we breathe only tested air'.[95]

Richland's history in part demonstrates the attraction of the Military Keynesian model that had helped to reshape regional economies throughout the Cold War. The town, which was de facto segregated, provided its blue-collar workers with middle-class salaries and a very high standard of living, as corporate executives and government officials agreed that security could only be guaranteed through middle-class abundance. Uniquely, Richland had (until 1957) no private property, no free market, no local self-government and (less uniquely for a company town) no trade unions.[96] Paradoxically, Richland showcased the American Dream of middle-class living but did so only thanks to extensive government intervention.

---

[92] Nathan Hodge and Sharon Weinberger, *A Nuclear Family Vacation: Travels in the World of Atomic Weaponry* (New York: Bloomsbury USA, 2008), 25.

[93] United States Congress Senate Committee on Armed Services, *Civil Defense Program: Hearings before the Subcommittee on Civil Defense of the Committee on Armed Services, United States Senate, Eighty-Fourth Congress, First Session, on Operations and Policies of the Civil Defense Program* (U.S. Government Printing Office, 1955), 245.

[94] Kate Brown, *Plutopia: Nuclear Families, Atomic Cities, and the Great Soviet and American Plutonium Disasters*, repr. edn (Oxford: Oxford University Press, 2015), 223.

[95] Brown, *Plutopia*, 223.

[96] Brown, *Plutopia*, 4.

Beneath this veneer though, the Hanford Site was what Brown has called a 'slow motion disaster'. General Electric and the Atomic Energy Commission had allocated 'more money to Richland's school system than to waste management, public health monitoring, or scientific research at the plant'.[97] The plant was emitting huge quantities of radioactive isotopes into both the water and air, where they entered the food chain. Eventually, millions of curies worth of radiation were released into the environment, causing significant health problems for the residents of Richland. The medical monitoring offered to the town's residents did them little good, as one study estimated that fallout from the plant had led to a total of 3,200 excess deaths, while thousands more suffered from illness and birth defects.[98] The secrecy surrounding Hanford didn't help, as it took decades to declassify these reports, and then only in the face of sustained grassroots political pressure.

Richland was only the most extreme example of this phenomenon. Toxic materials from nuclear missile silos leaked into groundwater; Gulfport, Mississippi, where Agent Orange that was shipped to Vietnam was stored, had to contend with a huge clean-up operation, and the by 1993, the DoD listed approximately 19,000 contaminated sites in over 1,700 active military facilities in the United States.[99] The communities downwind of the Nevada test site who were reassured that they were 'active participants in national defence' saw elevated levels of leukaemia and thyroid cancer, and the government eventually paid out over $2 billion worth of compensation to those who had been exposed to radiation.[100] The environmental consequences of militarizing these spaces would take decades to unfold. Much as communities in Vietnam, the Philippines and the Marshall Islands had to contend with environmental damage caused by military operations, the same issues were playing out at home as well.

The environmental history of militarized spaces, though, should not be understood as simply a monolithic march towards more secrecy and more ecological degradation. The damage caused by nuclear testing was certainly immense, so much so that in 1993, the scholar Mike Davis referred to this part

---

[97] Brown, *Plutopia*, 221.
[98] Brown, *Plutopia*, 276–80.
[99] Martini, *Agent Orange*, 115–17; McNeill and Painter, 'The Global Environmental Footprint of the U.S. Military, 1789–2003', 23.
[100] 'Justice Department Surpasses $2 Billion in Awards under the Radiation Exposure Compensation Act', 2 March 2015, https://www.justice.gov/opa/pr/justice-department-surpasses-2-billion-awards-under-radiation-exposure-compensation-act; Howard Ball, 'Downwind from the Bomb', *New York Times*, 9 February 1986, sec. Magazine, https://www.nytimes.com/1986/02/09/magazine/downwind-from-the-bomb.html.

of the country as 'the dead west'.[101] As several historians have noted, though, communities in the rural West did not simply accept the imposition of the National Security State willingly. With varying degrees of success, they sought to remake these landscapes and challenge military domination.[102] Conservative ranchers and environmental activists often worked together to resist the DoD's appropriation of lands. While they achieved very little in the early years of the Cold War – as the futile attempts of South Dakotan ranchers to negotiate the location of Minuteman silos on their land show – the end of the Cold War provided an opening to remake these spaces.[103] Many former military bases required Environmental Protection Agency clean-ups before being converted to civilian use, but campaigners sought to take advantage of the lack of intensive agriculture and industry in these areas to restore wildlife and some biodiversity. The Rocky Mountain Arsenal outside of Denver, Colorado, which had been a chemical weapons facility, became the Rocky Mountain Arsenal National Wildlife Refuge in 1992. Meanwhile, the largest military facility in the country, the White Sands Missile Range in New Mexico (an area bigger than Rhode Island and Delaware combined), gradually became a site of wildlife conservation where several endangered species thrived, as the DoD was pressured by environmentalists and ranchers to comply with federal environmental regulations.[104] White Sands is the home of the Trinity Site, where the first nuclear device was detonated in July 1945, and is still an active bombing range where thousands of weapons are test fired. But even here, the logic of the National Security State has not gone completely unchallenged, and military geographies have been reshaped by the activism of local communities who have worked to redefine their surrounding landscapes.

* * *

White Sands' transformation into a site of conservation under pressure from local activists highlights how the politics of military land use in the Southwest were complicated by competing interests. The relative success of ranchers and environmentalists though is also telling when contrasted with the fate of other groups who found their interests at odds with those of the military. The Western

---

[101] Mike Davis, 'The Dead West: Ecocide in Marlboro Country', *New Left Review*,. I/200 (July/August 1993): 49–73.

[102] Ryan H. Edgington, *Range Wars: The Environmental Contest for White Sands Missile Range* (Lincoln: University of Nebraska Press, 2014); Sarah Alisabeth Fox, *Downwind: A People's History of the Nuclear West* (Lincoln: University of Nebraska Press, 2014); Heefner, *The Missile Next Door*.

[103] For an account of ranchers' attempts to negotiate the relocation of missile silos, see Heefner, *The Missile Next Door*, 92–108.

[104] Edgington, *Range Wars*.

Shoshone, for instance, fought a long and mostly unsuccessful struggle against nuclear testing on their lands, and Western Shoshone reservations downwind of the Nevada Test site suffered from the effects of fallout.[105] Similarly, some communities downrange of the White Sands Missile Range had to reckon with the military's presence while having no say in how its activities affected them. American missiles landed south of the Mexican border several times after the opening of the range, starting with a V-2 rocket that landed in Juarez in 1947. In 1970, an Athena missile launched in Utah and destined for White Sands overshot its target and landed 400 kilometres south of the border in Durango. The missile had been carrying the radioactive isotope cobalt-57, which necessitated an extensive clean-up effort that involved removing hundreds of tonnes of soil from the crash site.[106]

The parallel frustrations of the Western Shoshone and communities in Mexico who found themselves having to deal with stray missiles illustrate what's distinctive about the Southwestern United States: it's not only an area with extensive military training ranges but it's also been the site of the 'frontier' and then the border with Mexico.[107] Historian Greg Grandin has distinguished between the two concepts by arguing that the frontier represented the endless possibilities of expansion and provided a safety valve for social problems, but that the concept of the border reflects a turning inwards and a closing of the gate where political passions can no longer be displaced outwards. Reflecting on the construction of prototypes of President Trump's proposed border wall with Mexico, Grandin argues that 'today the frontier is closed, the safety valve shut. Whatever metaphor one wants to use, the country has lived past the end of its myth. Where the frontier symbolised perennial rebirth, a culture in springtime, those eight prototypes in Otay Mesa loom like tombstones.'[108] The transition from frontier to border has involved the progressive militarization of spaces in the Southwest, as the United States moved to control the flow of migration and prevent unwanted people from entering into the country.

---

[105] Taylor N. Johnson, '"The Most Bombed Nation on Earth": Western Shoshone Resistance to the Nevada National Security Site', *Atlantic Journal of Communication* 26, no. 4 (8 August 2018): 224–39, https://doi.org/10.1080/15456870.2018.1494177.

[106] Edgington, *Range Wars*, 106–13.

[107] Lisa Meierotto has argued that conservation and immigration enforcement efforts have combined to effect much of the landscape of the Southwest in unique ways. Lisa Meierotto, 'A Disciplined Space: The Co-Evolution of Conservation and Militarization on the US-Mexico Border', *Anthropological Quarterly; Washington* 87, no. 3 (Summer 2014): 637–64, http://dx.doi.org/10.1353/anq.2014.0039.

[108] Grandin, *The End of the Myth*, 270.

While the frontier consisted of an expanding network of military outposts, the militarization associated with the border has been both more extensive and, paradoxically, less directly associated with the military itself. The impetus to control the flow of people over the southern border began in the 1940s and the first border fence was erected in California in 1945. Consisting of 4,500 feet of chain-link fence recycled from a Japanese internment camp, the southern border fence and many of the structures that followed were more concerned with preventing cattle from straying than preventing people from entering the United States.[109] Instead, immigration enforcement came through Border Patrol–led crackdowns and round-ups, such as Operation Wetback, which deported millions of migrant workers from 1954 onwards, and Operation Intercept, the Nixon-era anti-drug campaign that effectively shut down all border crossings between the United States and Mexico. In the 1970s and 1980s, border enforcement became more systematic, as the director of the Immigration and Naturalization Service, the retired Marine Corps General Leonard Chapman, decried what he called a 'growing, silent invasion of illegal aliens'.[110] An expanded Border Patrol was accompanied by vigilante groups such as the Ku Klux Klan, who set up a 'border watch' in San Ysidro in 1977.[111] With the passage of Immigration Reform and Control Act of 1986, and President Ronald Reagan's National Security Decision Directive (NSDD) 221 of the same year, which sanctioned a 'war on drugs', border enforcement escalated still further.

Nonetheless, even as he was calling for more action on the border, Chapman conceded that 'no one wants to see our country hemmed in by a Berlin Wall. And we can't have a huge army of immigration officers stopping people on the streets to check for citizenship'.[112] Anthropologists Josiah Heyman and Howard Campbell argue that the militarization of the border that began in the 1970s was not 'an omniscient, omnipotent control strategy, but rather a repetitive and somewhat clumsy template used by U.S. political elites (and relatedly, Mexican elites) to address dynamic and disruptive challenges in Latin America and related regions of the United States'.[113] They note that this militarization occurred even

---

[109] Grandin, *The End of the Myth*, 99–100.
[110] Cited in Douglas S. Massey, Jorge Durand and Karen A. Pren, 'Why Border Enforcement Backfired', *American Journal of Sociology* 121, no. 5 (1 March 2016): 1557–600, https://doi.org/10.1086/684200. Massy, Durand and Pren argue that Chapman's efficiency had the unintended consequence of increasing illegal immigration, as the newfound difficulty in crossing the border meant that what had been a circular flow of male workers migrated seasonally become a large population of settled families north of the border.
[111] Grandin, *The End of the Myth*, 223.
[112] Grandin, *The End of the Myth*, 223.
[113] Josiah Heyman and Howard Campbell, 'The Militarization of the United States-Mexico Border Region', *Revista de Estudos Universitários - REU* 38, no. 1 (2012): 75.

though the United States and Mexico have had a peaceful relationship with no major disputes. Instead of being aimed at Mexico itself, it was a response to transnational social processes stretching across Latin America that the United States struggled to contain.

This militarization increased in tandem with the increase in economic inequalities along the border. The military itself became formally involved in border operations in 1989, with the establishment of Joint Task Force Six at Fort Bliss, Texas. While its mission was to support the counter-drug operations of other federal agencies, this task force also conducted armed reconnaissance patrols along the border until 1997, when a Marine patrol shot dead Esequiel Hernández, an American high school student, in Redford, Texas.[114] After that incident, the military ended armed patrols and focused instead on surveillance and intelligence operations. In their stead though, law enforcement agencies at the border became steadily militarized from the Clinton era onwards. The Border Patrol launched a series of high-visibility operations in urban areas, like Operation Gatekeeper in San Diego and Operation Hold the Line in El Paso, forcing migrants into harsher and more dangerous terrain.[115] Between 1992 and 2012, the number of Border agents increased more than fivefold, from 4,139 to 21,444.[116] This was accompanied by a huge increase in the use of surveillance technology, including watch towers, blimps, light aircraft and (later) drones. The Secure Fence Act of 2006 authorized the construction of seven hundred miles of fencing along the border, along with 'virtual fence' known as SBInet (the Secure Border Initiative network), which was to consist of towers with long-range cameras, thermal imaging, seismic detection and motion detectors. SBInet was cancelled in 2010 after $1 billion had already been spent on the programme.[117]

Thus, the Trump-era focus on the border as a national security threat was only a continuation and acceleration of already-existing trends. Trump's promise to build a wall along the length of the border and his theatrical deployment of large numbers of troops to the border in 2018 were more extreme iterations

---

[114] Timothy J. Dunn, 'Border Militarization via Drug and Immigration Enforcement: Human Rights Implications', *Social Justice* 28, no. 2 (84) (2001): 7–30.

[115] Timothy J. Dunn, *Blockading the Border and Human Rights: The El Paso Operation That Remade Immigration Enforcement*, 1st edn (Austin: University of Texas Press, 2010); Jeremy Slack et al., 'The Geography of Border Militarization: Violence, Death and Health in Mexico and the United States', *Journal of Latin American Geography* 15, no. 1 (31 March 2016): 7–32, https://doi.org/10.1353/lag.2016.0009.

[116] Daniel E. Martinez, Josiah Heyman and Jeremy Slack, 'Border Enforcement Developments since 1993 and How to Change CBP' (The Center for Migration Studies of New York (CMS), 24 August 2020), https://cmsny.org/publications/border-enforcement-developments-since-1993-and-how-to-change-cbp/.

[117] Julia Preston, 'Homeland Security Cancels "Virtual Fence" after $1 Billion Is Spent', *New York Times*, 14 January 2011, sec. U.S., https://www.nytimes.com/2011/01/15/us/politics/15fence.html.

of the policies of previous presidents.[118] As national security fears increased, though, the very size of what could be called the border increased with it. The border expanded outwards, with deeper US involvement with counter-drug and anti-migration measures south of the border, and inwards, as Border Patrol and later Immigration and Customs Enforcement (ICE) officials conducted searches, raids and checkpoints well into United States territory. By 2018, the American Civil Liberties Union (ACLU) was highlighting the existence of a 100-mile deep 'border zone', which encompassed 65.3 per cent of the entire US population, where different standards about search warrants, check points, detention and questioning about suspected immigration violations apply.[119] The controversy over the extent of border zone demonstrates how some of the same rhetoric of security that impelled the United States to build military bases all over the world could also call forth a highly militarized form of policing within the United States itself. Attempts to create a hard border in the Southwest brought with them new legal regimes and new ways of governing spaces, but these practices themselves were drawn from the long American experience of controlling militarized zones overseas.

* * *

In the final passages of *The Soldier and the State*, his classic 1957 book on civil–military relations in the United States, the political scientist Samuel Huntington reflected on the United States' relationship with its military by comparing the United States Military Academy at West Point with the neighbouring village of Highland Falls. Contrasting 'the tiresome monotony and incredible variety and discordancy of small-town commercialism' of Highland Falls with the 'ordered serenity' of the Military Academy, where 'beauty and utility are merged in grey stone', Huntington declared West Point to be 'a bit of Sparta in the midst of Babylon'.[120] As this chapter has demonstrated though, Huntington's binary view of military *versus* civilian spaces is a crude oversimplification. The imposing architecture and uniform grey stone of West Point may hint at order and unity, and indeed it is true that militarized spaces are the sites and subjects of intensive order, but such spaces are also locations of conflict and disturbances, where

---

[118] Michael D. Shear and Thomas Gibbons-Neff, 'Trump Sending 5,200 Troops to the Border in an Election-Season Response to Migrants', *New York Times*, 29 October 2018, https://www.nytimes.com/2018/10/29/us/politics/border-security-troops-trump.html.

[119] 'The Constitution in the 100-Mile Border Zone', American Civil Liberties Union, accessed 21 February 2020, https://www.aclu.org/other/constitution-100-mile-border-zone.

[120] Samuel P. Huntington, *The Soldier and the State* (Cambridge, MA: Harvard University Press, 1957), 464–5.

local communities seek to harness economic benefits while trying to mitigate environmental or societal disruption.

Relatedly, and more crucially, the notion of Highland Falls as a Babylon that exists independently of the isolated Sparta that adjoins it completely misses the ways in which places like Highland Falls are shaped by militarization. Military activities and purposes do not just exert control over spaces that belong to the military. The sheer scale of American preparation for war, especially during the Cold War, has meant that spaces at home and overseas were governed or informed by military logics in profound ways. From oil pipelines in Western Europe to technology parks in North Carolina to nature preserves in Colorado, all manner of different locations owe their existence to the interaction between the military and broader society. Of course, in the case of Highland Falls, this relationship is even easier to delineate. The very collection of commercial ventures that Huntington accuses of being 'motley, disconnected collection of frames coincidentally adjoining each other, lacking common unity or purpose' in fact largely existed to service the needs of West Point.[121] The architecture of Main Street may not have hinted at it, but these various businesses certainly had a clear unity of purpose: to support and constitute the commercial life of a small town dedicated to servicing the needs of the Military Academy. The story of Highland Falls has been replicated a thousand times over, as military spending has had an immense impact on the economic and social life of specific villages, towns, cities and regions.

With its origins as a Revolutionary War–era fortification, West Point represents one of the earliest examples of how, in Gretchen Heefner's formulation, American power was rationalized and made visible in specific locations. Taken together, the scholarship that has mapped and traced the histories of these locations does a number of important things. First, it demonstrates that militarization of space abroad was mirrored by similar processes at home; as the Empire of Bases expanded overseas, so too did the acreage dedicated to military uses in the United States itself. Secondly, it shows that the narrative of militarization knits together the histories of diverse places. The suburbs, the border wall, environmental refuges and toxic waste dumps alike all owe their existence in some way to the American state's preparations for war and its quest for security. Finally, by focusing on specific locations, this scholarship demonstrates that even the most omnipotent-seeming process has been affected by contingency and resistance. From rioters in Okinawa to ranchers and environmental

---

[121] Huntington, *The Soldier and the State*, 465.

protestors in New Mexico, militarized control over space was contested and subjected to other logics. This is not simply a question of righteous anti-war resistance. If we look at the ways in which the Army adapted its mobilization plans in 1918 to account for the challenges of locating so many of training camps in the segregated South, we can see how military necessity had to content with other political forces. Militarized landscapes, then, have been constituted by the interaction between the immense power of the military state and local actors with their own concerns and priorities. These interactions were virtually always highly unequal, but served to shape and legitimize the process of militarization as it ebbed and flowed through environments all over the world.

4

Militarized encounters: Armed Americans abroad

In late August 1942, three American fliers came ashore on the small Pacific atoll of Sikaiana in the Solomon Islands. Ensign Harold L. Bingaman (Ben), Aviation Radiomen Paul W. Knight and Calvin ('Clyde') P. Crouch, whose torpedo bomber had been shot down during the Battle of the Eastern Solomons, were lucky to be alive. The sea was calm that day, which allowed them to reach the shore through the roughest part of the reef. They were even more fortunate that the island was inhabited: the Polynesian people of the island sheltered them, fed them and tended to their wounds until a Navy seaplane came to rescue them several days later. After the departure of the three Americans, the women of the island composed a series of songs to commemorate their stay. In an inversion of the typical Western exoticization of 'tropical beauties', the women taunted the young men of the island by celebrating the beauty of the American fliers:

> I want the very white skin of Ben to sleep with me
> I want the fragrant skin of Paul to sleep with me
> You are disgusting to me
> You are disgusting to Clyde
> You are simply disgusting.[1]

Contacted by an American anthropologist forty years later, Paul W. Knight remembered the incident well. He had been severely wounded in the crash and attributed his survival to the people of Sikaiana nursing his wounds. By way of thanks, the crew of the rescue seaplane gave them several cartons of cigarettes, and the rescued fliers gifted them the whistle from their life raft.

---

[1] William W. Donner, '"Far Away" and "Close Up": World War II and Sikaiana Perceptions of Their Place in the World', in *The Pacific Theater: Island Representations of World War II*, ed. Geoffrey M. White and Lamont Lindstrom (Honolulu: University of Hawaii Press, 1989), 153.

The incident on Sikaiana represents the most benign form of military encounter with civilians abroad. The Americans were deeply grateful to their hosts and left on friendly terms. This minor event, though, contains within it several themes common to the way that armed Americans interacted with strangers. Firstly, it demonstrates just how far-reaching American military power could be. Even if it came in the rather pathetic form of three drenched and wounded fliers, armed only with pistols, the US military had a presence in one of the most remote places on earth. Secondly, in the form of playful verses of the women of Sikaiana, the encounter was sexualized and, in some small way, changed social relations on the island. Finally, the material plenty of the United States was in evidence throughout. The Americans left behind their rubber life raft and their emergency rations and expressed their gratitude in the forms of cartons of cigarettes.

Elsewhere in the South Pacific, encounters were much more fraught and more complicated. After the outbreak of war with Japan in December 1941, some 2 million Americans moved quickly into the sparsely populated region to the east of Australia, where they built bases, moved supplies and fought battles. Such was the speed with which they moved that when the joint Army/Navy task force departed Charleston in January 1942 to build a supply depot on the island of Bora-Bora, the planners had no maps of the island to work with, but only a reel of a 1930s Hollywood film that had been shot there.[2] Within months though, the French colonial possession – with a pre-war population of 1,500 – hosted an American base with 4,600 troops and workers, concrete docks, ammunition bunkers, four batteries of coastal artillery and several huge fuel tanks. On New Caledonia, another French colonial possession, the Americans built an even larger base and made it the headquarters of their South Pacific Fleet. The pre-war population of 57,000 was overwhelmed by more than 100,000 Americans. The French colonial governor complained that Noumea, New Caledonia's capital, had been transformed 'into an American town: noisy, filled with snack bars, and populated with drunken sailors and soldiers'.[3] He also remonstrated that African American soldiers had terrified the French civilian population, listing a series of bar fights and traffic accidents as instances of grievances caused by the Americans, as well as protesting at more serious crimes such as rape and murder.

---

[2] John T. Mason Jr, *Pacific War Remembered: An Oral History Collection* (Annapolis: Naval Institute Press, 2013), 43.
[3] Kim Munholland, 'Yankee Farewell: The Americans Leave New Caledonia, 1945', *Proceedings of the Meeting of the French Colonial Historical Society* 16 (1992): 187.

On New Caledonia, Bora-Bora and elsewhere, American military officials worked with or through colonial administrators to manage relations with indigenous labourers. On Guadalcanal, Major General Alexander M. Patch issued a memorandum decrying practices 'prejudicial to the full utilization of native labour and the control of natives by British authorities'. Such practices included 'over-payment for services or commodities, employment of casual labour without adequate supervision or control … and permitting casual natives to wander through camps and military areas and encouraging the latter bad practice by feeding or making gifts to these casual natives'.[4] French colonial administrators in New Caledonia insisted that the Americans turn over their payroll funds to the French Native Affairs Office, who would manage payments to indigenous workers, as they had done in pre-war times.[5] The work itself was tough and draining. One veteran of the Solomon Islands Native Labour Corps recalled that 'we became so absorbed with work that we did not know which day was Sunday or which one was Saturday. Every week was just like the one before. Every day was just the same. We had no time to rest. We just worked.'[6] Whether they wanted to participate or not, indigenous workers were enlisted in the war effort. Throughout the war, New Caledonia was hit by several strikes; to American military officials, these were not simply work stoppages but instances of 'desertion' that should be addressed with military discipline.[7] French troops put these protests down with considerable force.[8]

Nonetheless, if American officials were eager to cooperate with colonial administrators to keep wages down and to leave colonial labour systems intact, most of the 2 million Americans in the South Pacific were ordinary men and women, themselves sucked up into the war effort with little choice. These troops had little knowledge of pre-war conventions on the islands and no particular interest in protecting the colonial system. Patch's memo on Guadalcanal, after all, sought to limit fraternization that had already begun to occur (Figure 4.1). Even as workers went on strike in New Caledonia, Tannese workers on the

---

[4] Lamont Lindstrom and Geoffrey M. White, 'War Stories', in *The Pacific Theater: Island Representations of World War II*, ed. Geoffrey M. White and Lamont Lindstrom (Honolulu: University of Hawaii Press, 1989), 10.

[5] Lamont Lindstrom, 'Working Encounters: Oral Histories of World War II Labor Corps from Tanna, Vanuatu', in *The Pacific Theater: Island Representations of World War II*, ed. Geoffrey M. White and Lamont Lindstrom (Honolulu: University of Hawaii Press, 1989), 400.

[6] David W. Gegeo and Karen Ann Watson-Gegeo, 'World War II Experience and Life History: Two Cases from Malaita, Solomon Islands', in *The Pacific Theater: Island Representations of World War II*, ed. Geoffrey M. White and Lamont Lindstrom (Honolulu: University of Hawaii Press, 1989), 361.

[7] Andrew Friedman, 'US Empire, World War 2 and the Racialising of Labour', *Race & Class*, 4 April 2017, 29, https://doi.org/10.1177/0306396816685024.

[8] Munholland, 'Yankee Farewell', 191.

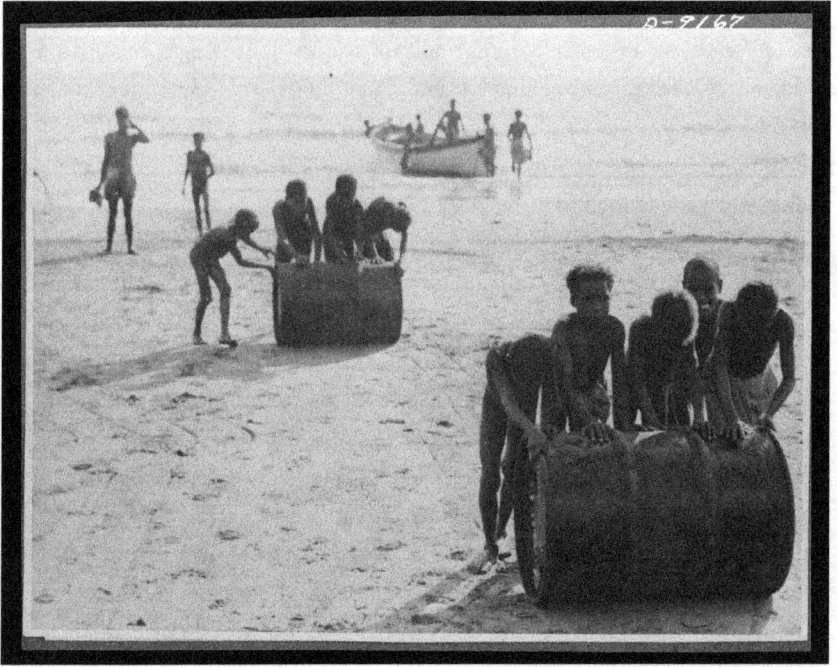

Figure 4.1 Papuan boys help unload petrol drums on a beach during an Allied offensive in Papua New Guinea, 1943. Credit: Library of Congress, Prints and Photographs Division, Farm Security Administration/Office of War Information Black-and-White Negatives.

Solomon Islands found wartime to be a time of plenty: 'When America was here, no problems with food, cigarettes, and money. There were a lot of them all the time ... You did not have to pay anything. Things were given freely – lolly, crackers – when you went to [the camp at] Ekasik. You did not ask for these things, they wanted to give them to you.'[9] Some observers noted that the entire male population of the region 'appeared to be clothed from US Army and Navy supplies.'[10]

Styling themselves as latter-day pioneers, American military personnel in the South Pacific eagerly catalogued local wildlife, took photographs and reported on the habits of indigenous people in letters home to their families.[11] They

[9] Charles De Burlo, 'Islanders, Soldiers, and Tourists: The War and Shaping of Tourism in Melanesia', in *The Pacific Theater: Island Representations of World War II*, ed. Geoffrey M. White and Lamont Lindstrom (Honolulu: University of Hawaii Press, 1989), 304.

[10] Munholland, 'Yankee Farewell', 190.

[11] Peter Schrijvers, *The GI War against Japan: American Soldiers in Asia and the Pacific during World War II* (New York: New York University Press, 2005), 3–25.

created a rudimentary tourist economy, buying shell necklaces and grass skirts, prompting locals to set up impromptu markets to barter with the Americans, even on Christianized islands where no one actually wore grass skirts any longer.[12] On Vanuatu, Americans and indigenous workers ate together in the same canteens, and, surprisingly, some even admired how Black and white American soldiers seemed to work together without any problems, in stark contrast to colonial racial hierarchies. Even in the 1980s, an American anthropologist visiting the remote island of Vanatinai in Papua New Guinea was asked 'how is the American Negro doing?', touching upon wartime connections made decades ago.[13]

At the end of the war, this vast tide of military personnel rolled back to the United States. Behind them, they left not only memories but also the runways and concrete docks that would be vital to the 1960s jet travel tourism boom. They also left behind some four thousand mixed race children, the legacy of relations between American men and indigenous women.[14] They left behind profoundly transformed labour and political relations, as wage labour became more common throughout the region and nationalist movements worked to dismantle colonialism. Perhaps the most striking political and social legacy of the American encounter with indigenous societies is the presence of 'cargo cults' on several archipelagos, such as Vanuatu. The paleness and relative generosity of the Americans led many indigenous people to conclude that they were the ghosts of their ancestors, who had returned to help them in their anti-colonial struggles. Some of these cults – which mixed indigenous religion with millenarian Christianity – predated the war but were given new impetus by both the sight of vast quantities of American 'cargo' coming ashore on beaches or docks or being dropped from the sky, or the terrible spectacle of battle, where Islanders heard the thunder of the guns, saw huge ships sink into the ocean and witnessed stricken aircraft trailing black smoke as they plunged into the sea. After the Americans and their 'cargo' had left, these movements worked to bring them back, clearing air strips in the jungle and building control towers manned by indigenous air traffic controllers, solemnly waving non-existent aircraft in to land.[15] Even today, every February 15th, many people on the island of Tanna

---

12 De Burlo, 'Islanders, Soldiers, and Tourists', 309.

13 Maria Lepowsky, 'Soldiers and Spirits: The Impact of World War II on a Coral Sea Island', in *The Pacific Theater: Island Representations of World War II*, ed. Geoffrey M. White and Lamont Lindstrom (Honolulu: University of Hawaii Press, 1989), 218, 222.

14 Judith A. Bennett and Angela Wanhalla, eds, *Mothers' Darlings of the South Pacific: The Children of Indigenous Women and U.S. Servicemen, World War II* (Honolulu: University of Hawaii Press, 2016).

15 Lamont Lindstrom, 'Cargo Cults', *Cambridge Encyclopedia of Anthropology*, 29 March 2018, https://www.anthroencyclopedia.com/entry/cargo-cults.

celebrate 'John Frum', a mythical African American soldier who lives inside the island's volcano and promises material plenty to his followers, with a military-style parade.[16] Nearly eighty years later, the arrival of armed Americans in the South Pacific still resonates in profound ways.

We are able to recount these stories because of the work undertaken by scholars in recent decades to highlight the importance of these seemingly mundane encounters. As anthropologists Lamont Lindstrom and Geoffrey White noted in the 1980s, previous generations of military historians 'writing about the Pacific War ... ignored wholesale the people living on the islands over which the armies were "hopping"'.[17] In more recent years, this has no longer been true. Feminist historians in particular have emphasized just how significant everyday encounters were, and how we can use them to get a broader, clearer picture of the realities and consequences of American foreign policy.[18] Historians have argued that the history of Americans abroad can tell us much about the history of the United States itself.[19] Here, we focus on *armed* Americans abroad. Of course, American soldiers had intervened on virtually every continent since independence, but after 1941 the sheer number of Americans abroad increased dramatically and stayed that way throughout the Cold War and beyond. What is striking about the histories of US soldiers overseas is how lightly their arms seemed to weigh on them, and – conversely – how heavily they weighed on local communities. Americans often saw themselves in benign terms, whether as liberators, tourists, explorers or allies. And while local populations sometimes did think highly of Americans, especially during the Second World War, they rarely saw the presence of armed foreigners, whether in wartime or peacetime, as a self-evidently good thing.

These encounters could be commercial, sexual or even violent, and they all in some way involved the remaking of local cultures, while service members were also vehicles for the transmission of foreign ideas back to the United States. Whether as armed tourists, military occupiers or in senior roles such as attaché or advisor, armed Americans overseas were, for many, the embodiment of US foreign policy. This chapter provides an overview of these interactions. Often, as in the South

---

[16] Marc Tabani, 'Ritualisation du changement et célébration des continuités: les cérémonies John Frum du 15 février à Tanna (Vanuatu)', *Journal de la Societe des Oceanistes* 142–3, no. 1 (2016): 143–58.

[17] Lindstrom and White, 'War Stories', 6.

[18] Cynthia Enloe, *Bananas, Beaches and Bases: Making Feminist Sense of International Politics* (Berkeley: University of California Press, 2014); Cynthia Enloe, *Maneuvers: The International Politics of Militarizing Women's Lives* (Berkeley: University of California Press, 2000).

[19] Brooke L. Blower, 'Nation of Outposts: Forts, Factories, Bases, and the Making of American Power', *Diplomatic History* 41, no. 3 (1 June 2017): 439–59, https://doi.org/10.1093/dh/dhx034.

Pacific, Americans came 'armed with abundance' and symbolized the strengths of American consumerism, while on other occasions, their interactions were much less benign and far more violent, particularly and most obviously during wartime. The military did not just send soldiers overseas, however, and the families and dependents that travelled to these bases are also worthy of study, particularly for the ways in which they sought to re-create some version of the United States abroad. Finally, the chapter outlines the flow of people and ideas that went in the other direction – whether it be ideas about civil rights that African American soldiers brought home from Europe, the Second World War 'war brides' or the large flows of refugees produced by American wars overseas. By studying these more personal encounters and the movement of people to and from the United States, we can better understand the transnational dimensions of militarization.

* * *

As in the Pacific theatre, when Americans went to war in Europe in the Second World War, they did so amid a vast outpouring of industrial production. They were borne across the Atlantic on a fleet of mass-produced troop ships; once in battle, they relied upon fire support from enormous quantities of highly effective artillery and air support, and they were sustained by a quartermaster corps that by the end of the war was responsible for feeding over seven and a half million people.[20] GIs were given a ration of 4,050 calories a day, which compared favourably to the German ration of 2,700 daily calories per soldier.[21] The sheer scale of logistics in the Second World War was unprecedented and provided a model for future conflicts. Planners worked to ensure that Americans going to war would have every material need met, and – with very rare exceptions – they were able to succeed in doing so.[22] Every time they deployed abroad, US military personnel were well fed, well paid and – wherever it was feasible – had ample opportunities

---

[20] William F. Ross and Charles F. Romanus, *The Quartermaster Corps: Operations in the War against Germany*, CMH Pub 10-15 (Washington, DC: US Army Center of Military History, 2004), vii.

[21] Ross and Romanus, *The Quartermaster Corps*, 295, 534. During the Vietnam War, this ration increased to 4,500 calories a day. Meredith H. Lair, *Armed with Abundance: Consumerism and Soldiering in the Vietnam War* (Chapel Hill: University of North Carolina Press, 2014), 75.

[22] Several scholars have argued that Americans in the Second World War pursued a strategy of annihilation based on industrial capacity. John Ellis, *Brute Force: Allied Strategy and Tactics during the Second World War* (London: Viking, 1990); Thomas Zeiler, *Annihilation: A Global Military History of World War II*, 1st edn (New York: Oxford University Press, 2010); Jeffrey Fear, 'War of the Factories', in *Cambridge History of the Second World War, Vol. 3. Total War: Economy, Society and Culture*, ed. Michael Geyer and Adam Tooze, vol. 3 (Cambridge: Cambridge University Press, 2015), 94–121. Russell Weigley, *The American Way of War: A History of United States Military Strategy and Policy* (New York: Macmillan, 1973), 269–362. For an account that demonstrates how central anxieties about American economic strength were to Hitler's calculations, see Adam Tooze, *The Wages of Destruction: The Making and Breaking of the Nazi Economy* (London: Penguin, 2007).

for entertainment and leisure. As General Robert L. Eichelberger bragged during the occupation of Japan, 'our government has made this the best fed, the best clothed and the best entertained army in history'.[23] While this might not sit easily with a picture of haggard combat troops sheltering in foxholes and eating barely digestible K-rations, the majority of American troops who served abroad in every war since 1941 did not see combat. They were clerks, drivers, accountants, laborers and engineers. In their free time, they were tourists and consumers too.

As historian Meredith Lair points out, the Vietnam War marked an acceleration of this trend, as military leaders sought to ensure that the deprivations of war would minimally affect troops deployed to Southeast Asia, who 'brought with them high standards for what constituted comfort and satiety, standards that had been cultivated by the ethos of abundance in which so many of them were reared'.[24] In Vietnam, unlike the Second World War, there was no need to ration supplies like petrol or ammunition and supply lines between the continental United States and depots in Japan and the Philippines remained open and unimpeded. The US military operated dozens of ice plants in South Vietnam and flew in hundreds of tonnes of fresh food and vegetables (only 30 per cent of the produce served to American soldiers came from Vietnam itself), as the military command sought to raise morale not by dealing with doubts about the war but by improving material circumstances.[25]

The advent of the All-Volunteer Force only increased this emphasis on soldier morale and welfare, as a force that depended solely on recruiting in the marketplace had to offer a lifestyle that would persuade service members to re-enlist.[26] Indeed, this question was foremost in the minds of military planners, given the low pay and low morale of the 1970s-era military. In one of the rare exceptions to the global image of the affluent GI, the drop in the value of dollar relative to the Deutschmark meant American military wages had decreased purchasing power in Germany. Germans were beginning to comment on the fact that American service personnel deployed to West Germany tended to live in substandard accommodation and drive beat-up cars, even while their counterparts in places like Long Binh in South Vietnam lived in luxury.[27] As

---

[23] Susan L. Carruthers, *The Good Occupation: American Soldiers and the Hazards of Peace* (Cambridge, MA: Harvard University Press, 2016), 235.

[24] Lair, *Armed with Abundance*, 10.

[25] Lair, *Armed with Abundance*, 75–7.

[26] Beth Bailey, *America's Army: Making the All-Volunteer Force* (Cambridge, MA: Harvard University Press, 2009); Beth Bailey, 'The Army in the Marketplace: Recruiting an All-Volunteer Force', *Journal of American History* 94, no. 1 (2007): 47–74, https://doi.org/10.2307/25094776; Jennifer Mittelstadt, *The Rise of the Military Welfare State* (Cambridge, MA: Harvard University Press, 2015).

[27] Maria Höhn, 'The Racial Crisis of 1971 in the US Military: Finding Solutions in West Germany and South Korea', in *Over There: Living with the U.S. Military Empire from World War Two to the Present*,

the military worked to fix these problems, they invested even more in the idea that it was imperative to provide material comfort to American soldiers abroad. Thus, by the time American troops deployed to Iraq in the mid-2000s, they had access to air-conditioned accommodation, generous portions in the dining hall and reliable internet connections, and those stationed at the many American bases abroad were living in what were effectively versions of American suburbia transplanted to Okinawa or northern Italy.[28] This combination of a style of war-making that emphasized overwhelming force and personnel policies that prioritized the highest standard of living possible meant that armed Americans abroad became symbols of American consumer culture, in all its abundance and wastefulness.

In one sense, this abundance performed a service for the United States. American soldiers simply had more material goods than anyone else and, when they were willing to share, GIs became ambassadors for the American way of life and consumer capitalism more broadly.[29] The historian and populariser of 'greatest generation' narratives, Stephen Ambrose, argues,

> In the spring of 1945, around the world, the sight of a twelve-man squad of teenage boys, armed and in uniform, brought terror to people's hearts. … But there was an exception: a squad of GIs, a sight that brought the biggest smiles you ever saw to people's lips, and joy to their hearts. Around the world, this was true, even in Germany, even – after September 1945 – in Japan. This was because GIs meant candy, cigarettes, C-rations, and freedom. [30]

Sometimes, this image was intentionally fostered to great effect. The most famous example of the propaganda value of food was 'Operation Little Vittles' during the Berlin Airlift. Throughout the crisis, Air Force Lieutenant Gail Halvorsen, acting at first on his own initiative and then with the support of the Air Force, parachute-dropped 23 tonnes of candy to the children of West

---

ed. Maria Höhn and Seungsook Moon (Durham, NC: Duke University Press, 2010), 267–9; Howard J. De Nike, 'The US Military and Dissenters in the Ranks', in *GIs in Germany: The Social, Economic, Cultural, and Political History of the American Military Presence*, ed. Thomas W. Maulucci and Detlef Junker (Washington, DC: German Historical Institute; Cambridge University Press, 2013), 277.

28 For accounts of life on US military bases in Iraq, see Rajiv Chandrasekaran, *Imperial Life in the Emerald City: Inside Iraq's Green Zone*, 1st edn (New York: Alfred A. Knopf, 2006); Leonard Wong, *CU @ the FOB: How the Forward Operating Base Is Changing the Life of Combat Soldiers* (Carlisle, PA: Strategic Studies Institute, U.S. Army War College, 2006). For the literature on American bases, see Chapter 3.

29 Bruce Makoto Arnold, '"Your Money Ain't No Good o'er There": Food as Real and Social Currency in the Pacific Theater of World War II', *Food and Foodways* 25, no. 2 (3 April 2017): 107–22, https://doi.org/10.1080/07409710.2017.1311160.

30 Stephen Ambrose, *Citizen Soldiers: The U.S. Army from the Normandy Beaches to the Bulge* (New York: Simon & Schuster, 2013), 485–6.

Berlin, a practice that was enormously popular, both with German and domestic American audiences.[31] Thus, both planned demonstrations of American largesse and everyday encounters with well-fed, well-clothed GIs who came bearing gifts underscored the power of the American economy and the US military, even if – as British historian David Reynolds has pointed out – many of the soldiers deployed to Britain during the Second World War were 'living far better in the wartime Army than they had been in Depression America'.[32]

American wealth was not without its problems though. South Vietnam suffered from hyperinflation due to the massive impact of American spending on its economy, while elsewhere the US military often sucked up scarce resources. In order to contain GI consumerism, military authorities rushed to establish Post Exchanges (PXs) wherever American troops were stationed. These well-stocked military-run stores would keep soldiers' pay from over-heating local economies while also sending some of this money back into the military system and maintaining soldier morale by allowing troops access to luxuries that might be scarce locally. Certainly, PXs were important to morale, as evidenced by the fact that the bare shelves that appeared in Korean PXs in 1946 became the subject of Congressional inquiry.[33] They also however exacerbated local jealousies and provided fodder for black market entrepreneurs. In his history of the occupation of post-war Japan, John Dower records not only how American occupation authorities in Japan declared numerous stores, theatres, hotels and recreation facilities off-limits to the Japanese but also how 'there was always a crowd of Japanese outside the PX … watching the customers come in and out, flattening their noses against the shop windows, gazing in silent awe at the display of merchandise: the souvenirs, candy bars, milk shakes, shoes, wool sweaters, silk kimonos and guaranteed curios of the orient'.[34] Not only that, but PXs could also become sites of corruption. In South Vietnam, the manager of the Saigon PX was found to be in possession of 142,000 cans of hair spray, even though there were only 720 women in the city who had PX privileges at the time.[35] The hair spray had evidently been destined for the black market, which thrived under the American occupation of South Vietnam. In post-war Japan

---

[31] Kaete M. O'Connell, '"Uncle Wiggly Wings": Children, Chocolates, and the Berlin Airlift', *Food and Foodways* 25, no. 2 (3 April 2017): 142–59, https://doi.org/10.1080/07409710.2017.1311163.

[32] David Reynolds, *Rich Relations: The American Occupation of Britain 1942–1945* (London: Phoenix, 2001), 437.

[33] Carruthers, *The Good Occupation*, 244.

[34] John W. Dower, *Embracing Defeat: Japan in the Wake of World War II* (New York: W. W. Norton, 2000), 207, 209.

[35] Lair, *Armed with Abundance*, 203.

and Germany, American occupation authorities blamed black market activity on various 'out-groups' – Koreans in Japan and Jewish Displaced Persons in Germany – even though virtually everyone – occupier, occupied and refugee – participated in black market activities.[36] Black markets created extortionate prices for commodities easily available to Americans via the military logistics system.

As historian Susan Carruthers notes, American occupiers often saw bartering goods on the black market as a form of entertainment; because so many of their material needs were met, they had plenty of money with which to purchase souvenirs, both legal and illicit. American military consumption habits had a deep and long-lasting impact on local economies. For instance, American occupation soldiers in occupied Japan helped establish the reputation of Canon and then Nikon cameras in the United States and gave a huge boost to Suntory whiskey.[37] This impact wasn't restricted to buying souvenirs. For soldiers on occupation duty or not in combat, overseas deployments afforded ample opportunities for tourism and entertainment. In the Second World War Italy, the US Navy organized day trips to Capri, while the Army organized weeklong sight-seeing tours (used commandeered German buses) that allowed soldiers to see much of Italy. The Army's pocket handbook, *The Soldier's Guide to Italy*, envisioned soldier-tourism not just as a means of avoiding boredom and raising morale but as a means of cultural diplomacy as well, encouraging GIs to act in such a way that it would remind Italians that 'the German way isn't the only way of occupying a country'.[38] In Vietnam, the military not only set up in-country R&R facilities such as the China Beach resort for short breaks, but they afforded soldiers the opportunity for longer trips out of the country, to places like Bangkok and Hong Kong.[39] This created distorting consequences for these economies: between 1965 and 1970 Hong Kong hosted about 200,000 US personnel on holiday every year, earning the colony about $300–400 million per annum, while US military tourists on R&R from South Vietnam accounted

---

[36] Carruthers, *The Good Occupation*, 186–7.

[37] Dower, *Embracing Defeat*, 534.

[38] Andrew Buchanan, '"I Felt like a Tourist Instead of a Soldier": The Occupying Gaze – War and Tourism in Italy, 1943–1945', *American Quarterly* 68, no. 3 (21 September 2016): 595, https://doi.org/10.1353/aq.2016.0055.

[39] Chi-kwan Mark, 'Vietnam War Tourists: US Naval Visits to Hong Kong and British-American-Chinese Relations, 1965–1968', *Cold War History* 10, no. 1 (1 February 2010): 1–28, https://doi.org/10.1080/14682740902837001; Peter E. Hamilton, '"A Haven for Tortured Souls": Hong Kong in the Vietnam War', *International History Review* 37, no. 3 (27 May 2015): 565–81, https://doi.org/10.1080/07075332.2014.946948; Porphant Ouyyanont, 'The Vietnam War and Tourism in Bangkok's Development, 1960–70', *Japanese Journal of Southeast Asian Studies* 39, no. 2 (2001): 157–87, https://doi.org/10.20495/tak.39.2_157.

for some 20 per cent of tourist expenditure in Thailand from 1966 to 1968.[40] The US withdrawal from Vietnam subsequently prompted a 50 per cent drop in the number of bars in Bangkok.[41] The sheer scale of consumer expenditure by GIs and the logistics system that supported them had a profound effect on virtually every society that hosted them. In virtually all cases, material plenty helped shape local perceptions of armed Americans abroad and provided the backdrop to the relationships that Americans had with others.

* * *

Inevitably, many of those relationships were sexual. Wherever American soldiers went, they had sex with locals, which invariably caused tensions. These issues were ones that sometimes had to be dealt with at the highest levels of government. In 1951, General Dwight D. Eisenhower, the Supreme Commander of NATO forces in Europe, told a US Senate Committee that 'a very touchy problem' had been created across Western Europe because 'as usual, the American soldier could outspend his allied comrades on wine and women'.[42] Indeed, so touchy were these problems that a few years previously Eisenhower had spent the eve of the D-Day landings in 1944 reviewing the case of Leroy Henry, an African American soldier who had been convicted of the rape of a white British woman in Bath the previous month.[43] After an outcry on both sides of the Atlantic, Eisenhower overturned the verdict and affirmed Henry's innocence, while in the British and African American press his accuser was depicted as a prostitute who had simply attempted to extort Henry by playing on white American fears of Black hypersexuality. The Henry Case and the controversy around it demonstrated that sexual encounters between American servicemen and local women could be consensual, commercial or violent, but – given the context in which they occurred – they were all politicized in some way.

The politicization of these relationships occurred from both sides. Firstly, the ways in which GIs thought and spoke about sex had important political connotations. Secondly, the reaction of authorities – both American and local – and civil society to sexual encounters was entangled in both domestic

---

[40] Hamilton, '"A Haven for Tortured Souls"'; Ouyyanont, 'The Vietnam War and Tourism in Bangkok's Development, 1960–70', 164.

[41] Ouyyanont, 'The Vietnam War and Tourism in Bangkok's Development, 1960–70', 165.

[42] Quoted in Giora Goodman, '"Only the Best British Brides": Regulating the Relationship between US Servicemen and British Women in the Early Cold War', *Contemporary European History* 17, no. 4 (2008): 485.

[43] Mary Louise Roberts, 'The Leroy Henry Case: Sexual Violence and Allied Relations in Great Britain, 1944', *Journal of the History of Sexuality* 26, no. 3 (1 September 2017): 402–23, https://doi.org/10.7560/JHS26303; Reynolds, *Rich Relations*, 233–7.

and international politics. Perhaps the clearest example of the broader impact of intimate relations was the experience of GIs in post-war Germany. As Petra Goedde has argued, American soldiers radically altered their view of an 'aggressive, masculine wartime image of the Third Reich' when they moved into Germany in the spring of 1945 and mostly encountered women and children struggling to survive in a country in ruins.[44] As Goedde puts it, 'unable to conceive of women as the enemy, they saw themselves increasingly as providers and protectors of the starving, impoverished enemy population'.[45] While the American military government in Germany attempted to enforce a strict fraternization ban on relations with the enemy population, this ban quickly collapsed in the face of GI insistence that their relations with German women were apolitical. In many ways, these relationships smoothed the way for the transition of Germany from wartime enemy to Cold War ally.

This American tendency to understand a country through encounters with its women was far from unique to Germany. GIs often held particular sexualized images of the countries they visited, whether as allies or as invaders. As Mary Louise Roberts notes, soldiers preparing for the D-Day landings were encouraged to think about the beautiful, sexually experienced women waiting for them on the other side of the channel, while American soldiers in Vietnam were variously wary of dangerous 'dragon ladies' and attracted to Vietnamese women as helpless damsels in need of rescue.[46] Japan, like Germany, underwent a post-war conversion in the eyes of American service members, as its image changed from a dangerous and bestial enemy to a nation of pliant and defenceless Geishas.[47] Whether foreign women were seen as dangerous or alluring, or both, these visions helped to reshape foreign relations in important ways.

The GI perspective was not the only one that mattered, though. As Maria Höhn has demonstrated, German views of American men also had an effect on Cold War politics. Many Germans in garrison towns viewed GIs as far less masculine and warriorlike than their German counterparts and, while German

---

[44] Petra Goedde, *GIs and Germans: Culture, Gender and Foreign Relations, 1945–1949* (New Haven, CT: Yale University Press, 2003); Petra Goedde, 'From Villains to Victims: Fraternization and the Feminization of Germany, 1945–1947', *Diplomatic History* 23, no. 1 (1999): 1–20.

[45] Goedde, 'From Villains to Victims', 2.

[46] Mary Louise Roberts, *What Soldiers Do: Sex and the American GI in World War II France* (Chicago: University of Chicago Press, 2013), 15–56; Heather Marie Stur, *Beyond Combat: Women and Gender in the Vietnam War Era* (New York: Cambridge University Press, 2011), 17–63; Gregory A. Daddis, *Pulp Vietnam: War and Gender in Cold War Men's Adventure Magazines* (New York: Cambridge University Press, 2020), 174–217.

[47] John Dower, *War without Mercy: Race and Power in the Pacific War* (New York: Pantheon Books, 1986); Naoko Shibusawa, *America's Geisha Ally: Reimagining the Japanese Enemy* (Cambridge, MA: Harvard University Press, 2010).

women might enjoy dating American men, many Germans in the early 1950s worried about the ability of such soldiers to fight the Soviets if the Cold War ever turned hot.[48] Both local and American military authorities sought to maintain some control over these encounters. For instance, during the Second World War and the early Cold War, the British government sought to ensure that only 'decent' English girls would be brought to dances with American servicemen, enlisting voluntary organizations to help run these dances and provide safe entertainment.[49] The British worried that sexually aggressive working-class girls could damage the Atlantic alliance with their bad behaviour. Conversely, the same British authorities were uncomfortable with the American export of Jim Crow practices to Europe.[50]

The British government would not acquiesce to allowing the official segregation of facilities for American soldiers, but in practice, British dance halls and pubs became de facto segregated spaces to accommodate Americans, as small towns cooperated with the US Army's policy of 'black nights' and 'white nights', and certain spaces became Black- or white-only, while Whitehall initially suggested basing African American units near British population centres with an existing Black population (Figure 4.2).[51] These policies caused tensions not only with British civilians but within the military as well, leading to fistfights and brawls when Military Police endeavoured to enforce segregation in pubs. The most infamous of these incidents was the Battle of Bamber Bridge in 1943, where the attempted arrest of African American GIs in a pub by white Military Police led to a melee that escalated into a firefight between the Military Police and the GIs that left one dead and five wounded.[52]

While ordinary British people often objected to these practices, fears of miscegenation fuelled anti-fraternization movements elsewhere in Europe. In both Germany and Austria, an organized anti-fraternization movement aimed at ostracizing (and sometimes attacking) women who were in relationships

---

[48] Maria Höhn, '"The American Soldier Dances, the German Soldier Marchs": The Transformation of German Views on GIs, Masculinity, and Militarism', in *Over There: Living with the U.S. Military Empire from World War Two to the Present*, ed. Maria Höhn and Seungsook Moon (Durham, NC: Duke University Press, 2010).

[49] Goodman, '"Only the Best British Brides"'.

[50] Sonya O. Rose, 'Girls and GIs: Race, Sex, and Diplomacy in Second World War Britain', *International History Review* 19, no. 1 (1997): 146–60; Lucy Bland, 'Interracial Relationships and the "Brown Baby Question": Black GIs, White British Women, and Their Mixed-Race Offspring in World War II', *Journal of the History of Sexuality* 26, no. 3 (September 2017): 424–53, https://doi.org/10.7560/JHS26304; Reynolds, *Rich Relations*, 225–37.

[51] Reynolds, *Rich Relations*, 218.

[52] Reynolds, *Rich Relations*, 319.

Figure 4.2 African American soldiers dancing with local girls in a London nightclub, 1943. Credit: Hulton Deutsch.

with American soldiers, aiming in particular at women who had sex with Black soldiers.[53] These issues continued in Cold War–era West Germany, as both pub and nightclub owners and military authorities alike discriminated against African Americans, to the extent that these tensions contributed to a full-on crisis in the US Seventh Army in the early 1970s.[54]

These anti-fraternization movements were often as much about the social control of women as they were about anti-Americanism. In occupation-era Japan, a powerful anti-prostitution movement emerged in the 1950s in response to the phenomenon of *pan-pan* girls, the unregulated street prostitutes whose clients were primarily American military personnel.[55] These women were reviled by many Japanese commentators as overly materialistic and arrogant, and in

---

[53] Perry Biddiscombe, 'Dangerous Liaisons: The Anti-Fraternization Movement in the U.S. Occupation Zones of Germany and Austria, 1945–1948', *Journal of Social History* 34, no. 3 (2001): 628–9.

[54] Höhn, 'The Racial Crisis of 1971 in the US Military'; De Nike, 'The US Military and Dissenters in the Ranks'.

[55] Sarah Kovner, *Occupying Power: Sex Workers and Servicemen in Postwar Japan* (Stanford, CA: Stanford University Press, 2012); Robert Kramm, *Sanitized Sex: Regulating Prostitution, Venereal Disease, and Intimacy in Occupied Japan, 1945–1952* (Berkeley: University of California Press, 2017); M. McLelland, *Love, Sex, and Democracy in Japan during the American Occupation* (London: Palgrave Macmillan, 2012); Holly Sanders, 'Panpan: Streetwalking in Occupied Japan', *Pacific Historical Review; Berkeley* 81, no. 3 (August 2012): 404–31.

popular depictions they always wore high heels, nylon stockings, red lipstick and smoked American cigarettes, living symbols of the degeneration of traditional Japan under American occupation.[56] The Japanese government had established a formal system of government-sanctioned prostitution, the Recreation and Amusement Association (RAA), to cater to occupation forces, but this shut down in March 1946 due to the American military authority's concerns about venereal disease.[57] In place of these government-run brothels, a street-walking culture emerged instead, as young Japanese women moved to fill this gap. For conservative Japanese observers, these women were both deeply subversive of traditional gender norms and living examples of the humiliation inflicted by defeat. Scholars have variously emphasized the *pan-pan* as sexually liberated women who were drawn to the business by curiosity and operated with relative independence (since there were no brothel owners or pimps to control them) and noted the extent to which the destitution of post-war Japanese society drove these women to sex work.

Certainly, in places like South Vietnam and Korea, economic necessity was the driving force behind militarized prostitution. By contrast, West Germany saw relatively low numbers of prostitutes servicing American military garrisons after the economically strained post-years passed.[58] Along with their money, the sexual desires of American servicemen could reshape entire economies and societies. In South Vietnam, there were between 300,000 and 500,000 Vietnamese women working as prostitutes by 1972, while Olongapo, a Filipino city adjacent to the American naval base in Subic Bay, had 6,019 women registered as 'hostesses' in 1976.[59] In 1960s South Korea, prostitution was designated a 'special tourism industry' by the government because of the amount of valuable foreign currency it brought into the country.[60] Prostitution on this scale was not an ad hoc phenomenon; it was an industry that had a real economic impact and one that was subject to government policing and regulation.[61]

---

[56] Masakazu Tanaka, 'The Sexual Contact Zone in Occupied Japan: Discourses on Japanese Prostitutes or "Panpan" for U.S. Military Servicemen', *Intersections: Gender and Sexuality in Asia and the Pacific*, no. 31 (December 2012), http://intersections.anu.edu.au/issue31/tanaka.htm#n18.

[57] Dower, *Embracing Defeat*, 127–31.

[58] Maria Höhn, ' "You Can't Pin Sergeant's Stripes on an Archangel": Soldering, Sexuality, and US Army Policy in Germany', in *Over There: Living with the US Military Empire from World War Two to Present*, ed. Maria Höhn and Seungsook Moon (Durham, NC: Duke University Press, 2010), 136.

[59] Enloe, *Maneuvers*, 67, 74.

[60] Seungsook Moon, 'Regulating Desire, Managing the Empire: US Military Prostitution in South Korea, 1945–1970', in *Over There: Living with The US Military Empire from World War Two to Present*, ed. Maria Höhn and Seungsook Moon (Durham, NC: Duke University Press, 2010), 67.

[61] Katharine H. S. Moon, 'Resurrecting Prostitutes and Overturning Treaties: Gender Politics in the "Anti-American" Movement in South Korea', *Journal of Asian Studies* 66, no. 1 (February 2007): 129–57, https://doi.org/10.1017/S0021911807000046.

American military authorities typically had a hypocritical attitude towards prostitution, where they officially condemned it but unofficially worked with host governments to manage and control it. We can see an example of this hypocrisy in Second World War France, where Major General Charles Gebhardt, commander of the 29th Infantry Division ordered his staff to establish a brothel for his soldiers in September 1944. The 'Blue and Gray Corral', which offered 'riding lessons' for 100 Francs, lasted for a total of five hours before being shut down by military authorities.[62] If the Army would not directly run brothels though, they were happy to leave them to the French, even if the management of prostitution would prove to be a fractious issue in Franco-American relations.[63] For military authorities, control of venereal disease was the primary lens through which they saw prostitution, and this imperative to keep their troops healthy legitimated their partnerships with host governments to manage it. Local governments and Americans collaborated to police women's bodies, and women who had relations with American soldiers were frequently subjected to compulsory medical examination. In occupation-era Germany, this could take the form of joint Military Police/German police raids of nightclubs, where all women in attendance were arrested, loaded onto US Army trucks and then taken to German police stations and given gynaecological exams. In South Korea, the 'Camptown' system put similar policies on a more permanent footing. Seungsook Moon describes these specialized towns, which existed to provide prostitutes for American bases as 'virtually colonized spaces, where Korean sovereignty was suspended and replaced by the US military authorities, and GI's buying power ruled Korean residents, whose livelihoods depended on them'.[64] These spaces were closely regulated by American and Korean authorities, with women again subject to frequent medical examination and registration.[65] As South Korea experienced economic growth, Korean prostitutes gradually began to be replaced by Filipino and Russian women, creating a transnational economy of sex work centred around American bases.

Like German night clubs and British dance halls, these camptowns were also segregated spaces, with separate brothels for white troops and Black troops. Indeed, when it came to the regulation of sex work, the move to condone

---

[62] Roberts, *What Soldiers Do*, 159.

[63] Mary Louise Roberts, 'The Price of Discretion: Prostitution, Venereal Disease, and the American Military in France, 1944–1946', *American Historical Review* 115, no. 4 (2010): 1002–30.

[64] Moon, 'Regulating Desire, Managing the Empire', 54.

[65] During Second World War, these strictures were sometimes placed on prostitutes in the United States as well. See Beth L. Bailey and David Farber, *The First Strange Place: Race and Sex in World War II Hawaii* (Baltimore, MD: Johns Hopkins University Press, 1994), 95–132.

prostitution but to regulate its worst excesses frequently meant the targeting of Black-only bars and prostitutes who associated with Black men. As Maria Höhn argues in the case of West Germany, 'the combined efforts of German and American police officers to contain *all* prostitution turned instead into containment of interracial sexuality'.[66] Indeed, encounters with American soldiers did not only provoke already-existing local racism but directly imported American ideas about race as well. In Japan, *pan-pan* girls who associated with African American GIs were considered lower status than those who associated with Euro-American GIs.[67] Thus, American racial politics had a direct bearing on the societies in which American soldiers moved.

When we look at the history of sexual encounters between American military personnel and locals, we can see that these relationships were subject to military logics and imperatives. In the case of sex workers, these relationships were directly regulated and controlled by American military authorities, but authorities were intimately involved in the management of all sorts of relationships, from the ill-fated fraternization ban in Germany to efforts to find 'the right sort' of girls to attend dances in East Anglia. These relationships were also militarized because behind them lay the material abundance of the US military: GIs were an attractive proposition because of their relative wealth and ability to spend. Finally, these relationships were militarized because the Americans involved in them were agents of violence who had access to weapons and were trained in their use. This is not to say that the relationship between a GI and the German woman he met and married while on deployment was one primarily structured by violence, but it is worth noting that militaries are organizations whose primary role is the employment of armed force.

When it came to overt acts of sexual violence, women's bodies became the site of a variety of racial and nationalist politics. Again, American racial politics came to the fore overseas, as Black GIs frequently found themselves on trial for rape at disproportionate rates. For instance, in Second World War Europe, of the 904 men tried for rape, 391 were Black, representing over 40 per cent of those prosecuted, even though African American soldiers made up only 11 per cent of US Armed Forces.[68] Not only that, but Black GIs represented nearly

[66] Höhn, '"You Can't Pin Sergeant's Stripes on an Archangel"', 133.

[67] Michiko Takeuchi, '"Pan-Pan Girls" Performing and Resisting Neocolonialism(s) in the Pacific Theater: US Military Prostitution in Occupied Japan, 1945–1952', in *Over There: Living with the US Military Empire from World War Two to Present*, ed. Maria Höhn and Seungsook Moon (Durham, NC: Duke University Press, 2010), 92.

[68] Ruth Lawlor, 'American Soldiers and the Politics of Rape in World War II Europe' (Cambridge: University of Cambridge, 2019); United States Selective Service System, *Selective*

two-thirds of those found guilty and 87 per cent of those who were executed for rape.[69] White soldiers were not only less likely to be tried for rape they were far more likely to have their sentences commuted or overturned. As scholars such as Mary Louise Roberts and J. Robert Lilly have argued, these statistics were largely the product of a racist military justice system, where white jurists presided over courts martial that were rushed and reached verdicts that were predicated on flimsy evidence.[70] African American troops were also overwhelmingly service troops working in rear areas, and thus more likely to be prosecuted in France and Germany than combat soldiers who were operating in a more chaotic environment where crimes were harder to document. The historian Ruth Lawlor however has argued that we need to understand this phenomenon as more than the simple export of Jim Crow practices to Europe. Local agency mattered and, as Lawlor argues,

> An encounter between an American soldier, black or white, and a European woman, was rarely just a meeting, sometimes violent, of two individuals. It was also a point of contact between the U.S. military – as a political and legal entity – and the different publics of each of these European nations.[71]

The rape statistics from the Second World War do more than tell a story of racial discrimination though. The 904 men put on trial represent a tiny fraction of the some 4 million Americans under arms who were at some point under the jurisdiction of US military courts in the European Theatre of Operations. While estimates of the number of women raped by American soldiers vary wildly – J. Robert Lilly claims the number is approximately 14,000, while historian Miriam Gebhardt claims that there were 190,000 rapes committed by American soldiers in Germany alone – it seems clear that the number of soldiers who were court-martialled bears little relation to the actual number of crimes committed.[72] This points to one of the fundamental problems faced by historians who write about sexual violence: the written record, which consists

Service and Victory: The 4th Report of the Director of Selective Service, 1944–1945, with a Supplement for 1946–1947 (Washington: U.S. Government Printing Office, 1948), 187.

[69] Lawlor, 'American Soldiers and the Politics of Rape in World War II Europe'.

[70] Roberts, *What Soldiers Do*, 195–254; J. Lilly, *Taken by Force: Rape and American GIs in Europe during World War II* (Basingstoke: Palgrave Macmillan, 2007). See also William I. Hitchcock, *The Bitter Road to Freedom: The Human Cost of Allied Victory in World War II Europe* (New York: Free Press, 2009), 50–5.

[71] Lawlor, 'American Soldiers and the Politics of Rape in World War II Europe'. See also Ruth Lawlor, 'Contested Crimes: Race, Gender, and Nation in Histories of GI Sexual Violence, World War II', *Journal of Military History* 84, no. 2 (2020): 541–70.

[72] Lilly, *Taken by Force*; Miriam Gebhardt, *Crimes Unspoken: The Rape of German Women at the End of the Second World War* (Cambridge: Polity Press, 2016).

almost entirely of court martial records, police reports and the occasional oral history, is fragmentary and partial. Rape is an under-reported crime under any circumstance, and doubly so in a wartime environment. Recovering and centring women's voices in these histories can be a difficult challenge, especially when the only place where these voices can be reliably found is the court martial transcript, where their testimony served a specific and narrow legal purpose.[73]

These difficulties can help to explain why the historiography on American military sexual violence is relatively limited. While there is an emerging literature on rape in the Second World War, the scholarship on other conflicts and time periods is much less well-developed. Sexual violence might appear in social histories of the Korean and Vietnam Wars, as well as the Cold War, but rarely is it the core focus of analysis.[74] Such scholarship that we do have tends to focus on well-known war crimes, where soldiers raped as well as murdered civilians. In the Vietnam War, this means the My Lai massacre; in the Iraq War, the Mahmudiyah rape and killings.[75] When it comes to American military occupation, the kidnap and rape of a schoolgirl by three US servicemen serving on Okinawa in 1995 stands out as a political flashpoint.[76] While it is of course vital to study these incidents, they only represent a fraction of the crimes committed and there remains an enormous amount of work to do to uncover these stories and tell the broader story of militarized American sexual violence.

Telling these stories matters not just because they can help us to better understand the experiences of women who were raped, or because sexual violence often sits on the fracture lines of racial or nationalist politics, but

---

[73] On the issue of women's voices being mediated in the court-room, see Atina Grossmann, 'A Question of Silence: The Rape of German Women by Occupation Soldiers', *October* 72 (1995): 43–63, https://doi.org/10.2307/77892. For a broader reflection on the difficulties of writing about sexual violence, see Amy Stanley, 'Writing the History of Sexual Assault in the Age of #MeToo', *Perspectives on History*, 24 September 2018, https://www.historians.org/publications-and-directories/perspectives-on-history/november-2018/writing-the-history-of-sexual-assault-in-the-age-of-metoo.

[74] Nick Turse, 'Rape Was Rampant during the Vietnam War. Why Doesn't US History Remember This?', *Mother Jones* (blog), 19 March 2013, https://www.motherjones.com/politics/2013/03/rape-wartime-vietnam/. For attempts to uncover histories of sexual violence in the post–Second World War period see Jennifer V. Evans, 'Protection from the Protector: Court-Martial Cases and the Lawlessness of Occupation in American-Controlled Berlin, 1945–48', in *GIs in Germany: The Social, Economic, Cultural, and Political History of the American Military Presence*, ed. Thomas W. Maulucci and Detlef Junker (Washington, DC: German Historical Institute; Cambridge University Press, 2013), 212–36; Gina Marie Weaver, *Ideologies of Forgetting: Rape in the Vietnam War* (Albany, NY: SUNY Press, 2012).

[75] Michal R. Belknap, *The Vietnam War on Trial: The My Lai Massacre and the Court-Martial of Lieutenant Calley* (Lawrence: University Press of Kansas, 2002), https://muse.jhu.edu/book/55581; Kendrick Oliver, *The My Lai Massacre in American History and Memory* (Manchester: Manchester University Press, 2006); Jim Frederick, *Black Hearts: One Platoon's Descent into Madness in Iraq's Triangle of Death* (London: Pan, 2011).

[76] Chalmers Johnson, 'The Okinawan Rape Incident and the End of the Cold War in East Asia', *California Western International Law Journal* 27 (1997): 389.

because systematically examining this phenomenon can shed light on how the US military as an institution has dealt with misogyny in its culture. Legal scholar Madeline Morris observed in the 1990s that while the rate of violent crime in the US military was often far lower than rates of violent crimes by civilians (controlling for age and gender), there is a 'rape differential', where military rape rates were in fact much closer to their civilian counterparts.[77] Moreover, Morris argued that at certain time periods in the Second World War, such as the breakout in France in 1944 and in Germany in 1945, the military rape rate jumped to more than four times the civilian rape rate. Explanations for this 'rape differential' tend to centre on military culture and particularly militarized forms of misogyny. By studying intimate as well as spectacular forms of violence, we can get a more complete picture of the behaviour of American troops overseas. Much as the wealth of armed Americans abroad helped structure their relationships with others, the fact that they were armed and were part of a huge military force had consequences as well. When it came to both intimate relationships and sexual violence, martial imperatives mattered, and military legal and regulatory frameworks helped to shape these encounters in important ways.

* * *

Because these encounters could be fraught and could have negative consequences, both politically and culturally, American military leaders often tried to minimize them or to prevent them from happening at all. To that, they enlisted civilian American women and private organizations to bring the home front to the battlefield and the Cold War outpost. As historian Kara Dixon Vuic recounts, groups such as the American Red Cross and the United Services Organizations (USO) mobilized ordinary people and celebrities alike to provide entertainment and relief to American GIs overseas.[78] These efforts ranged from the American Red Cross Clubmobile Service of the Second World War, which sent women around the battlefield in mobile kitchens to provide donuts and hot chocolate, to large-scale USO shows involving celebrities such as Bob Hope and Marilyn Monroe. From the 'donut dollies' of the Second World War or the Vietnam War to jobbing entertainers in Korea and Kuwait, these women were expected to affirm home front support for the troops and, especially during the First World War and the Second World War, to remind

---

[77] Madeline Morris, 'By Force of Arms: Rape, War, and Military Culture', *Duke Law Journal* 45, no. 4 (1996): 651–781, https://doi.org/10.2307/1372997.

[78] Kara Dixon Vuic, *The Girls Next Door: Bringing the Home Front to the Front Lines* (Cambridge, MA: Harvard University Press, 2019).

Figure 4.3 Actress Ann-Margret entertaining GIs in Long Binh, South Vietnam, 23 December 1968. Credit: Bettmann.

American service personnel overseas of the virtues of American womanhood and to help bring civilization to far-off places (Figure 4.3).[79]

The American Red Cross, in particular, made an effort to recruit 'the right sort' of women and to provide wholesome entertainment and comfort to the troops while alleviating their loneliness and feminizing the all-male military environment. Unlike the Red Cross and USO, which largely promoted a 'girl next door' image, groups that had less of a long-standing institutional relationship with the military embraced a more overtly sexualized form of entertainment. For instance, in 1966, Playboy sent Jo Collins, the 1965 Playmate of the Year, to tour South Vietnam and, more subversively, ran 'Operation Playmate', an effort to send signed photos of playmates to American soldiers deployed to Saudi Arabia during Operation Desert Shield.[80] Whether it was through providing donuts and hot chocolate or sexualized entertainment, the military enlisted

[79] Vuic, *The Girls Next Door*, 58–137; Heather Stur, 'Perfume and Lipstick in the Boonies: Red Cross SRAO and the Vietnam War', *The Sixties* 1, no. 2 (1 December 2008): 151–65, https://doi.org/10.1080/17541320802457079.

[80] Christian G. Appy, *Vietnam: The Definitive Oral History Told from All Sides* (London: Ebury, 2008), 28–30; Amber Batura, 'How Playboy Explains Vietnam', *New York Times*, 28 February 2017, https://www.nytimes.com/2017/02/28/opinion/how-playboy-explains-vietnam.html; Vuic, *The Girls Next Door*, 260. In the wake of the 9/11 attacks, 'Operation Playmate' was relaunched for a new generation of soldiers.

these civilian women to help raise morale and to keep soldiers away from vice and the temptation of foreign bars and foreign women.

In addition to providing wholesome entertainment, military leaders attempted to improve the behaviour and morale of American troops overseas by sending wives and families to accompany them. Much as with the 'donut dollies' of the Red Cross and the entertainers of the USO, military officials hoped that the presence of women and children would appropriately feminize the environment and – quite literally – domesticate their soldiers. In the wake of the Second World War, thousands of American women and children were sent to join their husbands and fathers who were stationed on overseas bases; by 1960, 600,000 armed forces personnel were deployed overseas, along with 462,000 military family members.[81] As historian Donna Alvah argues, military wives in particular also served an important role of 'unofficial ambassadors' during the Cold War, when they were encouraged to forge ties with local communities, run women's clubs, church and school events, and demonstrate American benevolence to allies and host countries.[82] Even children could be enlisted as ambassadors. A 1950s Army pamphlet for families stationed overseas made it clear that the Army considered public diplomacy to be a family affair: 'your children too, you must remember are just as much ambassadors of good will as you are ... Spoiled youngsters ... hamper our best efforts at promoting good relations abroad.'[83]

Children, however, were far from the greatest concern when it came to Americans making a bad impression overseas. Especially in the early years of the American occupation of Germany and Japan, the vast material gulf between the living circumstances of American and local families was manifest. Beginning in 1946, as families crossed the Atlantic and Pacific, US military authorities worked to improve the quality of overseas military housing to make it fit for family occupation, creating a series of 'little Americas' that contrasted sharply with rubble-strewn cities. As with the PX system, the living arrangements of American military families made clear just how well resourced the American military was. Senior officers lived in neo-colonial splendour in Japan, occupying some of the best houses in Tokyo and equipping their households with local servants, while ordinary military families were able to take advantage of the generous PX system and the strong dollar to live very comfortably.[84] As Susan Carruthers argues, the

[81] Donna Alvah, *Unofficial Ambassadors: American Military Families Overseas and the Cold War, 1946–1965* (New York: New York University Press, 2007), 2.
[82] Alvah's analysis builds on Cynthia Enloe's foundational work on the hidden role of diplomatic wives in the conduct of foreign policy. Enloe, *Bananas, Beaches and Bases*, 181–210.
[83] Alvah, *Unofficial Ambassadors*, 199.
[84] Dower, *Embracing Defeat*, 207–9.

presence of military families and the construction of special housing for them 'did more to exaggerate the socioeconomic gulf between occupiers and occupied than to close it'.[85] Later in the Cold War, such communities became a security concern, as terrorist groups targeted military housing in Germany, straining US–German relations and putting military families at the centre of geopolitics.[86]

While hundreds of thousands of military family members moved overseas in the aftermath of the Second World War, these numbers were dwarfed by the flow of people moving inwards, as the actions of the United States in the world produced militarized migration networks that spanned continents and, in some cases, decades.[87] Even as ships full of military families crossed the Atlantic in 1946, passenger liners brought thousands of European brides of GIs in the other direction. Transporting these women quickly became a logistical and political headache, as thousands of British wives of American soldiers marched on the US embassy in October 1945 with cries of 'we want transport' and 'we want our husbands'.[88] Congress rushed to pass the War Brides Act in December 1945, easing immigration restrictions to allow families to reunite. Beginning in January 1946, the US military shipped 38,723 dependents from the United Kingdom to the United States in what the press dubbed 'Operation Diaper Run'.[89] The RMS *Queen Mary* alone transported some 2,300 women in one trip, with the now-empty indoor swimming pool converted into a drying room for nappies.[90] Meanwhile, in the United States, American wives of GIs still stationed overseas and awaiting demobilization protested the use of scarce shipping resources for these women, arguing that the return of their husbands should be prioritized instead. All told, at least 125,000 GI marriages resulted from the Second World War.

The War Brides Act itself enabled 114,000 wives to enter the United States. Of those, the overwhelming majority – 85,000 of them – were Europeans, and

[85] Carruthers, *The Good Occupation*, 286.

[86] 'U.S. Military Housing Area in Germany Is Bombed', *New York Times*, 1 November 1982, https://www.nytimes.com/1982/11/01/world/us-military-housing-area-in-germany-is-bombed.html; Daniel J. Nelson, *Defenders or Intruders?: The Dilemmas Of U.S. Forces in Germany* (Abingdon: Routledge, 1987).

[87] For two excellent surveys of the literature on the links between war, militarization and migration in US history, see Paul A. Kramer, 'The Geopolitics of Mobility: Immigration Policy and American Global Power in the Long Twentieth Century', *American Historical Review* 123, no. 2 (1 April 2018): 393–438, https://doi.org/10.1093/ahr/123.2.393; Ellen D. Wu, 'It's Time to Center War in U.S. Immigration History', *Modern American History* 2, no. 2 (July 2019): 215–35, https://doi.org/10.1017/mah.2019.6.

[88] Reynolds, *Rich Relations*, 418.

[89] Reynolds, *Rich Relations*, 420.

[90] Jenel Virden, *Good-Bye, Piccadilly: British War Brides in America* (Urbana: University of Illinois Press, 1996), 77; Reynolds, *Rich Relations*, 420.

white English-speaking women (not only from Britain and Ireland but also Canada, Australia and New Zealand) accounted for over half of all immigrating war brides.[91] After the fraternization ban was lifted, these women were joined by a large number of Germans, with Germany providing the second largest number of war brides after Britain.[92] The stories told in the press about these women, both in the United States and Europe, depicted them as successful new Americans: stylish, modern wives and paragons of the 'American Dream'.[93] As the statistics suggest though, the overwhelming whiteness of post–Second World War brides indicates the structural barriers put in the way of African American soldiers and non-white women alike. Military commanders often refused to sanction interracial marriages and women were refused entry to the United States due to racist immigration laws.[94] This stance only began to soften with the McCarren–Walter Act of 1952, which abolished racial bars to entry and citizenship (although it still maintained racial quotas). In part, these changes could be attributed not only to the needs of the Cold War propaganda campaigns but also to the activism of both veterans and GIs and the arguments that they made about military service, patriotism and the need to re-unify military families.[95]

The politics of family reunification were also complicated by the children of GIs. Everywhere American soldiers went, they left behind children produced by their relationships with local women. These children often faced difficult upbringings, especially when they were mixed-race. In post-Second World War Britain, nearly half of these 'brown babies' were given to children's homes, but few were adopted.[96] In Germany, these children faced stigmatization and discrimination while the West German government, deeming Germany incapable of absorbing them, made efforts to have them adopted by African American military families and brought to the United States.[97] Mixed-race children in Japan faced possibly

---

[91] Susan Zeiger, *Entangling Alliances: Foreign War Brides and American Soldiers in the Twentieth Century* (New York: New York University Press, 2010), 72.

[92] Raingard Esser, '"Language No Obstacle": War Brides in the German Press, 1945–49', *Women's History Review* 12, no. 4 (1 December 2003): 582, https://doi.org/10.1080/09612020300200375.

[93] Esser, '"Language No Obstacle"'.

[94] Zeiger, *Entangling Alliances*, 132–6.

[95] Angela Lynn Tudico, '"They're Bringing Home Japanese Wives": Japanese War Brides in the Postwar Era' (University of Maryland, 2009); Philip E. Wolgin and Irene Bloemraad, '"Our Gratitude to Our Soldiers": Military Spouses, Family Re-Unification, and Postwar Immigration Reform', *Journal of Interdisciplinary History* 41, no. 1 (2010): 27–60.

[96] Lucy Bland, *Britain's 'Brown Babies': The Stories of Children Born to Black GIs and White Women in the Second World War* (Manchester: Manchester University Press, 2019).

[97] Stephanie Siek, 'Germany's "Brown Babies": The Difficult Identities of Post-War Black Children of GIs', *Spiegel Online*, 13 October 2009, sec. International, https://www.spiegel.de/international/germany/germany-s-brown-babies-the-difficult-identities-of-post-war-black-children-of-gis-a-651989.html; Sabine Lee, 'A Forgotten Legacy of the Second World War: GI Children in

the most difficult upbringing, as US military authorities largely ignored them while Japanese nationalists railed against the 'blood mixing' that these children represented and argued that both foreign troops and mixed-race children be expelled from Japan so that it might be reconstructed as a 'pure-blood' nation.[98]

Concern for the plight of GI babies, especially those born in Asia, moved groups to campaign for emergency measures to evacuate them. As historian Arissa Oh has documented, the very practice of organized international adoption has its origins in the aftermath of the Korean War, as veterans' groups and Christian organizations worked to have the unwanted Korean children of American soldiers adopted in the United States.[99] The Vietnam War produced similar dynamics. In April 1975, as the People's Army of Vietnam closed in on Saigon, the US Air Force evacuated two thousand Vietnamese orphans (many of them fathered by US military personnel) in Operation Babylift, a mission that was sold as a form of national redemption in the face of defeat in Southeast Asia.[100] President Gerald Ford personally greeted one flight of 325 Vietnamese orphans when it landed in San Francisco Airport.[101] This spectacle was eventually followed on a policy level by the Amerasian Immigration Act of 1982 and the Amerasian Homecoming Act of 1987, which allowed the children of US servicemen to resettle in the United States.[102]

These orphans represented only the tip of the iceberg though. In the aftermath of the Vietnam War, over 1 million Vietnamese, Hmong and Cambodians migrated to the United States, constituting, as historian Ellen Wu observes, the largest refugee resettlement programme in American history.[103] Therefore, to

Post-War Britain and Germany', *Contemporary European History* 20, no. 2 (May 2011): 157–81, https://doi.org/10.1017/S096077731100004X.

[98] Kristin Roebuck, 'Orphans by Design: "Mixed-Blood" Children, Child Welfare, and Racial Nationalism in Postwar Japan', *Japanese Studies* 36, no. 2 (3 May 2016): 191–212, https://doi.org/10.1080/10371397.2016.1209969.

[99] Arissa Oh, *To Save the Children of Korea: The Cold War Origins of International Adoption* (Stanford, CA: Stanford University Press, 2015).

[100] Allison Varzally, *Children of Reunion: Vietnamese Adoptions and the Politics of Family Migrations* (Chapel Hill: University of North Carolina Press, 2017); Heather Marie Stur, '"Hiding behind the Humanitarian Label": Refugees, Repatriates, and the Rebuilding of America's Benevolent Image after the Vietnam War', *Diplomatic History* 39, no. 2 (1 April 2015): 223–44, https://doi.org/10.1093/dh/dht128.

[101] Bob Sigall, 'Pan Am Flight Out of Saigon in '75 Changed Lives Forever', *Honolulu Star - Advertiser*, 12 August 2016, sec. Business, http://search.proquest.com/docview/1811054028/abstract/A2D32FC019DE4280PQ/17.

[102] Jana K. Lipman, '"The Face Is the Road Map": Vietnamese Amerasians in U.S. Political and Popular Culture, 1980-1988', *Journal of Asian American Studies* 14, no. 1 (23 February 2011): 33–68, https://doi.org/10.1353/jaas.2011.0009; Jana K. Lipman, 'A Refugee Camp in America: Fort Chaffee and Vietnamese and Cuban Refugees, 1975-1982', *Journal of American Ethnic History* 33, no. 2 (2014): 57–87, https://doi.org/10.5406/jamerethnhist.33.2.0057.

[103] Wu, 'It's Time to Center War in U.S. Immigration History', 4.

fully understand the sort of migration prompted by American war-making, we need to look beyond intimate relations and examine how the destruction and economic demands of war alike shaped US immigration history in profound ways. While Southeast Asian refugees were facilitated by the US government, refugees fleeing violence in Central America fuelled by US paramilitary and covert assistance received no such welcome.[104] The Reagan administration routinely refused asylum to applicants attempting to escape right-wing violence in El Salvador and Guatemala, while they and other administrations welcomed anti-communist refugees from places like Cuba and Hungary. Where the US government has been able to blame its enemies for violence, refugees have been more welcome than when the United States itself was culpable. Such sentiments, along with Islamophobia, might explain why between 2003 and 2007 the United States only admitted 701 refugees from Iraq out of a total displaced population of 2 million. As Wu argues, this policy has exacerbated the global refugee problem caused by the US 'war on terror'.[105]

Historian Paul Kramer has contended that the different treatment meted out to different categories of war refugees reveals that 'modern state boundaries are best imagined not as walls but as filters, usually seeking less to block human movement entirely than to select, channel, and discipline it'. Kramer argues that the geopolitics of militarized migration has led to the construction of 'an institutional matrix that has sought to streamline migration in the interests of state and corporate power through active recruitment, sponsorship, visa policies, and transport infrastructure'.[106] Certainly, military necessity prompted different types of migration. Operation Paperclip, the mass relocation of German scientists and engineers after the Second World War to work on US aerospace programmes, represents one end of the scale; the *bracero* programme that imported temporary Mexican farmworkers into the US Southwest to address wartime labour shortages, the other.[107] Notably, the German scientists, even though many were Nazis, were well-treated and offered permanent residency and even citizenship. The Mexican labourers suffered low pay, poor working conditions and were given no such path to permanency before the programme ended in 1964. Both programmes were designed to maximize the military power of the United States. The history

---

[104] Wu, 'It's Time to Center War in U.S. Immigration History', 4.
[105] Wu, 'It's Time to Center War in U.S. Immigration History', 5.
[106] Kramer, 'The Geopolitics of Mobility', 399.
[107] Annie Jacobsen, *Operation Paperclip: The Secret Intelligence Program That Brought Nazi Scientists to America* (New York: Little, Brown, 2014); Mae M. Ngai, *Impossible Subjects: Illegal Aliens and the Making of Modern America* (Princeton, NJ: Princeton University Press, 2014), 127–66.

of migration associated with the US military, however, also suggests that such flows of people cannot always be disciplined. Whether it was the establishment of post–Second World War Samoan migrant labour networks centred on American naval bases in Hawai'i and California, or English war brides marching on to the US embassy in protest at their separation from their husbands, people's desire to cross borders created challenges for the functioning of American power.[108] If the United States is popularly understood as being a nation of immigrants, it was worth noting just how much of that immigration was caused by war and military necessity.

* * *

The activities of the American military in the world certainly generated a global flow of people moving both to and from the United States, but ideas as well as people crossed borders. American veterans returning from war brought new concepts and customs with them. These ranged from the deeply political to the very ordinary, but all had their own impact on domestic politics. Often, these new ideas related to identity. For many, the experience of military service overseas was about thinking more deeply about what it meant to be American.[109] But the context in which this process of reflection occurred matters: being overseas, these GIs also inevitably compared themselves to the people they interacted with. As they travelled through foreign lands, their ideas about American identity and society changed in sometimes unpredictable ways. Unlike earlier wars, few military units in the Second World War or subsequent conflicts were organized along regional lines, so troops encountered fellow Americans of different regions, ethnicities and races. As historian Gary Gerstle has argued, the Second World War movie trope of the multicultural 'melting pot' platoon of white soldiers of different ethnicities points to how these experiences were supposed to produce national unity.[110] The problem of race was not so easily solved, however. The military of the Second World War remained largely segregated, to the point where Red Cross blood supplies were racially segregated, so that white soldiers could never receive Black blood and vice versa.[111]

[108] Robert W. Franco, 'Samoan Representations of World War II and Military Work: The Emergence of International Movement Networks', in *The Pacific Theater: Island Representations of World War II*, ed. Geoffrey M. White and Lamont Lindstrom (Honolulu: University of Hawaii Press, 1989).

[109] For a superb account about 'becoming American' overseas, see Brooke L. Blower, *Becoming Americans in Paris: Transatlantic Politics and Culture between the World Wars* (New York: Oxford University Press, 2011).

[110] Gary Gerstle, *American Crucible: Race and Nation in the Twentieth Century*, repr. edn (Princeton, NJ: Princeton University Press, 2017), 204–6.

[111] Thomas A. Guglielmo, ' "Red Cross, Double Cross": Race and America s World War II-Era Blood Donor Service', *Journal of American History* 97, no. 1 (2010): 63–90.

African American experience of segregation overseas fed back into the civil rights movement at home. The 'Double-V' campaign that promoted victory over fascism abroad and over racism at home positioned African Americans to comingle participation in the war effort with protest.[112] Touring the Mediterranean and European Theatres at the behest of the War Department in 1944, Walter White, the chairman of the NAACP, observed that American race relations in Italy were far better than in England. The difference was that, in Italy, white and Black troops fought in combat together, whereas in England they did not.[113] Integration was hardly a panacea though, and frustration at its uneven implementation in the Korean War led to a decline in African American support for that conflict.[114] Nor did overseas service always straightforwardly lead African American GIs to more loudly advocate for Civil Rights in the broader sense. At times, this overseas experience certainly pushed them to reflect more on the flaws of American society for, as Martin Klimke has argued, in Germany, 'the experience of black GIs in the immediate postwar period was one of liberation from the legal and social constraints that confined them in American society'.[115] By contrast, Michael Cullen Green has claimed that the experience of African American troops in the Pacific in the aftermath of the Second World War in fact led them to adopt the same racialized attitudes towards Asians held by their white counterparts and led many of them to support the expansion of the American military presence in Asia.[116]

The experience of war in Vietnam soured these benign views of American military power. As it did at home, discontent about the war spread among African American soldiers stationed on bases overseas. In Germany, over 1,000 Black Panther GIs attended an anti-war protest in Heidelberg on 4 July 1970, where they were closely monitored by military intelligence.[117] Discontent also stemmed from the racial discrimination that Black GIs faced from the military justice system and German civilians alike. One Army Sergeant summed up the depth of frustration: 'The black man's got no business being in the Army if this

---

[112] For a broader discussion of the integration of the armed forces and the place of African Americans within the military, see Chapter 5.

[113] Gerstle, *American Crucible*, 228.

[114] Mitchell Lerner, ' "Is It for This We Fought and Bled?": The Korean War and the Struggle for Civil Rights', *Journal of Military History* 82, no. 2 (April 2018): 515–45.

[115] Martin Klimke, 'The African-American Civil Rights Struggle and Germany, 1945–1989', *GHI Bulletin*, no. 43 (Fall 2008): 96.

[116] Michael Cullen Green, *Black Yanks in the Pacific: Race in the Making of American Military Empire after World War II*, 1st edn (Ithaca, NY: Cornell University Press, 2010).

[117] Höhn, 'The Racial Crisis of 1971 in the US Military', 316; De Nike, 'The US Military and Dissenters in the Ranks', 308.

mess keeps up. They keep killing our people back home and we're still being sent out to the Nam! We fight there and then we're shipped to Germany and we fill the jails here.'[118] If being a Black American in post–Second World War Germany meant experiencing more freedom and equality than at home, then the experience of the 1970s seemed to be about a deepening sense of alienation on the part of African American GIs instead. Radical GIs made contact with the German student movement, while others drew inspiration from the West German soldiers' movement and the experience of Dutch soldiers who had recently won the right to collective bargaining.[119] Both American military authorities and the German government moved to try to head off radicalism; German Chancellor Willy Brandt and Minister for Defence Helmut Schmidt publicly decried racism against Black GIs, while the US Seventh Army worked to diversify both unit command and the curriculum in schools for the children of military personnel.[120] These concerted efforts did manage to succeed in diminishing Black GI militancy, but the fact that they necessitated the intervention of the German Chancellor speaks both to the depth of the crisis and the fact that it was one with international ramifications.

The experience of the Vietnam War did not just lead African American soldiers to rethink how they related to the rest of the country. As Kathleen Belew documents in her book *Bring the War Home*, the contemporary White Power movement also had its origins in the Vietnam experience. White supremacists such as Louis Beam were radicalized by the conflict and saw themselves as continuing the war against a non-white 'other' at home. Claiming they were betrayed by an American government that lost the war in Vietnam, returning veterans re-energized movements like the Ku Klux Klan.[121] Indeed, the Texas branch of the Klan focused their energies on burning out the fishing boats of recently resettled Vietnamese refugees in Galveston Bay, a stark illustration of the ways in which these violent white supremacists understood themselves to be bringing the war home.[122] As Belew argues, the actions of the Oklahoma City

---

[118] Christian G. Appy, *Working-Class War: American Combat Soldiers and Vietnam* (Chapel Hill: University of North Carolina Press, 1993), 19; James E. Westheider, *Fighting on Two Fronts: African Americans and the Vietnam War* (New York: New York University Press, 1999), 11–16.

[119] Maria Höhn, 'The Black Panther Solidarity Committees and the Voice of the Lumpen', *German Studies Review* 31, no. 1 (2008): 133–54; De Nike, 'The US Military and Dissenters in the Ranks', 303–4.

[120] Höhn, 'The Racial Crisis of 1971 in the US Military', 320–2.

[121] Kathleen Belew, *Bring the War Home: The White Power Movement and Paramilitary America* (Cambridge, MA: Harvard University Press, 2018).

[122] Belew, *Bring the War Home*, 40–52.

bomber, Gulf War veteran Timothy McVeigh, fit into this broader pattern of a militarized White Power movement drawing inspiration from overseas wars by attacking the federal government at home.[123]

More recently, we saw an even more direct attempt to bring the war home with the attack on the US Capitol building on 6 January 2021. Estimates vary, but between 10 per cent and 20 per cent of those charged for their role in the attempt to overturn the results of a democratic election were either veterans or active-duty military, and many of them were veterans of Iraq or Afghanistan.[124] Certainly, the point is not that these insurrectionists were representative of the military as a whole, but the comments of some of the rioters that they had a right to be on the Senate floor because they were veterans is telling.[125] As the journalist Spencer Ackerman argues, many of the practices and paranoid tendencies of the War on Terror were brought home into American politics, and militia membership numbers surged, as they did in the aftermath of the Vietnam War.[126] Scholars still have much work to do to unpack the ideologies behind the events of that day, particularly when it comes to these connections between foreign war and domestic insurrection, but we see how complicated their task will be just by looking at who was represented in the crowds that surged into the halls of Congress. Among the flags waving on the steps of the Capitol was none other than the yellow and red of the Republic of Vietnam (RVN), a polity that has been defunct since 1975.[127] The presence of Vietnamese Americans at what has rightly been termed a white supremacist insurrection gives some sense of how the effects of American wars have reverberated in strange ways, and of how the wartime flow of both people and ideas has had unexpected consequences.

* * *

[123] Belew, *Bring the War Home*, 209–34. While Belew uncovers a history of organized White Power violence within the United States, Kyle Burke has demonstrated how American anti-communist paramilitaries in the Cold War often explicitly attempted to export white supremacist ideas abroad. Kyle Burke, *Revolutionaries for the Right: Anticommunist Internationalism and Paramilitary Warfare in the Cold War* (Chapel Hill: University of North Carolina Press, 2018).

[124] Tom Dreisbach and Meg Anderson, 'Nearly 1 in 5 Defendants in Capitol Riot Cases Served in the Military', NPR.org, 5, accessed 24 June 2021, https://www.npr.org/2021/01/21/958915267/nearly-one-in-five-defendants-in-capitol-riot-cases-served-in-the-military; Marshall Cohen, '1 in 10 Defendants from US Capitol Insurrection Have Military Ties', CNN, 28 May 2021,https://www.cnn.com/2021/05/28/politics/capitol-insurrection-veterans/index.html.

[125] Jennifer Steinhauer, 'In the Battle for the Capitol, Veterans Fought on Opposite Sides', *New York Times*, 8 February 2021, sec. U.S., https://www.nytimes.com/2021/02/08/us/politics/capitol-riot-trump-veterans-cops.html.

[126] Spencer Ackerman, *Reign of Terror: How the 9/11 Era Destabilized America and Produced Trump* (New York: Viking, 2021).

[127] Viet Thanh Nguyen, 'There's a Reason the South Vietnamese Flag Flew during the Capitol Riot', *Washington Post*, 14 January 2021, https://www.washingtonpost.com/outlook/2021/01/14/south-vietnam-flag-capitol-riot/.

Klan attacks on Vietnamese fishermen in Galveston and RVN flags on the steps of the Capitol illustrate two of the ways in which the presence of armed Americans overseas reshaped the United States itself: both attacks highlighted both how American wars and the presence of the US military abroad inspired international migration on a mass scale, and how the experience of being overseas prompted veterans to think anew about American identity. This particular rethinking may have led to the reinforcement of white supremacist ideas, but at other times, veterans took more internationalist lessons from their time abroad. When thinking about the experience of armed Americans overseas though, the effect of these encounters on the United States pales in comparison with the effect they had elsewhere. The image of the United States was closely tied up with the impression made by military personnel overseas. Military commanders were very much aware of this fact, as we have seen in the example of the attempt to enlist the children of American soldiers serving in Europe into Cold War public diplomacy. However, such encounters were too numerous and too various for government authorities to be able to control them in such a way as to provide any unified message.

As Susan Carruthers has observed of the post–Second World War occupation forces, 'members of America's "after-armies" were variously, and sometimes simultaneously, guards, police, judges, teachers, aid workers, athletes, actors, tourists, and students'.[128] Historians have done important work in excavating how they fulfilled these roles in various places and at various times. Taken together, these histories demonstrate that the actions of military forces overseas had profoundly important consequences beyond the battlefield. Sometimes intentionally, often by accident, American soldiers reshaped the politics, economies, societies and cultures of the countries they lived or fought in, even as local actors resisted or shaped American policies for their own ends. From the camptowns of South Korea to the black markets of Saigon to the dance halls of East Anglia, the everyday actions of American military personnel had political consequences.

In sketching the histories of these everyday encounters though, we should not forget that behind their roles as tourists, consumers, aid givers or romantic partners, American GIs abroad were, in the final reckoning, soldiers who belonged to an enormous military machine. Much as the nostalgic retelling of the Second World War by scholars like Stephen Ambrose might suggest otherwise, what foreigners noticed the most about the Americans among them

---

[128] Carruthers, *The Good Occupation*, 241.

was not their generosity in dispensing chocolate bars or their wealth but their raw martial power. David Reynolds notes that one of the things that ordinary British people most remembered about the American military presence during the Second World War was the build to the D-Day landings, where they observed 'the truly awesome sight of American power wending its way down to the ports of southern England'.[129] In telling the stories of armed Americans abroad, it is important to keep the military power that shaped these encounters at the forefront of our minds.

---

[129] Reynolds, *Rich Relations*, 438.

5

Military service and the meanings of citizenship

In November 1990, the US Supreme Court brought a remarkable legal saga to an end when it upheld, without comment, the ruling of the Court of Appeals for the Ninth Circuit in *Watkins vs United States Army*. That court had ordered the Army to reinstate Staff Sergeant Perry Watkins into its ranks, and awarded him back pay, retirement benefits and retroactive promotion to Sergeant First Class five years after he had been dismissed from military service for being a declared homosexual. What made Watkins different from the many other service members dismissed from the military for their sexuality is that he had been openly gay since his enlistment in 1967; indeed, his induction papers noted that he was a homosexual and he again declared his sexuality when he successfully re-enlisted in the Army in 1971.[1] The fact that Watkins had told his superiors that he was gay on several occasions and yet continued to serve in an exemplary fashion for fourteen years was the key factor in convincing the courts to overturn the Army's decision to dismiss him.

So how did Watkins manage a long and (until his dismissal) successful career in the Army in an era where gay men and women were prohibited from military service? After being drafted in August 1967, Watkins had checked the box on his medical history chart at his pre-induction physical examination that indicated that he had homosexual tendencies. The examining psychologist evidently did not believe him and designated him as qualified for induction. Watkins twice requested discharge because he was gay and was denied both times, even though he had been removed from Chaplain's Assistant training school after basic

---

[1] Randy Shilts, *Conduct Unbecoming: Lesbians and Gays in the U.S. Military: Vietnam to the Persian Gulf* (New York: St. Martin's Press, 1993), 61–3. Shilts's book contains the most detailed treatment of Watkins's career and his case against the US Army. To date, it is the only long-form account of the case.

training because he was an admitted homosexual. Years later, Watkins made it clear he believed that race was a factor in the Army's decision-making:

> Every white person that I know ... who checked that box yes, was told 'Nope, you can't go in.' This was not just an isolated case. This was probably very common practice, particularly among people who felt like, oh, well yes, let's send all the blacks to Vietnam. I mean ... The reason I was drafted is simply because they didn't expect me to be here in twenty years to talk about it.[2]

Watkins went on to re-enlist, again marking 'yes' to having homosexual tendencies in his medical questionnaire. He served two tours in Korea and one in Germany. While serving in Germany, he performed in drag as 'Simone' in Army clubs throughout Europe. He received several commendations for his work and was described as an 'exemplary soldier' by his commanding officer. Later, in court testimony, several of his former commanders noted that his sexuality had had no detrimental impact whatsoever on his performance.[3]

As the Army tightened its regulations on homosexuality, he found that his career began running into difficulties. In 1975, without warning, his then-commanding officer unsuccessfully attempted to discharge him for homosexuality, beginning a years-long administrative and legal ordeal. On several occasions, the Army attempted to remove Watkins's 'secret' security clearance, although the fact that Watkins was openly gay helped him win an appeal on this front, as military authorities had to admit that it was very unlikely that he could be blackmailed over his sexuality when he had never denied it in the first place. Finally, in 1979, his security clearance was permanently revoked, and the Army began proceedings to discharge him in 1981. In 1983, with his dismissal still working its way through the courts, the Army barred him from performing in drag on military bases.[4] Watkins was forced out with an honourable discharge when his enlistment expired in 1984, although he continued to fight the case in court. Finally, in 1989, the Ninth Circuit voted 7–4 to order the Army to allow Watkins to re-enlist. The decision was a narrowly constructed one, as it didn't make any pronouncement on whether or not homosexuals had the right to serve in the military but instead focused on the fact that the Army had initially been content to let Watkins enlist and then re-enlist as a gay man, only to change its mind later.[5] After the Supreme Court affirmed the verdict, Watkins took a

[2] Eric Marcus, 'Perry Watkins', Making Gay History: The Podcast, accessed 30 March 2020, https://makinggayhistory.com/podcast/perry-watkins/.
[3] Watkins v. United States Army, 721 F. 2d 687 (Court of Appeals, 9th Circuit 1983).
[4] 'No Dancing Allowed', Jet, 10 January 1983.
[5] Watkins v. US Army, 875 F. 2d 699 (Court of Appeals, 9th Circuit 1988).

settlement and opted for an honourable discharge and retirement rather than re-enlistment.[6] He marched in uniform as a Grand Marshal at San Francisco Pride in 1993 but did not live to enjoy his legal victory for long, passing away from complications due to AIDS in 1996.[7] Although he has been less celebrated than the white gay veterans who came after him, such as Leonard Matlovich in the Air Force and Keith Meinhold in the Navy, Watkins's long military career as an openly gay man and a drag artist is perhaps one of the most remarkable stories in the history of the long battle to end the exclusion of gay men and women from military service.

Watkins's story may have been unique but it also points to broader themes that this chapter will explore. Firstly, the Army's decision to induct Watkins despite his declared homosexuality has to be understood not only in terms of his race but also in light of the organization's manpower needs during the Vietnam War. The military has always had a history of tightening or loosening its enlistment requirements depending on the size of the pool of men (and later women) available to it. Watkins had had no desire to join the military, but he was nonetheless drafted and then found that an escape route frequently used by middle-class men – a declaration of homosexuality – was denied to him. Secondly, even if Watkins did not initially choose the military as a career, he chose to re-enlist because he found it to be a useful vehicle for socio-economic advancement. Years later, he told an interviewer: 'I worked in personnel, I went to college and got a four year degree. I travelled, I lived in Europe for eight years, I lived in Korea for two, I learned a lot about people, I learned a lot about myself, I enjoyed my life, I enjoyed my work.'[8] Thirdly, the Army's efforts to eventually dismiss Watkins demonstrate how an institution that frequently declared that it was not in the business of 'social engineering' worked hard to promote and enforce its own ideas about gender and sexual norms, even at the cost of dismissing a soldier who was, by their own admission, exemplary in the performance of his duties. After his dismissal from the Army, Watkins lost the house that he had bought with his middle-class wages and spent years in poverty trying to recover the life denied to him by the Army's disapproval of his homosexuality.

---

[6] 'Ending Long Fight, Ousted Gay Soldier Settles with Army', *New York Times*, 31 January 1991, https://www.nytimes.com/1991/01/31/us/ending-long-fight-ousted-gay-soldier-settles-with-army.html.

[7] David W. Dunlap, 'Perry Watkins, 48, Gay Sergeant Won Court Battle with Army', *New York Times*, 21 March 1996, sec. New York, https://www.nytimes.com/1996/03/21/nyregion/perry-watkins-48-gay-sergeant-won-court-battle-with-army.html.

[8] Marcus, 'Perry Watkins'.

Above all else though, Watkins's story demonstrates the deep ties between military service and concepts of citizenship. Broader debates over what rights and obligations Americans had as citizens often played out with reference to military service, and the needs of the national security state often shaped the state's approach to these questions as well. In the Watkins case, while the Ninth Circuit's decision ultimately avoided broader questions about civil rights, Judge William Allen Norris, in a concurring opinion, went beyond the majority's focus on administrative fairness, and intervened in the debate over citizenship and rights, arguing that the Army's treatment of Watkins violated the Equal Protection clause of the Constitution. Norris compared the Army's position on homosexuals to earlier racial discrimination and accused the Army of 'catering to private biases'. He noted the Army's professed fear that allowing openly gay soldiers to serve could cause hostilities in the ranks struck 'an all-too-familiar chord' and argued that while 'for much of our history, the military's fear of racial tension kept black soldiers separated from whites ... today is unthinkable that the judiciary would defer to the Army's prior "professional" judgment that black and white soldiers had to be segregated to avoid interracial tensions'.[9] Thus, the Watkins case demonstrated how tightly bound up military service was with questions about the rights and obligations of citizenship. Marginalized groups have frequently asserted their right to serve in the military as a way of affirming their full membership of American society. At the same time, the burdens of military service have often fallen heavily on some of those same groups, creating a tension between desires to don a uniform in order to stake a claim for full rights and complaints that not everyone shared the burdens of war equally.

Military service was not the only way in which the preparation for war affected citizenship. At various times, the American state promoted scientists, factory work, the nuclear family and civil defence preparedness as essential to national defence. Given the breadth of activities and roles that could be considered as vital to American security, it is no surprise that militarization shaped the relationship between the federal government and American citizens, and indeed notions of what it meant to be American in the first place. From managing draft exemptions in a way that channelled manpower to the right parts of the economy, to social welfare policies specifically targeting military personnel and veterans, to civil defence plans that emphasized private responsibility and the primacy of the nuclear family, the American state acted to promote, sometimes inadvertently, a militarized form of citizenship.

---

[9] Watkins v. US Army, 875 F. 2d at 728–9 Norris, W. concurring.

This chapter traces that evolving relationship between citizenship and militarization by examining how the changing nature of military service and expanded concepts of national security shaped American ideas about what citizenship meant. The transformation wrought by the Second World War on the American state meant not only that citizen soldiers were elevated to previously unseen heights in public regard but also that social policy was ever more shaped around the needs of those citizen soldiers, as a federal government made more activist by the needs of the war moved to ensure both that soldiers would have the materiel they needed to fight the war and that they would be looked after when they returned home. Consequently, the GI Bill shaped post-war federal welfare policies, while debates over Universal Military Training and the implementation of desegregation and Selective Service meant that the military both became an important engine for social change and reaffirmed military service as a rite of passage and a marker of full citizenship for men, even as the broader needs of Cold War preparedness opened up different ways for Americans to serve.

The failures of the Vietnam War effectively brought an end to that particular form of militarized citizenship. In a reflection of growing doubts about the value of military service, the African American press went from celebrating the number of Black GIs proudly serving their country to decrying a system that seemed to put those same GIs in harm's way at a much greater rate than it did white soldiers. The war also exposed the iniquities of a draft system that conscripted working-class men at high rates while offering generous exemptions to the middle class and the wealthy. Not only that, but groups such as scientists, university administrators and even labour unions who had seen themselves as playing a part in national defence now baulked at the militarized understanding of their role.

The end of the draft and the advent of the All-Volunteer Force profoundly changed the relationship between the military and broader American society. The citizen soldier was effectively relegated to a rhetorical trope, even as the military began to meaningfully open its ranks to the half of the population that had been excluded from military service when it began removing barriers that had prevented women from serving in large numbers. As it did so, the military found itself competing with other employers in the marketplace, and military service became the preserve of fewer and fewer Americans. Given concerns that the military would fail to fill its ranks without a draft to support it, the All-Volunteer Force necessitated the construction of a more generous military welfare state to support it and also had the contradictory effect of placing soldiers on pedestals as 'warriors' while at the same time promoting what sociologist Charles Moskos called 'occupationalism' within the military – the sense that the military was 'just another job'.[10] The long years of war in Iraq, Afghanistan and elsewhere only further deepened the divide between what were now termed 'warriors' and the American public that they ostensibly served. Even if the military was smaller and more insular, it was still a site where Americans contested citizenship and identity, as the Trump administration's ban on transgender people from serving in the military and its attempts to close off military service as a pathway for immigrants to become citizens demonstrates. Thus, even as the nature of military service changed, militarization continued to have a profound impact on notions of citizenship as well as the nature of the American state.

* * *

As many scholars have argued, the Second World War cemented a consensus on the need for a stronger and more activist federal government, a matter that had been up for debate during the earlier years of the New Deal.[11] What had been controversial in the Depression-era 1930s became a necessity during the wartime 1940s. Increased taxation, more overt government coordination of the economy and increased federal protections for citizens became commonplace, as we saw in Chapter 2. In his book, *Warfare State*, though, historian James Sparrow notes that it was striking that all of these developments were symbolically oriented around the needs of the combat soldier.[12] For instance, much of the federal government's wartime spending was financed via war bonds, which were marketed directly to the public as a patriotic duty. Bond drives would often have communities 'buy' specific pieces of equipment, offering them a tangible connection to the frontlines through the B-17 bomber or Sherman tank that they had purchased for the troops.[13] Not only were civilians encouraged to see themselves as connected to the battlefield, they were also invited to think about the repercussions of their actions – whether it be wasting food or making a mistake on the production line – for the combat soldier. And while labour unions promoted the notion that factory workers were 'home front soldiers of

---

[10] Charles C. Moskos, ed., *The Postmodern Military: Armed Forces after the Cold War* (New York: Oxford University Press, 2000).

[11] David Goldfield, *The Gifted Generation: When Government Was Good* (New York: Bloomsbury USA, 2017); Walter W. Heller, 'Activist Government: Key to Growth', *Challenge* 29, no. 1 (1986): 4–10; James T. Sparrow, *Warfare State: World War II Americans and the Age of Big Government* (Oxford: Oxford University Press, 2011); Mark R. Wilson, *Destructive Creation: American Business and the Winning of World War II* (Philadelphia: University of Pennsylvania Press, 2016).

[12] James T. Sparrow, ' "Buying Our Boys Back": The Mass Foundations of Fiscal Citizenship in World War II', *Journal of Policy History* 20, no. 2 (April 2008): 263–86, https://doi.org/10.1353/jph.0.0015.

[13] Sparrow, *Warfare State*, 149.

production', they ranked behind soldiers in terms of public esteem. Conversely, surveys of GIs revealed that the public's fondness for them was not reciprocated. Many 'felt instinctive revulsion at what they perceived to be pseudo patriotism among civilians, who enjoyed high paying war jobs and did not face the hardship of military life.[14] Even if they regarded military life with some ambivalence, GIs felt their own military service was a crucible 'of both their manhood and their national citizenship, which together established their Americanism.[15]

This hierarchy carried over into the post-war era and into social policy when President Franklin Delano Roosevelt's plans for a 'second Bill of Rights' guaranteeing full employment, access to education, medical care and decent housing found material form in the Servicemen's Readjustment Act of 1944, or GI Bill. Whereas Roosevelt had wanted a means-tested programme that would focus on lifting poor people out of poverty, the GI Bill, which was championed by the American Legion, instead focused on offering much more generous, non-means-tested benefits, but only to one particular group: returning veterans.[16] The programme offered unemployment insurance, low-cost mortgages and loans, and tuition and living expenses payments to attend college or vocational school, and had profoundly important redistributive effects, as it expanded the socio-economic horizons of a whole generation of men.[17] By 1948, the GI Bill accounted for 15 per cent of the federal budget and veterans constituted nearly half of the student body of colleges and universities around the country.[18] The nature of the Bill, though, means that its benefits were targeted at specific groups. It offered its most generous benefits to married men, while the allowances granted to women were comparatively meagre and women faced barriers when dealing with the veteran's organizations that helped many male veterans obtain their GI Bill benefits. African American men also fared less well than their white counterparts.[19] At the insistence of Southern lawmakers, local officials were left to administer the programme, which meant that banks were free to decline to lend to African American veterans, while Southern colleges and

---

[14] Sparrow, *Warfare State*, 212.
[15] Sparrow, *Warfare State*, 203.
[16] Kathleen J. Frydl, *The G.I. Bill* (New York: Cambridge University Press, 2009), 102–44.
[17] Michael Bennett, *When Dreams Came True* (Washington, DC: Potomac Books, 1996); Suzanne Mettler, *Soldiers to Citizens: The G.I. Bill and the Making of the Greatest Generation* (New York: Oxford University Press, 2007); Edward Humes, *Over Here: How the G.I. Bill Transformed the American Dream* (Orlando: Harcourt, 2006), http://archive.org/details/overhere00edwa.
[18] Joshua Freeman and Eric Foner, *American Empire: The Rise of a Global Power, the Democratic Revolution at Home, 1945–2000* (New York: Penguin Books, 2013), 33–4.
[19] Lizabeth Cohen, *A Consumers' Republic: The Politics of Mass Consumption in Postwar America* (New York: Random House, 2008), 141.

universities outside of the already-oversubscribed Historically Black Colleges and Universities (HBCU) system refused to enrol them. This was not solely a southern problem. According to political scientist Ira Katznelson, of the 67,000 mortgages insured by the GI Bill in New York and New Jersey, fewer than 100 were issued to non-whites.[20]

Part of what differentiated the GI Bill from previous federal veteran's benefits programmes was its generosity, both in terms of the suite of benefits it offered and the fact that it was available to all those who served on active duty during the war for at least ninety days, and who had not been dishonourably discharged. A total of 7.8 million veterans (out of a Second World War veteran population of 16 million) took advantage of the Bill's educational supports, while the Veterans Administration backed 2.4 million home loans for veterans between 1944 and 1952.[21] Over one-fifth of all single-family homes built between the end of the Second World War and 1966 were financed by GI Bill loans.[22] The very scale of the Bill meant that it had important consequences for notions of citizenship, especially when it came to who was included or excluded from its benefits. The GI Bill elevated the concept of martial citizenship to new heights. The social compact implied by the Bill was that eligible men would serve in the military whenever the state needed them, and in return the state would ensure that they had access to jobs, cheap credit, education and housing. This version of martial citizenship tightly bound together military service obligations with a particular set of rights and privileges accorded to those who served.

The power of military authorities to offer someone an honourable or dishonourable discharge became freighted with even more importance in these circumstances. In 1945, the Veterans Administration barred any soldier who had been administratively discharged 'because of homosexual acts or tendencies' from receiving benefits, which meant that the military had to strive to offer a definition of what 'homosexual tendencies' might be.[23] As historian Margot Canaday argues, this was not only part of a process by which the federal government actively created the categories of homosexual and heterosexual through its regulations as it worked to make the demarcation between the two clear enough to be useful to bureaucrats deciding on discharges, but that it also

[20] Ira Katznelson, *When Affirmative Action Was White: An Untold History of Racial Inequality in Twentieth-Century America* (New York: W. W. Norton, 2006), 140.

[21] 'History and Timeline – Education and Training', United States Department of Veteran Affairs, accessed 5 June 2020, https://www.benefits.va.gov/gibill/history.asp.

[22] Cohen, *A Consumers' Republic*, 141.

[23] Margot Canaday, *The Straight State: Sexuality and Citizenship in Twentieth-Century America* (Princeton, NJ: Princeton University Press, 2011), 150.

led to 'the construction of a closet in federal welfare policy', as it encouraged those who experienced homosexual desire but went undetected to 'pass' as straight so as to claim benefits. According to Canaday, 'the World War II policy on homosexuality thus provided not only for formal exclusion, in other words, but also for a degraded kind of inclusion in citizenship ... the stakes of being included – on any terms at all – were only made higher by the magnitude of the GI Bill'.[24]

Therefore, the growth of the American state in the Second World War and its aftermath was associated with a form of martial masculine citizenship where military service was of central importance and where a huge range of values and norms were refracted through the lens of national security. One of the pivotal moments in the elevation of this form of citizenship came in 1940, when the Roosevelt administration instituted the first peacetime draft in the nation's history and met with almost no public outcry, in stark contrast to the First World War, where conscription was not introduced until the United States joined the war and was met with some resistance.[25] By requiring that all young men register with their local draft board, the Selective Service Act of 1940 meant that the draft would impact on the lives of all American men until its end in 1973. Even if they did not serve in the military, they faced a reckoning with the state, which would declare them unacceptable, offer them a deferment or decide that they were indeed eligible for service.

As historian Amy Rutenberg has noted, even at the height of martial citizenship during the Second World War, men eagerly sought deferments, even if they did not openly resist or protest the draft. The decisions that legislators, federal officials and local draft board members made on who should serve and who should not made clear what they valued when it came to the rights and responsibilities of masculine citizenship. Throughout the war, there were tensions surrounding whether or not married fathers should be drafted, while others complained that fit young men flocked to even low-paying civilian jobs that had been deemed as essential to national security.[26] While debates about what constituted war-essential work were fundamentally about security and military necessity, the reluctance to draft fathers – which resulted in a nine-month-long battle within the Roosevelt administration – spoke to how the state

---

[24] Canaday, *The Straight State*, 142.

[25] Amy J. Rutenberg, *Rough Draft: Cold War Military Manpower Policy and the Origins of Vietnam-Era Draft Resistance* (Ithaca, NY: Cornell University Press, 2019), 5; Christopher Capozzola, *Uncle Sam Wants You: World War I and the Making of the Modern American Citizen* (Oxford: Oxford University Press, 2010), 21–54.

[26] Rutenberg, *Rough Draft*, 26–35.

valued and promoted the role of men as breadwinners and the moral compasses of their families.

Concerns about tensions between military necessity and societal values did not disappear after the end of the war. In a break with previous experiences, the draft was extended until 1947, as the United States sought to navigate the uncertainties of the post-war world. To replace it, the Truman administration proposed Universal Military Training (UMT), a system where every able-bodied man would undergo some form of military training, producing a vast pool of trained manpower that could be called upon when war broke out.[27] The initial impetus for UMT came from military leaders who, as early as 1943, began to fear that the United States would quickly demobilize after the war and reduce the military to the state it had been in prior to the Second World War.[28] They argued that the United States was vulnerable in a way it had not been before and that it needed to be able to rapidly mobilize armies in the event of another war. President Truman agreed with that assessment, but he also saw UMT as a cost-effective way to maintain preparedness, while avoiding the spectre of an overly large standing army. Truman also thought that UMT could offer social benefits, and pushed the notion that the training could improve physical and mental health while also providing trainees with new skills.[29] Opponents instead argued that UMT constituted a 'time tax' on American youth that would deprive them of their freedom and put the United States on the road to fascism.[30] Unions and the NAACP saw some benefit in the social uplift that Truman offered, but preferred that it not be offered through militarized means, while Southern representatives insisted that UMT would have to be racially segregated.[31] Faced with these contradictions and a military leadership that had grown lukewarm about the idea – large standing armies seemed less useful in the age of nuclear war – Truman dropped the idea and instead signed the Selective Service Act of 1948, which modernized and extended the draft.

The failure of UMT amid fears that it might help establish a garrison state did not mean that Americans began to delink citizenship from responsibilities for the defence of the United States. On the contrary, the shadow of the atomic bomb

---

[27] Michael J. Hogan, *A Cross of Iron: Harry S. Truman and the Origins of the National Security State, 1945–1954* (Cambridge: Cambridge University Press, 2000), 119–58; William A. Taylor, *Every Citizen a Soldier: The Campaign for Universal Military Training after World War II* (College Station: Texas A&M University Press, 2014).

[28] Taylor, *Every Citizen a Soldier*, 27–32.

[29] Rutenberg, *Rough Draft*, 48.

[30] Hogan, *A Cross of Iron*, 142.

[31] Taylor, *Every Citizen a Soldier*, 136–7.

meant that the state attempted to enlist ordinary civilians in the effort to support national security.[32] The Federal Civil Defense Administration (FCDA) solicited mass participation in national defence by asking citizens to take responsibility for protecting their homes and neighbourhoods from nuclear attack. They were asked to undergo training in evacuation drills, build bomb shelters on their properties and to stock up on the supplies they would need to survive nuclear fallout. Unlike UMT, which had solely focused on male citizens, the FCDA saw women as crucial participants in protecting their families and organizing self-help within their neighbourhoods. However, as historian Laura McEnaney argues, this early Cold War–era programme faced the same tensions as the failed UMT proposal. Even as federal officials asked Americans to adopt military hierarchies and training styles into their daily rituals, promoting the notion of civil defence as a way of life, they were wary of creating a large programme that would resemble Soviet-style 'big government' and of promoting preparedness in such a way that would lead to an overly powerful military. Therefore, FCDA planners endorsed 'self-help' and rejected plans to build extensive networks of public shelters, instead urging private citizens to build these shelters in their own backyard.[33] Of course, shifting the financial burden of civil defence from the state to the individual assumed that citizens could afford to build shelters and even that they had backyards in which to site them. Instead of emphasizing the collective, the private family unit was eventually put at the core of all civil defence planning. According to FCDA advertising, not having a well-provisioned fallout shelter was the marker of an inadequate breadwinner and citizen.[34] These policies had their parallels in the Cold War propaganda that underlined how the material abundance and security of white American family life in modern suburbs was a sign of the superiority of the American system of governance.[35]

This capacious understanding of national security and the role of the family within it meant that sustaining a vibrant civilian society through the long haul of the Cold War became an important goal for policymakers. As historian Amy Rutenberg points out, this had implications for how the draft functioned. Not

[32] Thomas Bishop, *Every Home a Fortress* (Amherst: University of Massachusetts Press, 2020); Thomas Bishop, '"The Struggle to Sell Survival": Family Fallout Shelters and the Limits of Consumer Citizenship', *Modern American History* 2, no. 2 (July 2019): 117–38, https://doi.org/10.1017/mah.2019.8; Kenneth D. Rose, *One Nation Underground: The Fallout Shelter in American Culture* (New York: New York University Press, 2001), McEnaney, *Civil Defense Begins at Home: Militarization Meets Everyday Life in the Fifties* (Princeton, NJ: Princeton University Press, 2000).
[33] McEnaney, *Civil Defense Begins at Home*, 6–8.
[34] McEnaney, *Civil Defense Begins at Home*, 37.
[35] Elaine T. May, *Homeward Bound* (New York: Basic Books, 1988), 12–13.

only did it mean that married fathers would be exempted from military service, in keeping with the emphasis on the nuclear family, but it also meant that there was subtle shift from a focus on what a man could currently contribute to what his future contributions to national security might be.[36] Eisenhower cut the size of the military while various reforms improved retention, meaning that the military's manpower needs fell at the same time the size of the population was rising.[37] The increased size of the manpower pool relative to the needs of the military services meant that Selective Service officials could be more targeted in who they called into service. The Second World War had demonstrated a huge need for scientists, which was only reinforced by the Cold War. Thus, planners used the draft as a form of manpower channelling to encourage young men to attend college, particularly STEM programmes.[38] Student deferments became a popular means by which to promote higher education and the idea that men could be more valuable to the military as students and civilians than as soldiers. Rutenberg argues that the student deferment programme helped to 'militarize the scientific fields by tying them to the nation's defence efforts. It privileged civilian forms of masculine citizenship at the same time that it militarized them'.[39] Not only that, but it effectively created a class-stratified draft where middle-class men could opt to attend college rather than be drafted, making military service appear more and more like a choice.

While college campuses welcomed thousands of young men on student deferments and supported National Defense Education Act scholarships, they also hosted large numbers of young men in uniform. Universities broadly welcomed the post-Second World War expansion of the Reserve Officer Training Corps (ROTC) programme as it transitioned from providing a smattering of military training to college students and sending its graduates to the reserves to becoming the main pipeline for active duty officers in the Cold War military.[40] Far from being an imposition on reluctant civilians, ROTC was a programme sustained by the enthusiasm of college administrators who wanted to offer an education in moral and civil values to their students and saw ROTC as an ideal vehicle for this project. It also ensured that the military would remain rooted in the civic republican citizen soldier tradition. If the ranks of the officer corps were

---

[36] Rutenberg, *Rough Draft*, 71.
[37] Brian McAllister Linn, *Elvis's Army: Cold War GIs and the Atomic Battlefield* (Cambridge, MA: Harvard University Press, 2016), 156–9.
[38] Rutenberg, *Rough Draft*, 95–7.
[39] Rutenberg, *Rough Draft*, 91.
[40] Michael S. Neiberg, *Making Citizen-Soldiers: ROTC and the Ideology of American Military Service* (Cambridge, MA: Harvard University Press, 2001), 2–4.

predominantly filled by graduates of the nation's civilian universities rather than the elite service academies, then the United States could have a large, standing military while avoiding the dangers of militarism. In many ways, ROTC shared with the FCDA and UMT the goals of providing civic and moral education to citizens while avoiding an overly powerful professional military class.

The military of the early Cold War reflected these citizen soldier impulses while also dealing with the complications of the nuclear battlefield and the highly technical challenges posed by their own sophisticated and complicated equipment. This meant that the draftees who filled the ranks of the 1950s Army required extensive technical training. Even repairing trucks now required a lot of expertise, while many military technical specialist roles, such as missile maintenance, had no civilian equivalents, which meant that the military needed to create its own highly skilled workforce.[41] In this sense, while middle-class students could avoid the draft by going to college, conscription became an even more important vehicle for social mobility for young working-class men. Historian Brian Linn has argued that 'the US Army of the 1950s was the most diverse, representative, and in some ways egalitarian peacetime organization in the nation's history'.[42] Notwithstanding the popularity of student deferments, the sight of Elvis Presley, the biggest cultural icon of the 1950s, serving as an ordinary draftee GI in Cold War West Germany helped validate faith that military service was a national obligation, and press reports about his boot camp training in Fort Hood, Texas, highlighted the brutal egalitarianism of basic training.[43] While much had changed since the Second World War bond drives celebrated GIs as the symbol around which a national imagined community could be built, Private Elvis Presley's stint in the Army represented the still-enduring connection between male citizenship and military service. Even as the needs of the Cold War meant that there were other ways to serve the state, military service obligations were a central part of what it meant to be an American man in the 1950s.

* * *

If the US military of the 1950s was a relatively egalitarian organization by the standards of that decade, then this was a very recent development indeed. As African American contributions to the debate over UMT made clear, the military was both a place where they could justify claims of full citizenship, and an

---

[41] Linn, *Elvis's Army*, 121–3.
[42] Linn, *Elvis's Army*, 3.
[43] Linn, *Elvis's Army*, 195.

institution that diverted resources away from more worthy social programmes. For more radical internationalist Black thinkers, the military could never be an adequate vehicle for civil rights, as they saw violence overseas and racial oppression at home as deeply intertwined.[44] Unlike the First World War, where figures such as WEB DuBois encouraged full Black participation in the war effort as a means of asserting claims for citizenship, African Americans were more cautious in their embrace of the war effort during the Second World War. Some, such as the activist Malcolm X and the historian John Hope Franklin, refused to serve in a segregated military, while many others framed the fight against fascism as only part of a broader fight against racism at home.[45] This 'Double V' campaign centred on advancing civil rights for African American war workers and on desegregating the military.[46] Black organizations petitioned President Franklin Delano Roosevelt to fire Secretary of War Henry Stimson because the latter was a strong supporter of a segregated military and refused to countenance Black combat units, even as American forces in Europe faced looming manpower shortages as the war ground on (Figure 5.1).[47]

Despite segregation, more than 1.2 million African Americans served in the military during the Second World War, and these soldiers and veterans returned from their wartime experiences and fought for voting rights, desegregation, the integration of education and economic opportunity.[48] They did so as wartime civil rights gains were rolled back in the immediate aftermath of the war. A demobilizing Marine Corps only allowed African Americans to remain in service if they accepted positions as stewards, serving food.[49] Meanwhile, the Fair Employment Practice Committee (FEPC), established to prevent discrimination in war-related work in 1941, was dissolved in 1946, and Black soldiers and veterans who wore their military uniforms were attacked across the south. In the most famous case, Sergeant Isaac Woodward

---

[44] Penny M. Von Eschen, *Race against Empire: Black Americans and Anticolonialism, 1937–1957* (Ithaca, NY: Cornell University Press, 1997).

[45] Douglas Bristol, 'Terror, Anger and Patriotism: Understanding the Resistance of Black Soldiers during World War II', in *Integrating the US Military: Race, Gender and Sexual Orientation since World War II*, ed. Douglas Bristol and Heather Marie Stur (Baltimore, MD: Johns Hopkins University Press, 2017), 12.

[46] Patrick S. Washburn, 'The Pittsburgh Courier's Double V Campaign in 1942', *American Journalism* 3, no. 2 (1 April 1986): 73–86, https://doi.org/10.1080/08821127.1986.10731062.

[47] Kimberley L. Phillips, *War! What Is It Good For?: Black Freedom Struggles and the U.S. Military from World War II to Iraq* (Chapel Hill: University of North Carolina Press, 2012), 26.

[48] Peter C. Baker, 'The Tragic, Forgotten History of Black Military Veterans', *New Yorker*, 27 November 2016, https://www.newyorker.com/news/news-desk/the-tragic-forgotten-history-of-black-military-veterans.

[49] Steven Morris, 'How Blacks Upset the Marine Corps: "New Breed" Leathernecks Are Tackling Racists Vestiges', *Ebony*, December 1969, 58.

Figure 5.1 Tuskegee Airmen from the 332nd Fighter Group attending a briefing in Ramitelli, Italy, March 1945. Credit: Library of Congress/Toni Frissell.

was pulled off a bus and arrested by South Carolina police just hours after his discharge from the military in February 1946. The police beat him so badly that the attack left him permanently blind.[50] Outrage at both the attack and the acquittal of the police officer who blinded Woodward prompted President Harry Truman, who was himself appalled by the assault on a veteran, to establish the President' Committee on Civil Rights, which published its report, *To Secure These Rights*, in 1947.[51] Among the report's recommendation

---

[50] Phillips, *War! What Is It Good For?*, 88.
[51] President's Committee on Civil Rights, 'To Secure These Rights: The Report of the President's Commission on Civil Rights' (Washington, DC: Government Printing Office, 1947).

was the desegregation of the military, which Truman implemented by issuing Executive Order 9981 in July 1948.[52]

The Executive Order marked a victory for Civil Rights activists such as A. Philip Randolph, who had campaigned against segregation in the military since the early 1940s. Randolph had threatened to advise young Black men to resist the draft unless segregation in the military was ended. He warned Truman in March 1948 of the potentially dire consequences of not pursuing integration, telling him that 'I can tell you the mood among Negroes of this country is that they will never bear arms again until all forms of bias and discrimination are abolished.'[53]

Its success was also partly due to the experiences of the Second World War, where surveys revealed that white soldiers had a much higher opinion of their Black comrades after serving with them, and the few Black combat units that were established performed well.[54] This paralleled the experience of Japanese Americans, where the performance of the all-*Nisei* 442nd Infantry Regiment in Europe was seen as a marker of loyalty to the United States, even as their families were interned in concentration camps. Truman's address to the 442nd on their return to the United States captured this spirit well: 'You fought not only the enemy, but you fought prejudice – and you won. Keep up that fight, and we will continue to win – to make this great republic stand for what the Constitution says it stands for: "The welfare of all the people all the time."'[55] However, Truman's integrationist rhetoric and even his Executive Order did not by themselves transform the military. While the Navy and the new Air Force moved relatively quickly to desegregate, and the military as a whole dropped racial draft quotas in the Selective Service Act of 1948, the Army refused to desegregate, slow-rolling its implementation of the order until the manpower crisis of the Korean War forced it to finally integrate its combat units in 1951.[56] The Marines followed suit in 1952, but kept Black Marines from certain assignments, such as recruiting or embassy duty, until the late 1950s.[57]

---

[52] For the complete history of the integration of the US military, see Morris J. MacGregor, *Integration of the Armed Forces, 1940–1965* (Washington, DC: US Army Center of Military History, 1981).

[53] Jervis Anderson, *A. Philip Randolph: A Biographical Portrait* (Berkeley: University of California Press, 1986), 276.

[54] Tanya L. Roth, '"An Attractive Career for Women": Opportunities, Limitations, and Women's Integration in the Cold War Military', in *Integrating the US Military: Race, Gender and Sexual Orientation since World War II*, ed. Douglas Bristol and Heather Marie Stur (Baltimore, MD: Johns Hopkins University Press, 2017), 28.

[55] Cited in Ronald R. Krebs, *Fighting for Rights: Military Service and the Politics of Citizenship* (Ithaca, NY: Cornell University Press, 2006), 170.

[56] Phillips, *War! What Is It Good For?*, 111.

[57] Morris, 'How Blacks Upset the Marine Corps'.

This integration process was uneven, especially outside of wartime conditions, but African American enlistment rates surged during and after the Korean War. Of the 1.5 million men inducted during the Korean War, 25 per cent of those were African American, with a roughly even split between those who were drafted and those who voluntarily enlisted. The enlistment rate for African Americans remained well above the African American share of the population well after the war ended.[58] This reflected not so much attempts to assert full citizenship via military service as the fact that military service provided good wages, opportunities for education or job training and general social mobility. The experience of African Americans in the newly desegregated military seemed to bear out some of the predictions advocates of UMT had made about social uplift and military service in the 1940s. Thus, many liberal political leaders saw increasing the number of poor men, and African American men in particular, in the ranks as a worthy policy goal.

When John F. Kennedy ran for office, he emphasized re-establishing national strength in the aftermath of Sputnik and the stalemate in Korea. His administration valued manly service of all kinds, from volunteering in the newly established Peace Corps to enlisting in Green Beret special forces units.[59] As part of their policy agenda, they were interested in reducing the number of men that the military had to reject from draft inductions.[60] Criticisms of the draft in the early 1960s emphasized that it was unfair because it denied the poor the opportunity to serve, and by 1963, draft boards were rejecting up to half of those called up for failing either their mental or physical exam. To remedy this, the Kennedy administration proposed offering literacy, numeracy and healthcare services to poor men rejected by draft boards to bring them up to the standard required of inductees. Assistant Secretary for Labor Daniel Patrick Moynihan saw such interventions as crucial in breaking the cycle of poverty in African American communities.[61] Moynihan thought military service could be the saviour of Black men, given that it offered the full benefits of martial citizenship, such as the GI Bill, veterans hospitals and federally backed mortgages. Most importantly, for Moynihan it would provide a way for these men to rediscover their masculinity. Moynihan believed that Black poverty could be explained by cultural pathology and the prevalence of single-mother families in Black

---

[58] Phillips, *War! What Is It Good For?*, 147.
[59] Robert D. Dean, 'Masculinity as Ideology: John F. Kennedy and the Domestic Politics of Foreign Policy', *Diplomatic History* 22, no. 1 (January 1998): 29–62, https://doi.org/10.1111/1467-7709.00100.
[60] Rutenberg, *Rough Draft*, 136–44.
[61] Daniel Geary, *Beyond Civil Rights: The Moynihan Report and Its Legacy* (Philadelphia: University of Pennsylvania Press, 2015), 42–78.

communities and, in his influential 1965 report, *The Negro Family: The Case for National Action*, he argued that 'given the strains of disorganized and matrifocal family life in which so many Negro youth come of age, the armed forces are a dramatic and desperately needed change; a world away from women, a world run by strong men and unquestioned authority'.[62]

While the Moynihan Report was heavily criticized by the NAACP and the broader civil rights movement, its recommendations found their way into government policy. Project 100,000, launched by Secretary of Defense Robert McNamara in October 1966, was a crucial part of the effort to induct more African American draftees.[63] The Pentagon lowered induction standards for both draftees and volunteers to ensure that men who would have previously been rejected were able to serve. The plan was to admit 100,000 men into the military each year who had failed the qualifying exam. These personnel would then receive remedial training, learn valuable job skills and would later return to civilian life and help break the poverty cycle. Rejection rates dropped from 50 per cent to 34 per cent between 1965 and 1966, and fell even further in 1967. Although the programme was part of President Lyndon Johnson's 'war on poverty', few of these inductees received any dedicated numeracy or literacy training, as inductees in earlier pilot programmes had. Only 6 per cent of the 240,000 men enlisted under Project 100,000 between 1966 and 1968 received any remedial training, and even that training only raised their reading skills to a fifth-grade level.[64] Further, the Project 100,000 men were distributed across training centres and weren't even aware that they were part of the project.[65] Because of their inadequate literacy and numeracy skills, many of these men failed their technical training courses and ended up in infantry units. About 40 per cent of those inducted via the programme were trained for combat, compared to only 25 per cent for all enlisted men. Black men made up 10 per cent of the entire military, but constituted 40 per cent of the Project 100,000 inductees.[66] Such results help explain why, along with liberal reformers and civic republicans such as McNamara, Hershey and Moynihan, more openly racist politicians such

[62] United States Department of Labor and United States Department of Labor Office of Policy Planning and Research, *The Negro Family: The Case for National Action* (Washington, DC: U.S. Government Printing Office, 1965), 42.

[63] Janice H. Laurence and Peter F. Ramsberger, *Low-Aptitude Men in the Military: Who Profits, Who Pays?* (New York: Praeger, 1991).

[64] Christian G. Appy, *Working-Class War: American Combat Soldiers and Vietnam* (Chapel Hill: University of North Carolina Press, 1993), 32.

[65] Rutenberg, *Rough Draft*, 149.

[66] Edward J. Drea, *McNamara, Clifford, and the Burdens of Vietnam 1965–1969* (Washington, DC: Historical Office, Office of the Secretary of Defense, 2011), 269.

as Senator Richard Russell of Georgia supported the programme. Russell was happy to offer his support, as he correctly believed that it would ensure that more Black soldiers were sent to Vietnam.[67]

Ironically, during the early stages of the American war in Vietnam, many in the Black press shared Russell's objective. Outlets like *Ebony* and *Jet* celebrated the fact that this was the first war where African Americans would serve as fully equal participants in an integrated force.[68] However, as American involvement in Southeast Asia intensified and casualties mounted, the war's uneven toll became clear.[69] In the early years of the war, Black soldiers accounted for 20 per cent of all deaths, about twice their proportion in the US civilian population. Moreover, Black soldiers also found themselves subject to capricious military discipline, and received 'Article 15' nonjudicial punishments at much higher rates than white soldiers.[70] African Americans accounted for only 2 per cent of officers in Vietnam and generally experienced much lower rates of promotion throughout the ranks.[71] Frustrations about structural racism within the military combined with lack of progress on Civil Rights at home led to a series of soldier uprisings in 1971, with large demonstrations taking place in Okinawa, Germany, Vietnam and on bases throughout the United States, such as Fort Ord and Travis Air Force Base, California, and Fort McClelland, Alabama.[72]

It was also not lost on some Civil Rights leaders that Black soldiers were ostensibly fighting for rights that they still did not enjoy at home. In his 'Beyond Vietnam' speech where he laid out his opposition to the war, Rev. Martin

---

[67] Rutenberg, *Rough Draft*, 151.

[68] 'Special Issue: The Black Soldier', *Ebony*, August 1968; Simeon Booker, '"An American Is an American", Say Fightingest GIs in Vietnam', *Jet*, 30 June 1966; Gerald F. Goodwin, 'Black and White in Vietnam', *New York Times*, 18 July 2017, sec. Opinion, https://www.nytimes.com/2017/07/18/opinion/racism-vietnam-war.html.

[69] For scholarship on the African-American experience in Vietnam, see James E. Westheider, *Fighting on Two Fronts: African Americans and the Vietnam War* (New York: New York University Press, 1999); James E. Westheider, *The African American Experience in Vietnam: Brothers in Arms* (Lanham, MD: Rowman & Littlefield, 2008); Phillips, *War! What Is It Good For?*, 188–227; Wallace Terry, *Bloods: An Oral History of the Vietnam War* (New York: Random House, 1984); Herman Graham, *The Brothers' Vietnam War: Black Power, Manhood, and the Military Experience* (Gainesville: University Press of Florida, 2003).

[70] Denton L. Watson, 'The NAACP: Defender of Black Servicemen', *The Crisis* 80, no. 4 (June–July 1973): 204–10.

[71] Appy, *Working-Class War*, 22; Isaac Hampton, *The Black Officer Corps: A History of Black Military Advancement from Integration through Vietnam* (London: Routledge, 2013).

[72] Richard R. Moser, *The New Winter Soldiers: GI and Veteran Dissent during the Vietnam Era* (New Brunswick, NJ: Rutgers University Press, 1996), 76; Ron Carver, David Cortright and Barbara Doherty, eds, *Waging Peace in Vietnam: US Soldiers and Veterans Who Opposed the War* (New York: New Village Press, 2019); David Cortright, *Soldiers in Revolt: GI Resistance during the Vietnam War* (Chicago: Haymarket Books, 2005); Derek Seidman, 'Vietnam and the Soldiers' Revolt', *Monthly Review* (blog), 1 June 2016, https://monthlyreview.org/2016/06/01/vietnam-and-the-soldiers-revolt/.

Luther King Jr. spoke of the 'cruel irony of watching Negro and white boys on TV screens as they kill and die together for a nation that has been unable to seat them together in the same schools' and of the 'brutal solidarity' of an interracial military burning huts in Vietnamese villages but who 'would hardly live on the same block in Chicago'.[73] King's opposition to the war signalled the re-emergence of a Black internationalism that had waned in the early Cold War years. Citizenship based on equal participation in the armed forces had less meaning if that citizenship was based on the oppression of others. King noted,

> As I have walked among the desperate, rejected, and angry young men, I have told them that Molotov cocktails and rifles would not solve their problems. I have tried to offer them my deepest compassion while maintaining my conviction that social change comes most meaningfully through nonviolent action. But they ask – and rightly so – what about Vietnam? They ask if our own nation wasn't using massive doses of violence to solve its problems, to bring about the changes it wanted. Their questions hit home, and I knew that I could never again raise my voice against the violence of the oppressed in the ghettos without having first spoken clearly to the greatest purveyor of violence in the world today – my own government.[74]

Mohammed Ali, perhaps the most famous draft resister of the Vietnam War era, expressed a similar sense of international solidarity:

> My conscience won't let me go shoot my brother, or some darker people, or some poor hungry people in the mud for big powerful America. And shoot them for what? They never called me nigger, they never lynched me, they didn't put no dogs on me, they didn't rob me of my nationality, rape and kill my mother and father. … Shoot them for what?[75]

Ali's application for conscientious objector status was somewhat atypical in that it was an option open to relatively few African American or working-class men. The Selective Service system was not designed to make the armed forces mirror the composition of society as a whole, and the fact that decision-making was devolved to thousands of local draft boards meant that the preferences of the upper-middle-class white men who overwhelmingly constituted those boards held sway.[76] Similarly, slots in Reserve and National Guard units, which were

---

[73] Martin Luther King, 'Beyond Vietnam' (Riverside Church, New York City, 4 April 1967), https://kinginstitute.stanford.edu/encyclopedia/beyond-vietnam.

[74] King, 'Beyond Vietnam'.

[75] DeNeen L. Brown, '"Shoot Them for What?" How Muhammad Ali Won His Greatest Fight', *Washington Post*, 16 June 2018, https://www.washingtonpost.com/news/retropolis/wp/2018/06/15/shoot-them-for-what-how-muhammad-ali-won-his-greatest-fight/.

[76] Rutenberg, *Rough Draft*, 163.

generally not sent to Southeast Asia, were awarded to those with connections. Mississippi presents an extreme example of this state of affairs: in a state where African Americans constituted 42 per cent of the population and the National Guard had a strength of 10,365, only one Black man was admitted to the Guard.[77] Historian Christian Appy estimates that the enlisted ranks in Vietnam were 25 per cent poor, 55 per cent working class, and 20 per cent middle class, with only a negligible number of wealthy serving.[78] According to Appy, the map of American casualties in Vietnam is a map of class: 'Most Americans in Vietnam were nineteen-year-old high school graduates. They grew up in the white, working-class enclaves of South Boston and Cleveland's West Side; in the black ghettos of Detroit and Birmingham; in the small rural towns of Oklahoma and Iowa; and in the housing developments of working-class suburbs.'[79]

For young men in these communities, seeking conscientious objector status was both socially frowned upon and logistically difficult. The Vietnam War was unique in that it produced a mini 'beat the draft' industry with the emergence of draft counsellors who could advise on ways to avoid military service. But, like college deferments and sympathetic doctors who would diagnose draft-exempting ailments, these were seldom available to working-class men. The sort of masculinity that draft counsellors promoted – one that emphasized embracing moral convictions rather than martial bravery – was one that did not always resonate in working-class neighbourhoods. Amy Rutenberg has argued that middle-class men who had grown accustomed to seeing the draft as a choice due to the wide range of exemptions built into the system turned to draft counsellors to reassert control over their lives.[80] This notion that military service was a choice was not one that was shared by the working-class and poor men who did a hugely disproportionate share of the fighting and dying in Southeast Asia.

* * *

Even if opposition to conscription formed a major part of the anti-war movement, the end of the draft did not come at the hands of protestors. The crucial impetus for change came not from African American draftees or white middle-class college students but from libertarian economics professors.[81] The libertarian argument against Selective Service echoed the critiques of UMT in the 1940s

---

77 Appy, *Working-Class War*, 37.
78 Appy, *Working-Class War*, 27.
79 Appy, *Working-Class War*, 27–8.
80 Rutenberg, *Rough Draft*, 183–6.
81 The best account of this development is Beth Bailey, *America's Army: Making the All-Volunteer Force* (Cambridge, MA: Harvard University Press, 2009), 1–33; Bernard D. Rostker and K. C. Yeh, *I Want You!: The Evolution of the All-Volunteer Force* (Santa Monica, CA: Rand Corporation, 2006), 15–42.

that had called conscription a 'time tax'. For economists like Alan Greenspan and Milton Friedman, the draft was an infringement on liberty, and arguments about the obligations of citizenship had little meaning in this world view.[82] Influenced by the Columbia University economist Martin Anderson, Richard Nixon called for an end to the draft during his successful run for the presidency in 1968 and, on taking office, he established the Gates Commission to put together a plan of action for ending the draft. The Commission's report, delivered in 1970, argued that military recruitment was essentially a labour market issue that could be solved by the free market by offering adequate pay and benefits to recruits rather than on relying on the coercive 'hidden tax' of conscription.[83] Even if liberals did not buy into the economic rationale for opposing the draft, they did see it as a vehicle for inequality and some even thought that the cost of an All-Volunteer Force would make it more difficult for the United States to go to war in the future.

The military did not share in Nixon's enthusiasm for abolishing the draft. While they did not rely wholly on draftees, much of their recruitment was driven by draft-motivated volunteers, who joined in order to get a better assignment than they would if they were conscripted.[84] The Army, in particular, depended heavily on Selective Service and senior leaders seriously doubted that they could find enough volunteers for combat units. Nonetheless, a combination of resignation of the political inevitability of the end of the draft and dissatisfaction at the quality of draftees in the early 1970s meant that the Army put in place plans for improving the quality of soldiers' lives. This included relaxing haircut regulations, ending morning reveille formations, allowing beer in barracks and giving soldiers individual rooms rather than having them live in open barracks along with dozens of other soldiers.[85] The Army also began to heavily invest in advertising, increasing its $3 million ad account by 600 per cent.[86] New advertisements emphasized the Army as an opportunity rather than an obligation. This campaign highlighted job training opportunities, invited recruits to 'take the Army's European tour' and told them that 'we care more about how you think than how you cut your hair'. All of these ads ran under the controversial umbrella slogan of 'Today's Army Wants to Join You', a statement

[82] Milton Friedman, 'Why Not a Volunteer Army?', *New Individualist Review* 4, no. 4 (1967): 3–6.
[83] Gates Commission, 'The Report of the President's Commission on an All-Volunteer Armed Force', Washington, DC: US Government Printing Office, 1970.
[84] Bailey, *America's Army*, 36.
[85] Bailey, *America's Army*, 54–7; Robert K. Griffith, *US Army's Transition to the All-Volunteer Force, 1968–1974* (Washington, DC: Center of Military History, 1996), 101–14.
[86] Bailey, *America's Army*, 67.

that seemed designed to inflame the feelings of the Army's career NCOs and officers.[87]

Notwithstanding the Army's reforms and recruiting campaign, when the last draftee entered training on 30 June 1973, the military as a whole faced significant challenges with the transition to the All-Volunteer Force. Morale remained low, as the institution dealt with drug problems and racial tensions.[88] Observers began to worry about the quality of incoming recruits, concerns that were deeply entwined with race. By 1974, 30 per cent of all Army recruits were Black and the Marines imposed racial quotas on recruitment again as they worried that all-Black rifle companies would lead to disproportionate African American casualties in the event of war.[89] By 1981, complaints the All-Volunteer Military was 'too dumb, too black, and too costly' were pervasive.[90] At this stage, 50 per cent of all Army recruits were classed as Category IV in intelligence tests.[91] This drop in quality, though, was driven by an influx of poor white soldiers. Black recruits scored much higher on intelligence tests and critics such as Representative Charles Rangel argued that the military was creaming off the most promising lower-middle-class Black men.[92] In response to the racial crisis of the early 1970s, the Department of Defense had established the Defense Race Relations Institute and began an effective programme of Affirmative Action that greatly improved the prospects of Black officers and NCOs.[93] Caught between concerns about the exploitation of poor Black citizens and the imperative to offer opportunities in well-paying federal jobs to Black people, policymakers vacillated on the best approach, eventually deciding to move recruiting stations

---

[87] Melissa T. Brown, *Enlisting Masculinity: The Construction of Gender in US Military Recruiting Advertising during the All-Volunteer Force*, Oxford Studies in Gender and International Relations (Oxford: Oxford University Press, 2012), 47–52; Beth Bailey, 'The Army in the Marketplace: Recruiting an All-Volunteer Force', *Journal of American History* 94, no. 1 (2007): 47–74, https://doi.org/10.2307/25094776.

[88] Richard Lock-Pullan, '"An Inward Looking Time": The United States Army, 1973–1976', *Journal of Military History* 67, no. 2 (April 2003): 483–511, https://doi.org/10.2307/3093465; Cecil Currey, *Self-Destruction: The Disintegration and Decay of the United States Army during the Vietnam Era* (New York: W. W. Norton, 1981); Richard A. Gabriel and Paul Savage, *Crisis in Command: Mismanagement in the Army* (New York: Hill and Wang, 1978); Stuart H. Loory, *Defeated: Inside America's Military Machine* (New York: Random House, 1973); Richard Boyle, *The Flower of the Dragon: The Breakdown of the U.S. Army in Vietnam.* (San Francisco, CA: Ramparts Press, 1972).

[89] Bailey, *America's Army*, 110, 115.

[90] Bailey, *America's Army*, 121.

[91] Bailey, *America's Army*, 125.

[92] Charles C. Moskos and John Sibley Butler, *All That We Can Be: Black Leadership and Racial Integration the Army Way* (New York: Basic Books, 1996).

[93] Isaac Hampton, 'Reform in the Ranks: The History of the Defense Race Relations Institute, 1971–2014', in *Integrating the US Military: Race, Gender and Sexual Orientation since World War II*, ed. Douglas Bristol and Heather Marie Stur (Baltimore, MD: Johns Hopkins University Press, 2017), 122–41.

to white middle-class suburbs in order to make sure that the military looked more like society as a whole.[94]

A crucial part of these efforts was the array of benefits available to military service members. Secretary of the Army 'Bo' Calloway thought that offering financial support for college was more important than offering cash bonuses to recruits, as the former would attract more intelligent and ambitious recruits.[95] Thus, the revitalization of the GI Bill, whose benefits had become much less generous in the Vietnam era and then lapsed entirely in 1976, became an important tool in making sure that the All-Volunteer Force was a success.[96] As historian Jennifer Mittelstadt has argued, there was a huge irony in the fact that in order to solve the 'labour market problem' posed to it by the libertarian architects of the AVF, the military turned to the very social welfare institutions that those same libertarians were trying to dismantle. There has been a long historical connection between military service and social welfare, with many parts of the social safety net having their origins in obligations to care for war widows and veterans before being expanded to cover the rest of the population.[97] In this era, though, the military social welfare system grew more elaborate and generous, while the civilian safety net shrank. Indeed, Ronald Reagan drastically cut college financial aid even as he pushed for a GI Bill expansion for military personnel. In Reagan's world view, military service was not just a job; military personnel veterans belonged to a special and elevated category that entailed significant economic benefits not available to other citizens.[98] Thus, in the All-Volunteer Force era, military service entailed special rights and privileges.

The military used its newly generous social welfare system to recruit and, just as importantly, retain personnel. Army leaders were fond of the slogan that the Army 'recruited soldiers, but retained families'. Certainly, the AVF required a broader focus on family welfare, as it attracted older, longer-serving members who had a much higher marriage rate than their predecessors in the Selective Service Era.[99] High marriage rates might have been associated with increased welfare spending, but families were seen as an important way of moderating

---

[94] Bailey, *America's Army*, 115.

[95] Jennifer Mittelstadt, *The Rise of the Military Welfare State* (Cambridge, MA: Harvard University Press, 2015), 98, 104.

[96] Mark Boulton, *Failing Our Veterans: The G.I. Bill and the Vietnam Generation* (New York: New York University Press, 2014).

[97] Theda Skocpol, *Protecting Soldiers and Mothers: The Political Origins of Social Policy in the United States* (Cambridge, MA: Harvard University Press, 1995).

[98] Mittelstadt, *The Rise of the Military Welfare State*, 94–119.

[99] John Worsencroft, 'A Family Affair: Military Service in the Postwar Era' (PhD diss., Philadelphia, Temple University, 2017), 125.

soldier behaviour, and conservatives celebrated military families as moral exemplars that could be contrasted with the decaying civilian family.[100] Indeed, right-wing Christians worked with some military leaders within the armed forces to push conservative values into military welfare programmes such as marriage counselling and addiction treatment services.[101]

Military families, though, were not just a vehicle for traditionalist values. Army spouses banded together to make sure that the military welfare state adequately supported them as well. Along with housing and healthcare benefits, a key demand was that the institution do a better job of facilitating the independent careers of the wives who frequently had to give up their jobs in order to follow their husbands to new postings.[102] While they celebrated military families, Army leaders were uneasy about such activism, and family support programmes were among the first to be targeted as the military welfare state began to be cut back in the 1990s. Some leaders even argued that families were too much of a burden on the military after all, and the Marine Corps – concerned about the impact of failed marriages on military readiness – made an abortive attempt to ban married persons from enlisting, a policy that was rescinded by the Clinton administration within hours of its announcement in August 1993.[103] The tension between idealized visions of a military family surrounded the protections afforded by the military welfare state and the Marines' apparent preference for a combat force made up of young men unencumbered by familial responsibilities was one that was never fully resolved.

This tension, which had always been present in some form, became all the more acute in the 1970s when more and more roles within the military were opened up to women. Women had always been part of the American military establishment in some sense and, as the military became larger and more bureaucratic, it needed to fill more jobs that were ordinarily considered 'women's work'.[104] Unlike its predecessor organization from the First World War era, the Women's Army Corps (WAC) was retained after the end of the Second World War and women were accepted as permanent, regular members of the armed forces after the passage of the Women's Armed Services Integration Act of 1948.

---

[100] Mittelstadt, *The Rise of the Military Welfare State*, 167; Natasha Zaretsky, *No Direction Home: The American Family and the Fear of National Decline, 1968-1980* (Chapel Hill: University of North Carolina Press, 2010).

[101] Anne C. Loveland, *American Evangelicals and the U.S. Military, 1942-1993* (Baton Rouge: Louisiana State University Press, 1996).

[102] Mittelstadt, *The Rise of the Military Welfare State*, 120–47.

[103] Worsencroft, 'A Family Affair: Military Service in the Postwar Era', 239–57.

[104] Leisa D. Meyer, *Creating GI Jane: Sexuality and Power in the Women's Army Corps during World War II* (New York: Columbia University Press, 1996).

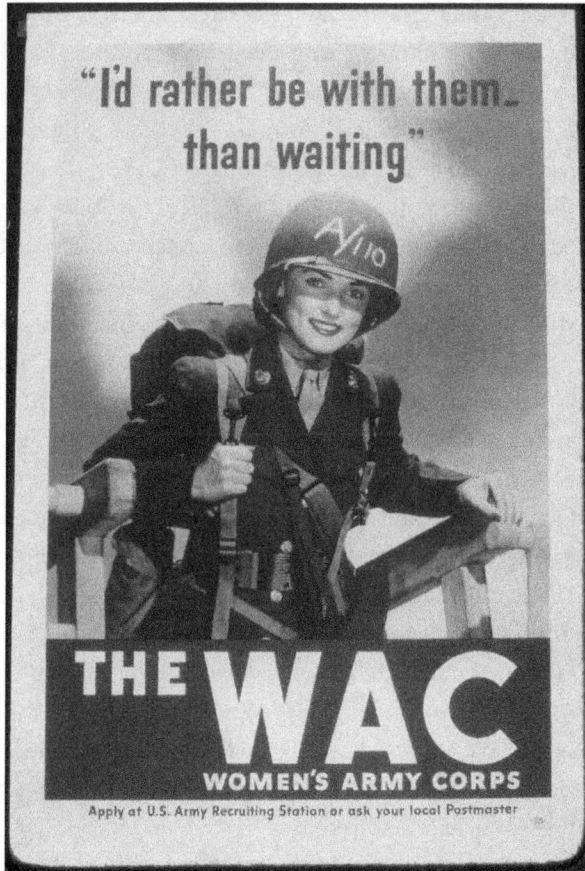

Figure 5.2 US Women's Army Corps Recruiting Poster, Second World War. Credit: US National Archives/Office of War Information.

The Act capped the number of women in the military at 2 per cent of the overall strength of active-duty forces, and WAC leadership, haunted by stories from the Second World War of lesbianism and promiscuity in their ranks, took a very conservative approach to both recruiting and discipline.[105] Advertisements for WACs emphasized femininity, respectability and marriage prospects, while the Marine Corps partnered with Pan-Am in the 1960s to help with grooming and diet advice (Figure 5.2).[106]

Servicewomen had pushed at the boundaries of these strictures long before the advent of second-wave feminism, but they had greater success in their fight

---

[105] Bailey, *America's Army*, 144.
[106] Roth, '"An Attractive Career for Women"', 77–82.

for equality as the broader women's liberation movement built up momentum in the late 1960s. The cap on the number of women in the armed forces was lifted in 1968 and, as the Department of Defense watched the Equal Rights Amendment secure passage through Congress and move to seemingly inevitable ratification by the States, it moved to integrate women more fully into the military and do away with separate women's organizations altogether.[107] This coincided with the birth of the All-Volunteer Force and planners also realized that they would need to massively expand the recruitment of women to help make up for the shortfall in numbers after the end of the draft.[108] Advertising began to change too: although some ads in the 1970s still held out the prospect of military service leading to a good marriage, more of them instead emphasized that the military could provide a steady job, and good educational and training prospects, a similar message to that targeted at men.[109] This change in direction met with some success when it came to recruiting: in 1971, women made up 1.3 per cent of enlisted ranks in the Army; this increased to 7.6 per cent in 1979, a figure that indicated that the military could no longer function effectively without women.[110]

Notwithstanding this success, these changes provoked a conservative backlash. When women were admitted to the service academies in 1975, they underwent combat training as part of the curriculum, opening up the prospect of women as wartime combatants. While Representative Patricia Schroeder campaigned to open roles in combat units to women, conservative activists like Phyllis Schlafly used the prospect of women being forced into serving in combat via a renewed draft as a successful tactic with which to prevent the ratification of the Equal Rights Amendment. Schlafly sought to preserve traditional gender roles and argued that 'our young women have a constitutional right to be treated like American ladies.'[111] Within the military, conservatives conflated the presence of women with the concerns over quality and readiness that were roiling the armed forces in the 1970s. Critics like Marine veteran and Reagan's Secretary of the Navy James Webb thought that the presence of women undermined the fundamental mission of the military by weakening camaraderie and undermining physical standards. Webb argued that the service academies

---

[107] Bailey, *America's Army*, 157.
[108] Bailey, *America's Army*, 154.
[109] Brown, *Enlisting Masculinity*, 67–8.
[110] Bailey, *America's Army*, 133.
[111] Phyllis Schlafly, 'Hearings on H.R. 6569, Registration of Women', Military Personnel Subcommittee of the House Committee on Armed Services, 96th Cong., 2nd sess, 5 March 1980; Bailey, *America's Army*, 159.

should shut down rather than accept women.[112] In a similar vein, the Army even went so far as to institute a 'womanpause' in 1981, halting the recruitment of women altogether.[113]

Women were now integral to the functioning of the military, so this 'womanpause' did not last long, and questions about women in combat became more pronounced as the Cold War ended. Captain Linda Bray, a Military Police officer, became the first American woman to command troops in combat during the invasion of Panama in 1989, and 41,000 women deployed overseas during the Persian Gulf War of 1990/1.[114] Following that conflict, a presidential Commission again looked at the question of opening up combat roles to woman. The Commission declined to do so, but it did open up a broader variety of roles and the Army and the Navy introduced gender-integrated basic training. Even these moves became culture war flashpoints, as conservatives again argued that the presence of women in the ranks undermined traditional gender norms and led to poor military performance.[115]

This debate was intertwined with the conversation over whether or not to allow openly gay personnel to serve in the military. This particular struggle had been ongoing for decades but came to a head when the incoming Clinton administration pledged to end the gay ban.[116] The ensuing controversy – which resulted in the Don't Ask, Don't Tell compromise and a defeat for progressives – centred on notions of morality and unit cohesion but it also highlighted a contradictory strain of thinking within the military, where senior leaders both argued that the armed forces should not be considered a social laboratory, where policymakers could attempt to make changes that would be repugnant to the rest of society,

---

[112] Jim Webb, 'Women Can't Fight', *Washingtonian*, 1 November 1979, https://www.washingtonian.com/1979/11/01/jim-webb-women-cant-fight/.

[113] Bailey, *America's Army*, 171; Jeanne Holm, *Women in the Military: An Unfinished Revolution* (Novato, CA: Presidio Press, 1992), 387–95.

[114] Michael R. Gordon, 'Noriega's Surrender: Army; For First Time, a Woman Leads G.I.'s in Combat', *New York Times*, 4 January 1990, https://www.nytimes.com/1990/01/04/world/noriega-s-surrender-army-for-first-time-a-woman-leads-gi-s-in-combat.html; 'Report to the Secretary of Defense: Women in the Military: Deployment in the Persian Gulf' (Washington, DC: General Accounting Office, 1993), http://archive.gao.gov/t2pbat5/149552.pdf.

[115] Stephanie Gutman, *The Kinder, Gentler Military: Can America's Gender-Neutral Fighting Force Still Win Wars?* (New York: Scribner, 2000); Lorry Fenner and Marie deYoung, *Women in Combat: Civic Duty or Military Liability?* (Washington, DC: Georgetown University Press, 2001); Megan MacKenzie, *Beyond the Band of Brothers: The US Military and the Myth That Women Can't Fight* (New York: Cambridge University Press, 2015).

[116] Aaron Belkin and Geoffrey Bateman, *Don't Ask, Don't Tell: Debating the Gay Ban in the Military* (Boulder, CO: Lynne Rienner, 2003); Nathaniel Frank, 'What's Love Got to Do with It? The Real Story of Military Sociology and "Don't Ask, Don't Tell"', *Lingua Franca* 10, no. 7 (October 2000): 71–81; Charles C. Moskos Papers, Northwestern University Archives; Nathaniel Frank, *Unfriendly Fire: How the Gay Ban Undermines the Military and Weakens America* (New York: Thomas Dunne Books, 2009); Shilts, *Conduct Unbecoming*, 734–50.

and that the military was an institution apart, where its special purpose as an instrument of violence meant that issues like cohesion and combat effectiveness made it essentially alien to civilian society and exempt from many of the obligations placed on other institutions.[117]

The military lost its particular arguments about gays and women in the long run: the Obama administration finally ended Don't Ask Don't Tell and the combat exclusion policy for women in 2010 and 2013 respectively. But the argument about the military as a place apart from civilian society, which was one advanced by many others as well, had much more staying power. Far from the 'hollow force' of the 1970s, the military of the 1990s and the early 2000s was venerated as the most successful institution in the United States. Victory on the battlefield in the Persian Gulf War was greeted with scenes of mass adulation as most major American cities staged homecoming parades, and generals became celebrity figures.[118] The notion of military personnel as inherently deserving of thanks reached a fever pitch with the US reaction to the attacks of 11 September 2001 and the invasion of Afghanistan and Iraq. The phrase 'thank you for your service' became both ubiquitous and the object of derision among military personnel who were perpetually being given discounts at coffee outlets but also required to spend years away from their families on multiple deployments.[119] As the overall share of Americans serving in the military shrank, and the number of personnel whose parents also served in the military grew, military leaders began to worry about the growing gap between the military and civilian society.[120] Ironically, as concerns within the military about their future as a 'warrior caste' grew, these leaders reversed some of their earlier arguments about the military as an exceptional institution. While the military's treatment of women in its

---

[117] Beth Bailey, 'The Politics of Dancing: "Don't Ask, Don't Tell", and the Role of Moral Claims', *Journal of Policy History* 25, no. 1 (2013): 89–113; Jacqueline E. Whitt and Elizabeth A. Perazzo, 'The Military as Social Experiment: Challenging a Trope', *Parameters* 48, no. 2 (22 June 2018): 5.

[118] David Fitzgerald, 'Support the Troops: Gulf War Homecomings and a New Politics of Military Celebration', *Modern American History* 2, no. 1 (March 2019): 1–22, https://doi.org/10.1017/mah.2019.1; Dana Priest, *The Mission: Waging War and Keeping Peace with America's Military* (New York: W. W. Norton, 2004), 61–120; Norman Schwarzkopf, *It Doesn't Take a Hero: The Autobiography of General H. Norman Schwarzkopf* (New York: Bantam, 1993); Colin L. Powell and Joseph E. Persico, *My American Journey: An Autobiography* (New York: Random House, 1995).

[119] David Finkel, *Thank You for Your Service* (New York: Sarah Crichton Books, 2013); David Finkel, *The Good Soldiers* (New York: Picador, 2010); Ben Fountain, *Billy Lynn's Long Halftime Walk* (New York: Ecco, 2012); Kenneth T. MacLeish, *Making War at Fort Hood: Life and Uncertainty in a Military Community* (Princeton, NJ: Princeton University Press, 2013); David Kieran, *Signature Wounds: The Untold Story of the Military's Mental Health Crisis* (New York: New York University Press, 2019).

[120] Thom Shanker, 'Admiral Mullen Urges West Point Graduates to Bridge Gap With Public', *New York Times*, 21 May 2011, http://www.nytimes.com/2011/05/22/us/22mullen.html; Jim Mattis and Kori N. Schake, eds, *Warriors and Citizens: American Views of Our Military* (Stanford, CA: Hoover Institution Press, 2016).

ranks continued to lag far behind the norms and expectations of civilian society, the end of Don't Ask Don't Tell brought forth none of the breakdown in cohesion that opponents of gays in the military had feared, and it was noteworthy that when the Trump administration moved to ban the accession of transgender recruits, it was the Joint Chiefs of Staff who objected, in a stark reversal of roles from Clinton administration days.[121]

Even as military leaders moved to reassert their connections to broader society, the status of veterans and serving military personnel within American society continued to grow. Military service conferred not only special rights and privileges but, increasingly, a special social status as well. This state of affairs was the logical outcome of the success of the All-Volunteer Force. The military welfare state and the fact that only a small number of Americans now deployed to fight the nation's wars helped to create a class of citizens apart. Even if Cold War–era martial citizenship had long since faded away, the elevated status of the military meant that concepts relating to military service, its obligations, its rights and its privileges continued to figure in discussions over citizenship.

* * *

We can observe this enduring connection between military service and questions of citizenship in the fact that the military continues to be a site of contestation in the ongoing culture wars, and as different groups continue their efforts to open up military service to more parts of society. What is striking, though, is the campaigns to fully open the ranks of the military to women and allow gay personnel to serve openly displayed few of the tensions that had wracked Black civil rights organizations in previous eras. These contemporary campaigns emphasized that excluding citizens from military service on the basis of gender and sexuality was inherently wrong, while making no critique of the role of the military in American life, or indeed in the world more broadly. The relative absence of such tensions within these modern-day civil rights movements points to how successful the move to the All-Volunteer Force was in removing concerns about war-making from mainstream conversations.

The year 1973, then, represents an important inflection point in that it changed how Americans thought about military service. While the targeted way in which the draft functioned meant that many thought about military service as a choice rather than an obligation long before the end of conscription, the

---

[121] Tara Copp, 'All 4 Service Chiefs on Record: No Harm to Units from Transgender Service', *Military Times*, 25 April 2018, https://www.militarytimes.com/news/your-military/2018/04/24/all-4-service-chiefs-on-record-no-harm-to-unit-from-transgender-service/.

very existence of Selective Service and the sheer number of men who went through that system meant that the draft had a profound influence on American society during its lifetime. At its apogee during the early Cold War, the citizen soldier ideal was one that was almost universally promoted and celebrated. From its origins in the build-up to American intervention in the Second World War to its demise in the aftermath of American withdrawal from Vietnam, the draft channelled generations of American men either into the military or into college, while policymakers used it to single out particular groups, from married fathers to young men born into poverty, for particular attention and to promote particular familial and masculine ideals. Added to this, social policies designed to reward military personnel meant that military service had as much to do with the material rewards of citizenship as it did its obligations, and ensured that the draft had an impact on American society that was broader than questions of who should serve and who should not.

These questions seemed to become significantly less fraught with the end of the draft. Widespread martial citizenship faded at the same time as the New Deal did, and the military joined the marketplace, while it strengthened its own welfare programmes in order to ensure that it could continue to recruit enough personnel in the absence of conscription. Thus, the All-Volunteer Force was a vehicle for social mobility, even as it still worked to exclude those who, like Sergeant Perry Watkins, it deemed to represent values that it wished to condemn. While military service and militarized understandings of the role of institutions like universities and labour unions became less central to American life, what endured was the notion of the soldier as a form of model citizen. Marginalized groups continued to fight for access to military service as a marker of full citizenship, and the American public began to ostentatiously celebrate soldiers as inherently heroic in a way that arguably surpassed even the height of such glorification during the Second World War. In acting as a vehicle for idealized projections of what it meant to be American, the All-Volunteer Force – although now quite distant from the civilian society that it served – continued to inform discussions about the meanings of citizenship and American identity.

6

War in the American imagination

In early August 1990, the US Marines at Twentynine Palms learned of Iraq's invasion of Kuwait and were immediately put on standby for deployment to the Middle East. The sniper platoon of the Second Battalion, Seventh Marines began preparing themselves for war. First, they marched to the base barber to get fresh haircuts, and then they sent some of the platoon into the nearby town to 'rent all the war movies they [could] get their hands on'.[1] As memoirist Anthony Swofford recounts, the platoon spent three days watching and re-watching these movies, especially Vietnam films, as they waited for more news about their coming deployment. In an effort to prepare themselves for the brutality and excitement of war, they endlessly replayed famous scenes from *Apocalypse Now*, *Platoon* and *Full Metal Jacket*. For Swofford, 'Vietnam war films are all pro-war, no matter what the supposed message, what Kubrick or Coppola or Stone intended.' Civilians might watch these films and 'weep and decide once and for all that war is inhumane and terrible, and they will tell their friends at church and their family this', but the military personnel who 'watch the same films and are excited by them, because the magic brutality of the films celebrates the terrible and despicable beauty of their fighting skills'.[2]

Swofford's memoir of the Persian Gulf War, *Jarhead*, is filled with observations like these. For Swofford and his peers, their expectations for and experiences of war were mediated through cultural depictions of past wars, especially the United States' most recent war in Vietnam. Throughout the book, though, there is also a marked tension between these expectations – of violence and drama and sex – and the Marines' lived experiences of war in the Persian Gulf, which more often centred on discomfort and boredom. Swofford and his fellow snipers look for combat, for the opportunity to demonstrate their skills and to experience

[1] Anthony Swofford, *Jarhead: A Marine's Chronicle of the Gulf War and Other Battles* (New York: Scribner, 2003), 5.
[2] Swofford, *Jarhead*, 6–7.

the excitement of battle, but they are always foiled by the American airpower that precedes them and destroys Iraqi forces before the advancing ground forces can engage them. Even the cultural associations from the Vietnam War begin to bother Swofford as he complains about a psychological operations unit playing loud music on the battlefield: 'It was fine in the movies, on the boat with Martin Sheen going up the fake Vietnamese Congo or with the grunts patrolling the Ho Chi Minh and as they take a hill and heavy casualties, but I don't need the Who and the Doors in my war.'[3] What *Jarhead* captures very well is that there was a disjuncture between Swofford's wartime experiences and those of American veterans of the Vietnam War and of earlier conflicts. It was as if the reality of war was disappearing from view in the gloom of smoke from Kuwaiti oilfield fires, where even snipers found it difficult to perceive it clearly.

If Swofford and his comrades experienced war as both an embodied episode and as a set of imaginative associations, then for most Americans, the Gulf War was an entirely cultural event. Famously, it was the first war of the era of the 24-hour news channel, and networks like CNN provided steams of dramatic footage from Baghdad and Kuwait to inform and entertain their viewers.[4] News broadcasts also made heavy use of coalition-supplied footage from bomb and missile cameras to show the perspective of the actual machinery of war.[5] The French postmodern theorist Jean Baudrillard took note of this development and identified a similar rupture to Swofford, going so far in a series of essays to declare that the Gulf War 'will not take place', 'is not taking place' and 'did not take place'.[6] Baudrillard thought that this 'promotional, speculative, virtual' war no longer corresponded to old understandings of war, and that what was truly at stake was not a question of conquest or domination but 'war itself: its status, its meaning, its future'.[7] War had 'lost much of its credibility' during the long Cold War and now the Western protagonists of the Gulf War were attempting to demonstrate its utility once more, through a series of heavily stage-managed events.[8] Whether or not the leaders of the military coalition assembled to fight

---

[3] Swofford, *Jarhead*, 213; Andrea Porter, '"Jarhead" and the Failure of the Vietnam Myth', *CEA Critic* 73, no. 1 (2010): 1–14.

[4] Douglas Kellner, *The Persian Gulf TV War* (Boulder, CO: Westview Press, 1992); Hamid Mowlana, George Gerbner and Herbert Schiller, eds, *Triumph of the Image: The Media's War in the Persian Gulf, a Global Perspective* (Boulder, CO: Routledge, 1992); W. Lance Bennett and David L. Paletz, eds, *Taken by Storm: The Media, Public Opinion, and U.S. Foreign Policy in the Gulf War* (Chicago: University of Chicago Press, 1994).

[5] News networks and wire services were far more reluctant to show the effects of those weapons. Torie Rose DeGhett, 'The War Photo No One Would Publish', *The Atlantic*, 8 August 2014, https://www.theatlantic.com/international/archive/2014/08/the-war-photo-no-one-would-publish/375762/.

[6] Jean Baudrillard, *The Gulf War Did Not Take Place* (Indianapolis: Indiana University Press, 1995).

[7] Baudrillard, *The Gulf War Did Not Take Place*, 30, 32.

[8] Baudrillard, *The Gulf War Did Not Take Place*, 32.

the war consciously shared the objectives that Baudrillard ascribed to them, they certainly worked hard to manage the images that emerged from the war, heavily restricting press access and remaining acutely aware of the scenes that ran on news networks.

Americans did experience the war as more than grainy images of high-tech missiles hitting their targets, though. In the run-up to the opening of hostilities between the coalition and the Iraqis, there was a boom in what one commentator has called 'imperial folk art', including wildly popular t-shirts depicting Bart Simpson doing violence to Saddam Hussein, and 'Iraqi' calendars that showed the year ending on 15 January 1991, the date of the UN ultimatum for the withdrawal of Iraqi forces from Kuwait.[9] This jingoist commercialism was also paired with a more civic-nationalist-oriented appreciation of the armed forces. As historian Melani McAlister has argued, news coverage venerated a form of 'military multiculturalism' and highlighted the fact that the force deployed to Saudi Arabia contained a wide cross section of American society, including, for the first time, many women.[10] Not only was this an indication of the social progress that Americans had made over the past few decades, but it invested the military with moral authority and made them positive examples for the rest of the world. Swofford and his fellow Marines may not have felt that way, but Americans certainly embraced them as paragons of the best of the nation throughout 1990 and 1991.

Americans did not just consume the war; they also participated in it as a cultural event. From letter writing campaigns and organizing mass care packages to the prominent display of yellow ribbons (the first time this practice was associated with the troops) to the millions who attended victory parades in American cities and towns in the aftermath of the war, large segments of the population actively displayed their support for the war or, more accurately, their support for the troops.[11] The war may indeed have largely been no more than a

---

[9] Matt Stieb, 'Operation Desert Shirt: Revisiting the Civilian Souvenirs of the Gulf War, Thirty Years On', The Baffler, 18 January 2021, https://thebaffler.com/latest/operation-desert-shirt-stieb; David Fitzgerald, 'Supporting the Troops, Debating the War: The Persian Gulf War in Kentucky', *Register of the Kentucky Historical Society* 117, no. 3 (2019): 580, https://doi.org/10.1353/khs.2019.0093.

[10] Melani McAlister, *Epic Encounters: Culture, Media, and U.S. Interests in the Middle East since 1945* (Berkeley: University of California Press, 2005), 235–59.

[11] George Mariscal, 'In the Wake of the Gulf War: Untying the Yellow Ribbon', *Cultural Critique*, no. 19 (1991): 97–117, https://doi.org/10.2307/1354309; Jack Santino, 'Yellow Ribbons and Seasonal Flags: The Folk Assemblage of War', *Journal of American Folklore* 105, no. 415 (1992): 19–33, https://doi.org/10.2307/541997; David Fitzgerald, 'Support the Troops: Gulf War Homecomings and a New Politics of Military Celebration', *Modern American History* 2, no. 1 (March 2019): 1–22, https://doi.org/10.1017/mah.2019.1.

spectacle for the vast majority of Americans, but they could tell themselves that they played some part in it.

It is all the more curious, then, that the Gulf War has not lived long in the cultural memory of the United States. Swofford's memoir was a bestseller and was made into an equally successful movie, and there have been a few other attempts at cinematic renderings of the war, such as *Three Kings* and *Courage under Fire*, but troops preparing to depart for Iraq or Afghanistan in the mid-2000s were far more likely to be watching the Second World War or Vietnam films as they prepared for their own deployments.[12] The Gulf War burned very brightly in the American imagination for a brief period of time, and then faded away.

The relative impermanence of the Gulf War in American culture is indicative of an important trend in the ways in which Americans have thought about war since the 1940s. By the end of the twentieth century, personal experience of war was something that was increasingly uncommon for Americans, who instead encountered it through the news media and through cultural representations. This chapter is concerned with delineating how Americans perceived and imagined war, and ultimately with describing how war as an experience began to slip out of the American imagination. It draws on the important work of scholars such as Marilyn Young, Andrew Bacevich, Mary Dudziak and Michael Sherry to show that often the consequences of war have been erased from American culture and memory.[13] As the Gulf War demonstrated, patriotism could still be mobilized in support of war, even as technology and changes in the news media made it into something akin to a spectator sport for many Americans.

This is not to say that we are solely concerned here with telling the story of that erasure, though. Historians have done immensely useful work in showing how war has, at various times, been centrally important to American culture and how the stories Americans told themselves about war were fundamental to their ideas about American identity and about the place of the United States in the world.[14] Therefore, the political stakes of war stories have always been

---

[12] Edward Zwick, *Courage under Fire* (Fox 2000 Pictures, Davis Entertainment, Joseph M. Singer Entertainment, 1996); David O. Russell, *Three Kings* (Warner Bros., Village Roadshow Pictures, Village-A.M. Partnership, 1999).

[13] Mark Philip Bradley and Mary L. Dudziak, eds, *Making the Forever War: Marilyn Young on the Culture and Politics of American Militarism* (Amherst: University of Massachusetts Press, 2021); Andrew J. Bacevich, *The New American Militarism: How Americans Are Seduced by War* (New York: Oxford University Press, 2005); Mary Dudziak, *War Time: An Idea, Its History, Its Consequences* (New York: Oxford University Press, 2012); Michael Sherry, *In the Shadow of War: The United States since the 1930s* (New Haven, CT: Yale University Press, 1995).

[14] Of course, this scholarship covers the entire span of American history. For a limited sample, see Jill Lepore, *The Name of War: King Philip's War and the Origins of American Identity* (New York: Vintage Books, 1999); Walter L. Hixson, *The Myth of American Diplomacy: National Identity and U.S. Foreign*

very high. While some scholars have emphasized culture as a battlefield where consent for military intervention might be either manufactured or withheld, others have noted that televisual, film and literary portrayals of combat have not only influenced how the American public thought about war, gender roles and race but have also shaped, in subtle ways, the world views of strategists and policymakers.[15] Much as Swofford tried (and failed) to make sense of his own experiences in the Persian Gulf through the tropes of Vietnam movies, the way that war has figured in the imaginations of policymakers has in turn affected how they have made decisions on intervention and waged their wars.

As with other chapters in this book, the Second World War features here as a crucial moment. The scale of the war and the United States' decisive role in the Allied victory meant that the war had cultural reverberations that still resonate. Hollywood, along with the rest of the country, mobilized for war, and, as historian Michael Sherry observes, the war film genre was effectively invented during the conflict.[16] The omnipresence of war in American culture during this era, though, should not be read as the product of open militarism. The stories Americans told about war implied that they were reluctant warriors, with a military composed of free-thinking citizen soldiers, in stark contrast to the militarized societies of Germany and Japan. It was only after the war, and with the dawn of the atomic age, that these stories began to change. With the threat of Soviet nuclear attack seeming far more real than any fears of German or Japanese bombers reaching American shores, war as a threat to the American way of life loomed larger in the imagination, and films, novels and comic books sold war (or the readiness for war) as a necessity, and more openly celebrated forms of military masculinity. At the same time, the experience of total war in the Second World War meant that few Americans could see war as taking any form but global, all-encompassing conflict. The cataclysm of the Second World War still loomed large in those years and formed the canvas on which ideas about war, identity and military masculinity were projected.

Policy (New Haven, CT: Yale University Press, 2008); Kristin L. Hoganson, *Fighting for American Manhood: How Gender Politics Provoked the Spanish-American and Philippine-American Wars* (New Haven, CT: Yale University Press, 1998); Philip Gleason, 'Americans All: World War II and the Shaping of American Identity', *Review of Politics* 43, no. 4 (1981): 483–518; Christopher Capozzola, *Uncle Sam Wants You: World War I and the Making of the Modern American Citizen* (Oxford: Oxford University Press, 2010); Eric Foner, 'Who Is an American? The Imagined Community in American History', *Centennial Review* 41, no. 3 (1997): 425–38.

15 Theo Farrell, 'Memory, Imagination and War', *History* 87, no. 285 (2002): 61–73; Adrian R. Lewis, *The American Culture of War: The History of U.S. Military Force from World War II to Operation Iraqi Freedom* (Abingdon: Routledge, 2006); David Ryan, *US Collective Memory, Intervention and Vietnam: The Cultural Politics of US Foreign Policy since 1969* (London: Routledge, forthcoming).

16 Sherry, *In the Shadow of War*, 158.

This trajectory of growing militarization in American culture was shattered by the experience of Vietnam, however. There, much as Swofford struggled to reconcile his Vietnam-derived images of war with his own experiences, young men raised on narrative of the good war were perplexed and horrified by what they experienced in Indochina as well. The Vietnam experience also gave rise to a cultural turn away from militarism, in parallel with the rise of a large and well-organized anti-war movement. Cooperation between Hollywood and the military hit a low ebb, and narratives of American innocence became much less common.

The backlash to this anti-war sentiment, in the form of the action movies of the 1980s along with broader struggles over the myths and memories of the war in Vietnam, didn't restore consensus but was rather indicative of a splintering in American culture, where disillusionment with the Vietnam experience coupled with the increasing distance between war and American life meant that war as a phenomenon began to lose its coherence, as many contested its utility and others only understood it as an abstraction. For policymakers and the public alike, this problem only became more acute with the end of the Cold War which, although nebulous in form, still offered something on which to anchor understandings of war, retaining as it did the Second World War–era notions of total, worldwide struggle. Even as American wars ground on overseas and war seemingly spilled out of its temporal boundaries to become a 'forever war' in the years after the 9/11 attacks, while militarized culture became more pervasive, war became less real and its consequences faded further from view.[17]

* * *

As the historian Adrian Lewis has observed, when most Americans think of war, the Civil War and the Second World War immediately spring to mind. Both of these conflicts were huge, all-encompassing events that transformed the United States, and so they live on in collective consciousness. For Lewis, 'Americans believe they know what these wars were like, what they were about, and why they ended the way they did.' These two conflicts therefore provide the images for 'what real war ought to look like'.[18] Of the two, the Second World War arguably now looms larger, given both its status as the most participatory war of the twentieth century and its closer proximity to the present day. To understand how contemporary Americans have imagined war, then, it is vital

---

[17] Dudziak, *War Time*; Dexter Filkins, *The Forever War* (New York: Knopf, 2008).
[18] Adrian R. Lewis, 'The American Culture of War in the Age of Artificial Limited War', in *Warfare and Culture in World History*, ed. Wayne E. Lee (New York: New York University Press, 2011), 188.

to put the Second World War at the centre of our discussion. The outpouring of fictional depictions of the war has hardly let up since the early 1940s, and the continuing commemorations of the Second World War have been the subject of huge bodies of work in the fields of both history and memory studies.[19] While the Second World War has not been quite as all-consuming in the United States as it has been in other countries, where it is often referred to as simply 'the war', it certainly dominated American understandings of war for generations and arguably continues to do so, even if its image has been refracted through subsequent experiences.

Unlike the Civil War, the fighting in the Second World War took place almost exclusively elsewhere. There was combat in the sparsely populated Aleutian islands but, apart from the cursory attempts by Japanese submarines to shell facilities on the West coast and an equally unsuccessful Japanese 'balloon bomb' campaign, the Pearl Harbor attack was the only major battle that occurred in a heavily populated area in the United States or its incorporated territories.[20] Crucially, this meant that, in the words of historian Mary Dudziak, 'Americans at home could only look at World War II through the eyes of others.'[21] This meant that for the majority of Americans, while the war brought about immense social and cultural upheaval, they did not have first-hand experience of the terror of war in the way that civilians in Europe, Asia and elsewhere did. This marked a stark contrast with the Civil War, which was fought on American soil with evidence of destruction everywhere and came with a staggering death toll that meant that all parts of the nation were touched by it.[22] For Dudziak, 'the history

---

[19] Philip D. Beidler, *The Good War's Greatest Hits: World War II and American Remembering* (Athens: University of Georgia Press, 1998); John Bodnar, *The 'Good War' in American Memory* (Baltimore, MD: Johns Hopkins University Press, 2010); Patrick Finney, 'Politics and Technologies of Authenticity: The Second World War at the Close of Living Memory', *Rethinking History* 21, no. 2 (3 April 2017): 154–70, https://doi.org/10.1080/13642529.2017.1315967; Marc Gallicchio, 'World War II in Historical Memory', in *A Companion to World War II*, ed. Thomas Zeiler and Daniel M. DuBois (Hoboken, NJ: John Wiley, 2012), 978–98, https://doi.org/10.1002/9781118325018.ch57; Peter Schrijvers, 'War against Evil', in *Heroism and the Changing Character of War: Toward Post-Heroic Warfare?*, ed. Sibylle Scheipers (London: Palgrave Macmillan UK, 2014), 76–92, https://doi.org/10.1057/9781137362537_6; Penny Summerfield, 'Conflict, Power and Gender in Women's Memories of the Second World War: A Mass-Observation Study', *Miranda. Revue Pluridisciplinaire Du Monde Anglophone/Multidisciplinary Peer-Reviewed Journal on the English-Speaking World*, no. 2 (1 July 2010), https://doi.org/10.4000/miranda.1253.
[20] Bert Webber, *Silent Siege: Japanese Attacks against North America in World War II* (Fairfield, WA: Ye Galleon Press, 1984); Ross Coen, *Fu-Go: The Curious History of Japan's Balloon Bomb Attack on America* (Lincoln: University of Nebraska Press, 2014); Emily S. Rosenberg, *A Date Which Will Live: Pearl Harbor in American Memory* (Durham, NC: Duke University Press, 2003).
[21] Mary L Dudziak, '"You Didn't See Him Lying … beside the Gravel Road in France": Death, Distance, and American War Politics', *Diplomatic History* 42, no. 1 (1 January 2018): 1, https://doi.org/10.1093/dh/dhx087.
[22] Drew Gilpin Faust, *This Republic of Suffering* (New York: Knopf Doubleday Publishing Group, 2008).

of American war since the Civil War has been, in part, a history of losing a more intimate connection with the dead. Americans continued to kill and die in war, but the dying happened somewhere else.'[23]

During the Second World War, civilians had to rely on letters home, news reports and fictional depictions of combat in order to imagine what war was like. Letters home from soldiers, no matter how candid, could not capture the sensory experience of war, and even those whose profession was conveying meaning through words or pictures – the war correspondents – could not adequately convey the destruction that they saw.[24] In 1943, in an attempt to make the cost of the war clear to those at home, *Life* Magazine published George Strock's photo of three dead American soldiers on Buna beach, arguing that if GIs 'had the guts to take it, then we ought to have the guts to look at it'.[25] But Strock's photos could not tell the viewer that 'he rarely bathed when in New Guinea because he said the water tasted like dead bodies'.[26] Similarly, journalists such as Ernie Pyle and Bill Mauldin, whose deeply sympathetic portrayals of the hardship of military life made them beloved by the troops, were frustrated at their own inability to express what they really saw.[27] As Dudziak argues, this unbridgeable gap between those who experienced war and those who did not marks a midpoint in the long drift away from a public that engaged with death and suffering to one that was isolated from military violence and apathetic about war.

Ironically, military leaders worried about the possibility of apathy throughout the war in such a way that it meant that they quite often let reports that portrayed the horrors of combat slip through the censor's filters. Indeed, some commanders, such as Admiral Nimitz and General Eisenhower, expressed a preference for 'realistic' portrayals of war, especially after the fortunes of Allies changed for the better in 1943, so that the public might be steeled for the sacrifices to come.[28] In 1944, the Roosevelt administration even accentuated American monthly casualty figures in order to demonstrate to the Soviet Union that the United

---

[23] Dudziak, '"You Didn't See Him Lying … beside the Gravel Road in France"', 10.

[24] Susan L. Carruthers, 'Communications Media, the U.S. Military, and the War Brought Home', in *At War: The Military and American Culture in the Twentieth Century and Beyond*, ed. David Kieran and Edwin A. Martini (New Brunswick, NJ: Rutgers University Press, 2018), 258–78.

[25] 'Editorial: Three Americans', *LIFE Magazine*, 20 September 1943. The photo was only published after a lengthy battle with censors in the Office of War Information.

[26] Dudziak, '"You Didn't See Him Lying … beside the Gravel Road in France"', 3.

[27] Andrew J. Huebner, *Warrior Image: Soldiers in American Culture from the Second World War to the Vietnam Era* (Chapel Hill: University of North Carolina Press, 2008), 39–43; Susan A. Brewer, *Why America Fights: Patriotism and War Propaganda from the Philippines to Iraq* (Oxford: Oxford University Press, 2009), 120.

[28] John McCallum, 'U.S. Censorship, Violence, and Moral Judgement in a Wartime Democracy, 1941–1945', *Diplomatic History* 41, no. 3 (1 June 2017): 555, https://doi.org/10.1093/dh/dhw058.

States was pulling its weight.[29] This meant that while censorship was certainly extensive throughout the war – technical details of weaponry were out, as was any hint about war crimes committed by American soldiers – it began to ease in its later years, where military censors made little effort to minimize graphic descriptions of combat, including the deliberate targeting of enemy civilians in bombing raids.[30] By the end of the war, censors, journalists and even Hollywood producers were all emphasizing the need for a tough-minded attitude about what war demanded of its participants.

If these portrayals of combat were 'realistic', then they were still far from unsentimental. Wartime films such as *Wake Island, Bataan, Guadalcanal Diary* and *Thirty Seconds over Tokyo* all paired a relatively unflinching view of the harshness of battle with a compassionate portrayal of American soldiers.[31] News reports and films emphasized not only what they suffered but also their ordinariness. Almost universally, soldiers were portrayed as reluctant warriors, torn from their peaceful lives to fight fascism. In the words of radio broadcaster Norman Corwin, 'far-fling ordinary men, unspectacular but free, rousing out of their habits and their homes, got up early one morning, flexed their muscles, learned (as amateurs) the manual of arms, and set out across perilous plains and ocean to whop the bejesus out of the professionals'.[32] Oscar-winning films such as *Sergeant York* and *Casablanca* pushed for intervention by telling the story of reluctant Americans (a religious conscientious objector in the First World War in the case of *Sergeant York*, a cynical expat in Vichy Morocco in the case of *Casablanca*) moved to cast aside their doubts and embrace both internationalism and war.[33]

---

[29] Huebner, *Warrior Image*, 21.

[30] For the debate on the extent to which the press was self-censoring during the war, see George Roeder, *The Censored War: American Visual Experience during World War II: American Visual Experience during World War Two* (New Haven, CT: Yale University Press, 1995); Steven Casey, *The War Beat, Europe: The American Media at War against Nazi Germany* (New York: Oxford University Press, 2017); Sam Lebovic, *Free Speech and Unfree News: The Paradox of Press Freedom in America* (Cambridge, MA: Harvard University Press, 2016), 121–48; McCallum, 'U.S. Censorship, Violence, and Moral Judgement in a Wartime Democracy, 1941–1945'; Dudziak, ' "You Didn't See Him Lying … beside the Gravel Road in France" '.

[31] Tanine Allison, *Destructive Sublime: World War II in American Film and Media.* (New Brunswick, NJ: Rutgers University Press, 2018); Jeanine Basinger, 'The World War II Combat Film: Definition', in *The War Film*, ed. Robert Eberwein (New Brunswick, NJ: Rutgers University Press, 2004), 30–49.

[32] Norman Corwin, *On a Note of Triumph* (New York: Simon & Schuster, 1945), 11, http://archive.org/details/onnoteoftriumph00corw.

[33] The film historian Lary May has called this the 'conversion narrative'. Lary May, *The Big Tomorrow: Hollywood and the Politics of the American Way* (Chicago: University of Chicago Press, 2000), 139–74; Michael E. Birdwell, *Celluloid Soldiers: The Warner Bros. Campaign Against Nazism* (New York: New York University Press, 2000).

Americans defined themselves against the open militarism of the Germans and Japanese, and propaganda contrasted 'free societies' with 'slave societies'.[34] Director Frank Capra's *Why We Fight* documentary series, produced for the Department of War, sketched out the history of the rise of totalitarian militarism for US service members and the general public alike.[35] American soldiers were free men who took no pleasure in war, while the Germans and Japanese were automatons who attempted to excuse their crimes by claiming that they were just following orders. In his VE Day broadcast, 'On a Note of Triumph', Corwin celebrated the demise of this militarism at the hand of the common man, opening the transmission with the famous lines: 'take a bow, G.I., take a bow, little guy. The superman of tomorrow lies at the feet of you common men of this afternoon'.[36]

The language of the common man was very much a part of the vernacular of wartime American culture. The Roosevelt administration's invocation of the 'Four Freedoms' as the central aim of the war put liberal notions about universal ideals at the heart of the war effort, while Vice President Henry Wallace's 1942 speech proclaiming the 'century of the common man' was given musical expression in Aaron Copland's composition *Fanfare for the Common Man*.[37] The administration created the Office of War Information (OWI) as its official propaganda outlet in 1942, which promoted the idea of a 'people's war' and drew upon New Deal ideals to make the case for the war effort to Americans.[38] The OWI attempted to learn lessons from its First World War–era counterpart, the Committee for Public Information, and was far less heavy-handed in its censorship. Nonetheless, via its Bureau of Motion Pictures, it worked closely with Hollywood studios, reviewing movie scripts and offering suggestions on how they might better promote the war aims.[39]

Hollywood movies, official propaganda and commercial advertising all promoted some idealized notion of the small town filled with honest and ordinary people as the thing that the troops were fighting for.[40] Norman Rockwell

---

[34] Brewer, *Why America Fights*, 104.

[35] Frank Capra, *Why We Fight: Prelude to War*, accessed 11 March 2021, http://archive.org/details/PreludeToWar.

[36] Corwin, *On a Note of Triumph*, 9.

[37] Sean Wilentz, *Bob Dylan in America* (New York: Random House, 2011), 17–46.

[38] Allan M. Winkler, *Politics of Propaganda: Office of War Information, 1942–45* (New Haven, CT: Yale University Press, 1978); Lebovic, *Free Speech and Unfree News*, 122–8; Brewer, *Why America Fights*, 88–140.

[39] Brewer, *Why America Fights*, 102–3; Clayton R. Koppes and Gregory D. Black, 'What to Show the World: The Office of War Information and Hollywood, 1942–1945', *Journal of American History* 64, no. 1 (1977): 87–105, https://doi.org/10.2307/1888275.

[40] On advertising during the war, see John Bush Jones, *All-Out for Victory!: Magazine Advertising and the World War II Home Front* (Hanover, NH: Brandeis University Press, 2009); Inger L. Stole,

translated the universal ideals of Roosevelt's 'Four Freedoms' into small-town imagery in his famous series of paintings of the same name, depicting small-town Americans living out those freedoms.[41] The war only directly intrudes onto one of these images. In 'Freedom from Fear', a mother and father stand watchfully over their sleeping children; in the father's hand is a newspaper that features a headline about the German bombing of London.[42] More than anything else, this particular message about threat seems to have cut through. As historian John Bodnar notes, Roosevelt's war aims didn't necessarily mean a lot to those fighting – one 1943 survey of the troops indicated that only 13 per cent of them could name at least three of the four freedoms – but the vast majority accepted the notion that the United States must fight now if it wanted to protect itself from Axis aggression on its own soil.[43] As noted in Chapter 2, distance seemed to collapse during the Second World War and Americans felt directly threatened by foreign aggression in a way that they had not for well over a hundred years. Indeed, in his VE Day radio broadcast celebrating 'the little guy', Norman Corwin proclaimed that 'we've learned that our east coast is the west bank of the Rhine and that the defences of Seattle begin in Shanghai'.[44] For Corwin, there could be no return to pre-war normality, because 'vigilance pays interest and compounds into peace, whereas bland unconcern and the appeasing cheek draw blitzkrieg as a lightning rod attracts a thunderbolt'. He urged Americans 'to do a little civil thinking every day and not pass up the front page for the sports page as we did before'.[45]

This meant that while Americans certainly retained their self-image as reluctant and anti-militarist warriors, they would henceforth have to be prepared for conflict. The Second World War was a distant war for most Americans, experienced via letters home, radio broadcasts and movies, but it was such a massive and disruptive social event that it lodged in their minds as the archetype of war itself. For many, the lesson of the Second World War was that all wars could become world wars eventually, and the notion that war was necessarily a total and global phenomenon became central to how Americans imagined it.

* * *

Advertising at War: Business, Consumers, and Government in the 1940s (Urbana: University of Illinois Press, 2012).
[41] Brewer, *Why America Fights*, 119–21.
[42] Robert B. Westbrook, *Why We Fought: Forging American Obligations in World War II* (Washington, DC: Smithsonian Institution, 2010), 44–8.
[43] Bodnar, *The 'Good War' in American Memory*, 26.
[44] Corwin, *On a Note of Triumph*, 48.
[45] Corwin, *On a Note of Triumph*, 62.

The triumphalism of VE Day did not last. Although the defeat of Japan followed swiftly, the manner of that defeat made a return to pre-war normality almost impossible to imagine. As news of the atomic bombing of Hiroshima and Nagasaki reached Americans, they reacted with shock and fear.[46] While there was certainly a degree of vindictiveness and anti-Japanese racism in the coverage of the bombings mixed with relief that an invasion of Japan would no longer be necessary, most quickly grasped how much had changed.[47] On 6 August 1945, the day after the bombing of Hiroshima, the *St Louis Post-Dispatch* warned that science may have 'signed the mammalian world's death warrant and deeded an earth in ruin to ants'.[48] Even if the contours of the Cold War were not yet visible, the stakes of war now seemed higher than ever, and few seemed to think that the United States would maintain its nuclear monopoly for long. Historian Paul Boyer has pointed to a certain irony in this reaction: 'Physically untouched by the war, the United States at the moment of victory perceived itself as naked and vulnerable. Sole possessors and users of a devastating new instrument of mass destruction, Americans envisioned themselves not as a potential threat to other peoples, but as potential victims.'[49]

Part of this blindness to the consequences of American power surely stemmed from the American self-image of the United States as a nation of anti-militarists, reluctant to intervene overseas (Figure 6.1). In this telling, disaster had only been averted because German scientists had not managed to unlock the secrets of the bomb before the war ended. Elements of this narrative of innocence persisted into the 1960s. As historian Gretchen Heefner notes, the fact that United States named its first solid-fuel ICBM the 'Minuteman' hearkened back to colonial-era militias and implied a defensive purpose, as if Americans would never be the aggressor in a nuclear war.[50] More generally, though, fears of nuclear attack stemmed from a sense that the Second World War had proven that war was ineradicable. Reflecting on the end of the war on 17 August 1945, the radio commentator H. V. Kaltenborn was already thinking ahead as he asked his listeners to reflect on 'the mass murder which will come with World War III'.[51] News of the bomb prompted a renewal of

---

[46] Paul Boyer, *By the Bomb's Early Light: American Thought and Culture at the Dawn of the Atomic Age* (Chapel Hill: University of North Carolina Press, 1994), 3–26.

[47] On anti-Japanese sentiment and reactions to the atomic bomb, see Boyer, *By the Bomb's Early Light*, 12–13; Matthew Jones, *After Hiroshima: The United States, Race and Nuclear Weapons in Asia, 1945–1965* (Cambridge: Cambridge University Press, 2010), 8–9; John Dower, *War without Mercy: Race and Power in the Pacific War* (New York: Pantheon Books, 1986), 142.

[48] 'A Decision for Mankind', *St. Louis Post-Dispatch*, 7 August 1945.

[49] Boyer, *By the Bomb's Early Light*, 14.

[50] Gretchen Heefner, *The Missile Next Door: The Minuteman in the American Heartland* (Cambridge, MA: Harvard University Press, 2012), 36.

[51] Boyer, *By the Bomb's Early Light*, 7.

Figure 6.1 Mushroom cloud with ships below during Operation Crossroads nuclear weapons test on Bikini Atoll, July 1946. Credit: Library of Congress, Prints and Photographs Division.

campaigns for peace by international movements, but much as institutions like the United Nations were less ambitious in their hopes for permanent peace than the League of Nations had been, the notion that war could be eliminated never caught hold in the popular imagination as it did after the First World War.[52]

Given the seeming inevitability of nuclear war, there was an understandable impulse to attempt to normalize and domesticate nuclear weapons. From government-sponsored public service broadcasts and educational films that taught children to 'duck and cover' to the sale of fallout shelters, to commercial

---

[52] Petra Goedde, *The Politics of Peace: A Global Cold War History* (New York: Oxford University Press, 2019).

advertising that used mushroom clouds and metaphors about explosiveness to sell products, signs of a new atomic age were everywhere in American culture throughout the 1940s and 1950s.[53] These symbols even seeped into childhood. Alongside models of other products of the technological revolution of the Second World War, parents could buy their children replicas of nuclear submarines or water-powered 'ICBMs'. However, as cultural commentator Tom Engelhardt has observed, 'there was something palpably unplayful in "nuclear toys." For obvious reasons, one could not lose oneself in them.'[54] As Boyer has argued, the ubiquity of 'atomic ephemera' and attempts to make light of the bomb should not distract from the depth of anxiety and apprehension that its existence caused in American culture.[55]

This anxiety found expression in various forms of fiction. Comic books introduced superheroes who derived their powers from atomic energy, while the science fiction genre exploded into the mainstream, as audiences began to regard as prophetic those writers who had been speculating about atomic war for decades.[56] Few of these visions offered any reassurances about nuclear weapons. Ray Bradbury's 1950 best-selling short story collection, *The Martian Chronicles*, documents the destruction of human life on Earth after a global nuclear war, while films such as *On the Beach* (1959), *Fail-Safe* and *Dr Strangeglove* (both 1964) offered visions of nuclear apocalypse and stinging criticisms of the Cold War policies that risked global nuclear war.[57]

Of the three, *On the Beach* offers the most comprehensive portrait of a post-apocalyptic world. Set in Australia, the only remaining refuge for human life after the Third World War has devasted the northern hemisphere and killed

---

[53] Michael A. Amundson and Scott C. Zeman, eds, *Atomic Culture: How We Learned to Stop Worrying and Love the Bomb* (Boulder: University Press of Colorado, 2004); Margot A. Henriksen, *Dr. Strangelove's America: Society and Culture in the Atomic Age* (Berkeley: University of California Press, 1997); *The Atomic Cafe (1982) – IMDb*, accessed 11 February 2021, http://www.imdb.com/title/tt0083590/; Nathan Hodge and Sharon Weinberger, *A Nuclear Family Vacation: Travels in the World of Atomic Weaponry* (New York: Bloomsbury USA, 2008); Michael Scheibach, *Atomic Narratives and American Youth: Coming of Age with the Atom, 1945-1955* (Jefferson, NC: McFarland, 2003); Joyce Evans, *Celluloid Mushroom Clouds: Hollywood and Atomic Bomb* (London: Routledge, 2018).

[54] Tom Engelhardt, *The End of Victory Culture: Cold War America and the Disillusioning of a Generation* (Amherst: University of Massachusetts Press, 1998), 81.

[55] Boyer, *By the Bomb's Early Light*, 12; Allan M. Winkler, *Life under a Cloud: American Anxiety about the Atom* (Urbana: University of Illinois Press, 1999).

[56] Ferenc Morton Szasz, *Atomic Comics: Cartoonists Confront the Nuclear World* (Reno: University of Nevada Press, 2013); Steffen Hantke, *Monsters in the Machine: Science Fiction Film and the Militarization of America after World War II* (Jackson: University Press of Mississippi, 2016).

[57] Ray Bradbury, *The Martian Chronicles* (London: HarperCollins UK, 1950); Sidney Lumet, *Fail Safe* (Columbia Pictures, 1964); Stanley Kramer, *On the Beach* (Stanley Kramer Productions, Lomitas Productions, 1959); Stanley Kubrick, *Dr. Strangelove or: How I Learned to Stop Worrying and Love the Bomb* (Columbia Pictures, Hawk Films, 1964).

all humans there with nuclear fallout, it tells the story of surviving humans reckoning with death as air currents carry the radiation inexorably south. The Australian government has distributed suicide pills to the population and after a trip by a surviving US submarine to the US West Coast confirms that it is indeed devoid of human life, the film ends with its characters choosing various forms of suicide. Its closing frames show the deserted streets of Melbourne, where a Salvation Army banner that reads 'there is still time ... brother' flaps in the wind alongside a First World War memorial. The film's message about nuclear war was damaging enough that it ended up being the subject of a cabinet-level discussion chaired by Vice President Richard Nixon, while the US Information Agency and Atomic Energy Commission both produced briefing papers to counter its claims. That it provoked such a high-level reaction is testament to how haunting its depiction of atomic warfare was, and the extent to which visions of nuclear attack were pervasive in American culture in the 1950s.[58]

While visions of global nuclear war may have troubled American culture, these visions of imagined war ran in parallel to a real war in Korea. The lesson of the Second World War and the implications of the nuclear arms race seemed to be that all wars were necessarily global, unlimited and high-tech, and yet the experience of combat in Korea – and crucially, the manner in which it was portrayed – was different. Initially, the outbreak of war on the Korean peninsula in 1950 did seem to fit within the parameters defined by the Second World War. In the words of historian Marilyn Young, 'to be sure, it was all happening in a country most people could neither visualise nor locate. But thick arrows moving relentlessly across clearly defined borders were familiar markers on the geography of American imagination'.[59] Expecting wartime shortages, Americans rushed to buy spare tyres and new cars before the anticipated rationing regime began.[60]

Soon though, it was apparent that Korea was no Second World War. As discussed in Chapter 2, no declaration of war from the Truman administration was forthcoming, and indeed the administration strove to ensure that Americans *didn't* understand Korea as a total war.[61] The imperative to keep the conflict from escalating into a general war with the Soviet Union or China meant that

---

[58] Mick Broderick, 'Fallout on the Beach', *Screening the Past*, no. 36 (2013), http://www.screeningthepast.com/issue-36-first-release/fallout-on-the-beach/#_edn40.

[59] Marilyn B. Young, 'Hard Sell: The Korean War', in *Selling War in a Media Age: The Presidency and Public Opinion in the American Century*, ed. Kenneth Osgood and Andrew K Frank (Gainesville: University Press of Florida, 2011), 115.

[60] Brewer, *Why America Fights*, 151.

[61] Steven Casey, *Selling the Korean War: Propaganda, Politics, and Public Opinion in the United States, 1950–1953* (Oxford: Oxford University Press, 2010).

they described the conflict as a 'police action' and had to push back against the demands of figures like General Douglas MacArthur, who declared that there 'was no substitute for victory' while advocating for the atomic bombing of China. Opinion polling seemed to suggest that the public agreed with MacArthur: wars should be won outright or wound up quickly.[62]

And yet the administration persisted in prosecuting a bloody conflict with a conscript army without much in the way of strong public support. News coverage of the war was gloomy. In the early months of the conflict, journalists ran stories about officers looking on with exhaustion as they learned that their ammunition had run out, and even official newsreel footage from the Army signal corps tended to depict weary and exhausted GIs, with few signs of smiles or thumbs-up gestures.[63] As Andrew Huebner notes, this coverage was in some ways a continuation of earlier trends. Worries about reintegrating broken veterans after 1945 and downbeat post-war novels like Norman Mailer's *The Naked and the Dead* had combined in the aftermath of the war to produce a discourse about soldiers and war that undermined some of the more optimistic portrayals of the Second World War.[64] Photo exhibitions and magazine stories on Korea showed soldiers crying, breaking down and suffering in a way that added complexity to the warrior image and showed the ugliness of the war.[65] Cinematic depictions of the war were ambivalent too. Films like *The Steel Helmet* (1951) portrayed racial tensions and strife between the enlisted ranks and officers and generally depicted soldiers as unfortunate victims put into difficult situations.[66]

Downbeat coverage of the war and of GIs provoked a backlash, not against the coverage itself but against the state of American society. Marine general Chesty Puller complained about the softness of the current generation, claiming that 'our country won't go on forever, if we stay as soft as we are now. There won't be an America – because some foreign soldiers will invade us and take our women and breed a hardier race.'[67] Public concern about the possible 'brainwashing' of American POWs held by the North Koreans stemmed from worries about 'momma's boys' who were too soft to handle captivity and related to broader worries about the danger of 'menticide', or the destruction

---

[62] Casey, *Selling the Korean War*, 253–4; Michael D. Pearlman, *Truman and MacArthur: Policy, Politics, and the Hunger for Honor and Renown* (Bloomington: Indiana University Press, 2008), 199–234.

[63] Huebner, *Warrior Image*, 104–5.

[64] Huebner, *Warrior Image*, 88–91.

[65] Huebner, *Warrior Image*, 125.

[66] Young, 'Hard Sell: The Korean War', 117; Huebner, *Warrior Image*, 149.

[67] Brewer, *Why America Fights*, 152.

of individual autonomy.[68] Cold War pageantry brought the dangers of invasion and totalitarian rule closer to home. For instance, the American Legion staged a mock 'invasion' of Mosinee, Wisconsin, by Soviet forces, where local officials played Stalinist officials, people were searched on the streets, religious leaders were locked up in a concentration camp and restaurants served nothing but black bread and potato soup.[69]

In this atmosphere, militarism became something of a necessity, even if few would deny the ugliness of war. Hollywood films may not have portrayed war as glorious, but, as Christian Appy argues, films of the 1950s tended to contain a sort of sentimental militarism that depicted Americans freely (and temporarily) submitting to military authority, even as they resisted permanent militarization.[70] Meanwhile, men's magazines of the 1950s and 1960s openly celebrated a form of hypermasculine militarism that retold stories from the Second World War that melded war and sex in unique ways.[71] Largely marketed to white working-class teenagers, these pulp magazines encouraged teens to emulate the wartime adventures of their fathers. The pulps were a crucial part of the upbringing of the generation who went to war in Vietnam. Divorced from the grim reality of war in Korea or fears of nuclear holocaust, these narratives of war glorified combat as the crucible of manhood. In his study of pulp magazines, Gregory Daddis argues that we need to pay attention to these hypermasculine and militarist stories as much as we do the subtexts of anxiety that permeated Cold War culture in the United States if we are to understand the visions of war that Americans took with them to Vietnam. The early Cold War was neither a time of straightforward triumphalist militarism nor sustained anti-war activism. Instead, an incoherence crept into American understandings of war, as they were simultaneously preoccupied by the threat of nuclear annihilation, troubled by an unsuccessful and grinding war in Korea, and encouraged to think of American success in the Second World War as the wellspring for post-war prosperity.

* * *

---

[68] Susan L. Carruthers, *Cold War Captives: Imprisonment, Escape, and Brainwashing* (Berkeley: University of California Press, 2009); Charles S. Young, *Name, Rank, and Serial Number: Exploiting Korean War POWs at Home and Abroad* (New York: Oxford University Press, 2014).

[69] Richard M. Fried, *The Russians Are Coming! The Russians Are Coming!: Pageantry and Patriotism in Cold-War America* (New York: Oxford University Press, 1999), 67–86.

[70] Christian G. Appy, "'We'll Follow the Old Man": The Strains of Sentimental Militarism in Popular Films of the Fifties', in *Rethinking Cold War Culture*, ed. Peter J Kuznick and James Burkhart Gilbert (Washington, DC: Smithsonian Institution Press, 2001).

[71] Gregory A. Daddis, *Pulp Vietnam: War and Gender in Cold War Men's Adventure Magazines* (New York: Cambridge University Press, 2020).

Whether it was images from pulp magazines or from films like *The Sands of Iwo Jima*, American soldiers took visions of the Second World War with them to Vietnam. The memoirs of Vietnam veterans are full of references to their fathers' war. The author Tim O'Brien put it that he 'grew out of one war and into another'. He recalled re-enacting the Second World War in games with his childhood friends:

> In patches of weed and clouds of imagination, I learned to play army games. Friends introduced me to the Army Surplus Store off main street. We bought dented relics of our fathers' history, rusted canteens and olive-scented, scarred helmet liners. Then we were our fathers, taking on the Japs and the Krauts along the shores of Lake Okabena, on the flat fairways of the golf course. I rubbed my fingers across my father's war decorations, stole a tiny battle star off one of them, and carried it in my pocket.[72]

Whether they were drafted or volunteered for the war, many GIs went to war with similar romantic notions, built on the sentimental militarism of the 1950s.[73] Marine veteran Philip Caputo complained that 'we went overseas full of illusions, for which the intoxicating atmosphere of those years was as much to blame as our youth'.[74] Caputo was among the first group of combat troops to deploy to Vietnam in March 1965, and the disorienting character of their beach landing in Da Nang – where Marines in full combat gear waded from their landing craft onto the shore where they were greeted by sightseers, Vietnamese girls with Leis and South Vietnamese officers – marked a sharp contrast with the violent and dramatic amphibious landings in Normandy and Inchon. For those who served in Vietnam, the gap between the wartime narratives they grew up with and their own experiences was immediately apparent. The literature from the Vietnam War, both memoirs and fiction, is marked by regret, trauma and feelings of futility.[75] The narrative structure of these accounts often reflects the disorienting nature of the war: timelines are out of sequence, stories are only

---

[72] Tim O'Brien, *If I Die in a Combat Zone: Box Me Up and Ship Me Home* (New York: Crown, 2011), 12.

[73] John Hellmann, *American Myth and the Legacy of Vietnam* (New York: Columbia University Press, 1989), 104–5; Christian G. Appy, *Working-Class War: American Combat Soldiers and Vietnam* (Chapel Hill: University of North Carolina Press, 1993), 60–2.

[74] Philip Caputo, *A Rumor of War: The Classic Vietnam Memoir*, 40th anniversary edn (London: Picador, 2017), xxii.

[75] O'Brien, *If I Die in a Combat Zone*; Tim O'Brien, *The Things They Carried* (London: Flamingo, 1991); Tim O'Brien, *Going after Cacciato*, repr. edn (New York: Crown, 1999); Robert Mason, *Chickenhawk* (New York: Random House, 2012); Karl Marlantes, *Matterhorn* (New York: Atlantic Books, 2010); Tobias Wolff, *In Pharaoh's Army: Memories of the Lost War*, Later Printing edn (New York: Vintage, 1995); Gregory Daddis, 'Mansplaining Vietnam: Male Veterans and America's Popular Image of the Vietnam War', *Journal of Military History* 82, no. 1 (1 January 2018): 181–207.

told in snatches and fiction blends with fact to produce a sense of the confusion and violence of war.

Journalistic accounts of the war – works of creative nonfiction like Michael Herr's *Dispatches* aside – not only tended to be more traditional in their structure but also emphasized the blurred lines of the war, particularly the difficulty of distinguishing friend from foe. Here, the efforts of the Johnson administration to evoke the example of the Second World War in order to bolster support for the war proved to be counterproductive, as they only served to draw attention to the lack of clear front lines and the less than heroic character of the United States' South Vietnamese allies.[76] This is not to say that journalists were necessarily opposed to the war itself. In the early years of the war, they often critiqued American methods in Vietnam but rarely the American presence in South Vietnam. News outlets gave lots of space to official statements about the war and fewer than 5 per cent of TV news reports from Vietnam actually showed violence, but interviews with individual GIs were a staple of both TV and newspaper reporting.[77] Here, to an even greater degree than the Second World War or Korea, soldiers related the drudgery and misery of war, and coverage often portrayed less as heroic than as characters deserving of sympathy, sent to fight a difficult war that few fully understood.[78]

As the war wore on, though, the lack of censorship of American reporting in Vietnam meant that reporters could talk freely about incidents that did not cast a favourable light on the US military or its South Vietnamese ally. Morley Safer's 1965 broadcast for CBS which depicted Marines burning down huts in a Vietnamese village was an outlier at the time, but footage of combat, including American casualties, became much more common as the number of American troops in South Vietnam climbed higher and higher.[79] Trust between the military authorities and journalists began to fray as military press briefings became more and more misleading, and journalists more openly challenged these official narratives.[80] The chaotic scenes of the 1968 Tet Offensive, where

---

[76] Daniel C. Hallin, 'The Media, the War in Vietnam, and Political Support: A Critique of the Thesis of an Oppositional Media', *Journal of Politics* 46, no. 1 (1984): 1–23; Daniel C. Hallin, *The Uncensored War: The Media and Vietnam* (Berkeley: University of California Press, 1989); Kathleen J. Turner, *Lyndon Johnson's Dual War: Vietnam and the Press* (Chicago: University of Chicago Press, 1985).

[77] Brewer, *Why America Fights*, 181.

[78] Huebner, *Warrior Image*, 210.

[79] Huebner, *Warrior Image*, 180.

[80] Chester Pach, '"We Need to Get a Better Story to the American People": LBJ, The Progress Campaign, and the Vietnam War on Television', in *Selling War in a Media Age: The Presidency and Public Opinion in the American Century*, ed. Kenneth Osgood and Andrew K Frank (Gainesville: University Press of Florida, 2011), 180–1.

the Johnson administration's message of progress was undermined by images of fighting in the streets of Saigon and within the walls of the US embassy, further underlined the extent to which this war could not be understood on the same terms as previous conflicts.[81]

The growing criticism of the war in the press tracked, but did not lead, a steady decline in public support for the American presence in Vietnam. As American post-war economic growth began to stutter and the social and cultural cleavages of the 1960s deepened, the war gave rise to the first mass anti-war movement in the United States since the 1930s.[82] Crucially, this movement critiqued not only government policy in Vietnam but also the place of war in American society. In his 1967 speech, 'Beyond Vietnam', Rev. Martin Luther King Jr. directly challenged militarization when he critiqued a 'society gone mad on war', compared the war to 'some demonic, destructive suction tube' that took resources away from the poor and warned that 'if American's soul becomes totally poisoned, part of the autopsy must read "Vietnam".[83] King's views were shared by a broad cross section of society, as could be seen in the huge protests outside the Pentagon in October 1967 and with the 'Moratorium' protests of 1969, which involved nationwide protests in October and then a 500,000-strong march in Washington, DC, in November. Organizers of the moratorium centred 'moderate' elements of the anti-war movement, including church leaders, university faculty, business and union leaders, in efforts to underline just how widespread anti-war sentiment was.[84]

That the moratorium leadership felt the need to highlight moderate voices in 1969 spoke to the fact that, notwithstanding the unpopularity of the war in Vietnam, the movement itself was not particularly well-liked.[85] Both the Johnson and Nixon administrations worked hard to depict anti-war protestors

---

[81] David F. Schmitz, *The Tet Offensive: Politics, War, and Public Opinion* (Lanham, MD: Rowman & Littlefield, 2005); Peter Braestrup, *Big Story: How the American Press and Television Reported and Interpreted the Crisis of Tet 1968 in Vietnam and Washington* (Boulder, CO: Westview Press, 1977); Edwin Moise, *The Myths of Tet: The Most Misunderstood Event of the Vietnam War* (Lawrence: University Press of Kansas, 2017), 178–89.

[82] Charles DeBenedetti and Charles Chatfield, *An American Ordeal: The Antiwar Movement of the Vietnam Era* (Syracuse: Syracuse University Press, 1990); Melvin Small, *Antiwarriors: The Vietnam War and the Battle for America's Hearts and Minds* (Wilmington, Del: Scholarly Resources Books, 2002); Melvin Small, *At the Water's Edge: American Politics and the Vietnam War* (Chicago: Ivan R. Dee, 2005).

[83] Martin Luther Jr. King, 'Beyond Vietnam', The Martin Luther King, Jr., Research and Education Institute, Stanford University, 4 April 1967, https://kinginstitute.stanford.edu/king-papers/documents/beyond-vietnam.

[84] Simon Hall, 'The Response of the Moderate Wing of the Civil Rights Movement to the War in Vietnam', *Historical Journal* 46, no. 3 (2003): 669–701.

[85] Adam Garfinkle, *Telltale Hearts: The Origins and Impact of the Vietnam Anti-War Movement* (New York: Griffin, 1997).

as irresponsible, privileged college students in order to undermine the moral clarity of their argument against war.[86] The Nixon administration in particular, though, found it much harder to employ the same tactics against the growing number of veterans opposed to the war. The Vietnam Veterans Against the War organization counted around 25,000 members at its height, only a small fraction of the 3 million who went to Vietnam, but they were very prominent in protests from 1969 onwards.[87] In an inversion of the sort of Cold War pageantry seen in fake Soviet invasions of small town Wisconsin in the 1950s, Operation RAW saw anti-war veterans carrying out mock 'search and destroy' missions in small New Jersey towns on Labor Day weekend in 1970, where they brandished weapons, cleared homes and took and interrogated prisoners with the aid of actors playing civilians.[88] They further publicized US atrocities in Vietnam via their 'Winter Soldier investigation' of 1971, where over a hundred veterans gave testimony about war crimes they had witnessed or committed in Vietnam. In Operation Dewey Canyon III, over a thousand veterans spent a week protesting in Washington, DC, including marching to Arlington National Cemetery (where security initially turned them away), testifying before Congress and, in the most dramatic act of protest, throwing their medals and ribbons away on the steps of the Capitol building.[89]

While in the short term, anti-war Vietnam veterans provided an awkward problem for presidential administrations trying to shore up public support for the war, in the long run their identity as victims of the war ironically ended up nullifying some of their more fundamental critiques of militarization. In telling the stories of the violence they meted out abroad, they were attempting to highlight the immorality of American actions, but public discourse instead shifted to focus on the harm done to veterans.[90] Nowhere was this trajectory

---

[86] Sarah Thelen, 'Mobilizing a Majority: Nixon's "Silent Majority" Speech and the Domestic Debate over Vietnam', *Journal of American Studies* 51, no. 3 (August 2017): 887–914, https://doi.org/10.1017/S0021875816001936; Sarah Thelen, 'Give War a Chance: The Nixon Administration and Domestic Support for the Vietnam War, 1969–1973' (PhD dissertation, Washington, DC, American University, 2012); Sandra Scanlon, *The Pro-War Movement: Domestic Support for the Vietnam War and the Making of Modern American Conservatism* (Amherst: University of Massachusetts Press, 2013).

[87] Andrew E. Hunt, *The Turning: A History of Vietnam Veterans against the War* (New York: New York University Press, 1999), 197; Gerald Nicosia, *Home to War: A History of the Vietnam Veterans' Movement* (New York: Crown, 2001).

[88] Huebner, *Warrior Image*, 221.

[89] Tom Wells, *The War within: America's Battle over Vietnam* (New York: iUniverse, 2005), 481–91.

[90] Keith Beattie, *The Scar That Binds: American Culture and the Vietnam War* (New York: New York University Press, 2012); Jerry Lembcke, *The Spitting Image: Myth, Memory, and the Legacy of Vietnam* (New York: New York University Press, 2000); Richard Young, 'The "Real Victims" of the Vietnam War: Soldier versus State in American Comic Books', *Journal of Popular Culture* 50, no. 3 (2017): 561–84, https://doi.org/10.1111/jpcu.12548.

more apparent than in cinematic depictions of the war. Hollywood had remained unusually quiet during the war itself. While the Second World War saw over 450 films about the war run in American cinemas, the sole movie about Vietnam to be released during the conflict, 1968's John Wayne vehicle *The Green Berets*, was a commercial and critical failure that effectively tried to transpose Second World War good war narratives onto Indochina.[91] After the war, though, films began to come quickly. The 1970s efforts such as *Coming Home*, *The Boys in Company C*, *The Deer Hunter* and *Apocalypse Now*, along with another burst of Vietnam movies in the mid-to-late 1980s such as *Platoon*, *Full Metal Jacket* and *Born on the Fourth of July*, did not shy away from depictions of Americans visiting violence on Vietnamese civilians and tended to emphasize the futility of war, but all put the American combat soldier at the heart of the story and implied that they – and American innocence – were the real victims of the conflict.[92] As one of the protagonists of *Platoon* put it, 'we did not fight the enemy, we fought ourselves and the enemy was in us'.[93]

This practice extended to broader memorialization of the war. Maya Lin's Vietnam Veteran's Memorial in Washington DC is made up of the names of the 58,000 American dead, etched onto polished black granite and arranged into a shallow 'V' made up of twin memorial walls that point at the Washington monument and Lincoln memorial respectively. The memorial is sunken into the ground so that when a visitor approaches it, the panels are only at ankle height, and then rise over 3 metres at the apex, towering over the viewer. The wall says nothing about the war or its merits, but rather invites the visitors to read or even to touch the names.[94] The memorial only contains American names; if Vietnamese names were included, it would likely stretch the entire length of the National Mall. Moreover, such is the power of American narratives of the war in Vietnam, they overwhelm almost all other attempts to reckon with the war.[95] The Vietnamese-American literary scholar Viet Thanh Nguyen has spoken

[91]   Huebner, *Warrior Image*, 241.

[92]   Michael A. Anderegg, *Inventing Vietnam: The War in Film and Television* (Philadelphia, PA: Temple University Press, 1991); Linda Dittmar and Gene Michaud, *From Hanoi to Hollywood: The Vietnam War in American Film* (New Brunswick, NJ: Rutgers University Press, 1990).

[93]   Oliver Stone, *Platoon* (Hemdale, Cinema '84, Cinema 86, 1987).

[94]   Marita Sturken, 'The Wall, the Screen, and the Image: The Vietnam Veterans Memorial', *Representations*, no. 35 (July 1991): 118–42, https://doi.org/10.2307/2928719; Patrick Hagopian, *The Vietnam War in American Memory: Veterans, Memorials, and the Politics of Healing* (Amherst: University of Massachusetts Press, 2009); Kristin Ann Hass, *Sacrificing Soldiers on the National Mall* (Chapel Hill: University of North Carolina Press, 2013).

[95]   David Kieran has pointed out that the narrative power of the Vietnam War has also reshaped American remembrance of other wars. David Kieran, *Forever Vietnam: How a Divisive War Changed American Public Memory* (Amherst: University of Massachusetts Press, 2014).

about how American depictions of the war pervade the globe and structure understandings of the conflict everywhere, complaining that 'no matter where I go outside of Vietnam, if I want to discuss the war, even with intellectuals and academics, I often have to confront their encounters with American memories'.[96]

This means confronting a vision of the war where lost American innocence is the key theme and stories about the war are told in order to promote domestic reconciliation. The historian Marilyn Young has written about how the telling of these stories resulted in a 'transmogrification of defeat' where 'Vietnam was memorialized in public ceremonies such that US defeat was denied'.[97] These commemorations increasingly focused on what soldiers suffered rather than on what they did. The movement to bring back first the prisoners of war and then later the bodies of those who were missing in action performed a similar service. For the Nixon administration, this campaign first served the purpose of narrowing the goal of the war down to bringing the POWs home, and for later administrations, the arguments over recovering the remains of missing pilots (who were still alive in the imagination of some groups) were a wedge issue to prevent the normalization of relations with Vietnam.[98] Thus, there was a sharp edge to this reconciliation via remembrance. Americans could continue to disagree over the war, but all must agree that American soldiers had been poorly treated, both by the government that sent them there and by the public when they returned home. In this sense, the anti-war movement would have to disavow some of its critiques of the war and to channel its dissent through the language and gestures of patriotism. This rhetorical move did not succeed in putting back together the sort of consensus about the necessity to prepare for war that had pervaded American society in the 1950s, but it did mean that the sort of foundational reimagining of the role of the United States in the world (along with a sustained critique of the centrality of American military power) that had seemed possible by the end of the 1960s was deferred, seemingly indefinitely.

* * *

Efforts to recast the narrative of the Vietnam War as being about the suffering of American soldiers also opened up the possibility of a more explicitly militarist

---

[96] Viet Thanh Nguyen, *Nothing Ever Dies: Vietnam and the Memory of War* (Cambridge, MA: Harvard University Press, 2016), 116.

[97] Marilyn B. Young, 'How the United States Ends Wars', in *Not Even Past: How the United States Ends Wars*, ed. David Fitzgerald, David Ryan and John M. Thompson, 1st edn (New York: Berghahn Books, 2020), 253, 254.

[98] Michael J. Allen, *Until the Last Man Comes Home: POWs, MIAs, and the Unending Vietnam War* (Chapel Hill: University of North Carolina Press, 2009); Robert Schulzinger, *A Time for Peace: The Legacy of the Vietnam War* (New York: Oxford University Press, 2006).

retelling of the story of that war. The immensely popular *Rambo* film franchise, starring Sylvester Stallone as a mistreated Vietnam veteran, was typical of the trend. In *First Blood*, John Rambo arrives at a small rural American town in search of his Army buddy (who it transpires has died of cancer brought on by exposure to Agent Orange) only to find himself persecuted by the local sheriff, who is suspicious of Rambo's scruffy look and long hair. A series of gunfights ensues, with Rambo acting essentially as a lone guerrilla in the forest, fighting the forces of the state as the police and National Guard close in on him.[99] This inversion of wartime roles becomes even more explicit in the *Rambo: First Blood II*, where Rambo is sent back to Vietnam in search of POWs still being secretly held by the Vietnamese. Before he departs, he asks his old colonel, 'Do we get to win this time?'. Betrayed again by Army bureaucrats back in Washington, Rambo now takes on the combined might of the Vietnamese and Soviet armies, killing dozens of soldiers.[100]

The *Rambo* franchise (which included a third instalment where Rambo went to Afghanistan to fight with the *Mujahideen*) was the most straightforwardly revisionist cinematic depiction of the Vietnam War, but it was indicative of a militarist strain in American culture in the 1980s, as Hollywood producers celebrated individualist, anti-government masculinity in a variety of blockbuster action movies, starring hard-bodied men like Stallone who were portrayed in a straightforwardly heroic light.[101] Alongside these films, subcultures built around popular magazines such as *Soldier of Fortune* and new hobbies such as paintball and airsoft, which centred on military simulation, celebrated martial virtues and sought to rehabilitate the notion of a masculine warrior mystique.[102] In many ways, these were the heirs to the men's pulp magazines of the 1950s and 1960s, portraying war as a great adventure that made men and offered them the chance to re-assert their dominant role in the social order.

While these subcultures thrived in the 1980s, most of the reshaping of the memory of the Vietnam War took place on a loftier plane. As candidate for president, Ronald Reagan had declared the war to be a 'noble cause', and, as president, he emphasized American virtue and innocence at every turn,

---

[99] Ted Kotcheff, *First Blood* (Anabasis, NV, Cinema '84, Elcajo Productions, 1982).
[100] Peter MacDonald and Russell Mulcahy, *Rambo III*, Action, Adventure (Carolco Pictures, 1988).
[101] Susan Jeffords, *Hard Bodies: Hollywood Masculinity in the Reagan Era* (New Brunswick, NJ: Rutgers University Press, 1994); Susan Jeffords, 'Hollywood's Hard Bodies', in *A Companion to the Action Film* (Hoboken, NJ: John Wiley, 2019), 256–69, https://doi.org/10.1002/9781119100744.ch13.
[102] James William Gibson, *Warrior Dreams: Violence and Manhood in Post-Vietnam America* (New York: Hill & Wang, 1994).

rhetorically folding the Vietnam experience into a broader narrative that told of American wars as acts of liberation.[103] Standing before D-Day veterans in Normandy in 1984, Reagan claimed that 'there is a profound, moral difference between the use of force for liberation and the use of force for conquest'.[104] Later that year, he made the same claims about the Vietnam War, urging a Veteran's Day audience at the Vietnam Veteran's Memorial to 'resolve to always stand for freedom, as those who fought did'.[105] Even if subsequent presidents didn't always agree with Reagan that the war had indeed been a noble cause, all were in accord that the soldiers who fought there were noble. At his presidential inauguration in 2009, Barack Obama added the Vietnam War to the pantheon of events that contributed to American greatness, telling an audience of 2 million on the National Mall that 'for us, [American soldiers] fought and died in places like Concord and Gettysburg, Normandy and Khe Sanh'.[106]

The celebration of veterans of all wars took place alongside renewed cultural interest in the Second World War as the 'good war'.[107] From Tom Brokaw's book-length tribute to Second World War veterans *The Greatest Generation*, and Steven Spielberg's film *Saving Private Ryan*, to Stephen Ambrose's series of popular histories of the Second World War and the Ambrose/Spielberg collaboration that resulted in the *Band of Brothers* TV mini-series, depictions of the 'good war' became pervasive in American culture in the 1990s.[108] As historian Gary Gerstle has noted, this should not be read as a conservative initiative, however much Reagan liked to talk about the Second World War in his speeches, but rather as a project aimed at rehabilitating a form of liberal nationalism.[109] These works tended to celebrate citizen soldiers in a way that might have been familiar to

[103] Ronald Reagan, 'Peace: Restoring the Margin of Safety' (Veterans of Foreign Wars Convention, Chicago, 18 August 1980), http://www.reagan.utexas.edu/archives/reference/8.18.80.html.

[104] Ronald Reagan, 'Remarks at a Ceremony Commemorating the 40th Anniversary of the Normandy Invasion, D-Day' (Normandy, France, 6 June 1984), https://www.presidency.ucsb.edu/documents/remarks-ceremony-commemorating-the-40th-anniversary-the-normandy-invasion-d-day.

[105] Ronald Reagan, 'Remarks at Dedication Ceremonies for the Vietnam Veterans Memorial Statue' (Washington, DC, 11 November 1984), https://www.reaganlibrary.gov/archives/speech/remarks-dedication-ceremonies-vietnam-veterans-memorial-statue.

[106] Barack Obama, 'Inaugural Address' (Washington, DC, 21 January 2009), https://obamawhitehouse.archives.gov/blog/2009/01/21/president-barack-obamas-inaugural-address.

[107] Bodnar, *The 'Good War' in American Memory*.

[108] Stephen E. Ambrose, *Citizen Soldiers: The U.S. Army from the Beaches of Normandy to the Surrender of Germany* (New York: Simon & Schuster, 1997); Stephen E. Ambrose, *Band of Brothers: E Company, 506th Regiment, 101st Airborne from Normandy to Hitler's Eagle Nest* (New York: Simon & Schuster, 2001); Steven Spielberg, *Saving Private Ryan*, 1998, http://www.imdb.com/title/tt0120815/; *Band of Brothers* (DreamWorks, DreamWorks Television, HBO Films, 2001).

[109] Gary Gerstle, 'In the Shadow of War: Liberal Nationalism and the Problem of War', in *Americanism: New Perspectives on the History of an Ideal*, ed. Michael Kazin and Joseph A. McCartin (Chapel Hill: University of North Carolina Press, 2006), 128–52.

their counterparts in the 1940s. The GIs in these books and films were reluctant to fight and averse to cruelty. Like Norman Corwin's 'little guys', they fought out of a sense of duty and obligation. These works did not directly glorify war, often depicting battle in an extraordinarily gruesome way, most notably in the 30-minute opening sequence in *Saving Private Ryan*, which was unflinching in its portrait of the violence on Omaha Beach. They also offered a different vision of masculinity and of heroism; certainly, the slightly paunchy Tom Hanks in *Saving Private Ryan* is no Sylvester Stallone.

As the historian John Bodnar has argued, there is also something very modern about these portrayals of war.[110] Missing is the fact that the call to patriotic sacrifices during the World Wars was very much tied up with Roosevelt's vision for a fairer post-war order, even if those storming the beaches at Normandy couldn't necessarily recite the four freedoms on demand. In Spielberg and Ambrose's world, the soldier rather than the broader community is at the heart of things. While Ambrose's books fully emphasize the decency and humanity of the GIs that he writes about, he ends up contending that they 'fought because they had to. What held them together was not country and flag, but unit cohesion.'[111]

Coincidentally, the first episode of *Band of Brothers* aired on 9 September 2001, so Americans watched the series in the aftermath of the 9/11 attacks and the upsurge of nationalism that accompanied it.[112] The show's emphasis on duty, collective sacrifice and patriotism chimed well with the mood of the time. The series' other key message – that soldiers fought because of the comrades in the foxhole next to them – was similarly affirmed by the films and TV that came out of the Wars on Terror. In Sam Mendes's 2005 film version of *Jarhead*, a sergeant cuts off debate about the moral justification for the Gulf War with the retort: 'Fuck politics. We're here. Everything else is bullshit.'[113] This stance was implicitly echoed in much of the work depicting the war in Iraq. From mini-series such as *Generation Kill* that emphasized grimy verisimilitude to Hollywood productions such as *The Hurt Locker* that presented war as addictive, screenwriters and directors put the everyday experiences and preoccupations of

[110] John Bodnar, 'Saving Private Ryan and Postwar Memory in America', *American Historical Review* 106, no. 3 (June 2001): 805, https://doi.org/10.2307/2692325.
[111] Ambrose, *Citizen Soldiers*, 473.
[112] Rick Lyman, 'Fewer Soldiers March Onscreen; After Attacks, Filmmakers Weigh Wisdom of Military Stories', *New York Times*, 16 October 2001, sec. Movies, https://www.nytimes.com/2001/10/16/movies/fewer-soldiers-march-onscreen-after-attacks-filmmakers-weigh-wisdom-military.html.
[113] Sam Mendes, *Jarhead* (Universal Pictures, Red Wagon Entertainment, Neal Street Productions, 2005).

the troops at the heart of their stories and largely avoided taking overt political positions on the war.[114]

This pattern was mirrored in media coverage of the post-9/11 wars. While the self-censorship of the early post-9/11 years, where TV networks largely avoided airing dissent about American military intervention, didn't last, what did endure was a focus on the troops as human interest stories. The Pentagon took stock of its fractious relationship with the news media after the Vietnam War, and went through a variety of strategies for controlling wartime coverage, ranging from attempts to prevent the press from reaching the scene of the action at all, like during the 1983 invasion of Grenada where the US Navy threatened to sink a boat carrying journalists on their way to the island, to tightly controlling their access via a heavily managed press pool system, as in the Gulf War.[115] With the 2001 invasion of Afghanistan, military leaders hit upon a new and very successful strategy of embedding journalists with particular units. Embedded journalists could offer their audiences an authentic sense of what war 'on the ground' looked like but would inevitably always do so from the perspective of American soldiers.[116]

The troops themselves could provide such images, as helmet cam footage offered a visceral, seemingly intimate, first-person view of combat. Images released from these cameras became a staple of military press conferences, intercut with video feeds from drones and aircraft to offer dramatic depictions of firefights and Special Forces raids on enemy compounds. In many ways, this footage resembled the first-person shooter video games which were themselves trying to emulate the combat experience.[117] One of the most popular franchises

---

[114] *Generation Kill* (Boom, Blown Deadline Productions, Company Pictures, 2008); Kathryn Bigelow, *The Hurt Locker* (Voltage Pictures, Grosvenor Park Media, Film Capital Europe Funds (FCEF), 2008); Marilyn B. Young, 'The Hurt Locker: War as a Video Game', *Perspectives on History*, 1 November 2009, https://www.historians.org/publications-and-directories/perspectives-on-history/november-2009/the-hurt-locker-war-as-a-video-game; Susan L. Carruthers, 'Limited Engagement: The Iraq War on Film', in *The Wiley-Blackwell History of American Film*, ed. Roy Grundmann, Cynthia Lucia and Art Simon (Hoboken, NJ: Wiley-Blackwell, 2011), https://doi.org/10.1002/9780470671153.wbhaf092; Andrew C. McKevitt, '"Watching War Made Us Immune": The Popular Culture of the Wars', in *Understanding the U.S. Wars in Iraq and Afghanistan*, ed. Beth Bailey and Richard H. Immerman (New York: New York University Press, 2015), 238–58, http://www.jstor.org/stable/j.ctt13x0q17.

[115] Thomas Rid, *War and Media Operations: The US Military and the Press from Vietnam to Iraq* (London: Routledge, 2007).

[116] Shahira Fahmy and Thomas J. Johnson, '"How We Performed": Embedded Journalists' Attitudes and Perceptions towards Covering the Iraq War', *Journalism & Mass Communication Quarterly* 82, no. 2 (1 June 2005): 301–17, https://doi.org/10.1177/107769900508200205; Elana J. Ziede, 'In Bed with the Military: First Amendment Implications of Embedded Journalism Note', *New York University Law Review* 80, no. 4 (2005): 1309–44.

[117] Matthew Thomas Payne, 'Marketing Military Realism in Call of Duty 4: Modern Warfare', *Games and Culture* 7, no. 4 (1 July 2012): 305–27, https://doi.org/10.1177/1555412012454220.

in this genre, *Call of Duty*, debuted in 2003 and evolved alongside the War on Terror, releasing games set first during the Second World War and then later in fictional Middle Eastern countries that closely resemble Iraq.[118] If the pulp magazines of the 1950s offered a vicarious experience of war through vivid imagery, video games offered a much more immersive, participatory experience.

These games have proven to be vastly more popular than any cinematic or TV representations of the wars on terror, and, to date, are the only fictional depictions of these wars that have achieved true blockbuster success status. The analyst and combat veteran Andrew Exum has noted the wide disparity between actual and vicarious experience of war. He pointed out that in September 2010, there were 80,000 Americans deployed to Afghanistan (at the time the largest US overseas mission), while at the same time 2.2 million people per day were logging on to play a fictionalized version of that war in *Call of Duty: Modern Warfare 2* on Xbox Live.[119] In a war that had begun with a plea from President George W. Bush for Americans to 'go shopping' and to 'get down to Disney World in Florida', it seemed inevitable that war itself would disappear from American life to the extent that vastly more people would experience it in gamified form than would in reality.[120]

* * *

The growing erasure of war from the American imagination can give the impression that there was an overt attempt by political elites to conceal its realities from the American public. Certainly, if we look to the history of government censorship, wartime propaganda and arguments over cultural depictions of war, we can see a pattern of obfuscation and excision. This, however, is only part of the story. For while policymakers were working to maintain narratives of American innocence and to minimize public understanding of the costs of war, they were also themselves struggling to grasp what was becoming a slippery concept. After 1945, it seemed as if the 'real war' of the Third World War was a possibility that never actually materialized, as so they needed to turn to fiction and to predictions about the future in order to imagine war.[121] Given the apparently decisive break

---

[118] Frédérick Gagnon, "'Invading Your Hearts and Minds": Call of Duty® and the (Re)Writing of Militarism in U.S. Digital Games and Popular Culture', *European Journal of American Studies* 5, no. 3, (27 June 2010), https://doi.org/10.4000/ejas.8831.

[119] Chris Suellentrop, 'War Games', *New York Times*, 9 September 2010, https://www.nytimes.com/2010/09/12/magazine/12military-t.html.

[120] George W. Bush, 'Remarks by the President to Airline Employees' (O'Hare International Airport, Chicago, Illinois, 27 September 2001), https://georgewbush-whitehouse.archives.gov/news/releases/2001/09/20010927-1.html.

[121] Lawrence Freedman, *The Future of War: A History* (London: Penguin UK, 2017).

between the present and the past character of war caused by nuclear weapons, it was these visions of future war, as much as historical analogies, that informed policymakers' understandings of what war was.

Nowhere was this more apparent than in the extensive network of think tanks, academic programmes and long-range military planning staffs that emerged along with the national security state and focused on the question of how to fight a nuclear war. The fact that the speed and scale of destruction inherent to these wars made them unlike anything anyone had previously experienced meant that historical experience seemed less relevant and that resources needed to be poured into wargames that attempted to map out the particular scripts such conflicts might follow. Inevitably, debates over the results of these wargames caused tensions between civilian academics and military leaders. The flippant remark by the economist Alain Enthoven, responding to a critique by an Air Force general during a debate over nuclear weapons in the 1960s Pentagon, 'General, I've fought just as many nuclear wars as you have', gives a sense of just how uncharted this territory was for strategists and policymakers.[122]

The mathematical modelling produced by theorists like Enthoven reduced war to an abstraction and allowed strategists to do their work while being shielded from the horrors of nuclear war, but was ripe for satire. Biting critiques of nuclear war planning, such as *Dr Strangeglove*, had little influence on policymaking, but military and civilian leaders did sometimes depend on more earnest fictional representations of the Third World War to help them see through the fog. Much of the literature on the Cold War during the 1950s and 1960s came from the genre of the spy thriller, where authors like Graham Greene and John le Carré emphasized the moral ambiguities of the Cold War, but it was the later fiction of Tom Clancy, who wrote immensely popular military thriller novels, that stuck in the mind of policymakers, notably in the Reagan administration.[123] Clancy's early work, notably his novels *The Hunt for the Red October* (1984) and *Red Storm Rising* (1986), depicted the Cold War from the perspective of the people charged with waging it, and was a vehicle for both straightforward tales of American heroism and intensely detailed descriptions of military hardware.[124]

---

[122] Matthew Connelly et al., "'General, I Have Fought Just as Many Nuclear Wars as You Have'': Forecasts, Future Scenarios, and the Politics of Armageddon', *American Historical Review* 117, no. 5 (1 December 2012): 1431–60, https://doi.org/10.1093/ahr/117.5.1431.

[123] Walter L. Hixson, "'Red Storm Rising": Tom Clancy Novels and the Cult of National Security', *Diplomatic History* 17, no. 4 (1 October 1993): 599–614, https://doi.org/10.1111/j.1467-7709.1993.tb00601.x.

[124] Tom Clancy, *Red Storm Rising: A Suspense Thriller* (New York: Berkley, 1987); Tom Clancy, *The Hunt for Red October* (New York: Berkley Books, 1984).

In *Red Storm Rising*, the Third World War actually breaks out, when an oil-starved Soviet Union lashes out at its Western adversaries and is defeated by technologically sophisticated NATO forces. American stealth technology proves to be a decisive factor, with a Soviet general bemoaning 'those damned invisible bombers of yours' in conversation with his American counterpart during ceasefire negotiations.[125] In Clancy's telling, the war remained conventional, but otherwise his representations of how war with the Soviet Union might play out were remarkably close to those of Pentagon wargames. The success of *Hunt for the Red October* earned Clancy an invitation first to the Pentagon, where he dined with Navy admirals, and then the Reagan White House, where he met with the president on several occasions, Reagan having read Clancy's novel over Christmas 1984, declaring it a 'hell of a yarn'. Clancy was invoked as an expert on national security more than he was as a novelist, such as when Senator Dan Quayle intervened in a Senate debate on anti-satellite weapons technology by noting that this technology won the war in *Red Storm Rising*.[126] In the aftermath of the 9/11 attacks, Clancy was again invited to the Pentagon along with Hollywood producers in order to brainstorm what future terrorist attacks might look like.[127]

What is quite revealing is that even when Clancy wrote about the Cold War getting hot, he still could not imagine its end. *Red Storm Rising* ends with a KGB coup that arrests the militants in the Politburo. The new government then sues for peace and returns things to the status quo, with the Soviet Union itself still standing intact, albeit with the hint of reforms to come. The historian Matthew Connelly has argued that the Pentagon's wargames had a similar flaw, in that they made it virtually impossible to imagine the end of the Cold War except through total nuclear war. Thus, when the Soviet Union began to break up and the Cold War actually did come to an end, intelligence agencies and planning staffs – those who were charged with imagining the future – were caught completely off guard.[128]

The end of the Cold War posed other challenges for those professionally tasked with imagining war. American military doctrine had been entirely predicated on the relative strategic stability that the Cold War had offered, and when the military worked to rebuild itself in the wake of the Vietnam War, they

---

[125] Clancy, *Red Storm Rising*, 722.

[126] Hixson, '"Red Storm Rising"', 613.

[127] Michael C. Frank, 'At War with the Unknown: Hollywood, Homeland Security, and the Cultural Imaginary of Terrorism after 9/11', *Amerikastudien/American Studies* 60, no. 4 (2015): 485–504.

[128] Connelly et al., '"General, I Have Fought Just as Many Nuclear Wars as You Have"', 1457.

emphasized the sort of technological and tactical excellence that appeared in Clancy's fiction. What they did not do, though, was rethink their fundamental assumptions about war. Their focus was instead on battle and the act of combat, rather than on strategy and the relationship between politics and war. The military historian Hew Strachan has been a long-standing critic of what he argues is a decline of strategic thinking in the United States, and he pins much of the blame on this turn towards what the military called 'the operational level of war': in theory, this is the level of command that connects strategy and tactics, but in reality it's a zone that sits just above the tactical level.[129] Military commanders who embraced the operational level of war concept imagined themselves to be operating in a clearly defined 'policy-free zone' where their technical expertise could hold sway.[130] Ironically, even though this intellectual construct came from the military's inability to assert its ownership over planning for future nuclear war, it led to doctrine writers returning to the past for inspiration. However, they did so by focusing on narrow histories of campaigns, such as German *blitzkrieg* operations during the Second World War, that were stripped of all political and social context.[131] Thus, American generals, even those who had experienced combat in Vietnam, imagined war as simply something that was confined to the battlefield and that ended quickly and cleanly.

This tendency only accelerated after the end of the Cold War, when a putative 'Revolution in Military Affairs' promised seamless integration between weapons systems, extensive usage of precision munitions and an ability to lift the fog of war using highly sophisticated surveillance systems.[132] This vision of war was a fundamentally optimistic one very much in keeping with the atmosphere of the 1990s. The military commentator Ralph Peters channelled this exuberance in a 1997 essay for the journal of the US Army War College where he declared that 'everybody is afraid of us. They really believe we can do all the stuff in the movies. If the Trojans "saw" Athena guiding the Greeks in battle, then the

---

[129] Hew Strachan, 'Strategy or Alibi? Obama, McChrystal and the Operational Level of War', *Survival* 52, no. 5 (1 October 2010): 157–82, https://doi.org/10.1080/00396338.2010.522104.

[130] Strachan has elaborated on the critique in a number of essays. Hew Strachan, *The Direction of War: Contemporary Strategy in Historical Perspective* (Cambridge: Cambridge University Press, 2014).

[131] William Astore, 'American Blitzkrieg: Loving the German War Machine to Death', HuffPost, 20 April 2010, https://www.huffpost.com/entry/american-blitzkrieg-lovin_b_467329.

[132] William J Gregor, *Toward a Revolution in Civil-Military Affairs: Understanding the United States Military in the Post-Cold War World* (Cambridge, MA: John M. Olin Institute for Strategic Studies, 1996); James Kitfield, *War and Destiny: How the Bush Revolution in Foreign and Military Affairs Redefined American Power* (Washington, DC: Potomac Books, 2007); Arthur K. Cebrowski and John H. Gartska, 'Network-Centric Warfare – Its Origin and Future', *Proceedings, United States Naval Institute* 124, no. 1 (January 1998), https://www.usni.org/magazines/proceedings/1998/january/network-centric-warfare-its-origin-and-future.

Figure 6.2 US Air Force combat aircraft flying over the burning oil fields of Kuwait during Operation Desert Storm, 1991. Credit: United State Air Force.

Iraqis saw Luke Skywalker precede McCaffrey's tanks.'[133] Peters may have been unusually excitable, but it is true that the future of American war seemed bright. This optimism took cultural form in films like *Top Gun*, a celebration of the skill of US Navy fighter pilots who take to the sky to engage in what the scholar Andrew Bacevich has called a high-tech throwback to the days of knighthood, where there was a series of individual duels and skirmishes (Figure 6.2). Combat in *Top Gun* is literally black and white. The unnamed enemy are depicted flying in black aircraft, wearing black helmets with opaque visors.[134]

War in *Top Gun* is also clean. The brief aerial battle at the movie's finale ends quickly and with a decisive American victory. Its message about the promise of air power was one that was shared by many 'Revolution in Military Affairs' theorists, such as Air Force Colonel John Warden, who argued that American air power could quickly paralyse and defeat opponents by hitting important targets, notably enemy leadership.[135] In this form of warfare, risk to the lives of American soldiers could be contained and objectives achieved with minimal

---

[133] Ralph Peters, 'Constant Conflict', *Parameters: Journal of the US Army War College*, Summer 1997, 13.

[134] Tony Scott, *Top Gun*, Action, Drama (Paramount Pictures, Don Simpson/Jerry Bruckheimer Films, 1986); Bacevich, *The New American Militarism*, 113.

[135] John Andreas Olsen, *John Warden and the Renaissance of American Air Power* (Washington, DC: Potomac Books, 2011).

casualties. Later, policymakers would argue that the risk to civilians could be mitigated in these forms of war as well.[136] A combination of surveillance technology, precision weapons and elaborate targeting processes that were overseen by military lawyers would ensure that violence would only be visited on enemy combatants.[137] While it is not true to say that this turned war into something trivial for those engaged in it – pilots who carried out drone strikes in Afghanistan from their station at Nellis Air Force Base, Nevada, reported high rates of post-traumatic stress disorder even though they were able to drive home through Las Vegas traffic to their families after their shift ended – it did make it extraordinarily easy for policymakers to turn to air power and remote warfare to carry out military interventions that felt almost frictionless.[138]

These confident visions of war were deeply influential in the planning for the invasion of Iraq in 2003. Strategists drafted campaign plans that emphasized precision and speed and that characterized war as nothing more than a series of tactical engagements that would quickly lead to the enemy's capitulation.[139] On the eve of war in March 2003, General Tommy Franks, the commander of the invasion forces, gathered his staff together to watch a screening of the opening sequence of the Ridley Scott film, *Gladiator*.[140] The opening scenes show Russell Crowe as a Roman general in command of a legion fighting Germanic tribes on the edge of the Empire. The film's prologue explains that 'a twelve-year campaign against barbarian tribes … [is] drawing to and end [and] just one final stronghold stands in the way of Roman victory and the promise of peace throughout the Empire'. Crowe's heavily armoured legion quickly defeats the barbarian tribes in a display of technological wizardry, with the forest-covered battlefield lit up by flaming arrows streaking through the sky and explosions toppling trees and scattering barbarians.[141] The message that Franks was trying to convey to his

---

[136] Martin Shaw, *The New Western Way of War: Risk-Transfer War and Its Crisis in Iraq* (London: Polity Press, 2005).

[137] Matthew Evangelista and Henry Shue, eds, *The American Way of Bombing: Changing Ethical and Legal Norms, from Flying Fortresses to Drones* (Ithaca, NY: Cornell University Press, 2014); Rebecca A. Adelman and David Kieran, *Remote Warfare: New Cultures of Violence* (Minneapolis: University of Minnesota Press, 2020).

[138] Derek Gregory, 'From a View to a Kill: Drones and Late Modern War', *Theory, Culture & Society* 28, nos. 7–8 (1 December 2011): 188–215, https://doi.org/10.1177/0263276411423027; Derek Gregory, 'Lines of Descent', in *From Above: War, Violence and Verticality*, ed. Peter Adey, Mark Whitehead, and Alison Williams (Oxford: Oxford University Press, 2014), https://oxford.universitypressscholarship.com/view/10.1093/acprof:oso/9780199334797.001.0001/acprof-9780199334797-chapter-3.

[139] Thomas E. Ricks, *Fiasco: The American Military Adventure in Iraq* (London: Allen Lane, 2006); Michael R. Gordon, *Cobra II: The Inside Story of the Invasion and Occupation of Iraq*, 1st edn (New York: Pantheon Books, 2006).

[140] Mike Rossiter, *Target Basra* (New York: Random House, 2008), 100.

[141] Ridley Scott, *Gladiator* (Dreamworks Pictures, Universal Pictures, Scott Free Productions, 2000).

staff was not subtle: technology and a highly professional military would make short work of their foes. That the optimism of the early weeks of the Iraq War soon gave way to the series of failures that had scholars of strategy deploring American strategic illiteracy and myopia can surely be in some sense connected to how policymakers and military leaders alike struggled to hold a coherent vision of war in their mind's eye as they got further and further away from the archetype of the Second World War.

* * *

The failures of the United States in Iraq and Afghanistan can be put down in part to over-confidence and an inability to understand the limits of military force, but what is more remarkable than the world's most powerful military repeatedly failing to achieve its objectives over more than twenty years of war is that these failures attracted very little attention on the part of the American public. The wars were broadly unpopular but, as had been the case with the Korean War, that didn't seem to be a barrier for their continued prosecution. The lack of a draft and the fact that these wars could be paid for through borrowing rather than taxation meant that a significant anti-war movement never emerged. Despite very large anti-war demonstrations in March 2003, the post-9/11 wars produced more cynicism than outrage on the part of the broader public. In cultural terms, this meant not only that war was portrayed in ways that give very little sense of its real costs, but often that it wasn't portrayed at all.

The journalist Chris Hedges has argued that 'it is impossible to know war if you do not stand with the mass of the powerless caught in its maw'.[142] By that measure, virtually no Americans have known war in recent decades. We can see some of the effects of this disconnect in the trajectory of President Donald Trump's foreign policy.[143] Throughout his four-year term, Trump claimed that he was an anti-war leader who was bringing the troops home and ending what were now termed 'the forever wars'. Trump's rhetoric was effective enough in attracting the support of some commentators who had built their career around opposition to American wars, but it was belied by the fact that Afghan civilian casualties from air strikes increased by 330 per cent under his tenure.[144] Such

---

[142] Chris Hedges, 'What War Looks Like', *New York Times*, 20 May 2009, https://www.nytimes.com/2009/05/24/books/review/Hedges-t.html.

[143] Adam Serwer, 'Donald Is No Dove', *The Atlantic*, 11 September 2020, https://www.theatlantic.com/ideas/archive/2020/09/donald-no-dove/616264/.

[144] Neta Crawford, 'Afghanistan's Rising Civilian Death Toll Due to Airstrikes, 2017–2020', Costs of War (Brown University: Watson Institute for International and Public Affairs, Brown University, 7 December 2020), https://watson.brown.edu/costsofwar/papers/2020/AirstrikesAfghanistan.

was the gap between symbolism and material reality that Trump merely saying he was anti-war and having a poor relationship with the military and intelligence services was enough in the eyes of some.

American media commentators were perhaps not well equipped to make this distinction. On the night in April 2017 that the Trump administration launched missile strikes on Syria, NBC news anchor Brian William spoke over footage of cruise missiles being launched from a US Navy destroyer: 'We see these beautiful pictures at night from the decks of these two US Navy vessels in the eastern Mediterranean. I am tempted to quote the great Leonard Cohen: "I am guided by the beauty of our weapons." ' Williams went on: 'And, they are beautiful pictures of fierce armaments making, what is for them, a brief flight over to this airfield. What did they hit?'[145] While Williams's question was picked up by a military analyst who went on to discuss battle damage assessments, the issue of what the missiles actually hit seemed quite secondary in his soliloquy.

As war became more distant for Americans, it also became less coherent. Americans moved from a self-image of a nation of reluctant warriors forced to fight totalitarian militarism in an unlimited global war to having that self-image shattered in Vietnam. This shattering came not only from the evidence that Americans were hardly reluctant or innocent participants, but that the war in Vietnam, like Korea before it, destabilized notions of war as an essentially unlimited phenomenon that would be fought until total victory. In the aftermath of Vietnam, despite attempts by policymakers to restore narratives of both American innocence and competence, no one was able to put the pieces back together. There was certainly a strongly militarist undercurrent in American culture, but it never dominated the popular imagination in the way it had in the 1950s.

Certainly, after the end of the Cold War, most Americans did not think about war that frequently or deeply at all, beyond reflexive support for the troops. Military leaders found their highly technological visions of war confounded on the battlefield, and then struggled to articulate any alternative and coherent visions with which to replace Tom Clancy and *Top Gun*. In *Age of Fracture*, his intellectual history of late-twentieth-century life and thought in the United States, Daniel Rodgers argued that in his vague and optimistic presidential

---

[145] Derek Hawkins, 'Brian Williams Is "Guided by the Beauty of Our Weapons" in Syria Strikes', *Washington Post*, accessed 12 March 2021, https://www.washingtonpost.com/news/morning-mix/wp/2017/04/07/beautiful-brian-williams-says-of-syria-missile-strike-proceeds-to-quote-leonard-cohen/.

addresses that centred on individualism and freedom rather than mobilization, vigilance and responsibility, Ronald Reagan had 'lost the words of the Cold War'.[146] In reviewing the history of how Americans imagined war, spoke about and depicted it, it is clear that during that time period they lost the words of war altogether and let its substance slip away as well.

[146] Daniel T. Rodgers, *Age of Fracture* (Cambridge, MA: Harvard University Press, 2011), 15–40.

Conclusion

On 1 May 2020, two B-52H Stratofortress bombers from Barksdale Air Force base, Louisiana, accompanied by two F-15 fighter jets from the Louisiana Air National Guard, flew low and slow over medical facilities in New Orleans and Baton Rouge. As the aircraft passed overhead, healthcare workers emerged from their hospital facilities to take in the tribute that, in a reversal of the norms of the post-9/11 years, the military was paying to them.[1] The flyover was part of a weeks-long joint Air Force–Navy tribute to the 'essential workers fighting on the front lines' against the deadly first wave of the Covid-19 pandemic. Dubbed 'Operation America Strong', the programme saw dozens of display flights take place over American cities, with both the Air Force's Thunderbird and Navy's Blue Angel display squadrons and operational combat squadrons and wings deployed to put on display over the places that had been hit hardest by the virus.[2] The sight of billions of dollars' worth of aircraft, each with minimum running costs of $60,000 an hour, streaking over hospitals where healthcare workers were using bin bags as personal protective equipment due to supply shortages, had the unintended effect of demonstrating not so much patriotic unity as the stark disparities in the American state's long-term priorities.[3]

The sixty-year-old B-52s that flew over New Orleans cost roughly $25 million a year to operate, while below them, the city of New Orleans was experiencing

---

[1] 'Barksdale AFB B-52 Bombers, LANG F-15s to Fly over New Orleans and Baton Rouge in Salute to COVID-19 Essential Workers', US Air Force Resilience, accessed 30 April 2021, https://www.resilience.af.mil/News/Article-Display/Article/2171508/barksdale-afb-b-52-bombers-lang-f-15s-to-fly-over-new-orleans-and-baton-rouge-i/.

[2] Dan Lamothe, 'Pentagon Plans to Dispatch Blue Angels and Thunderbirds in Coronavirus Tribute', *Washington Post*, 23 April 2020, https://www.washingtonpost.com/national-security/2020/04/22/pentagon-plans-dispatch-blue-angels-thunderbirds-coronavirus-response/.

[3] Ursula Perano, 'Navy Blue Angels and Air Force Thunderbirds to Show National Unity in Multi-City Tour', Axios, Arlington, United States: Newstex, 22 April 2020, http://search.proquest.com/docview/2428081939/citation/D850FAB688884F88PQ/9.

a spike in deaths twice as intense as that of New York City, the other epicentre of the first wave of the pandemic.[4] Public health experts attributed this extraordinary mortality rate to a high prevalence of poverty-linked conditions in New Orleans, such as diabetes, hypertension and obesity.[5] Given the devastation that was playing out in New Orleans and elsewhere, the B-52 flyover seemed to be something of a futile gesture. In that moment, with the federal government floundering in its efforts to deal with the pandemic, it appeared not just as though the government had lost the capacity to act quickly to protect public health, but that the language of political gestures was so impoverished that the state fell back on the only symbol it still knew how to deploy: an ersatz salute to the troops now turned around to acknowledge those who were facing a deadly threat at home.

Outside of the realm of symbolism, though, the government mobilized aspects of the national security state to deal with the crisis. Early on, commentators called on the Trump administration to invoke the Defense Production Act of 1950, a piece of legislation that dated from the Truman administration's efforts to mobilize the economy for the Korean War.[6] The Defense Production Act granted the president emergency powers to direct private companies to prioritize orders from the federal government, prevent the hoarding of supplies and to 'allocate materials, services, and facilities' for national defence purposes.[7] Long after their demise, faint echoes of the wartime economic controls that had been vested in the War Industries Board of the First World War and the War Production Board and the Office of Price Administration of the Second World War could be heard in arguments over whether or not factories should be made to produce cotton swabs and whether or not chemical reagents necessary for test kits should be exported overseas. The Trump administration made some limited use of the Defense Production Act before the Biden administration more systematically harnessed its powers to boost supplies for vaccine production.[8]

4　Niall McCarthy, 'The Mammoth Cost of Operating America's Combat Aircraft', Forbes, 26 November 2020, https://www.forbes.com/sites/niallmccarthy/2020/11/26/the-mammoth-cost-of-operating-americas-combat-aircraft-infographic/.

5　Brad Brooks, 'Why Is New Orleans' Coronavirus Death Rate Twice New York's? Obesity Is a Factor', Reuters, 2 April 2020, https://news.yahoo.com/why-orleans-coronavirus-death-rate-100627119.html.

6　Aishvarya Kavi, 'Virus Surge Brings Calls for Trump to Invoke Defense Production Act', New York Times, 22 July 2020, https://www.nytimes.com/2020/07/22/us/politics/coronavirus-defense-production-act.html.

7　Anshu Siripurapu, 'What Is the Defense Production Act?', Council on Foreign Relations, 26 January 2021, https://www.cfr.org/in-brief/what-defense-production-act.

8　Andrew Jacobs, 'Despite Claims, Trump Rarely Uses Wartime Law in Battle against Covid', New York Times, 22 September 2020, https://www.nytimes.com/2020/09/22/health/Covid-Trump-Defense-Production-Act.html; Isaac Stanley-Becker, 'Biden Harnesses Defense Production Act to Speed

These actions accelerated the vaccination programme in the United States but led to worldwide complaints about Americans hoarding supplies that were in short supply elsewhere.[9]

Both the military flyovers of the spring of 2020 and the controversy over vaccine stockpiling in the following spring highlight the enormous costs of militarization and its temptations. The Covid-19 pandemic seemed to make it clear that the trillions of dollars that the United States had spent to fight its wars in the twenty-first century had done nothing to protect the country from arguably the greatest threat it had known in eighty years, while the crisis simultaneously demonstrated that the language of security and emergency could be immensely useful in helping to unlock legislative gridlock and in mobilizing resources to face imminent dangers. The pandemic was not the only crisis where this paradox was evident. Even as the Biden administration declared that the climate emergency would be its number one priority, it was torn between the need to cooperate with China in order to rapidly reduce global carbon emissions and the impulse to invoke the language of 'great power competition' to rally Americans into unifying around rebuilding projects at home and the mission to retain American military hegemony overseas.[10] These twin crises point to the difficult questions the United States will face in the years to come. If there is to be 'another American century', a phrase and promise beloved of Washington think tanks, then military power will hardly be its driving force. The answer to the question of how the United States can mobilize to deal with serious challenges that look nothing like war will go a long way towards determining what level of influence it will have in the world and what sort of quality of life it can promise to its own citizens.

What this book has demonstrated is that the process for preparing and mobilizing for war has been enormously consequential for both the United States and its relations with the world. Indeed, some political theorists have even argued that the political instability seen in the United States in the twenty-first century could be partly attributed to militarization losing its moorings with the end of the Cold War, which meant that American political factions would no longer unify around confronting the political and military threat posed by the

Vaccinations and Production of Protective Equipment', *Washington Post*, 5 February 2021, https:// www.washingtonpost.com/health/2021/02/05/biden-vaccines-tests-gloves/.

[9] 'American Export Controls Threaten to Hinder Global Vaccine Production', *The Economist*, 22 April 2021, https://www.economist.com/science-and-technology/2021/04/22/american-export-controls-threaten-to-hinder-global-vaccine-production.

[10] Adam Tooze, 'Biden's China Strategy: A Chronology. Chartbook Newsletter #23', Chartbook, 19 June 2021, https://adamtooze.substack.com/p/chartbook-newsletter-23.

Soviet Union. The militarization of the United States, however, extended beyond the Cold War. Once the logic of national security took hold in the early 1940s, it became and remained a centrally important priority for the state, both crowding out other imperatives and becoming a necessary reference point for political coalitions that wanted to harness the rhetoric and logic of national security in order to advance their goals.[11]

This logic also produced what Eisenhower famously called the military–industrial complex, an entity that, as scholars such as Michael Brenes have shown, created durable political coalitions in favour of higher defence spending that could withstand any transient public disquiet with militarization.[12] Both the defeat in Vietnam and the end of the Cold War seemed to open up possibilities for a change to the status quo, but these moments passed without any fundamental changes to the national security state. The pull of militarization also meant that many of the debates over the rights and obligations of citizenship were conducted with reference to military service, as marginalized groups worked to gain admission to the ranks in order to claim their full rights, while the government targeted the draft to create the sort of Cold War male citizen that they wanted. Not only that, but federal welfare policies were constantly being tuned to meet the needs of the military and veterans, through the post-war expansion of the welfare state via the GI Bill, the Kennedy and Johnson administration's efforts to use welfare programmes to produce better recruits for the military and to use the military to produce better citizens, or through the more targeted creation of a military welfare state to ensure that the All-Volunteer Force could attract and retain enough recruits to remain viable.

Ironically, the end of the draft, the advent of the All-Volunteer Force and the decrease in the number of Americans exposed to military service gave militarism a better environment in which to thrive, as these ideals could be celebrated without reference to the drudgery of military life or the scars of war. As early as the 1980s, the sociologist Michael Mann labelled this a culture of 'spectator sport militarism', where the combination of professional militaries and technological advances to weaponry meant that Western publics could comfortably view war from afar.[13] This isn't to say that the United States was ever

---

[11] International Relations theorists have produced a body of work dedicated to exploring this phenomenon, which they label 'securitization'. The classic work is Barry Buzan, Ole Waever and Jaap de Wilde, *Security: A New Framework for Analysis* (Boulder, CO: Lynne Rienner, 1998).

[12] Michael Brenes, *For Might and Right: Cold War Defense Spending and the Remaking of American Democracy* (Amherst: University of Massachusetts Press, 2020).

[13] Michael Mann, 'The Roots and Contradictions of Modern Militarism', *New Left Review* 1, no. 162 (1987): 35–50.

completely dominated by an overt or uniform form of militarism. Certainly, the sentimental celebration of reluctant citizen soldiers during the early Cold War, along with the widespread veneration of the rather less reluctant professional warriors of the post-9/11 years indicated that different forms of militarism could gain purchase in American culture, but these cultures of militarism flourished in specific historical moments and were not a constant, unchanging presence on the social and cultural landscape. What was constant was the ever-increasing distance between Americans and the physical realities of war. Cultural depictions of soldiers and war reflected this, as even those with lived experience of combat struggled to convey its meaning, through reportage, fiction or film. This produced an opaqueness in the way that Americans imagined war, a vagueness that meant that they found it very difficult to describe what it in fact was, even as they spent vast fortunes preparing for it and subordinated important parts of society and culture to those preparations.

Of course, it is not true to say that war's meaning was obscure for all. The shrinking but still significant population of veterans in the United States contains within it many who have known war, death and injury, but war and militarization's realities have generally been more apparent to non-Americans who encountered American military power overseas. From the political leaders at negotiations who realized that of the group of Americans sitting across the table from them, it was the generals rather than the diplomats who had access to bigger budgets and more resources; to civilians on the receiving end of weapons provided by American military aid; to the ordinary people who encountered armed Americans in mundane ways in their everyday lives, people often perceived the United States through a militarized lens. The deployment of American military power in their countries, whether during peace or wartime, has invariably had profound social, economic, political and cultural effects. However, much as Americans have liked to tell themselves stories about how they were reluctant soldiers or tourists who happened to be overseas on military duty, from the perspective of others, they have frequently been seen as being part of an immensely powerful and potentially (or actually) violent military machine.

When we speak of these encounters with armed Americans or of the effects of militarization within the United States, it is important to remember they tended to cluster in specific places. Bases and training ranges both in the United States and overseas were obviously sites where civilians came into contact with both military personnel and the power of the state. Because of both security imperatives and the tensions that these sorts of encounters can cause, those spaces have often tended to be governed by restrictive legal regimes. They have also been the sites of protests about the behaviour of soldiers, the conduct of American foreign policy and long-term environmental damage caused by military operations. These are the places where militarization's effects on both social relations and the physical environment are most clear. As this book has also shown, though, to more fully account for militarization's sources and effects, we need to also look at other places, from office buildings and research parks to the suburbs and highway systems, in order to produce a full inventory of the various facets of everyday life that have been touched by militarization. For historians who wish to precisely account for militarization's sources and effects, studying what has happened in these spaces can be immensely valuable, as trends and processes that can seem diffuse and vague in their operation and logic are densely compressed into particular times and spaces, and suddenly made visible and all too clear.

This sort of historical work can sometimes cut against the grain of American self-understanding. In the same essay where she called for historians 'to make war visible', Marilyn Young argued that the 'constancy of war' in American history was accompanied by its 'constant erasure'.[14] In response to this, Young argued that it was the work of historians 'to speak and write so that a time of war [would] not be mistaken for peacetime, nor waging war for making peace'.[15] As this book has hopefully made clear, scholars have taken this task seriously, and done much important work to highlight how war has been an important and constant thread for much of American history. Historians from across a huge range of subfields in the discipline have worked to uncover how militarization has shaped different places and stories and greatly enhanced our understanding of much of modern American history.

As Americans once more debate their role in the world and the meanings of 'national security', historical scholarship on militarization may be of particular value. This is not because historians have any particular talent for prediction but because so much of the work of historians is dedicated to exploring change over time and to explaining how deep structural forces have interacted with contingency and individual agency to produce the world that we live in. Often, historical work emphasizes how tangled and messy these interactions were and thus, if not always directly, demonstrates how uncertain these outcomes have been and offers glimpses of other possible trajectories or roads not taken.

---

[14] Marilyn B. Young, "'I Was Thinking, as I Often Do These Days, of War": The United States in the Twenty-First Century', *Diplomatic History* 36, no. 1 (1 January 2012): 2, https://doi.org/10.1111/j.1467-7709.2011.01004.x.

[15] Young, "'I Was Thinking, as I Often Do These Days, of War"', 15.

To return to the image of the B-52s over New Orleans – immensely expensive bomber aircraft designed to bring mass death but flying over a city where thousands were struggling to breathe in what was surely a fruitless effort to boost morale – it would be entirely understandable to look at the weight of historical evidence and to think that such an outcome was inevitable. After all, we have a rich body of scholarship that has described with some care the depth and power of militarization's hold on the course of American history since the Second World War. However, that same scholarship also demonstrates that this state of affairs was not always so and suggests that, at different times, alternative paths through the American Century seemed feasible, and that even the power of militarization had its limits and was occasionally turned back or subverted. In telling the specific story of the growth of the social and political order that led those B-52s to fly on their useless tribute, we can also imagine how other orders founded on different assumptions and values might be possible.

Selected Bibliography

Adelman, Rebecca A., and David Kieran. *Remote Warfare: New Cultures of Violence.* Minneapolis: University of Minnesota Press, 2020.

Allen, Michael J. *Until the Last Man Comes Home: POWs, MIAs, and the Unending Vietnam War.* Chapel Hill: University of North Carolina Press, 2009.

Allen, Robert L. *The Port Chicago Mutiny: The Story of the Largest Mass Mutiny Trial in U.S. Naval History.* Berkeley, CA: Equal Justice Society, 1989.

Allison, Tanine. *Destructive Sublime: World War II in American Film and Media.* New Brunswick, NJ: Rutgers University Press, 2018.

Alvah, Donna. *Unofficial Ambassadors: American Military Families Overseas and the Cold War, 1946–1965.* New York: New York University Press, 2007.

Ambrose, Stephen E. *Band of Brothers: E Company, 506th Regiment, 101st Airborne from Normandy to Hitler's Eagle Nest.* New York: Simon and Schuster, 2001.

Ambrose, Stephen E. *Citizen Soldiers: The U.S. Army from the Beaches of Normandy to the Surrender of Germany.* New York: Simon & Schuster, 1997.

Amundson, Michael A., and Scott C. Zeman, eds. *Atomic Culture: How We Learned to Stop Worrying and Love the Bomb.* Boulder: University Press of Colorado, 2004.

Anderegg, Michael A. *Inventing Vietnam: The War in Film and Television.* Philadelphia, PA: Temple University Press, 1991.

Anderson, Fred, and Andrew Cayton. *The Dominion of War: Empire and Liberty in North America, 1500–2000.* New York: Penguin Books, 2005.

Andrianopoulos, Gerry Argyris. *Kissinger and Brzezinski: The NSC and the Struggle for Control of US National Security Policy.* Basingstoke: Palgrave Macmillan, 2016.

Appy, Christian G. *Vietnam: The Definitive Oral History Told from All Sides.* London: Ebury, 2008.

Appy, Christian G. '"We'll Follow the Old Man": The Strains of Sentimental Militarism in Popular Films of the Fifties'. In *Rethinking Cold War Culture*, edited by Peter J. Kuznick and James Burkhart Gilbert, 74–105. Washington, DC: Smithsonian Institution Press, 2001.

Appy, Christian G. *Working-Class War: American Combat Soldiers and Vietnam.* Chapel Hill: University of North Carolina Press, 1993.

Arnold, Bruce Makoto. '"Your Money Ain't No Good o'er There": Food as Real and Social Currency in the Pacific Theater of World War II'. *Food and Foodways* 25, no. 2 (3 April 2017): 107–22.

Bacevich, Andrew J. *The New American Militarism: How Americans Are Seduced by War.* New York: Oxford University Press, 2005.

Bailey, Beth. *America's Army: Making the All-Volunteer Force*. Cambridge, MA: Harvard University Press, 2009.

Bailey, Beth. 'The Army in the Marketplace: Recruiting an All-Volunteer Force'. *Journal of American History* 94, no. 1 (2007): 47–74. https://doi.org/10.2307/25094776.

Bailey, Beth. 'The Politics of Dancing: "Don't Ask, Don't Tell", and the Role of Moral Claims'. *Journal of Policy History* 25, no. 1 (2013): 89–113.

Bailey, Beth L., and David Farber. *The First Strange Place: Race and Sex in World War II Hawaii*. Baltimore, MD: Johns Hopkins University Press, 1994.

Balko, Radley. *Rise of the Warrior Cop: The Militarization of America's Police Forces*. New York: PublicAffairs, 2013.

Banks, William C. 'First Use of Nuclear Weapons: The Constitutional Role of a Congressional Leadership Committee'. *Journal of Legislation* 13, no. 1 (1986): 1–21.

Basinger, Jeanine. 'The World War II Combat Film: Definition'. In *The War Film*, edited by Robert Eberwein, 30–49. New Brunswick, NJ: Rutgers University Press, 2004.

Baudrillard, Jean. *The Gulf War Did Not Take Place*. Indianapolis: Indiana University Press, 1995.

Baum, Dan. *Smoke and Mirrors: The War on Drugs and the Politics of Failure*. Boston, MA: Back Bay Books, 1997.

Beattie, Keith. *The Scar That Binds: American Culture and the Vietnam War*. New York: New York University Press, 2012.

Beidler, Philip D. *The Good War's Greatest Hits: World War II and American Remembering*. Athens, GA: University of Georgia Press, 1998.

Belew, Kathleen. *Bring the War Home: The White Power Movement and Paramilitary America*. Cambridge, MA: Harvard University Press, 2018.

Belkin, Aaron, and Geoffrey Bateman. *Don't Ask, Don't Tell: Debating the Gay Ban in the Military*. Boulder, CO: Lynne Rienner, 2003.

Belknap, Michal R. *The Vietnam War on Trial: The My Lai Massacre and the Court-Martial of Lieutenant Calley*. Lawrence: University Press of Kansas, 2002.

Bell, David A. *Men on Horseback: The Power of Charisma in the Age of Revolution*. New York: Farrar, Straus and Giroux, 2020.

Bell, Duncan. *Dreamworlds of Race: Empire and the Utopian Destiny of Anglo-America*. Princeton, NJ: Princeton University Press, 2020.

Bell, Jonathan. *The Liberal State on Trial: The Cold War and American Politics in the Truman Years*. New York: Columbia University Press, 2004.

Bennett, Judith A., and Angela Wanhalla, eds. *Mothers' Darlings of the South Pacific: The Children of Indigenous Women and U.S. Servicemen, World War II*. Honolulu: University of Hawai'i Press, 2016.

Bennett, W. Lance, and David L. Paletz, eds. *Taken by Storm: The Media, Public Opinion, and U.S. Foreign Policy in the Gulf War*. Chicago: University of Chicago Press, 1994.

Bensel, Richard Franklin. *Yankee Leviathan: The Origins of Central State Authority in America, 1859–1877*. Cambridge: Cambridge University Press, 2008.

Bessner, Daniel, and Fredrik Logevall. 'Recentering the United States in the Historiography of American Foreign Relations'. *Texas National Security Review* 3, no. 2 (2020): 38–55. https://doi.org/10.26153/tsw/8867.

Biddiscombe, Perry. 'Dangerous Liaisons: The Anti-Fraternization Movement in the U.S. Occupation Zones of Germany and Austria, 1945–1948'. *Journal of Social History* 34, no. 3 (2001): 611–47.

Birdwell, Michael E. *Celluloid Soldiers: The Warner Bros. Campaign against Nazism*. New York: New York University Press, 2000.

Bishop, Thomas. *Every Home a Fortress*. Amherst: University of Massachusetts Press, 2020.

Bland, Lucy. *Britain's 'Brown Babies': The Stories of Children Born to Black GIs and White Women in the Second World War*. Manchester: Manchester University Press, 2019.

Blight, David W. *Race and Reunion: The Civil War in American Memory*. Cambridge, MA: Harvard University Press, 2002.

Blower, Brooke L. *Becoming Americans in Paris: Transatlantic Politics and Culture between the World Wars*. New York: Oxford University Press, 2011.

Blower, Brooke L. 'From Isolationism to Neutrality: A New Framework for Understanding American Political Culture, 1919–1941'. *Diplomatic History* 38, no. 2 (1 April 2014): 345–76. https://doi.org/10.1093/dh/dht091.

Blower, Brooke L. 'Nation of Outposts: Forts, Factories, Bases, and the Making of American Power'. *Diplomatic History* 41, no. 3 (1 June 2017): 439–59. https://doi.org/10.1093/dh/dhx034.

Bodnar, John. 'Saving Private Ryan and Postwar Memory in America'. *American Historical Review* 106, no. 3 (June 2001): 805. https://doi.org/10.2307/2692325.

Bodnar, John. *The 'Good War' in American Memory*. Baltimore, MD: Johns Hopkins University Press, 2010.

Bönker, Dirk. *Militarism in a Global Age: Naval Ambitions in Germany and the United States before World War I*. Ithaca, NY: Cornell University Press, 2012.

Borgwardt, Elizabeth. *A New Deal for the World*. Cambridge, MA: Harvard University Press, 2007.

Boulton, Mark. *Failing Our Veterans: The G.I. Bill and the Vietnam Generation*. New York: New York University Press, 2014.

Bowie, Robert R., and Richard H. Immerman. *Waging Peace: How Eisenhower Shaped an Enduring Cold War Strategy*. Oxford: Oxford University Press, 2000.

Boyer, Paul. *By the Bomb's Early Light: American Thought and Culture at the Dawn of the Atomic Age*. Chapel Hill: University of North Carolina Press, 1994.

Bradley, Mark Philip, and Mary L. Dudziak, eds. *Making the Forever War: Marilyn Young on the Culture and Politics of American Militarism*. Amherst: University of Massachusetts Press, 2021.

Braestrup, Peter. *Big Story: How the American Press and Television Reported and Interpreted the Crisis of Tet 1968 in Vietnam and Washington*. Boulder, CO: Westview Press, 1977.

Brenes, Michael. *For Right and Might: Cold War Defense Spending the Remaking of American Democracy*. Amherst: University of Massachusetts Press, 2020.

Brewer, Susan A. *Why America Fights: Patriotism and War Propaganda from the Philippines to Iraq*. Oxford: Oxford University Press, 2009.

Bristol, Douglas, and Heather Marie Stur, eds. *Integrating the US Military: Race, Gender and Sexual Orientation since World War II*. Baltimore, MD: Johns Hopkins University Press, 2017.

Brooks, Rosa. *How Everything Became War and the Military Became Everything: Tales from the Pentagon*. New York: Simon & Schuster, 2017.

Brown, April L. 'No Promised Land: The Shared Legacy of the Castle Bravo Nuclear Test'. *Arms Control Today* 44, no. 2 (2014): 40.

Brown, Kate. *Plutopia: Nuclear Families, Atomic Cities, and the Great Soviet and American Plutonium Disasters*, repr. edn. Oxford: Oxford University Press, 2015.

Brown, Melissa T. *Enlisting Masculinity: The Construction of Gender in US Military Recruiting Advertising during the All-Volunteer Force*. Oxford Studies in Gender and International Relations. Oxford: Oxford University Press, 2012.

Buchanan, Andrew. '"I Felt Like a Tourist Instead of a Soldier": The Occupying Gaze—War and Tourism in Italy, 1943–1945'. *American Quarterly* 68, no. 3 (21 September 2016): 593–615. https://doi.org/10.1353/aq.2016.0055.

Burke, John P. *Honest Broker?: The National Security Advisor and Presidential Decision Making*. College Station: Texas A&M University Press, 2009.

Burke, Kyle. *Revolutionaries for the Right: Anticommunist Internationalism and Paramilitary Warfare in the Cold War*. Chapel Hill: University of North Carolina Press, 2018.

Canaday, Margot. *The Straight State: Sexuality and Citizenship in Twentieth Century America*. Princeton, NJ: Princeton University Press, 2011.

Capozzola, Chris, Andrew Huebner, Julia Irwin, Jennifer D. Keene, Ross Kennedy, Michael Neiberg, Stephen R. Ortiz, Chad Williams, and Jay Winter. 'Interchange: World War I'. *Journal of American History* 102, no. 2 (1 September 2015): 463–99. https://doi.org/10.1093/jahist/jav474.

Capozzola, Christopher. *Bound by War: How the United States and the Philippines Built America's First Pacific Century*. New York: Basic Books, 2020.

Capozzola, Christopher. *Uncle Sam Wants You: World War I and the Making of the Modern American Citizen*. Oxford: Oxford University Press, 2010.

Carroll, James. *House of War: The Pentagon and the Disastrous Rise of American Power*. Boston, MA: Houghton Mifflin, 2007.

Carruthers, Susan L. *Cold War Captives: Imprisonment, Escape, and Brainwashing*. Berkeley: University of California Press, 2009.

Carruthers, Susan L. *The Good Occupation: American Soldiers and the Hazards of Peace*. Cambridge, MA: Harvard University Press, 2016.

Carver, Ron, David Cortright, and Barbara Doherty, eds. *Waging Peace in Vietnam: US Soldiers and Veterans Who Opposed the War*. New York: New Village Press, 2019.

Casey, Steven. *Selling the Korean War: Propaganda, Politics, and Public Opinion in the United States, 1950–1953*. Oxford: Oxford University Press, 2010.

Casey, Steven. *The War Beat, Europe: The American Media at War against Nazi Germany*. New York: Oxford University Press, 2017.

Chambers, John Whiteclay. *The Oxford Companion to American Military History*. New York: Oxford University Press, 2000.

Chandrasekaran, Rajiv. *Imperial Life in the Emerald City: Inside Iraq's Green Zone*. New York: Alfred A. Knopf, 2006.

Chandrasekaran, Rajiv. *Little America: The War within the War for Afghanistan*. New York: Vintage Books, 2012.

Clark, J. P. *Preparing for War: The Emergence of the Modern U.S. Army, 1815–1917*. Cambridge, MA: Harvard University Press, 2017.

Clifford, J. Garry. *The Citizen Soldiers; the Plattsburg Training Camp Movement, 1913–1920*. Lexington: University Press of Kentucky, 1972.

Coates, Benjamin Allen. *Legalist Empire: International Law and American Foreign Relations in the Early Twentieth Century*. Oxford: Oxford University Press, 2016.

Coffman, Edward M. *The War to End All Wars: The American Military Experience in World War I*. Lexington: University Press of Kentucky, 1998.

Cohen, Lizabeth. *A Consumers' Republic: The Politics of Mass Consumption in Postwar America*. New York: Random House, 2008.

Cortright, David. *Soldiers in Revolt: GI Resistance during the Vietnam War*. Chicago: Haymarket Books, 2005.

Corwin, Norman. *On a Note of Triumph*. New York: Simon & Schuster, 1945. http://archive.org/details/onnoteoftriumph00corw.

Cosmas, Graham A. *An Army for Empire: The United States Army in the Spanish-American War*. Columbia, MO: University of Missouri Press, 1971.

Cowie, Jefferson. *Stayin' Alive: The 1970s and the Last Days of the Working Class*. New York: New Press, 2010.

Crackel, Theodore J. 'Jefferson, Politics, and the Army: An Examination of the Military Peace Establishment Act of 1802'. *Journal of the Early Republic* 2, no. 1 (1982): 21–38.

Craig, Campbell, and Fredrik Logevall. *America's Cold War: The Politics of Insecurity*. Cambridge, MA: Harvard University Press, 2008.

Currey, Cecil. *Self-Destruction: The Disintegration and Decay of the United States Army during the Vietnam Era*. New York: Norton, 1981.

Cypher, James M. 'The Origins and Evolution of Military Keynesianism in the United States'. *Journal of Post Keynesian Economics* 38, no. 3 (3 October 2015): 449–76.

Daalder, Ivo H., and I. M. Destler. *In the Shadow of the Oval Office: Profiles of the National Security Advisers and the Presidents They Served-From JFK to George W. Bush*. New York: Simon & Schuster, 2011.

Daddis, Gregory. 'Mansplaining Vietnam: Male Veterans and America's Popular Image of the Vietnam War'. *Journal of Military History* 82, no. 1 (1 January 2018): 181–207.

Daddis, Gregory A. *Pulp Vietnam: War and Gender in Cold War Men's Adventure Magazines*. New York: Cambridge University Press, 2020.

Davis, Sasha. *The Empires' Edge: Militarization, Resistance, and Transcending Hegemony in the Pacific*. Athens: University of Georgia Press, 2015.

Dean, Robert D. 'Masculinity as Ideology: John F. Kennedy and the Domestic Politics of Foreign Policy'. *Diplomatic History* 22, no. 1 (January 1998): 29–62.

DeBenedetti, Charles, and Charles Chatfield. *An American Ordeal: The Antiwar Movement of the Vietnam Era*. Syracuse: Syracuse University Press, 1990.

DeLay, Brian. 'How Not to Arm a State: American Guns and the Crisis of Governance in Mexico, Nineteenth and Twenty-First Centuries'. *Southern California Quarterly* 95, no. 1 (1 February 2013): 5–23. https://doi.org/10.1525/scq.2013.95.1.5.

Dittmar, Linda, and Gene Michaud. *From Hanoi to Hollywood: The Vietnam War in American Film*. New Brunswick, NJ: Rutgers University Press, 1990.

Dower, John. *Embracing Defeat: Japan in the Wake of World War II*. New York: W. W. Norton, 2000.

Dower, John. *War without Mercy: Race and Power in the Pacific War*. New York: Pantheon Books, 1986.

Downs, Gregory P. *After Appomattox: Military Occupation and the Ends of War*. Cambridge, MA: Harvard University Press, 2015.

Dudziak, Mary. *War Time: An Idea, Its History, Its Consequences*. New York: Oxford University Press, 2012.

Dudziak, Mary L. '"You Didn't See Him Lying … beside the Gravel Road in France": Death, Distance, and American War Politics'. *Diplomatic History* 42, no. 1 (1 January 2018): 1–16. https://doi.org/10.1093/dh/dhx087.

Edgington, Ryan H. *Range Wars: The Environmental Contest for White Sands Missile Range*. Lincoln: University of Nebraska Press, 2014.

Ellis, John. *Brute Force: Allied Strategy and Tactics during the Second World War*. London: Viking, 1990.

Engelhardt, Tom. *The End of Victory Culture: Cold War America and the Disillusioning of a Generation*. Amherst: University of Massachusetts Press, 1998.

Enloe, Cynthia. *Bananas, Beaches and Bases: Making Feminist Sense of International Politics*. Berkeley: University of California Press, 2014.

Enloe, Cynthia. *Maneuvers: The International Politics of Militarizing Women's Lives*. Berkeley: University of California Press, 2000.

Epstein, Katherine C. 'The Conundrum of American Power in the Age of World War I'. *Modern American History* 2, no. 3 (November 2019): 345–65. https://doi.org/10.1017/mah.2019.23.

Esser, Raingard. '"Language No Obstacle": War Brides in the German Press, 1945–49'. *Women's History Review* 12, no. 4 (1 December 2003): 577–603. https://doi.org/10.1080/09612020300200375.

Evangelista, Matthew, and Henry Shue, eds. *The American Way of Bombing: Changing Ethical and Legal Norms, from Flying Fortresses to Drones*. Ithaca NY: Cornell University Press, 2014.

Evans, Joyce. *Celluloid Mushroom Clouds: Hollywood and Atomic Bomb*. London: Routledge, 2018.

Fahmy, Shahira, and Thomas J. Johnson. "'How We Performed'": Embedded Journalists' Attitudes and Perceptions Towards Covering the Iraq War'. *Journalism & Mass Communication Quarterly* 82, no. 2 (1 June 2005): 301–17. https://doi.org/10.1177/107769900508200205.

Farish, Matthew. *The Contours of America's Cold War*. Minneapolis: University of Minnesota Press, 2010.

Faust, Drew Gilpin. *This Republic of Suffering*. New York: Knopf Doubleday Publishing Group, 2008.

Felbab-Brown, Vanda. *Shooting Up: Counterinsurgency and the War on Drugs*. Washington, DC: Brookings Institution Press, 2009.

Fenner, Lorry, and Marie deYoung. *Women in Combat: Civic Duty or Military Liability?* Washington, DC: Georgetown University Press, 2001.

Fergie, Dexter. 'Geopolitics Turned Inwards: The Princeton Military Studies Group and the National Security Imagination'. *Diplomatic History* 43, no. 4 (2019): 644–70. Accessed 16 July 2019. https://doi.org/10.1093/dh/dhz026.

Filkins, Dexter. *The Forever War*. New York: Knopf, 2008.

Finkel, David. *Thank You for Your Service*. New York: Sarah Crichton Books, 2013.

Finkel, David. *The Good Soldiers*. New York: Picador, 2010.

Fitzgerald, David. 'Support the Troops: Gulf War Homecomings and a New Politics of Military Celebration'. *Modern American History* 2, no. 1 (March 2019): 1–22. https://doi.org/10.1017/mah.2019.1.

Fitzgerald, David, David Ryan and John M. Thompson, eds. *Not Even Past: How the United States Ends Wars*. New York: Berghahn Books, 2020.

Foner, Eric. *Reconstruction: America's Unfinished Revolution, 1863–1877*. New York: HarperCollins, 2011.

Foner, Eric. 'Who Is an American? The Imagined Community in American History'. *Centennial Review* 41, no. 3 (1997): 425–38.

Fox, Sarah Alisabeth. *Downwind: A People's History of the Nuclear West*. Lincoln: University of Nebraska Press, 2014.

Frank, Michael C. 'At War with the Unknown: Hollywood, Homeland Security, and the Cultural Imaginary of Terrorism after 9/11'. *Amerikastudien/American Studies* 60, no. 4 (2015): 485–504.

Frank, Nathaniel. *Unfriendly Fire: How the Gay Ban Undermines the Military and Weakens America*. New York: Thomas Dunne Books, 2009.

Frederick, Jim. *Black Hearts: One Platoon's Descent into Madness in Iraq's Triangle of Death*. London: Pan, 2011.

Freedman, Lawrence. *The Future of War: A History*. London: Penguin UK, 2017.

Freeman, Joshua, and Eric Foner. *American Empire: The Rise of a Global Power, the Democratic Revolution at Home, 1945–2000*. New York: Penguin Books, 2013.

Fried, Richard M. *The Russians Are Coming! The Russians Are Coming!: Pageantry and Patriotism in Cold-War America*. New York: Oxford University Press, 1999.

Friedberg, Aaron L. *In the Shadow of the Garrison State: America's Anti-Statism and Its Cold War Grand Strategy*. Princeton, NJ: Princeton University Press, 2000.

Friedman, Andrew. *Covert Capital: Landscapes of Denial and the Making of U.S. Empire in the Suburbs of Northern Virginia*. Berkeley: University of California Press, 2013.

Friedman, Andrew. 'US Empire, World War 2 and the Racialising of Labour'. *Race & Class*, 4 April 2017. https://doi.org/10.1177/0306396816685024.

Gaddis, John Lewis. *Strategies of Containment: A Critical Appraisal of Postwar American National Security*. New York: Oxford University Press, 1982.

Gagnon, Frédérick. ' "Invading Your Hearts and Minds": Call of Duty® and the (Re) Writing of Militarism in U.S. Digital Games and Popular Culture'. *European journal of American studies* 5, no. 3 (27 June 2010). https://doi.org/10.4000/ejas.8831.

Gallicchio, Marc. 'World War II in Historical Memory'. In *A Companion to World War II*, edited by Thomas Zeiler and Daniel M. DuBois, 978–98. Hoboken, NJ: John Wiley, 2012. https://doi.org/10.1002/9781118325018.ch57.

Gans, John. *White House Warriors: How the National Security Council Transformed the American Way of War*. New York: Liveright, 2019.

Garfinkle, Adam. *Telltale Hearts: The Origins and Impact of the Vietnam Anti-War Movement*. New York: Griffin, 1997.

Gawthorpe, Andrew J. *To Build as Well as Destroy: American Nation Building in South Vietnam*. Ithaca, NY: Cornell University Press, 2018.

Geary, Daniel. *Beyond Civil Rights: The Moynihan Report and Its Legacy*. Philadelphia: University of Pennsylvania Press, 2015.

Geary, James. *We Need Men: The Union Draft in the Civil War*. Dekalb: Northern Illinois University Press, 1991.

Gebhardt, Miriam. *Crimes Unspoken: The Rape of German Women at the End of the Second World War*. Cambridge: Polity Press, 2016.

Gerstle, Gary. *American Crucible: Race and Nation in the Twentieth Century*, repr. edn. Princeton, NJ: Princeton University Press, 2017.

Gerstle, Gary. *Liberty and Coercion: The Paradox of American Government from the Founding to the Present*. Princeton, NJ: Princeton University Press, 2015.

Geyer, Michael. 'The Militarization of Europe, 1914–1945'. In *The Militarization of the Western World*, edited by John R. Gillis, 65–102. New Brunswick, NJ: Rutgers University Press, 1989.

Gibson, James William. *Warrior Dreams: Violence and Manhood in Post-Vietnam America*. New York: Hill & Wang, 1994.

Gillem, Mark L. *America Town: Building the Outposts of Empire*. Minneapolis: University of Minnesota Press, 2007.

Gleason, Philip. 'Americans All: World War II and the Shaping of American Identity'. *Review of Politics* 43, no. 4 (1981): 483–518.

Goedde, Petra. *GIs and Germans: Culture, Gender and Foreign Relations, 1945–1949.* New Haven, CT: Yale University Press, 2003.

Goedde, Petra. *The Politics of Peace: A Global Cold War History.* New York: Oxford University Press, 2019.

Goodman, Giora. '"Only the Best British Brides": Regulating the Relationship between US Servicemen and British Women in the Early Cold War'. *Contemporary European History* 17, no. 4 (2008): 483–503.

Graham, Herman. *The Brothers' Vietnam War: Black Power, Manhood, and the Military Experience.* Gainesville: University Press of Florida, 2003.

Grandin, Greg. *The End of the Myth: From the Frontier to the Border Wall in the Mind of America.* New York: Metropolitan Books, 2019.

Green, Michael Cullen. *Black Yanks in the Pacific: Race in the Making of American Military Empire after World War II.* Ithaca, NY: Cornell University Press, 2010.

Greenberg, Amy S. *A Wicked War: Polk, Clay, Lincoln, and the 1846 U.S. Invasion of Mexico.* New York: Vintage, 2013.

Gregor, William J. *Toward a Revolution in Civil-Military Affairs: Understanding the United States Military in the Post-Cold War World.* Cambridge, MA: John M. Olin Institute for Strategic Studies, 1996.

Gregory, Derek. 'From a View to a Kill: Drones and Late Modern War'. *Theory, Culture & Society* 28, nos. 7–8 (1 December 2011): 188–215. https://doi.org/10.1177/0263276411423027.

Griffith, Robert K. *US Army's Transition to the All-Volunteer Force, 1968–1974.* Washington, DC: Center of Military History, 1996.

Grossmann, Atina. 'A Question of Silence: The Rape of German Women by Occupation Soldiers'. *October* 72 (1995): 43–63. https://doi.org/10.2307/778926.

Guglielmo, Thomas A. '"Red Cross, Double Cross": Race and America s World War II-Era Blood Donor Service'. *Journal of American History* 97, no. 1 (2010): 63–90.

Hagopian, Patrick. *The Vietnam War in American Memory: Veterans, Memorials, and the Politics of Healing.* Amherst: University of Massachusetts Press, 2009.

Hall, Simon. 'The Response of the Moderate Wing of the Civil Rights Movement to the War in Vietnam'. *Historical Journal* 46, no. 3 (2003): 669–701.

Hallin, Daniel C. *The Uncensored War: The Media and Vietnam.* Berkeley: University of California Press, 1989.

Hämäläinen, Pekka. *Lakota America: A New History of Indigenous Power.* New Haven, CT: Yale University Press, 2019.

Hamilton, Peter E. '"A Haven for Tortured Souls": Hong Kong in the Vietnam War'. *International History Review* 37, no. 3 (27 May 2015): 565–81. https://doi.org/10.1080/07075332.2014.946948.

Hampton, Isaac. *The Black Officer Corps: A History of Black Military Advancement from Integration through Vietnam.* London: Routledge, 2013.

Hantke, Steffen. *Monsters in the Machine: Science Fiction Film and the Militarization of America after World War II*. Jackson: University Press of Mississippi, 2016.

Hass, Kristin Ann. *Sacrificing Soldiers on the National Mall*. Chapel Hill: University of North Carolina Press, 2013.

Hathaway, Oona A., and Scott J. Shapiro. *The Internationalists: How a Radical Plan to Outlaw War Remade the World*. New York: Penguin Books, 2017.

Haynes, Robert V. 'The Houston Mutiny and Riot of 1917'. *Southwestern Historical Quarterly* 76, no. 4 (1973): 418–39.

Hedges, Chris. 'What War Looks Like'. *New York Times*, 20 May 2009. https://www. nytimes.com/2009/05/24/books/review/Hedges-t.html.

Heefner, Gretchen. '"A Fighter Pilot's Heaven": Finding Cold War Utility in the North African Desert'. *Environmental History* 22, no. 1 (1 January 2017): 50–76. https://doi. org/10.1093/envhis/emw066.

Heefner, Gretchen. '"A Slice of Their Sovereignty": Negotiating the U.S. Empire of Bases, Wheelus Field, Libya, 1950–1954'. *Diplomatic History* 41, no. 1 (1 January 2017): 50–77. https://doi.org/10.1093/dh/dhv058.

Heefner, Gretchen. '"A Tract That Is Wholly Sand": Engineering Military Environments in Libya'. *Endeavour* 40, no. 1 (1 March 2016): 38–47. https://doi.org/10.1016/j. endeavour.2015.12.002.

Heefner, Gretchen. *The Missile Next Door: The Minuteman in the American Heartland*. Cambridge, MA: Harvard University Press, 2012.

Heller, Charles E. 'The U.S. Army, the Civilian Conservation Corps, and Leadership for World War II, 1933–1942'. *Armed Forces & Society* 36, no. 3 (1 April 2010): 439–53. https://doi.org/10.1177/0095327X09333944.

Hellmann, John. *American Myth and the Legacy of Vietnam*. New York: Columbia University Press, 1989.

Henriksen, Margot A. *Dr. Strangelove's America: Society and Culture in the Atomic Age*. Berkeley: University of California Press, 1997.

Herring, George C. *From Colony to Superpower: U.S. Foreign Relations since 1776*. New York: Oxford University Press, 2011.

Heyman, Josiah, and Howard Campbell. 'The Militarization of the United States-Mexico Border Region'. *Revista de Estudos Universitários – REU* 38, no. 1 (2012): 75–94.

High, Steven. *Base Colonies in the Western Hemisphere, 1940–1967*. Studies of the Americas. Basingstoke: Palgrave Macmillan, 2009. https://doi.org/10.1057/9780230618046.

Hiltner, Aaron. 'Friendly Invasions: Civilians and Servicemen on the World War II American Home Front'. PhD diss., Boston University, 2018. https://open.bu.edu/handle/2144/31691.

Hirshberg, Lauren. '"Navigating Sovereignty under a Cold War Military Industrial Colonial Complex: US Military Empire and Marshallese Decolonization"'. *History and Technology* 31, no. 3 (3 July 2015): 259–74. https://doi.org/10.1080/07341512.2015.1126408.

Hitchcock, William I. *The Bitter Road to Freedom: The Human Cost of Allied Victory in World War II Europe.* New York: Free Press, 2009.

Hixson, Walter L. "'Red Storm Rising": Tom Clancy Novels and the Cult of National Security.' *Diplomatic History* 17, no. 4 (1 October 1993): 599–614. https://doi.org/10.1111/j.1467-7709.1993.tb00601.x.

Hixson, Walter L. *The Myth of American Diplomacy: National Identity and U.S. Foreign Policy.* New Haven, CT: Yale University Press, 2008.

Hogan, Michael J. *A Cross of Iron: Harry S. Truman and the Origins of the National Security State, 1945–1954.* Cambridge: Cambridge University Press, 2000.

Hoganson, Kristin L. *Fighting for American Manhood: How Gender Politics Provoked the Spanish-American and Philippine-American Wars.* New Haven, CT: Yale University Press, 1998.

Höhn, Maria, and Seungsook Moon, eds. *Over There: Living with the U.S. Military Empire from World War Two to the Present.* Durham, NC: Duke University Press, 2010.

Holm, Jeanne. *Women in the Military: An Unfinished Revolution.* Novato, CA: Presidio Press, 1992.

Holmes, Amy Austin. *Social Unrest and American Military Bases in Turkey and Germany since 1945.* Cambridge: Cambridge University Press, 2014.

Howe, Daniel Walker. *What Hath God Wrought: The Transformation of America, 1815–1848.* Oxford: Oxford University Press, 2009.

Huebner, Andrew J. *Love and Death in the Great War.* Oxford: Oxford University Press, 2018.

Huebner, Andrew J. *Warrior Image: Soldiers in American Culture from the Second World War to the Vietnam Era.* Chapel Hill: University of North Carolina Press, 2008.

Hunt, Andrew E. *The Turning: A History of Vietnam Veterans against the War.* New York: New York University Press, 1999.

Huntington, Samuel P. *The Soldier and the State.* Cambridge, MA: Harvard University Press, 1957.

Immerman, Richard H. *Empire for Liberty: A History of American Imperialism from Benjamin Franklin to Paul Wolfowitz.* Princeton, NJ: Princeton University Press, 2010.

Immerwahr, Daniel. *How to Hide an Empire: A History of the Greater United States.* New York: Farrar, Straus and Giroux, 2019.

Inoue, Masamichi. *Okinawa and the U.S. Military: Identity Making in the Age of Globalization.* New York: Columbia University Press, 2017.

Irwin, Julia. *Making the World Safe: The American Red Cross and a Nation's Humanitarian Awakening.* Oxford: Oxford University Press, 2013.

Jacobsen, Annie. *Operation Paperclip: The Secret Intelligence Program That Brought Nazi Scientists to America.* New York: Little, Brown, 2014.

Jeffords, Susan. *Hard Bodies: Hollywood Masculinity in the Reagan Era.* New Brunswick, NJ: Rutgers University Press.

Johns, Andrew L. *Vietnam's Second Front: Domestic Politics, the Republican Party, and the War*. Lexington: University Press of Kentucky, 2010.

Johnson, Chalmers. 'The Okinawan Rape Incident and the End of the Cold War in East Asia'. *California Western International Law Journal* 27 (1997): 389.

Johnson, Taylor N. '"The Most Bombed Nation on Earth": Western Shoshone Resistance to the Nevada National Security Site'. *Atlantic Journal of Communication* 26, no. 4 (8 August 2018): 224–39. https://doi.org/10.1080/15456870.2018.1494177.

Jones, John Bush. *All-Out for Victory!: Magazine Advertising and the World War II Home Front*. Hanover, NH: Brandeis University Press, 2009.

Jones, Matthew. *After Hiroshima: The United States, Race and Nuclear Weapons in Asia, 1945–1965*. Cambridge: Cambridge University Press, 2010.

Kaplan, Robert D. *Imperial Grunts: On the Ground with the American Military, from Mongolia to the Philippines to Iraq and Beyond*. New York: Vintage Books, 2006.

Karp, Matthew. *This Vast Southern Empire: Slaveholders at the Helm of American Foreign Policy*. Cambridge, MA: Harvard University Press, 2016.

Karsten, Peter. 'The Nature of "Influence": Roosevelt, Mahan and the Concept of Sea Power'. *American Quarterly* 23, no. 4 (1971): 585–600. https://doi.org/10.2307/2711707.

Katznelson, Ira. *Fear Itself: The New Deal and the Origins of Our Time*. New York: W. W. Norton, 2013.

Katznelson, Ira. *When Affirmative Action Was White: An Untold History of Racial Inequality in Twentieth-Century America*. New York: W. W. Norton, 2006.

Kazin, Michael. *War against War: The American Fight for Peace, 1914–1918*. New York: Simon & Schuster, 2017.

Keene, Jennifer D. *Doughboys, the Great War, and the Remaking of America*. Baltimore, MD: Johns Hopkins University Press, 2003.

Kellner, Douglas. *The Persian Gulf TV War*. Boulder, CO: Westview Press, 1992.

Kemp, Geoffrey. 'The Continuing Debate Over U.S. Arms Sales: Strategic Needs and the Quest for Arms Limitations'. *Annals of the American Academy of Political and Social Science* 535, no. 1 (1 September 1994): 146–57. https://doi.org/10.1177/0002716294535001011.

Kennedy, David M. *Over Here: The First World War and American Society*. Oxford: Oxford University Press, 2004.

Kennedy, Ross A. 'Preparedness'. In *A Companion to Woodrow Wilson*, 270–85. New York: Wiley-Blackwell, 2013. https://doi.org/10.1002/9781118445693.ch14.

Khalili, Laleh. 'The Roads to Power: The Infrastructure of Counterinsurgency'. *World Policy Journal* 34, no. 1 (1 April 2017): 93–9.

Kieran, David. *Forever Vietnam: How a Divisive War Changed American Public Memory*. Amherst: University of Massachusetts Press, 2014.

Kieran, David. *Signature Wounds: The Untold Story of the Military's Mental Health Crisis*. New York: New York University Press, 2019.

Kieran, David, and Edwin A. Martini. *At War: The Military and American Culture in the Twentieth Century and Beyond*. New Brunswick, NJ: Rutgers University Press, 2018.

Kitfield, James. *War and Destiny: How the Bush Revolution in Foreign and Military Affairs Redefined American Power*. Washington, DC: Potomac Books, 2007.

Klare, Michael T. *American Arms Supermarket*. Austin: University of Texas Press, 1984.

Klimke, Martin. 'The African-American Civil Rights Struggle and Germany, 1945–1989'. *GHI Bulletin*, no. 43 (2008): 91–106.

Kohn, Richard H. *Eagle and Sword: The Federalists and the Creation of the Military Establishment in America, 1783–1802*, 1st edn. New York: Free Press, 1975.

Kohn, Richard H. 'The Inside History of the Newburgh Conspiracy: America and the Coup d'Etat'. *William and Mary Quarterly* 27, no. 2 (1970): 188–220. https://doi.org/10.2307/1918650.

Koistinen, Paul A. C. *Planning War, Pursuing Peace: The Political Economy of American Warfare, 1920–1939*. Lawrence: University Press of Kansas, 1998.

Koppes, Clayton R., and Gregory D. Black. 'What to Show the World: The Office of War Information and Hollywood, 1942–1945'. *Journal of American History* 64, no. 1 (1977): 87–105. https://doi.org/10.2307/1888275.

Kornbluh, Peter, and Malcolm Byrne. *The Iran-Contra Scandal: The Declassified History*. New York: New Press, 1993.

Kovner, Sarah. *Occupying Power: Sex Workers and Servicemen in Postwar Japan*. Stanford, CA: Stanford University Press, 2012.

Kramer, Paul A. 'The Geopolitics of Mobility: Immigration Policy and American Global Power in the Long Twentieth Century'. *American Historical Review* 123, no. 2 (1 April 2018): 393–438. https://doi.org/10.1093/ahr/123.2.393.

Kramm, Robert. *Sanitized Sex: Regulating Prostitution, Venereal Disease, and Intimacy in Occupied Japan, 1945–1952*. Berkeley: University of California Press, 2017.

Krebs, Ronald R. *Fighting for Rights: Military Service and the Politics of Citizenship*. Ithaca, NY: Cornell University Press, 2006.

Kreps, Sarah. *Taxing Wars: The American Way of War Finance and the Decline of Democracy*. New York: Oxford University Press, 2018.

Kutler, Stanley I. *American Inquisition: Justice and Injustice in the Cold War*. New York: Hill & Wang, 1984.

Kuzmarov, Jeremy. *The Myth of the Addicted Army: Vietnam and the Modern War on Drugs*. Amherst: University Massachusetts Press, 2009.

Lair, Meredith H. *Armed with Abundance: Consumerism and Soldiering in the Vietnam War*. Chapel Hill: University of North Carolina Press, 2014.

Lang, Andrew F. 'Republicanism, Race, and Reconstruction: The Ethos of Military Occupation in Civil War America'. *Journal of the Civil War Era* 4, no. 4 (2014): 559–89.

Lawlor, Ruth. 'American Soldiers and the Politics of Rape in World War II Europe'. PhD diss., Cambridge: University of Cambridge, 2019.

Lawlor, Ruth. 'Contested Crimes: Race, Gender, and Nation in Histories of GI Sexual Violence, World War II'. *Journal of Military History* 84, no. 2 (2020): 541–70.

Lebovic, Sam. *Free Speech and Unfree News: The Paradox of Press Freedom in America*. Cambridge, MA: Harvard University Press, 2016.

Lederman, Gordon Nathaniel, and Sam Nunn. *Reorganizing the Joint Chiefs of Staff: The Goldwater-Nichols Act of 1986*. Westport, CT: Greenwood Press, 1999.

Lee, Sabine. 'A Forgotten Legacy of the Second World War: GI Children in Post-War Britain and Germany'. *Contemporary European History* 20, no. 2 (May 2011): 157–81. https://doi.org/10.1017/S096077731100004X.

Leffler, Melvyn P. *A Preponderance of Power: National Security, the Truman Administration, and the Cold War*. Stanford, CA: Stanford University Press, 1993.

Leffler, Melvyn P. 'The American Conception of National Security and the Beginnings of the Cold War, 1945–48'. *American Historical Review* 89, no. 2 (April 1984): 346–81. https://doi.org/10.2307/1862556.

Lembcke, Jerry. *The Spitting Image: Myth, Memory, and the Legacy of Vietnam*. New York: New York University Press, 2000.

Lentz-Smith, Adriane. *Freedom Struggles: African Americans and World War I*. Cambridge, MA: Harvard University Press, 2010.

LeoGrande, William M. *Our Own Backyard: The United States in Central America, 1977–1992*. Chapel Hill: University of North Carolina Press, 2000.

Lerner, Mitchell. '"Is It For This We Fought And Bled?": The Korean War and the Struggle for Civil Rights'. *Journal of Military History* 82, no. 2 (April 2018): 515–45.

Lewis, Adrian R. *The American Culture of War: The History of U.S. Military Force from World War II to Operation Iraqi Freedom*. Abingdon: Routledge, 2006.

Lewis, Robert. 'World War II Manufacturing and the Postwar Southern Economy'. *Journal of Southern History* 73, no. 4 (2007): 837–66. https://doi.org/10.2307/27649570.

Lilly, J. Robert. *Taken by Force: Rape and American GIs in Europe during World War II*. Basingstoke: Palgrave Macmillan, 2007.

Lindstrom, Lamont. 'Cargo Cults'. *Cambridge Encyclopedia of Anthropology*, 29 March 2018. https://www.anthroencyclopedia.com/entry/cargo-cults.

Linn, Brian McAllister. *The Echo of Battle: The Army's Way of War*. Cambridge, MA: Harvard University Press, 2007.

Linn, Brian McAllister. *Elvis's Army: Cold War GIs and the Atomic Battlefield*. Cambridge, MA: Harvard University Press, 2016.

Linn, Brian McAllister. *The Philippine War, 1899–1902*. Lawrence: University Press of Kansas, 2000.

Lipman, Jana K. 'A Refugee Camp in America: Fort Chaffee and Vietnamese and Cuban Refugees, 1975–1982'. *Journal of American Ethnic History* 33, no. 2 (2014): 57–87. https://doi.org/10.5406/jamerethnhist.33.2.0057.

Lock-Pullan, Richard. "'An Inward Looking Time'": The United States Army, 1973–1976'. *Journal of Military History* 67, no. 2 (April 2003): 483–511. https://doi.org/10.2307/3093465.

Lotchin, Roger W. 'California Cities and the Hurricane of Change: World War II in the San Francisco, Los Angeles, and San Diego Metropolitan Areas'. *Pacific Historical Review* 63, no. 3 (1994): 393–420. https://doi.org/10.2307/3640972.

Loveland, Anne C. *American Evangelicals and the U.S. Military, 1942–1993*. Baton Rouge: Louisiana State University Press, 1996.

Lowen, Rebecca S. *Creating the Cold War University: The Transformation of Stanford*. Berkeley: University of California Press, 1997.

Luebke, Thomas E. *Palace of State: The Eisenhower Executive Office Building*. Washington, DC: U.S. Commission of Fine Arts, 2018.

Lutz, Catherine. *Homefront: A Military City and the American Twentieth Century*. Boston, MA: Beacon Press, 2002.

Lutz, Catherine. 'Making War at Home in the United States: Militarization and the Current Crisis'. *American Anthropologist* 104, no. 3 (2002): 723–35.

Lutz, Catherine. *The Bases of Empire: The Global Struggle against U.S. Military Posts*. New York: New York University Press, 2009.

MacGregor, Morris J. *Integration of the Armed Forces, 1940–1965*. Washington, DC: US Army Center of Military History, 1981.

MacKenzie, Megan. *Beyond the Band of Brothers: The US Military and the Myth That Women Can't Fight*. New York: Cambridge University Press, 2015.

MacLeish, Kenneth T. *Making War at Fort Hood: Life and Uncertainty in a Military Community*. Princeton, NJ: Princeton University Press, 2013.

Madsen, Grant. *Sovereign Soldiers: How the U.S. Military Transformed the Global Economy After World War II*. Philadelphia: University of Pennsylvania Press, 2018.

Mann, Michael. 'The Roots and Contradictions of Modern Militarism'. *New Left Review* 1, no. 162 (1987): 35–50.

Marcus, Eric. 'Perry Watkins'. Making Gay History: The Podcast. Accessed 30 March 2020. https://makinggayhistory.com/podcast/perry-watkins/.

Mariscal, George. 'In the Wake of the Gulf War: Untying the Yellow Ribbon'. *Cultural Critique*, no. 19 (1991): 97–117. https://doi.org/10.2307/1354309.

Mark, Chi-kwan. 'Vietnam War Tourists: US Naval Visits to Hong Kong and British-American-Chinese Relations, 1965–1968'. *Cold War History* 10, no. 1 (1 February 2010): 1–28. https://doi.org/10.1080/14682740902837001.

Markusen, Ann R., Peter Hall, Scott Campbell and Sabina Deitrick. *The Rise of the Gunbelt: The Military Remapping of Industrial America*. Oxford: Oxford University Press, 1991.

Martini, Edwin A. *Agent Orange: History, Science and the Politics of Uncertainty*. Amherst: University Massachusetts Press, 2012.

Martini, Edwin A., ed. *Proving Grounds: Militarized Landscapes, Weapons Testing, and the Environmental Impact of U.S. Bases*. Seattle: University of Washington Press, 2017.

Massey, Douglas S., Jorge Durand and Karen A. Pren. 'Why Border Enforcement Backfired'. *American Journal of Sociology* 121, no. 5 (1 March 2016): 1557–600. https://doi.org/10.1086/684200.

Mattis, Jim, and Kori N. Schake, eds. *Warriors and Citizens: American Views of Our Military*. Stanford, CA: Hoover Institution Press, 2016.

Maulucci, Thomas W., and Detlef Junker, eds. *GIs in Germany: The Social, Economic, Cultural, and Political History of the American Military Presence*. Cambridge: Cambridge University Press, 2013.

May, Elaine T. *Homeward Bound*. New York: Basic Books, 1988.

May, Ernest R., ed. *American Cold War Strategy: Interpreting NSC 68*. Boston, MA: Palgrave Macmillan, 1993.

May, Lary. *The Big Tomorrow: Hollywood and the Politics of the American Way*. Chicago: University of Chicago Press, 2000.

Mazzetti, Mark. *The Way of the Knife: The CIA, a Secret Army, and a War at the Ends of the Earth*. New York: Penguin Press, 2013.

McAlister, Melani. *Epic Encounters: Culture, Media, and U.S. Interests in the Middle East since 1945*. Berkeley: University of California Press, 2005.

McCallum, John. 'U.S. Censorship, Violence, and Moral Judgement in a Wartime Democracy, 1941–1945'. *Diplomatic History* 41, no. 3 (1 June 2017): 543–66.

McEnaney, Laura. *Civil Defense Begins at Home: Militarization Meets Everyday Life in the Fifties*. Princeton, NJ: Princeton University Press, 2000.

McKevitt, Andrew C. '"Watching War Made Us Immune": The Popular Culture of the Wars'. In *Understanding the U.S. Wars in Iraq and Afghanistan*, edited by Beth Bailey and Richard H. Immerman, 238–58. New York: New York University Press, 2015.

McLelland, Mark. *Love, Sex, and Democracy in Japan during the American Occupation*. London: Palgrave Macmillan, 2012.

McNeill, J. R., and Corinna R. Unger, eds. *Environmental Histories of the Cold War*. Cambridge: Cambridge University Press, 2010.

McNeill, J. R., and David S. Painter. 'The Global Environmental Footprint of the U.S. Military, 1789–2003'. In *War and the Environment: Military Destruction in the Modern Age*, edited by Charles E. Closmann, 10–31. College Station: Texas A&M University Press, 2009.

McPherson, James M. *Battle Cry of Freedom: The Civil War Era*. Oxford: Oxford University Press, 1988.

Meierotto, Lisa. 'A Disciplined Space: The Co-Evolution of Conservation and Militarization on the US-Mexico Border'. *Anthropological Quarterly; Washington* 87, no. 3 (Summer 2014): 637–64. http://dx.doi.org/10.1353/anq.2014.0039.

Meyer, Leisa D. *Creating GI Jane: Sexuality and Power in the Women's Army Corps during World War II*. New York: Columbia University Press, 1996.

Miller, Arthur S., and H. Bart Cox. 'Congress, the Constitution, and First Use of Nuclear Weapons'. *Review of Politics* 48, no. 3 (1986): 424–55.

Miller, Russell A. *US National Security, Intelligence and Democracy: From the Church Committee to the War on Terror*. London: Routledge, 2008.

Milne, David. *Worldmaking: The Art and Science of American Diplomacy*, repr. edn. New York: Farrar, Straus and Giroux, 2017.

Milward, Alan S. *War, Economy and Society, 1939–1945*. Berkeley: University of California Press, 1979.

Mittelstadt, Jennifer. *The Rise of the Military Welfare State*. Cambridge, MA: Harvard University Press, 2015.

Moïse, Edwin E. *Tonkin Gulf and the Escalation of the Vietnam War*. Chapel Hill: University of North Carolina Press, 1996. http://archive.org/details/isbn_9780807823002.

Moon, Katharine H. S. 'Resurrecting Prostitutes and Overturning Treaties: Gender Politics in the "Anti-American" Movement in South Korea'. *Journal of Asian Studies* 66, no. 1 (February 2007): 129–57. https://doi.org/10.1017/S0021911807000046.

Morgan, Matthew J. 'The Garrison State Revisited: Civil–Military Implications of Terrorism and Security'. *Contemporary Politics* 10, no. 1 (1 March 2004): 5–19.

Morris, Madeline. 'By Force of Arms: Rape, War, and Military Culture'. *Duke Law Journal* 45, no. 4 (1996): 651–781. https://doi.org/10.2307/1372997.

Moser, Richard R. *The New Winter Soldiers: GI and Veteran Dissent during the Vietnam Era*. New Brunswick, NJ: Rutgers University Press, 1996.

Mowlana, Hamid, George Gerbner and Herbert Schiller, eds. *Triumph of The Image: The Media's War in the Persian Gulf, A Global Perspective*. Boulder, CO: Routledge, 1992.

Munholland, Kim. 'Yankee Farewell: The Americans Leave New Caledonia, 1945'. *Proceedings of the Meeting of the French Colonial Historical Society* 16 (1992): 181–94.

Murphy, Paul L. *World War I and the Origin of Civil Liberties in the United States*. New York: W. W. Norton, 1979.

Murphy, William J. 'John Adams: The Politics of the Additional Army, 1798–1800'. *New England Quarterly* 52, no. 2 (1979): 234–49. https://doi.org/10.2307/364841.

Nash, Gerald D. *World War II and the West: Reshaping the Economy*. Lincoln: University of Nebraska Press, 1990.

Neiberg, Michael S. *Making Citizen-Soldiers: ROTC and the Ideology of American Military Service*. Cambridge, MA: Harvard University Press, 2001.

Nelson, Daniel J. *Defenders or Intruders?: The Dilemmas of U.S. Forces in Germany*. Abingdon: Routledge, 2019.

Ngai, Mae M. *Impossible Subjects: Illegal Aliens and the Making of Modern America – Updated Edition*. Princeton, NJ: Princeton University Press, 2014.

Nguyen, Viet Thanh. *Nothing Ever Dies: Vietnam and the Memory of War*. Cambridge, MA: Harvard University Press, 2016.

Nicosia, Gerald. *Home to War: A History of the Vietnam Veterans' Movement*. New York: Crown, 2001.

O'Connell, Kaete M. "'Uncle Wiggly Wings": Children, Chocolates, and the Berlin Airlift'. *Food and Foodways* 25, no. 2 (3 April 2017): 142–59. https://doi.org/10.1080/07409710.2017.1311163.

Oh, Arissa. *To Save the Children of Korea: The Cold War Origins of International Adoption*. Stanford, CA: Stanford University Press, 2015.

Oliver, Kendrick. *The My Lai Massacre in American History and Memory*. Manchester: Manchester University Press, 2006.

Olsen, John Andreas. *John Warden and the Renaissance of American Air Power*. Washington, DC: Potomac Books, 2011.

O'Mara, Margaret. *Cities of Knowledge: Cold War Science and the Search for the Next Silicon Valley*. Princeton, NJ: Princeton University Press, 2015.

O'Mara, Margaret. *The Code: Silicon Valley and the Remaking of America*. New York: Penguin, 2019.

Ortiz, Stephen R. 'Rethinking the Bonus March: Federal Bonus Policy, the Veterans of Foreign Wars, and the Origins of a Protest Movement'. *Journal of Policy History* 18, no. 3 (July 2006): 275–303. https://doi.org/10.1353/jph.2006.0010.

Osgood, Kenneth, and Andrew K Frank, eds. *Selling War in a Media Age: The Presidency and Public Opinion in the American Century*. Gainesville: University Press of Florida, 2011.

Ouyyanont, Porphant. 'The Vietnam War and Tourism in Bangkok's Development, 1960–70'. *Japanese Journal of Southeast Asian Studies* 39, no. 2 (2001): 157–87.

Pach, Chester J. *Arming the Free World: The Origins of the United States Military Assistance Program, 1945–1950*. Chapel Hill: University of North Carolina Press, 1991.

Payne, Matthew Thomas. 'Marketing Military Realism in Call of Duty 4: Modern Warfare'. *Games and Culture* 7, no. 4 (1 July 2012): 305–27. https://doi.org/10.1177/1555412012454220.

Pearlman, Michael D. *Truman and MacArthur: Policy, Politics, and the Hunger for Honor and Renown*. Bloomington: Indiana University Press, 2008.

Phillips, Kimberley L. *War! What Is It Good For?: Black Freedom Struggles and the U.S. Military from World War II to Iraq*. Chapel Hill: University of North Carolina Press, 2012.

Polenberg, Richard. *Fighting Faiths: The Abrams Case, the Supreme Court, and Free Speech*. Ithaca, NY: Cornell University Press, 1999.

Porter, Andrea. "'Jarhead" and the Failure of the Vietnam Myth'. *CEA Critic* 73, no. 1 (2010): 1–14.

Preston, Andrew. 'Monsters Everywhere: A Genealogy of National Security'. *Diplomatic History* 38, no. 3 (1 June 2014): 477–500. https://doi.org/10.1093/dh/dhu018.

Preston, Andrew. *The War Council: McGeorge Bundy, the NSC, and Vietnam*. Cambridge, MA: Harvard University Press, 2006.

Priest, Dana. *The Mission: Waging War and Keeping Peace with America's Military*. New York: W. W. Norton, 2004.

Raj, Christopher S. 'Controversial US AWACS Sale to Saudis'. *Strategic Analysis* 5, no. 8 (1 November 1981): 392–9. https://doi.org/10.1080/09700168109425826.

Regele, Lindsay Schakenbach. 'Manufacturing Advantage: War, the State, and the Origins of American Industry, 1790–1840'. *Enterprise & Society* 17, no. 4 (2016): 721–33.

Reynolds, David. *Rich Relations: The American Occupation of Britain 1942–1945*. London: Phoenix, 2001.

Rhode, Paul. 'The Nash Thesis Revisited: An Economic Historian's View'. *Pacific Historical Review* 63, no. 3 (1994): 363–92. https://doi.org/10.2307/3640971.

Richards, Leonard L. *Shays's Rebellion: The American Revolution's Final Battle*. Philadelphia: University of Pennsylvania Press, 2014.

Richardson, Heather Cox. *West from Appomattox: The Reconstruction of America after the Civil War*. New Haven, CT: Yale University Press, 2007.

Ricks, Thomas E. *Fiasco: The American Military Adventure in Iraq*. London: Allen Lane, 2006.

Rid, Thomas. *War and Media Operations: The US Military and the Press from Vietnam to Iraq*. London: Routledge, 2007.

Rietzler, Katharina. 'The War as History: Writing the Economic and Social History of the First World War*'. *Diplomatic History* 38, no. 4 (1 September 2014): 826–39. https://doi.org/10.1093/dh/dhu028.

Risen, Clay. *The Crowded Hour: Theodore Roosevelt, the Rough Riders, and the Dawn of the American Century*. New York: Simon & Schuster, 2020.

Roberts, Mary Louise. 'The Leroy Henry Case: Sexual Violence and Allied Relations in Great Britain, 1944'. *Journal of the History of Sexuality* 26, no. 3 (1 September 2017): 402–23. https://doi.org/10.7560/JHS26303.

Roberts, Mary Louise. *What Soldiers Do: Sex and the American GI in World War II France*. Chicago: University of Chicago Press, 2013.

Rodgers, Daniel T. *Age of Fracture*. Cambridge, MA: Harvard University Press, 2011.

Roebuck, Kristin. 'Orphans by Design: "Mixed-Blood" Children, Child Welfare, and Racial Nationalism in Postwar Japan'. *Japanese Studies* 36, no. 2 (3 May 2016): 191–212. https://doi.org/10.1080/10371397.2016.1209969.

Roeder, George. *The Censored War: American Visual Experience during World War II: American Visual Experience during World War Two*. New Haven, CT: Yale University Press, 1995.

Rofe, J. Simon. '"Under the Influence of Mahan": Theodore and Franklin Roosevelt and Their Understanding of American National Interest'. *Diplomacy & Statecraft* 19, no. 4 (16 December 2008): 732–45. https://doi.org/10.1080/09592290802564536.

Rohde, Joy. *Armed with Expertise: The Militarization of American Social Research during the Cold War*. Ithaca, NY: Cornell University Press, 2013.

Rose, Kenneth D. *One Nation Underground: The Fallout Shelter in American Culture*. New York: New York University Press, 2001.

Rose, Sonya O. 'Girls and GIs: Race, Sex, and Diplomacy in Second World War Britain'. *International History Review* 19, no. 1 (1997): 146–60.

Rosegrant, Susan. *Route 128: Lessons from Boston's High-Tech Community.* New York: Basic Books, 1993.

Rosen, Jonathan D. *Losing War, The: Plan Colombia and Beyond.* Albany: State University of New York Press, 2015.

Rosenberg, Emily S. *A Date Which Will Live: Pearl Harbor in American Memory.* Durham, NC: Duke University Press, 2003.

Rostker, Bernard D., and K. C. Yeh. *I Want You!: The Evolution of the All-Volunteer Force.* Santa Monica, CA: Rand Corporation, 2006.

Rothkopf, David. *Running the World: The Inside Story of the National Security Council and the Architects of American Power.* New York: Public Affairs, 2006.

Rutenberg, Amy J. *Rough Draft: Cold War Military Manpower Policy and the Origins of Vietnam-Era Draft Resistance.* Ithaca, NY: Cornell University Press, 2019.

Ryan, David. *US Collective Memory, Intervention and Vietnam: The Cultural Politics of US Foreign Policy since 1969.* London: Routledge, forthcoming.

Ryan, Maria. *Full Spectrum Dominance: Irregular Warfare and the War on Terror.* Stanford, CA: Stanford University Press, 2019.

Sanders, Holly. 'Panpan: Streetwalking in Occupied Japan'. *Pacific Historical Review; Berkeley* 81, no. 3 (August 2012): 404–31.

Santino, Jack. 'Yellow Ribbons and Seasonal Flags: The Folk Assemblage of War'. *Journal of American Folklore* 105, no. 415 (1992): 19–33. https://doi.org/10.2307/541997.

Scanlon, Sandra. *The Pro-War Movement: Domestic Support for the Vietnam War and the Making of Modern American Conservatism.* Amherst: University of Massachusetts Press, 2013.

Scheibach, Michael. *Atomic Narratives and American Youth: Coming of Age with the Atom, 1945–1955.* Jefferson, NC: McFarland, 2003.

Schmitz, David F. *The Tet Offensive: Politics, War, and Public Opinion.* Lanham, MD: Rowman & Littlefield, 2005.

Scholnick, Robert J. 'Extermination and Democracy: O'Sullivan, the Democratic Review, and Empire, 1837–1840'. *American Periodicals* 15, no. 2 (2005): 123–41.

Schrader, Stuart. *Badges without Borders: How Global Counterinsurgency Transformed American Policing.* Berkeley: University of California Press, 2019.

Schrecker, Ellen. *Many Are the Crimes: McCarthyism in America.* Princeton, NJ: Princeton University Press, 1999.

Schrijvers, Peter. *The GI War against Japan: American Soldiers in Asia and the Pacific during World War II.* New York: New York University Press, 2005.

Schulman, Bruce J. *From Cotton Belt to Sunbelt: Federal Policy, Economic Development, and the Transformation of the South 1938–1980.* Durham, NC: Duke University Press, 1994.

Schulzinger, Robert. *A Time for Peace: The Legacy of the Vietnam War*. New York: Oxford University Press, 2006.

Shaw, Martin. *The New Western Way of War: Risk-Transfer War and Its Crisis in Iraq*. London: Polity Press, 2005.

Sherry, Michael. *In the Shadow of War: The United States since the 1930s*. New Haven, CT: Yale University Press, 1995.

Sherry, Michael. 'War as a Way of Life'. *Modern American History* 1, no. 1 (March 2018): 93–6. https://doi.org/10.1017/mah.2017.12.

Shibusawa, Naoko. *America's Geisha Ally: Reimagining the Japanese Enemy*. Cambridge, MA: Harvard University Press, 2010.

Shilts, Randy. *Conduct Unbecoming: Lesbians and Gays in the U.S. Military: Vietnam to the Persian Gulf*. New York: St. Martin's Press, 1993.

Skeen, C. Edward, and Richard H. Kohn. 'The Newburgh Conspiracy Reconsidered'. *William and Mary Quarterly* 31, no. 2 (1974): 273–98. https://doi.org/10.2307/1920913.

Skocpol, Theda. *Protecting Soldiers and Mothers: The Political Origins of Social Policy in the United States*. Cambridge, MA: Harvard University Press, 1995.

Slack, Jeremy, Daniel E. Martínez, Alison Elizabeth Lee, and Scott Whiteford. 'The Geography of Border Militarization: Violence, Death and Health in Mexico and the United States'. *Journal of Latin American Geography* 15, no. 1 (31 March 2016): 7–32. https://doi.org/10.1353/lag.2016.0009.

Small, Melvin. *Antiwarriors: The Vietnam War and the Battle for America's Hearts and Minds*. Wilmington: Scholarly Resources Books, 2002.

Smith, Sherry L. 'Lost Soldiers: Re-Searching the Army in the American West'. *Western Historical Quarterly* 29, no. 2 (1 May 1998): 149–63. https://doi.org/10.2307/971327.

Sorenson, David S. *Shutting Down the Cold War: The Politics of Military Base Closure*. New York: Palgrave Macmillan, 1998.

Sparrow, James T. *Warfare State: World War II Americans and the Age of Big Government*. Oxford: Oxford University Press, 2011.

Stephanson, Anders. 'Fourteen Notes on the Very Concept of the Cold War'. In *Rethinking Geopolitics*, edited by Simon Dalby and Gearóid Ó Tuathail, 62–85. London: Routledge, 1998.

Stephanson, Anders. *Manifest Destiny: American Expansion and the Empire of Right*. New York: Hill and Wang, 1996.

Stewart, Richard W., ed. *American Military History, Volume 1: The United States Army and the Forging of a Nation, 1775–1917*. Washington, DC: US Army Center of Military History, 2005.

Stewart, Richard W., ed. *American Military History Volume 2: The United States Army in a Global Era, 1917?2008*. Washington, DC: US Army Center of Military History, 2010.

Stole, Inger L. *Advertising at War: Business, Consumers, and Government in the 1940s*. Urbana: University of Illinois Press, 2012.

Stone, Geoffrey R. *Perilous Times: Free Speech in Wartime: From the Sedition Act of 1798 to the War on Terrorism*. New York: W. W. Norton, 2005.

Stork, Joe. 'The Carter Doctrine and US Bases in the Middle East'. *Merip Reports* 90 (1980): 3–14.

Strachan, Hew. *The Direction of War: Contemporary Strategy in Historical Perspective*. Cambridge: Cambridge University Press, 2014.

Stuart, Douglas T. *Creating the National Security State: A History of the Law That Transformed America*. Princeton, NJ: Princeton University Press, 2009.

Stur, Heather Marie. *Beyond Combat: Women and Gender in the Vietnam War Era*. New York: Cambridge University Press, 2011.

Sturken, Marita. 'The Wall, the Screen, and the Image: The Vietnam Veterans Memorial'. *Representations*, no. 35 (July 1991): 118–42. https://doi.org/10.2307/2928719.

Summerfield, Penny. 'Conflict, Power and Gender in Women's Memories of the Second World War: A Mass-Observation Study'. *Miranda. Revue Pluridisciplinaire Du Monde Anglophone/Multidisciplinary Peer-Reviewed Journal on the English-Speaking World*, no. 2 (1 July 2010). https://doi.org/10.4000/miranda.1253.

Suskind, Ron. *The One Percent Doctrine: Deep Inside America's Pursuit of Its Enemies since 9/11*. New York: Simon & Schuster, 2007.

Swofford, Anthony. *Jarhead: A Marine's Chronicle of the Gulf War and Other Battles*. New York: Scribner, 2003.

Szasz, Ferenc Morton. *Atomic Comics: Cartoonists Confront the Nuclear World*. Reno: University of Nevada Press, 2013.

Tanaka, Masakazu. 'The Sexual Contact Zone in Occupied Japan: Discourses on Japanese Prostitutes or "Panpan" for U.S. Military Servicemen'. *Intersections: Gender and Sexuality in Asia and the Pacific*, no. 31 (December 2012). http://intersections.anu.edu.au/issue31/tanaka.htm#n18.

Taylor, Jonathan. 'Environment and Security Conflicts: The U.S. Military in Okinawa'. *Geographical Bulletin* 48 (2007): 3–13.

Taylor, William A. *Every Citizen a Soldier: The Campaign for Universal Military Training after World War II*. College Station: Texas A&M University Press, 2014.

Teague, Aileen. 'The United States, Mexico, and the Mutual Securitization of Drug Enforcement, 1969–1985'. *Diplomatic History* 43, no. 5 (1 November 2019): 785–812. https://doi.org/10.1093/dh/dhz035.

Terry, Wallace. *Bloods: An Oral History of the Vietnam War*. New York: Random House, 1984.

Thelen, Sarah. 'Mobilizing a Majority: Nixon's "Silent Majority" Speech and the Domestic Debate over Vietnam'. *Journal of American Studies* 51, no. 3 (August 2017): 887–914. https://doi.org/10.1017/S0021875816001936.

Thompson, John A. 'Conceptions of National Security and American Entry into World War II'. *Diplomacy & Statecraft* 16, no. 4 (1 December 2005): 671–97. https://doi.org/10.1080/09592290500331006.

Thompson, John A. 'The Exaggeration of American Vulnerability: The Anatomy of a Tradition'. *Diplomatic History* 16, no. 1 (1992): 23–43. https://doi.org/10.1111/j.1467-7709.1992.tb00482.x.

Thompson, Nicholas. *The Hawk and the Dove: Paul Nitze, George Kennan, and the History of the Cold War*. New York: Picador, 2010.

Tilly, Charles. 'War Making and State Making as Organized Crime'. In *Violence: A Reader*, edited by Catherine Besteman, 35–60. Basingstoke: Palgrave Macmillan, 2002.

Tooze, Adam. *The Deluge: The Great War and the Remaking of Global Order 1916–1931*. London: Penguin, 2015.

Tooze, Adam. *The Wages of Destruction: The Making and Breaking of the Nazi Economy*. London: Penguin, 2007.

Trask, David F. *The War with Spain in 1898*. Lincoln: University of Nebraska Press, 1996.

Turner, Kathleen J. *Lyndon Johnson's Dual War: Vietnam and the Press*. Chicago: University of Chicago Press, 1985.

Vanderbilt, Tom. *Survival City: Adventures among the Ruins of Atomic America*. Princeton: Architectural Press, 2002.

Varzally, Allison. *Children of Reunion: Vietnamese Adoptions and the Politics of Family Migrations*. Chapel Hill: University of North Carolina Press, 2017.

Vine, David. *Base Nation: How U.S. Military Bases Abroad Harm America and the World*. The American Empire Project. New York: Metropolitan Books, 2015.

Vine, David. *Island of Shame: The Secret History of the U.S. Military Base on Diego Garcia*. Princeton, NJ: Princeton University Press, 2011.

Virden, Jenel. *Good-Bye, Piccadilly: British War Brides in America*. Urbana: University of Illinois Press, 1996.

Vogel, Steve. *The Pentagon: A History*. New York: Random House, 2008.

Von Eschen, Penny M. *Race against Empire: Black Americans and Anticolonialism, 1937–1957*. Ithaca, NY: Cornell University Press, 1997.

Vuic, Kara Dixon. *The Girls Next Door: Bringing the Home Front to the Front Lines*. Cambridge, MA: Harvard University Press, 2019.

Washburn, Patrick S. 'The Pittsburgh Courier's Double V Campaign in 1942'. *American Journalism* 3, no. 2 (1 April 1986): 73–86. https://doi.org/10.1080/08821127.1986.10731062.

Weaver, Gina Marie. *Ideologies of Forgetting: Rape in the Vietnam War*. Albany, NY: SUNY Press, 2012.

Webber, Bert. *Silent Siege: Japanese Attacks against North America In World War II*. Fairfield, WA: Ye Galleon Press, 1984.

Weigley, Russell. *The American Way of War: A History of United States Military Strategy and Policy*. New York: Macmillan, 1973.

Wells, Tom. *The War Within: America's Battle over Vietnam*. New York: iUniverse, 2005.

Werry, Margaret. "'The Greatest Show on Earth': Political Spectacle, Spectacular Politics, and the American Pacific". *Theatre Journal* 57, no. 3 (2005): 355–82. https://doi.org/10.1353/tj.2005.0124.

Wertheim, Stephen. 'How Trump Brought Home the Endless War'. *New Yorker*, 1 October 2020. https://www.newyorker.com/news/our-columnists/how-trump-brought-home-the-endless-war.

Wertheim, Stephen. *Tomorrow, the World: The Birth of U.S. Global Supremacy*. Cambridge, MA: Harvard University Press, 2020.

Westbrook, Robert B. *Why We Fought: Forging American Obligations in World War II*. Washington, DC: Smithsonian Institution, 2010.

Westheider, James E. *Fighting on Two Fronts: African Americans and the Vietnam War*. New York: New York University Press, 1999.

Westheider, James E. *The African American Experience in Vietnam: Brothers in Arms*. Lanham, MD: Rowman & Littlefield, 2008.

White, Geoffrey M., and Lamont Lindstrom. *The Pacific Theater: Island Representations of World War II*. Honolulu: University of Hawaii Press, 1989.

Whitt, Jacqueline E., and Elizabeth A. Perazzo. 'The Military as Social Experiment: Challenging a Trope'. *Parameters* 48, no. 2 (22 June 2018): 5.

Williams, Chad. *Torchbearers of Democracy: African American Soldiers in the World War I Era*. Chapel Hill: University of North Carolina Press, 2013.

Williams, Chad. 'World War I in the Historical Imagination of W. E. B. Du Bois'. *Modern American History* 1, no. 1 (March 2018): 3–22. https://doi.org/10.1017/mah.2017.20.

Williams, David. *Bitterly Divided: The South's Inner Civil War*. New York: New Press, 2010.

Wills, Gary. *Bomb Power: The Modern Presidency and the National Security State*. New York: Penguin Books, 2011.

Wilson, Mark R. *Destructive Creation: American Business and the Winning of World War II*. Philadelphia: University of Pennsylvania Press, 2016.

Winkler, Allan M. *Life under a Cloud: American Anxiety about the Atom*. Urbana: University of Illinois Press, 1999.

Winkler, Allan M. *Politics of Propaganda: Office of War Information, 1942–45*. New Haven, CT: Yale University Press, 1978.

Wolfe, Audra J. *Competing with the Soviets: Science, Technology, and the State in Cold War America*. Baltimore, MD: Johns Hopkins University Press, 2013.

Wolff, Tobias. *In Pharaoh's Army: Memories of the Lost War*. Later Printing edition. New York: Vintage, 1995.

Wolgin, Philip E., and Irene Bloemraad. "'Our Gratitude to Our Soldiers": Military Spouses, Family Re-Unification, and Postwar Immigration Reform'. *Journal of Interdisciplinary History* 41, no. 1 (2010): 27–60.

Wong, Leonard. *CU @ the FOB: How the Forward Operating Base Is Changing the Life of Combat Soldiers*. Carlisle, PA: Strategic Studies Institute, U.S. Army War College, 2006.

Wood, Gordon S. *Empire of Liberty: A History of the Early Republic, 1789–1815*. Oxford: Oxford University Press, 2011.

Woodward, C. Vann. 'The Age of Reinterpretation'. *American Historical Review* 66, no. 1 (1960): 1–19. https://doi.org/10.2307/1845704.

Woodward, Rachel. *Military Geographies*. Malden, MA: Wiley-Blackwell, 2004.

Wooster, Robert. *The American Military Frontiers: The United States Army in the West, 1783–1900*. Albuquerque: University of New Mexico Press, 2012.

Worsencroft, John. 'A Family Affair: Military Service in the Postwar Era'. PhD diss., Temple University, 2017.

Wright, James Edward. *Those Who Have Borne the Battle: A History of America's Wars and Those Who Fought Them*. New York: Public Affairs, 2012.

Wu, Ellen D. 'It's Time to Center War in U.S. Immigration History'. *Modern American History* 2, no. 2 (July 2019): 215–35. https://doi.org/10.1017/mah.2019.6.

Yergin, Daniel. *Shattered Peace: The Origins of the Cold War and the National Security State*. Boston, MA: Houghton Mifflin, 1978.

Young, Charles S. *Name, Rank, and Serial Number: Exploiting Korean War POWs at Home and Abroad*. New York: Oxford University Press, 2014.

Young, Marilyn B. "'I Was Thinking, as I Often Do These Days, of War": The United States in the Twenty-First Century'. *Diplomatic History* 36, no. 1 (1 January 2012): 1–15. https://doi.org/10.1111/j.1467-7709.2011.01004.x.

Young, Marilyn B. 'The Hurt Locker: War as a Video Game'. *Perspectives on History*, 1 November 2009. https://www.historians.org/publications-and-directories/ perspectives-on-history/november-2009/the-hurt-locker-war-as-a-video-game.

Young, Richard. 'The "Real Victims" of the Vietnam War: Soldier versus State in American Comic Books'. *Journal of Popular Culture* 50, no. 3 (2017): 561–84. https:// doi.org/10.1111/jpcu.12548.

Zaretsky, Natasha. *No Direction Home: The American Family and the Fear of National Decline, 1968–1980*. Chapel Hill: University of North Carolina Press, 2010.

Zegart, Amy B. *Flawed by Design: The Evolution of the CIA, JCS, and NSC*. Stanford, CA: Stanford University Press, 2000.

Zeiger, Susan. *Entangling Alliances: Foreign War Brides and American Soldiers in the Twentieth Century*. New York: New York University Press, 2010.

Zeiler, Thomas. *Annihilation: A Global Military History of World War II*. New York: Oxford University Press, 2010.

Index

CPSIA information can be obtained
at www.ICGtesting.com
Printed in the USA
LVHW060717220322
713973LV00014B/30

9 781350 102224